MW01387883

Full Name	Age & Birthday

ABOUT ME

Today I am....

☐ Happy ☐ Bubbly ☐ Tickled ☐ Joyous

QUESTIONS	ANSWERS
Hair Color	
Eye Color	
Height	
Where were you born?	
Do you have any pets?	
What is your favorite food?	
Do you have any brothers and sisters?	

What do you want to be when you grow up?

What is your favorite subject in school?

What do you like to do in your free time?

What makes you unique? ______________________________

Score: ____________________

Date: ____________

Your Identity and Reputation Online

First, read over the entire passage(s). Then go back and fill in the blanks. You can skip the blanks you're unsure about and come back to them later.

persona	remarks	reputation	networking	repercussions
embarrassing	real-life	inappropriate	take-backs	derogatory

Your online identity grows every time you use a social network, send a text, or make a post on a website, for example. Your online ______________ may be very different from your real-world persona – the way your friends, parents, and teachers see you.

One of the best things about having an online life is trying on different personas. If you want to change how you act and show up to people, you can. You can also learn more about things that you like. Steps to help you maintain control on the internet can be taken just like in real life.

Here are some things to think about to protect your online identity and reputation:

Nothing is temporary online. The worldwide web is full of opportunities to connect and share with other people. It's also a place with no "____________________" or "temporary" situations. It's easy for other people to copy, save, and forward your information even if you delete it.

Add a "private" option for your profiles. Anyone can copy or screen-grab things that you don't want the world to see using social ____________________ sites. Use caution when using the site's default settings. Each site has its own rules, so read them to ensure you're doing everything you can to keep your information safe.

Keep your passwords safe and change them often. Someone can ruin your ____________________ by pretending to be you online. The best thing to do is pick passwords that no one can guess. The only people who should know about them are your parents or someone else who you can trust. Your best friend, boyfriend, or girlfriend should not know your passwords.

Don't put up pictures or comments that are __________________________ or sexually provocative. In the future, things that are funny or cool to you now might not be so cool to someone else, like a teacher or admissions officer. If you don't want your grandmother, coach, or best friend's parents to see it, don't post it. Even on a private page, it could be hacked or copied and sent to someone else.

Don't give in to unwanted advances. There are a lot of inappropriate messages and requests for money that teenagers get when they're on the web. These things can be scary, weird, or even

_________________________, but they can also be exciting and fun. Do not keep quiet about being bullied online. Tell an adult you trust right away if a stranger or someone you know is bullying you. It's never a good idea to answer. If you respond, you might say something that makes things even worse.

You can go to www.cybertipline.org to report bad behavior or other problems.

Avoid "flaming" by taking a break now and then. Do you want to send an angry text or comment to someone? Relax for a few minutes and realize that the _______________ will be there even if you have cooled off or change your mind about them.

People may feel free to write hurtful, _____________________, or abusive remarks on the internet if they can remain anonymous. We can be painful to others if we share things or make angry comments when we aren't facing someone. If they find out, it could change how they see us. If you wouldn't say it, show it, or do it in person, don't do it online.

Make sure you don't break copyright laws. Don't upload, share, or distribute copyrighted photographs, sounds, or files. Be aware of copyright restrictions. Sharing them is great, but doing so illegally runs the risk of legal ___________________________ down the road.

It's time for a self-evaluation. Take a look at your "digital footprint," which people can find out about you. When you search for your screen name or email address, see what comes up. That's one way to get a sense of what other people think of you online.

In the same way that your ___________________ identity is formed, your online identity and reputation are also formed. It's different when you're on the internet because you don't always have the chance to explain how you feel or what you mean. Thinking about what you're going to say and being responsible can help you avoid leaving an online trail that you'll later be sorry about.

History: Thomas Edison

Score: ______________________

Date: _____________

First, read the entire passage. After that, go back and fill in the blanks. You can skip the blanks you're unsure about and finish them later.

devices	teacher	dedicated	research	Morse
passed	hearing	invented	light	dream

Thomas Alva Edison was born in Milan, Ohio, on February 11, 1847. He developed _______________ loss at a young age. He was a creative and inquisitive child. However, he struggled in school, possibly because he couldn't hear his _______________. He was then educated at home by his mother.

Because of his numerous important inventions, Thomas Edison was nicknamed the "wizard." On his own or in collaboration with others, he has designed and built more than 1,000 _______________. The phonograph (record player), the lightbulb, and the motion-picture projector are among his most notable inventions.

Although Thomas did not invent the first electric ___________ bulb, he did create the first practical electric light bulb that could be manufactured and used in the home. He also _________________ other items required to make the light bulb usable in homes, such as safety fuses and on/off switches for light sockets.

As a teenager, Thomas worked as a telegraph operator. Telegraphy was one of the most important communication systems in the country at the time. Thomas was skilled at sending and receiving ___________ code messages. He enjoyed tweaking with telegraphic instruments, and he came up with several improvements to make them even better. By early 1869, he had left his telegraphy job to pursue his ___________ of becoming a full-time inventor.

Edison worked tirelessly with scientists and other collaborators to complete projects. He established _________________ facilities in Menlo Park, California, and West Orange, New Jersey. Finally, Edison established companies that manufactured and sold his successful inventions.

Edison's family was essential to him, even though he spent the majority of his life ___________________ to his work. He had six children from two marriages. Edison _____________ away on October 18, 1931.

Score: ______________________

Science: Invertebrates

Date:_______

Invertebrates can be found almost anywhere. Invertebrates account for at least 95% of all animals on the planet! Do you know what one thing they all have in common? Invertebrates lack a backbone.

Your body is supported by a backbone, which protects your organs and connects your other bones. As a result, you are a vertebrate. On the other hand, invertebrates lack the support of bones, so their bodies are often simpler, softer, and smaller. They are also cold-blooded, which means their body temperature fluctuates in response to changes in the air or water around them.

Invertebrates can be found flying, swimming, crawling, or floating and provide essential services to the environment and humans. Nobody knows how many different types of invertebrates there are, but there are millions!

Just because an invertebrate lacks a spinal column does not mean it does not need to eat. Invertebrates, like all other forms of animal life, must obtain nutrients from their surroundings. Invertebrates have evolved two types of digestion to accomplish this. The use of intracellular digestion is common in the most simple organisms. The food is absorbed into the cell and broken down in the cytoplasm at this point. Extracellular digestion, in which cells break down food through the secretion of enzymes and other techniques, is used by more advanced invertebrates. All vertebrates use extracellular digestion.

Still, all animals, invertebrates or not, need a way to get rid of waste. Most invertebrates, especially the simplest ones, use the process of diffusion to eliminate waste. This is merely the opposite of intracellular digestion. However, more advanced invertebrates have more advanced waste disposal mechanisms. Similar to our kidneys, specialized glands in these animals filter and excrete waste. But there is a happy medium. Even though some invertebrates do not have complete digestive tracts like vertebrates, they do not simply flush out waste through diffusion. Instead, the mouth doubles as an exit.

Scientists have classified invertebrates into numerous groups based on what the animals have in common. Arthropods have segmented bodies, which means that they are divided into sections. Consider an ant!

Arthropods are the most numerous group of invertebrates. They can live on land, as spiders and insects do, or in water, as crayfish and crabs do. Because insects are the most numerous group of arthropods, many of them fly, including mosquitoes, bees, locusts, and ladybugs.

They also have jointed legs or limbs to help them walk, similar to how you have knees for your legs and elbows for your arms. The majority of arthropods have an exoskeleton, tough outer skin, or shell that protects their body. Have you ever wondered why when you squish a bug, it makes that crunching sound? That's right; it's the exoskeleton!

Mollusks are the second most numerous group of invertebrates. They have soft bodies and can be found on land or in water. Shells protect the soft bodies of many mollusks, including snails, oysters, clams, and scallops. However, not all, such as octopus, squid, and cuttlefish, have a shell.

1. Invertebrates lack a ______.
   a. backbone
   b. tailbone

2. Invertebrates are also ____.
   a. cold-blooded
   b. warm-blooded

3. _____ can live on land, as spiders and insects do, or in water, as crayfish and crabs do.
   a. Vertebrates
   b. Arthropods

4. All animals, invertebrates or not, need a way to get rid of ____.
   a. their skin
   b. waste

5. _____ have soft bodies and can be found on land or in water.
   a. Arthropods
   b. Mollusks

6. Just because an invertebrate lacks a ______ column does not mean it does not need to eat.
   a. spinal
   b. tissues

7. Your body is supported by a backbone, which protects your ____ and connects your other bones.
   a. organs
   b. muscles

8. Invertebrates lack the support of bones, so their bodies are often simpler, ___, and smaller.
   a. softer and bigger
   b. softer and smaller

Score: ____________________

Weather and Climate

Date: ____________

The difference between weather and climate is simply a matter of time. Weather refers to the conditions of the atmosphere over a short period of time, whereas climate refers to how the atmosphere "behaves" over a longer period of time.

When we discuss climate change, we are referring to changes in long-term averages of daily weather. Today's children are constantly told by their parents and grandparents about how the snow was always piled up to their waists as they trudged off to school. Most children today have not experienced those kinds of dreadful snow-packed winters. The recent changes in winter snowfall indicate that the climate has changed since their parents were children.

Weather is essentially the atmosphere's behavior, particularly in terms of its effects on life and human activities. The distinction between weather and climate is that weather refers to short-term (minutes to months) changes in the atmosphere, whereas climate refers to long-term changes. Most people associate weather with temperature, humidity, precipitation, cloudiness, brightness, visibility, wind, and atmospheric pressure, as in high and low pressure.

Weather can change from minute to minute, hour to hour, day to day, and season to season in most places. However, the climate is the average of weather over time and space. A simple way to remember the distinction is that climate is what you expect, such as a very hot summer, whereas weather is what you get, such as a hot day with pop-up thunderstorms.

Use the word bank to unscramble the words!

Pressure	Density	Cloudy	Latitude	Elevation	Weather
Absorb	Humid	Precipitation	Windy	Forecast	Climate
Sunshine	Temperature				

1. IUMHD _ u _ _ _
2. UDLOYC _ l _ u _ _
3. FSEATOCR _ _ _ _ _ _ a _ t
4. UDLTITAE L _ _ _ _ u _ _
5. IEOCAIIPPTRNT _ _ _ _ _ _ _ t _ _ _ o n
6. TEEERPAURMT T _ _ _ e _ _ t _ _ _
7. RSEREUPS _ r e _ _ _ _ _
8. LEICATM _ _ i _ _ t _
9. SNNIEHUS S _ _ _ _ i _ _
10. OBBASR _ b s _ _ _
11. VETIEOANL _ _ _ _ a t _ _ _
12. EATWRHE W _ _ _ _ e _
13. NDWIY _ _ _ _ y
14. TYNEIDS _ _ _ _ i _ y

Health: The Food Groups

Score: ______________________

Date: ______________

First, read the entire passage. After that, go back and fill in the blanks. You can skip the blanks you're unsure about and finish them later.

produce	consume	yogurt	stored	bones
repair	water	portion	vitamins	fiber

Eating healthy foods is especially important for children because they are still developing. Children's bodies require nutrition to develop strong, healthy __________ and muscles. You will not grow as tall or as strong as you could if you do not get all the ________________ and minerals you require while growing.

Healthy food includes a wide variety of fresh foods from the five healthy food groups:

Dairy: Milk, cheese, and ____________ are the most critical dairy foods, which are necessary for strong and healthy bones. There aren't many other foods in our diet that have as much calcium as these.

Fruit: Fruit contains vitamins, minerals, dietary fiber, and various phytonutrients (nutrients found naturally in plants) that help your body stay healthy. Fruits and vegetables provide you with energy, antioxidants, and __________. These nutrients help protect you against diseases later in life, such as heart disease, stroke, and some cancers.

Vegetables and legumes/beans: Vegetables should account for a large ______________ of your daily food intake and should be encouraged at all meals (including snack times). To keep your body healthy, they supply vitamins, minerals, dietary fiber, and phytonutrients (nutrients found naturally in plants).

Grain (cereal) foods: choose wholegrain and/or high __________ bread, cereals, rice, pasta, noodles, and so on. These foods provide you with the energy you require to grow, develop, and learn. Refined grain products (such as cakes and biscuits) can contain added sugar, fat, and sodium.

Protein from lean meats and poultry, fish, eggs, tofu, nuts and seeds, and legumes/beans is used by our bodies to ______________ specialized chemicals such as hemoglobin and adrenalin. Protein also helps to build, maintain, and ____________ tissues in our bodies. Protein is the primary component of muscles and organs (such as your heart).

Calories are a unit of measurement for the amount of energy in food. We gain calories when we eat, which gives us the energy to run around and do things. If we ______________ more calories than we expend while moving, our bodies will store the excess calories as fat. If we burn more calories than we consume, our bodies will begin to burn the previously ____________ fat.

Score: ________________________

Music: The Piano

Date:_______

Bartolomeo Cristofori was the first to successfully develop a hammer-action keyboard instrument and hence deserves to be regarded as the creator of the piano.

Cristofori was dissatisfied with musicians' lack of control over the harpsichord's loudness level. Around 1700, he is credited for replacing the plucking mechanism with a hammer and thus creating the modern piano. Initially, the instrument was dubbed "clavicembalo con piano e forte" (literally, a harpsichord that can play soft and loud noises). This was later abbreviated to the now-common term "piano."

The piano possesses the characteristics of both a string and percussion instrument. A hammer strikes a string inside the piano (much like a percussion instrument). The piano's sounds and notes are produced by the vibration of these strings (like a string instrument).

The piano is commonly referred to as a keyboard instrument. This is because it is performed similarly to several other keyboard instruments, including the organ, harpsichord, electronic keyboards, and synthesizers.

The organ was the first keyboard instrument, dating back to the third century. However, the organ did not begin to use keys until much later. The harpsichord was invented in the 14th century and quickly gained popularity throughout Europe. The harpsichord plucked a string and resembled modern pianos in appearance. However, plucking the string did not allow for the playing of various volumes and expressions.

The term piano is derived from the Italian phrase pianoforte, which translates as "loud and soft." This is because you may now adjust the volume of notes played on the keyboard.

The grand piano and the upright piano are the two primary types of pianos.

Grand piano - a grand piano's strings and primary frame are horizontal. This enables longer strings and also aids in the piano's mechanics. However, grand pianos can consume a significant amount of room.

Upright piano - This piano style is more compact, making it ideal for use in a home. The strings and mainframe are arranged vertically.

Additionally, there are electronic pianos. While the keyboard and playing technique is typically identical to a standard piano, the sound is frequently quite different.

1. This piano style is more compact, making it ideal for use in a home.
   a. Upright piano
   b. Downright piano

2. A ____ strings and primary frame are horizontal.
   a. organ piano's
   b. grand piano's

3. The term piano is derived from the_____phrase pianoforte.
   a. English
   b. Italian

4. The ____ was invented in the 14th century.
   a. pianiochord
   b. harpsichord

5. The piano is commonly referred to as a ____ instrument.
   a. singer
   b. keyboard

6. The organ and harpsichord are keyboard instruments.
   a. organ
   b. guitar

English: Personal Pronouns

Score: ______________________

Date: ______________

Personal pronouns are words that are used to replace the subject or object of a sentence to make it easier for readers to understand.

To give a brief, personal pronouns are:

1. Replace nouns and other pronouns to make sentences easier to read and understand.

2. A sentence's subject or object can be either. For example, 'I' is the first-person subject pronoun, whereas 'me' is the first-person object pronoun.

3. It is possible to use the singular or plural form.

4. They must agree on gender and number with the words they are substituting.

1. Which of the following sentences has a plural subject pronoun and a plural object pronoun?
   a. She wants to live as long as she can, as long as she have someone by her side.
   b. While Tom believe everything will be fine, many don't agree with him.
   c. Whether we lived or died, it didn't matter to us either way.

2. Which of the following words would make the following sentence grammatically correct? '6th graders should check with their teachers before you leave the classroom.'
   a. Replace 'their' with 'they'
   b. Replace 'you' with 'they'
   c. Replace '6th graders' with 'they'

3. The pronoun 'my' is a . . .
   a. 1st person possessive pronoun
   b. 3rd person nominative pronoun
   c. 2nd person possessive pronoun

4. Which of the following correctly identifies the subjective and objective pronouns in the sentence here? 'Run away from the dinosaurs with the giant feet?' she asked. 'You don't have to tell me twice.'
   a. she - subject pronoun; you - subject pronoun; me - object pronoun
   b. she - object pronoun; you - object pronoun; me - object pronoun
   c. she - object pronoun; you - subject pronoun; me - object pronoun

5. The pronoun 'your' is a . . .
   a. 2nd person possessive pronoun
   b. 1st person possessive pronoun
   c. 2nd person objective pronoun

6. Which pronouns are found in the following sentence? 'I kept telling her that we would go back for John, but I knew we had left him behind. '
   a. I, we, knew, we, him
   b. I, her, we, I, we, him
   c. I, we, I, we, him

7. Kevin likes playing basketball. _________ is a very good player.
   a. Him
   b. He
   c. Their

8. The pronoun 'its' is a . . .
   a. 3rd person possessive pronoun
   b. 2nd person possessive pronoun
   c. 3rd person objective pronoun

9. The pronoun 'their' is a . . .
   a. 2nd person possessive pronoun
   b. 3rd person objective pronoun
   c. 3rd person possessive pronoun

10. Kimmy is a very good cook. _________ can cook any kind of food.
   a. She
   b. Hey
   c. Their

Reading Comprehension: Law Enforcement Dogs

Score: ______________________

Date: ____________

Police dogs are dogs that assist cops in solving crimes. In recent years, they have grown to be an essential part of law enforcement. With their unique abilities and bravery, police dogs have saved many lives. They are often regarded as an important and irreplaceable part of many police departments because they are loyal, watchful, and protective of their police officer counterparts.

Today, police dogs are trained in specific areas. They could be considered experts in their field. Some of the particular police dog roles are as follows:

Tracking: Tracking police dogs use their keen sense of smell to locate criminal suspects or missing people. Tracking dogs are trained for years and can track down even the most elusive criminal. Without police tracking dogs, many suspects would be able to elude capture.

Substance Detectors: Like tracking dogs, these police dogs use their sense of smell to assist officers. Substance dogs are trained to detect a specific substance. Some dogs are trained to detect bombs or explosives. These brave dogs are trained not only to detect explosives but also to respond (very carefully!) and safely alert their officer partner to the explosive location. Other dogs may be drawn to illegal drugs. By quickly determining whether an illegal substance is nearby, these dogs save officers from searching through luggage, a car, or other areas by hand.

Public Order - These police dogs assist officers in keeping the peace. They may pursue a criminal suspect and hold them until an officer arrives, or they may guard an area (such as a jail or prison) to prevent suspects from fleeing.

Cadaver Dogs: Although it may sound disgusting, these police dogs are trained to locate dead bodies. This is a critical function in a police department, and these dogs perform admirably.

A police dog is not just any dog. Police dogs require very special and specialized training. There are numerous breeds of dogs that have been trained for police work. What breed they are often determined by the type of work they will do. German Shepherds and Belgian Malinois are two of the most popular breeds today, but other dogs such as Bloodhounds (good for tracking) and Beagles (good for drug detection) are also used. Police dogs, regardless of breed, are typically trained to do their job from the time they are puppies.

Typically, police dogs are regarded as heroes. They frequently go to live with their human partner police officer. They've known this person for years and have grown to consider them family, which works out well for both the officer and the dog.

1. Tracking police dogs use their ______ to locate criminal suspects or missing people.

a. keen sense of training
b. keen sense of taste
c. keen sense of smell

2. Some substance dogs are trained to detect _____.

a. runaway children
b. bombs or explosives
c. metal and iron

3. Police dogs are trained in ___ areas.

a. many
b. a few
c. specific

4. Police dogs are dogs that assist cops in solving _____.

a. littering
b. homelessness
c. crimes

5. Substance dogs are trained to detect a specific ____.

a. substance
b. person
c. other police dogs

6. What type of police dog is trained pursue a criminal suspect and hold them until an officer arrives?

a. Crime Fighting dog
b. Tracking dog
c. Public Order dog

7. These police dogs are trained to locate dead bodies

a. Law and Order dogs
b. Cadaver dogs
c. Deadly Substance dogs

8. What are the two most popular police dogs used today?

a. German Shepherds and Belgian Malinois
b. Bloodhounds and German Shepherds
c. Belgian Malinois and Rottweiler

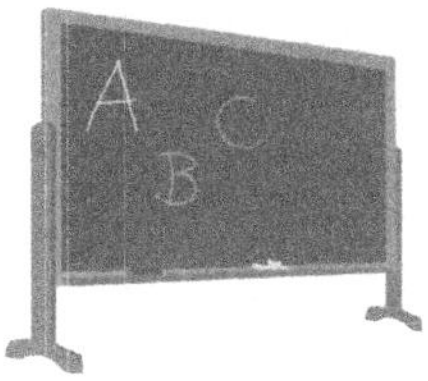

Spelling: How Do You Spell It? Part I

Score: ____________________

Date: ____________

Write and circle the correct spelling for each word.

		A	B	C	D
1.	________	grade	grrada	grrade	grada
2.	________	elementary	elenmentary	ellenmentary	ellementary
3.	________	marks	marrcks	marrks	marcks
4.	________	repurt	reporrt	report	repurrt
5.	________	schedolle	schedule	schedole	schedulle
6.	________	timetible	timetable	timettable	timettible
7.	________	highlight	highllight	hyghllight	hyghlight
8.	________	foell	foel	fuell	fuel
9.	________	instrucsion	insstruction	instruction	insstrucsion
10.	________	senttence	sentance	senttance	sentence
11.	________	vaccination	vacination	vaccinasion	vacinasion
12.	________	proof	prwf	prouf	proph
13.	________	mandatury	mandattury	mandatory	mandattory
14.	________	final	fynall	finall	fynal
15.	________	envellope	envelope	envellupe	envelupe
16.	________	equattor	eqauttor	eqautor	equator
17.	________	bllanks	blanks	blancks	bllancks
18.	________	honorible	honorrable	honorable	honorrible
19.	________	scaince	sceince	science	sciance
20.	________	mussic	mosic	muscic	music
21.	________	history	hisstory	hisctory	histury
22.	________	lissten	liscten	lysten	listen
23.	________	entrence	enttrance	enttrence	entrance
24.	________	especialy	especailly	especaily	especially
25.	________	mariage	maraige	marraige	marriage

Spelling: How Do You Spell It?
Part II

Score: ______________________

Date: ______________

Write and circle the correct spelling for each word.

		A	B	C	D
1.	____________	compllain	complian	complain	compllian
2.	____________	negattyve	negatyve	negative	negattive
3.	____________	importance	importence	imporrtance	imporrtence
4.	____________	encourragement	encouragement	encourragenment	encouragenment
5.	____________	shallves	shelves	shellves	shalves
6.	____________	mixture	mixttore	mixtore	mixtture
7.	____________	honorrable	honorable	honorible	honorrible
8.	____________	lagall	legall	lagal	legal
9.	____________	manar	mannar	manner	maner
10.	____________	encycllopedia	encyclopedia	encycllopedai	encyclopedai
11.	____________	repllacement	replacenment	repllacenment	replacement
12.	____________	medycie	medycine	medicine	medicie
13.	____________	experriance	experience	experiance	experrience
14.	____________	hunger	hunjer	hungerr	hunjerr
15.	____________	sallote	sallute	salote	salute
16.	____________	horrizon	hurizon	hurrizon	horizon
17.	____________	sestion	session	setion	sesion
18.	____________	shorrten	shurten	shorten	shurrten
19.	____________	fuacett	faucett	fuacet	faucet
20.	____________	haadache	haadace	haedache	headache
21.	____________	further	furrther	forrther	forther
22.	____________	injurry	injory	injury	injorry
23.	____________	disstance	distence	distance	disstence
24.	____________	rattio	ratio	rattoi	ratoi
25.	____________	independense	independence	independance	independanse

Spelling: How Do You Spell It? Part III

Score: ______________________

Date: ______________

Write and circle the correct spelling for each word.

		A	B	C	D
1.	______________	invitation	invittasion	invitasion	invittation
2.	______________	denuminator	denominator	denuminattor	denominattor
3.	______________	personal	perrsonal	perrsunal	persunal
4.	______________	rapkd	rapid	rahid	rapyd
5.	______________	oryginal	original	orryginal	orriginal
6.	______________	liquvd	liqiod	liqoid	liquid
7.	______________	desscendant	descendant	dessendant	desssendant
8.	______________	dissastrous	disastrous	dissastroos	disastroos
9.	______________	cooperasion	cooperation	coperation	coperasion
10.	______________	routine	roottine	routtine	rootine
11.	______________	earleist	earrleist	earrliest	earliest
12.	______________	acidentally	accidentally	acidentalli	accidentalli
13.	______________	rehaerrse	rehearrse	rehaerse	rehearse
14.	______________	quotte	qoote	quote	qootte
15.	______________	capablla	capablle	capable	capible
16.	______________	apointment	appointnment	apointnment	appointment
17.	______________	musscician	musscicain	musicain	musician
18.	______________	nomerrator	numerrator	numerator	nomerator
19.	______________	inquire	inqoire	inquirre	inqoirre
20.	______________	remote	remute	remutte	remotte
21.	______________	pryncipal	prrincipal	prryncipal	principal
22.	______________	sylent	sillent	syllent	silent
23.	______________	locatsion	locasion	location	locattion
24.	______________	edision	edition	editsion	edittion

Health: Check Your Symptoms

Score: ____________________

Date: ____________________

Healthy habits aid in the development of happy and healthy children as well as the prevention of future health issues such as diabetes, hypertension, high cholesterol, heart disease, and cancer.

Chronic diseases and long-term illnesses can be avoided by leading a healthy lifestyle. Self-esteem and self-image are aided by feeling good about yourself and taking care of your health.

Maintain a consistent exercise schedule.

No, you don't have to push yourself to go to the gym and do tough workouts, but you should be as active as possible. You can maintain moving by doing simple floor exercises, swimming, or walking. You can also remain moving by doing some domestic chores around the house.

What matters is that you continue to exercise. At least three to five times a week, devote at least twenty to thirty minutes to exercise. Establish a regimen and make sure you get adequate physical activity each day.

Be mindful of your eating habits.

You must continue to eat healthily in order to maintain a healthy lifestyle. Eat more fruits and vegetables and have fewer carbs, salt, and harmful fat in your diet. Don't eat junk food or sweets.

Avoid skipping meals since your body will crave more food once you resume eating. Keep in mind that you should burn more calories than you consume.

1. **I've got a pain in my head.**
    a. Stiff neck
    b. headache
2. **I was out in the sun too long.**
    a. Sunburn
    b. Fever
3. **I've got a small itchy lump or bump.**
    a. Rash
    b. Insect bite
4. **I might be having a heart attack.**
    a. Cramps
    b. Chest pain
5. **I've lost my voice.**
    a. Laryngitis
    b. Sore throat
6. **I need to blow my nose a lot.**
    a. Runny nose
    b. Blood Nose
7. **I have an allergy. I have a**
    a. Rash
    b. Insect bite
8. **My shoe rubbed my heel. I have a**
    a. Rash
    b. Blister
9. **The doctor gave me antibiotics. I have a/an**
    a. Infection
    b. Cold
10. **I think I want to vomit. I am**
    a. Nauseous
    b. Bloated

11. **My arm is not broken. It is**
    a. Scratched
    b. Sprained

12. **My arm touched the hot stove. It is**
    a. Burned
    b. Bleeding

13. **I have an upset stomach. I might**
    a. Cough
    b. Vomit

14. **The doctor put plaster on my arm. It is**
    a. Sprained
    b. Broken

15. **If you cut your finger it will**
    a. Burn
    b. Bleed

16. **I hit my hip on a desk. It will**
    a. Burn
    b. Bruise

17. **When you have hay-fever you will**
    a. Sneeze
    b. Wheeze

18. **A sharp knife will**
    a. Scratch
    b. Cut

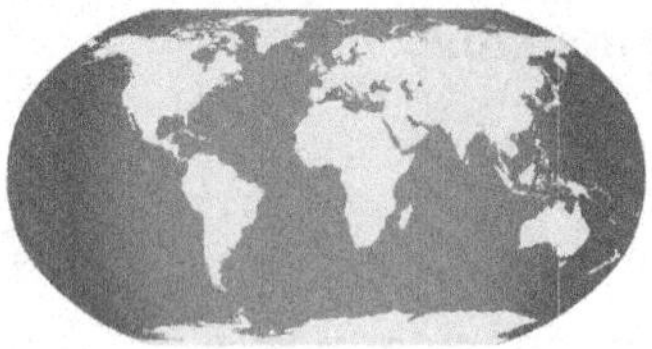

Geography: Know Your World

Score: ______________________

Date: ______________

Test your knowledge of global, national, and local geography, as well as the environment.

1. Spain can be found in which continent
   a. Europe
   b. New Zealand
   c. Bogota

2. Uganda can be found in which continent
   a. Canberra
   b. Africa
   c. Lake Taupo

3. Uruguay can be found in which continent
   a. South America
   b. Atlantic Ocean
   c. Bogota

4. Beijing is the capital city of
   a. China
   b. Samoa
   c. New York

5. Honshu is an island of what country
   a. Japan
   b. Suva
   c. New York

6. Apia is the capital city of
   a. Bogota
   b. Samoa
   c. Brasilia

7. The Amazon River can be found in which continent
   a. Suva
   b. Buenos Aires
   c. South America

8. The Southern Alps can be found in which country
   a. Portugal
   b. New Zealand
   c. Brasilia

9. The Andes Mountains can be found in which continent
   a. Brasilia
   b. South America
   c. Berlin

10. Lines of longitude run
   a. Vertical - North to South
   b. Wellington
   c. Samoa

11. Lines of latitude run
   a. Horizontal - East to West
   b. Suva
   c. Italy

12. The ocean between the Americas and Europe and Africa is the
   a. Africa
   b. Italy
   c. Atlantic Ocean

13. The capital city of France is
   a. Bogota
   b. Paris
   c. Buenos Aires

14. The capital city of Germany is
   a. Berlin
   b. New Zealand
   c. Moscow

15. The capital city of Russia is

a. Moscow
b. Buenos Aires
c. Paris

16. The capital city of the United States is

a. Brasilia
b. Washington D.C
c. China

17. The capital city of Fiji is

a. Suva
b. Portugal
c. Buenos Aires

18. Mt Everest can be found in what continent

a. Asia
b. Japan
c. Wellington

19. Switzerland is a country in

a. Europe
b. Wellington
c. Portugal

20. The capital city of Brazil is

a. Japan
b. China
c. Brasilia

21. The capital city of Colombia is

a. Spain
b. Bogota
c. Japan

22. The capital city of Argentina is

a. Buenos Aires
b. Portugal
c. Bogota

23. Vietnam can be found in what continent

a. Asia
b. Berlin
c. Vertical - North to South

24. Libya can be found in what continent

a. Africa
b. Bogota
c. New York

25. Rome is the capital city of which European country

a. Buenos Aires
b. Italy
c. Paris

26. Madrid is the capital city of which European country

a. Brasilia
b. Europe
c. Spain

27. Lisbon is the capital city of which European country

a. Samoa
b. Portugal
c. Buenos Aires

28. The Statue of Liberty can be found in what US city

a. Italy
b. New York
c. Paris

29. The capital city of New Zealand is

a. Canberra
b. Wellington
c. Washington D.C

30. The capital city of Australia is

a. China
b. Moscow
c. Canberra

31. What is the largest lake in New Zealand?

a. Spain
b. Lake Taupo
c. Washington D.C

Score: ____________________

Grammar: Is vs. Are

Date: ____________

Use **is** if the noun is singular. If the noun is plural or there are multiple nouns, use **are**.

1. _____ Billy?
1. Where are
2. Where's

2. _____ in the bed.
1. They're
2. He's

3. _____ Mum and Dad?
1. Where's
2. Where are

4. ______ in the kitchen.
1. She's
2. They're

5. _____ Grandpa?
1. Where are
2. Where's

6. _____ in the garden.
1. He's
2. She's

7. _____ Lucy and Lilly?
1. Where's
2. Where are

8. _____ in the park.
1. She's
2. They're

9. _____ my sister?
1. Where are
2. Where's

10. _____ in her bedroom.
1. He's
2. She's

11. _____ pupils?
1. Where are
2. Where's

12. _____ at school.
1. He's
2. They're

Grammar: Linking Verbs

Score: ____________________

Date: ______________

A linking verb links the topic of a phrase to a word that describes the subject, such as a condition or a relationship. They don't depict any action; instead, they serve to connect the subject to the rest of the phrase or sentence.

In a sentence, helping verbs always appear before the primary verb. They complete the structure of a phrase by adding information to the main verb. They can also help you understand how time is expressed in a sentence.

To connect nouns, pronouns, and adjectives, both the supporting and linking verb are utilized.

1. Which of the following examples best shows what a linking verb is?
   a. Shows action
   b. Connects a subject to the predicate
   c. Connects a noun and verb

2. How can you determine the difference between a helping verb and a linking verb?
   a. There is no difference between a helping verb and a linking verb.
   b. The helping verb is combined with an action verb.
   c. The helping verb or adverb shows action.

3. Which words belong to the category of state of being verbs?
   a. were, am, are, been
   b. flow, jump, bounce
   c. she, he, they, did

4. Which of the following examples does not connect subject and a predicate?
   a. Tiffany is an awesome student.
   b. She became the best mom ever!
   c. It danced quietly and smoothly.

5. What distinguishes a connecting verb from an action verb?
   a. It is an adjective.
   b. It shows no action.
   c. It shows action and no action.

6. The tomato smells rotten. Which is the linking verb in this sentence?
   a. rotten
   b. smells
   c. tomato

7. My brother is mad when he's hungry.
   a. is
   b. mad
   c. when

8. Identify the linking verb: The girl was frightened.
   a. girl
   b. was
   c. frightened

9. What is the linking verb in the sentence? Rob and Tony were class leaders.
   a. were
   b. class
   c. none

10. The Queen__________ busy laying eggs.
   a. is
   b. bee
   c. are

Score: ____________________

Date: ____________

History Reading Comprehension: Walt Disney

First, read the article. After that, go back and fill in the blanks. You can skip the blanks you're unsure about and finish them later. Don't try to do it all at one time. Break it down so that it's "do-able" and not so overwhelming. Take your time. Ask questions. Get help if you need it.

Mickey	Donald	sister	Hollywood	art
Red	Chicago	newspaper	friends	train
four	entertainment	White	Alice	Peter
Club	snacks	vacation	brother	theme

On December 5, 1901, Walter Elias Disney was born in ______________, Illinois. His family relocated to a farm outside of Marceline, Missouri, when he was ________ years old, thanks to his parents, Elias and Flora. Walt loved growing up on the farm with his three older brothers (Herbert, Raymond, and Roy) and younger ____________ (Ruth). Walt discovered his passion for drawing and art in Marceline.

The Disneys relocated to Kansas City after four years in Marceline. On weekends, Walt continued to draw and attend ______ classes. He even bartered his drawings for free haircuts with a local barber. Walt got a summer job on a train. On the __________, he walked back and forth, selling ____________ and newspapers. Walt had a great time on the train and would be fascinated by trains for the rest of his life.

Walt's family relocated to Chicago around the time he started high school. Walt studied at the Chicago Art Institute and worked as a cartoonist for the school __________________. Walt decided at the age of sixteen that he wanted to fight in World War I. Due to the fact that he was still too young to join the army, he decided to drop out of school and join the ______ Cross instead. He spent the next year in France driving ambulances for the Red Cross.

Disney returned from the war eager to launch his artistic career. He began his career in an art studio and later moved on to an advertising firm. During this time, he met artist Ubbe Iwerks and became acquainted with animation.

Walt aspired to create his own animated cartoons. He founded his own company, Laugh-O-Gram. He sought the help of some of his ______________, including Ubbe Iwerks. They made animated cartoons that were only a few minutes long. Despite the popularity of the cartoons, the business did not make enough money, and Walt was forced to declare bankruptcy.

Disney, on the other hand, was not going to be deterred by a single setback. In 1923, he relocated to _________________, California, and founded the Disney Brothers' Studio with his _____________ Roy. He enlisted the services of Ubbe Iwerks and a number of other animators once more. They created the well-known character Oswald the Lucky Rabbit. The company was a success. However, Universal Studios acquired the Oswald trademark and hired all of Disney's animators except Ubbe Iwerks.

Walt had to start all over again. This time, he came up with a new character called ___________ Mouse. He made the first animated film with sound. Steamboat Willie was the title of the film, which starred Mickey and Minnie Mouse. Walt provided the voices for Steamboat Willie. The movie was a huge success. Disney kept working, creating new characters like ___________ Duck, Goofy, and Pluto. With the release of the cartoon Silly Symphonies and the first color animated film, Flowers and Trees, he had even more success.

In 1932, Walt Disney decided to create a full-length animated film called Snow _________. People thought he was insane for attempting to create such a long cartoon. The film was dubbed "Disney's folly." However, Disney was confident that the film would be a success. The film, which was released in 1937, took five years to complete. The film was a huge box office success, becoming the most successful film of 1938.

Disney used the proceeds from Snow White to establish a film studio and produce other animated films such as Pinocchio, Fantasia, Dumbo, Bambi, _________ in Wonderland, and _________ Pan. During WWII, Disney's film production slowed as he worked on training and propaganda films for the United States government. Following the war, Disney began to produce live-action films alongside animated films. Treasure Island was his first major live-action film.

Television was a new technology that was taking off in the 1950s. Disney wished to be a part of the television industry as well. Disney's Wonderful World of Color, the Davy Crockett series, and the Mickey Mouse _______ was among the first Disney television shows to air on network television.

Disney, who is constantly coming up with new ideas, had the idea to build a _________ park featuring rides and entertainment based on his films. In 1955, Disneyland opened its doors. It cost $17 million to construct. Although it wasn't an immediate success, Disney World has since grown into one of the world's most popular _______________ destinations. Walt Disney World, a much larger park in Florida, would be built later by Disney. He contributed to the plans but passed away before the park opened in 1971.

Disney died of lung cancer on December 15, 1966. His legacy endures to this day. Every year, millions of people enjoy his films and theme parks. Every year, his company continues to produce fantastic films and _______________________.

Reading Comprehension
Multiple Choice: Walt Disney

Score: ____________________

Date: ____________

Make sure you go back and read the Disney article through to the very end. If you attempt to complete this assignment solely by scanning for answers, you will almost certainly pick the incorrect answer. Take your time. Ask questions. Get help if you need it. Good Luck!

1. Walter Elias Disney was born in Chicago, ____.
   a. Illinois
   b. Italy

2. Walter's parents names were Elias and Flora.
   a. True
   b. False

3. Walt got a summer job on a _____.
   a. train
   b. boat

4. Walt's younger sister name was ____.
   a. Ruby
   b. Ruth

5. Walt had _____ brothers.
   a. three
   b. two

6. In 1923, walt relocated to Hollywood, ______.
   a. Colorado
   b. California

7. Steamboat ____ was the title of the film, which starred Mickey and Minnie Mouse.
   a. William
   b. Willie

8. Walt spent the next year in France driving _____ for the Red Cross.
   a. taxi cabs
   b. ambulances

9. Walt and his friends created the well-known character Oswald the Lucky _____t.
   a. Dog
   b. Rabbi

10. Walt's first color animated film was____.
   a. Bears and Tigers
   b. Flowers and Trees

11. In ____, Disneyland opened its doors.
   a. 1955
   b. 1995

12. _____ was among the first Disney television shows to air on network television.
   a. Mickey Mouse Club
   b. Mickey and Friends

13. _____ was his first major live-action film.
   a. Treasure Island
   b. Treats Island

14. Walt Disney decided to create a full-length animated film called _____.
   a. Snow White
   b. Robin Hood

Grammar: some, any, a, an

Score: ____________________

Date: ____________________

A is used when the next word starts with a consonant sound.
AN is used when the next word starts with a vowel sound.
Some is generally used in positive sentences.
Any is generally used in negative sentences.

Rewrite the *scrambled words* so they form a complete *sentence.*

1. ______________________________

We · any · have · don't · apples.

2. ______________________________

make · some · lunch. · for · sandwiches · We · can

3. ______________________________

fridge. · in · There · the · isn't · any · milk

4. ______________________________

buy · I · to · tomatoes. · and · an · onion · need · some

5. ______________________________

carrots. · need · any · tomatoes · or · doesn't · She

6. ______________________________

have · any · we · potatoes? · Do

7. ______________________________

some · grapes. · We · have · don't · but · we · strawberries · any · have

8. ______________________________

There · any · isn't · sugar · in · bowl. · the

9. ______________________________

Can · a · I · banana, · have · please?

10. ______________________________

on · there · the · any · apples · counter? · Are

11. ______________________________

decision. · an · wasn't · easy · It

12. ______________________________

a · She · forced · smile.

13. ______________________________

an · I · appointment. · have

14. ______________________________

horseman, · you · excellent · He · an · is · know.

15. ______________________________

I · job, · an · easy · It's · expected. · like

16. ______________________________

That · was · no-brainer. · a

17. ______________________________

I · an · owe · me · think · you · explanation.

18. ______________________________

at · the · tree. · foot · of · he · stopped · a · Suddenly

Score: ____________________

History Reading Comprehension: John Hanson

Date: ____________

Many people do not realize that when we refer to the President of the United States, we are actually referring to presidents elected under the United States Constitution. Everyone knows that George Washington was the first president in that sense. However, the predecessor to the Constitution, the Articles of Confederation, also called for a president, albeit one with greatly limited powers. Under the Articles of Confederation, eight men were appointed to one-year terms as president. Under the Articles of Confederation, John Hanson became the first President of the United States in Congress Assembled in November 1781.

Many argue that John Hanson, rather than George Washington, was the first President of the United States, but this is not entirely correct. The United States had no executive branch under the Articles of Confederation. Within the Confederation Congress, the President of Congress was a ceremonial position. Although the job required Hanson to deal with correspondence and sign official documents, it was not the type of work that any President of the United States would have done under the Constitution.

Hanson disliked his job as well, finding it tedious and wishing to resign. Unfortunately, the Articles of Confederation did not account for succession, so his departure would have left Congress without a President. So he stayed in office because he loved his country and felt obligated to do so.

During his tenure, which lasted from November 5, 1781 to November 3, 1782, he was able to remove all foreign troops and flags from American soil. He also established the Treasury Department, as well as the first Secretary of War and Foreign Affairs Department. He led the flight to ensure the statehood of the Western Territories beyond the Appalachian Mountains, which had previously been controlled by some of the original thirteen colonies.

What's most intriguing is that Hanson is also credited with establishing Thanksgiving Day as the fourth Thursday of November.

Being the first person in this position as President of Congress was not an easy task. So it's amazing that Hanson was able to accomplish so much. Furthermore, instead of the current four-year term, Presidents under the Articles of Confederation served only one year. So, accomplishing anything in such a short period of time was a great accomplishment.

Hanson played an important role in the development of United States Constitutional History, which is often overlooked but is undeniably true. Hanson is frequently referred to as the "forgotten first President." According to Seymour Weyss Smith's biography of him, John Hanson, Our First President, the American Revolution had two primary leaders: George Washington in the military sphere and John Hanson in the political sphere. Despite the fact that one position was purely ceremonial and the other was more official, statues of both men can be found in the United States Capitol in Washington, D.C.

Hanson died at the age of 62 on November 15, 1783.

1. Hanson served from November 5, 1781 until December 3, 1782
   a. True
   b. False

2. Hanson really LOVED his job.
   a. True
   b. False

3. Under the Articles of Confederation, the United States had no ________.
   a. executive branch
   b. congress office

4. The President of Congress was a _____ position within the Confederation Congress.
   a. senate
   b. ceremonial

5. In November 1781, Hanson became the first President of the United States in Congress Assembled, under the _____.
   a. Articles of Congress
   b. Articles of Confederation

6. ____ men were appointed to serve one year terms as president under the Articles of Confederation.
   a. Eight
   b. Two

7. Hanson was able to remove all _____ troops from American lands.
   a. foreign
   b. USA

8. Hanson is also responsible for establishing _____ as the fourth Thursday in November.
   a. Christmas Day
   b. Thanksgiving Day

9. Instead of the four year term that current Presidents serve, Presidents under the Articles of Confederation served only ___ year.
   a. one
   b. three

10. Hanson died on November 15, 1783 at the age of ____.
    a. 64
    b. sixty-two

11. Both George Washington and Hanson are commemorated with ____ in the United States Capitol in Washington, D.C.
    a. houses
    b. statues

12. George Washington in the military sphere and John Hanson in the ____ sphere.
    a. presidential
    b. political

Score: ______________________

Date: ______________

Geography: Canada

Canada is the world's second-largest country, covering 10 million square kilometers. Canada's borders are bounded by three oceans: the Pacific Ocean to the west, the Atlantic Ocean to the east, and the Arctic Ocean to the north. The Canada-United States border runs along Canada's southern border.

Queen Victoria, Queen Elizabeth II's great-great-grandmother, chose Ottawa, which is located on the Ottawa River, as the capital in 1857. It is now the fourth largest metropolitan area in Canada. The National Capital Region, which encompasses 4,700 square kilometers around Ottawa, preserves and improves the area's built heritage and natural environment.

Canada is divided into ten provinces and three territories. Each province and territory has a separate capital city. You should be familiar with the capitals of your province or territory, as well as those of Canada.

Below are some of Canada's Territories, Provinces, and Capital Cities. Draw a line through each word you find.

R	L	U	G	M	A	N	I	T	O	B	A	N	K	M	E	X	L	S	P
W	K	A	K	B	B	H	A	L	B	E	R	T	A	G	D	K	P	R	R
Q	M	N	Y	N	X	W	I	S	Z	L	X	B	Q	E	K	B	T	X	I
I	Q	A	L	U	I	T	E	G	I	R	T	O	R	O	N	T	O	Y	N
A	B	R	I	T	I	S	H	C	O	L	U	M	B	I	A	E	C	E	C
V	N	N	R	S	Q	H	G	I	W	I	N	N	I	P	E	G	H	L	E
S	O	G	X	Z	G	A	O	N	T	A	R	I	O	F	B	R	A	L	E
T	V	Q	Z	E	D	M	O	N	T	O	N	C	D	F	W	Q	R	O	D
.	A	V	H	B	E	F	R	E	D	E	R	I	C	T	O	N	L	W	W
J	S	V	P	O	Q	U	E	B	E	C	C	I	T	Y	N	W	O	K	A
O	C	Y	J	R	W	S	H	V	C	V	Q	H	W	W	U	L	T	N	R
H	O	E	L	E	E	B	A	A	Z	O	U	Q	G	H	N	V	T	I	D
N	T	W	X	G	A	Q	L	S	T	J	E	F	H	I	A	I	E	F	I
'	I	K	M	I	D	C	I	L	X	L	B	U	V	T	V	C	T	E	S
S	A	C	P	N	C	O	F	T	Z	M	E	U	E	E	U	T	O	N	L
P	Q	Y	F	A	P	L	A	G	P	Y	C	F	M	H	T	O	W	B	A
I	W	S	D	R	Y	W	X	G	W	P	U	E	U	O	G	R	N	M	N
Y	N	E	W	B	R	U	N	S	W	I	C	K	T	R	P	I	C	R	D
R	X	B	T	E	R	V	Y	J	B	H	H	M	K	S	W	A	J	N	Z
G	F	S	A	S	K	A	T	C	H	E	W	A	N	E	Y	U	K	O	N

Yukon	Nunavut	Nova Scotia	Prince Edward Island	New Brunswick
Quebec	Ontario	Manitoba	Saskatchewan	Alberta
British Columbia	Victoria	Edmonton	Regina	Winnipeg
Toronto	Quebec City	Fredericton	Charlottetown	Halifax
St. John's	Iqaluit	Yellowknife	Whitehorse	

History: Henry VIII

Score: ____________________

Date: ____________

Read about Henry VIII and answer whatever questions you can.

Read here: https://www.britannica.com/biography/Henry-VIII-king-of-England (or Google "**Britannica.com Henry VIII**")

1. **Henry only became king because his elder brother died young.**
   a. True
   b. False

2. **The Tudors were an English royal dynasty in the 15th century.**
   a. True
   b. False

3. **The young Henry 8th was a weak and sickly young man.**
   a. True
   b. False

4. **His father, Henry 7th, was an unpopular king.**
   a. True
   b. False

5. **Henry tried to emulate his father's way of ruling.**
   a. True
   b. False

6. **Henry married Catherine of Aragon, his brother's wife.**
   a. True
   b. False

7. **Henry had a good relationship with his father-in-law, Ferdinand 2**
   a. True
   b. False

8. **Europe's unity at the time depended on a balance of power between Spain and France.**
   a. True
   b. False

9. **Cardinal Wolsey was a trusted advisor and friend of Henry 8.**
   a. True
   b. False

10. **Many thought that it was actually Wolsey who ruled England.**
    a. True
    b. False

11. **Henry disapproved of Wolsey's ambition of becoming the pope.**
    a. True
    b. False

12. **When Charles 5 came to power, Henry lost influence in Europe.**
    a. True
    b. False

13. **Wolsey lost power when his plans damaged English trade with the Netherlands**
    a. True
    b. False

14. **Ferdinand 2 of Aragon was Queen Catherine's grandfather.**
    a. True
    b. False

15. **By 1523 the English were becoming increasingly dissatisfied with the king.**
    a. True
    b. False

16. **By 1527 Wolsey's policies had brought England to the point of bankruptcy.**
    a. True
    b. False

17. **"The King's Matter" was a plan to break away from the Catholic Church.**
    a. True
    b. False

18. **Henry was a strong believer in the Catholic Church.**
    a. True
    b. False

19. **Both the pope and Henry believed he had been wrong to marry Catherine of Aragon.**
    a. True
    b. False

20. **The pope refused to annul Henry's marriage because a previous pope had allowed it.**
    a. True
    b. False

21. **Henry got rid of Wolsey because he couldn't find a solution to his marital problem.**
    a. True
    b. False

22. **Thomas More promised to help the king divorce.**
    a. True
    b. False

23. **Henry, with Thomas More, tried to preserve Catholicism in England.**
    a. True
    b. False

24. **Thomas More organized the break from Rome in 1532.**
    a. True
    b. False

25. **The split from Rome made the king the leader of the new church.**
    a. True
    b. False

26. **The king converted to protestantism because he no longer believed in the Catholic Church.**
    a. True
    b. False

27. **Henry created a completely new church based on his own religious beliefs.**
    a. True
    b. False

28. **Henry was a great admirer of Luther and used him for inspiration.**
    a. True
    b. False

29. **Henry was excommunicated by the pope.**
    a. True
    b. False

30. **Henry raised money by selling the Catholic Church's lands in England.**
    a. True
    b. False

Score: ____________________

Date: ____________________

Math Vocabulary Quiz

1. **algebraic equation**
    a. an arrangement of items or events in which order does not matter
    b. a relation in which each member of the domain is paired with exactly one member of the range
    c. equality of two expressions formulated by applying to a set of variables the algebraic operations

2. **direct evidence**
    a. evidence that, if believed, directly proves a fact
    b. one or more sets of numbers on a number line or coordinate/grid paper
    c. cause and effect relationships that keep a system working within its limits

3. **variable**
    a. two mathematical expressions are equal
    b. a symbol (usually a letter) standing in for an unknown numerical value in an equation
    c. the job or action of individual parts working together to form a whole

4. **scale factor**
    a. a method of writing very large or very small numbers by using powers of 10
    b. a graph with points plotted to show a possible relationship between two sets of data
    c. the ratio of the lengths of two corresponding sides of two similar polygons or solids

5. **computation**
    a. an object, event, idea, feeling, time period
    b. Finding an answer by using mathematics or logic
    c. numerical value in an equation

6. **equivalent**
    a. two meanings, numbers, or quantities that are the same
    b. symbol which works as a placeholder for expression
    c. one on each side of an equals numbers

7. **equation**
    a. changeable a variable climate
    b. two math expressions are equal (indicated by the sign =)
    c. simply a statement in math in which two things equal

8. **analyze**
    a. a number tendency or inclination: prejudice
    b. to study or determine the nature and relationship of the parts of (something) by analysis
    c. a verbal subtraction argument; a regulated discussion of a problem between two opposing sides

9. structure

a. the relation of a word to its base
b. a noun in the form of the present participle of a verb
c. the way that something is built, arranged, or organized

10. summarize

a. the result so obtain a number
b. 7 groups can be formed with 9 units
c. Express the most important facts or ideas about something or someone in a short and clear form

11. addends

a. the number resulting from the division
b. answer after we divide one number by another
c. A quantity to be added to another

12. place value

a. divide one number by another
b. multiplied by 100 between a test score and a standard value
c. the basis of our entire number system

13. difference

a. mathematical term that refers to the result of subtract
b. The result of subtracting one number from another.
c. quotient is the integer part of the result

14. divisor

a. a number by which another number is to be divided.
b. two variables, divided by a horizontal line

15. numerator

a. expression that identifies factors to be multiplied
b. number above the line of a fraction, showing the number of parts of the whole
c. two or more numbers when multiplied together

16. quotient

a. the result of an addition
b. result of multiplying two or more values
c. number obtained by dividing one number by another

Write sentences using words from above: Choose at least 5 different words.

1. ....

2. ....

3. ....

4. ....

5. ....

Name: ____________________

Math: Look It Up! Pop Quiz

Date: ____________

Learn some basic vocabulary words that you will come across again and again in the course of your studies in algebra. By knowing the definitions of most algebra words, you will be able to construct and solve algebra problems much more easily.

Find the answer to the questions below by *looking up each word. (The wording can be tricky. Take your time.)*

1. improper fraction
    a. a fraction that represents both positive and negative numbers that has a value more than 1
    b. a fraction in which the numerator is greater than the denominator, is always 1 or greater
    c. a fraction that the denominator is equal to the numerator

2. equivalent fraction
    a. a fraction that has a DIFFERENT value as a given fraction
    b. a fraction that has the SAME value as a given fraction
    c. a fraction that has an EQUAL value as a given fraction

3. simplest form of fraction
    a. an equivalent fraction for which the only common factor of the numerator and denominator is 1
    b. an equivalent fraction for which the only least factor of the denominator is -1
    c. an equal value fraction for which the only common factor of the numerator and denominator is -1

4. mixed number
    a. the sum of a positive fraction and a reciprocal
    b. the sum of a whole number and a proper fraction
    c. the sum of a variable and a fraction

5. reciprocal
    a. a number that can be multiplied by another number to make 1
    b. a number that can be divided by another number to make 10
    c. a number that can be subtracted by another number to make -1

6. percent
    a. a ratio that compares a number to 100
    b. a percentage that compares a number to 0.1
    c. a 1/2 ratio that equals a number to 100

7. sequence

a. a set of addition numbers that follow a operation

b. a set of letters & numbers divided by 5 that makes a sequence

c. a set of numbers that follow a pattern

8. arithmetic sequence

a. a sequence where ONE term is found by dividing or subtracting the exact same number to the previous term

b. a sequence where NO term is found by multiplying the exact same number to the previous term

c. a sequence where EACH term is found by adding or subtracting the exact same number to the previous term

9. geometric sequence

a. a sequence where each term is found by multiplying or dividing by the exact same number to the previous term

b. a sequence where each term is divided or subtracted by the same fraction to the previous term

c. a sequence where each term is solved by adding or dividing by a different number to the previous term

10. order of operations

a. the procedure to follow when simplifying a numerical expression

b. the procedure to follow when adding any fraction by 100

c. the procedure to follow when simplifying an equation with the same answer

11. variable expression

a. a mathematical phrase that contains numbers and operation symbols

b. a mathematical phrase that contains variables, addition, and operation sequence

c. a mathematical phrase that contains variables, numbers, and operation symbols

12. absolute value

a. a whole number on the number line from one to zero

b. the distance a number is from zero on the number line

c. the range a number is from one on the number line

13. integers

a. a set of numbers that equal to fractions line variables

b. a set of numbers that includes equal numbers and their difference

c. a set of numbers that includes whole numbers and their opposites

14. x-axis

a. the horizontal number line that, together with the y-axis, establishes the coordinate plane

b. the vertical number line that, together with the y-axis, establishes the coordinate plane

c. both horizontal & vertical number line that, together with the y-axis, establishes the coordinate plane

15. y-axis

a. the horizontal number line that, together with the x-axis, establishes the coordinate plane

b. the vertical number line that, together with the x-axis, establishes the coordinate plane

c. the vertical number line that, together with the x or y-axis, establishes the coordinate plane

16. coordinate plane

a. plane formed by two number lines (the horizontal x-axis and the vertical y-axis) intersecting at their zero points

b. plane formed by three number line (the vertical y-axis and the horizontal x-axis) intersecting at their two points

c. plane formed by one number line (the horizontal y-axis and the vertical x-axis) intersecting at their -1 points

17. quadrant

a. three sections on the axis plane formed by the intersection of the x-axis and the y-axis

b. one of four sections on the coordinate plane formed by the intersection of the x-axis and the y-axis

c. one of two sections on the four plane formed by the intersection of the x-axis

18. ordered pair

a. a pair of integer number sets that gives the range of a point in the axis plane. Also known as the "x-axis" of a point.

b. a pair of equal numbers that gives the range of a point in the axis plane. Also known as the "y-axis" of a point.

c. a pair of numbers that gives the location of a point in the coordinate plane. Also known as the "coordinates" of a point.

19. x-coordinate

a. the number that indicates the position of a point to the left or right of the y-axis

b. the number that indicates the range of a point to the left ONLY of the y-axis

c. the number that indicates the range of a point to both sides of the x-axis

20. y-coordinate

a. the number that indicates the value of a point only above the x-axis

b. the number that indicates the position of a point above or below the x-axis

c. the number that indicates the value or range of a point only above the y-axis

21. inverse operations

a. operations that divide evenly into each other

b. operations that undo each other

c. operations that equals to each other

22. inequality

a. a math sentence that uses a symbol (<, >, ≤, ≥, ≠) to indicate that the left and right sides of the sentence hold values that are different

b. a math sentence that uses a letter (x or y) to indicate that the left and right sides of the sentence hold values that are different

c. a math sentence that uses both numbers and letters (1=x or 2=y) to indicate that the left and right sides of the sentence hold values that are different

23. perimeter

a. the range around the outside or inside of a figure

b. the distance around the outside of a figure

c. the distance around the inside of a figure

24. circumference

a. the distance around a circle

b. the cube squared value around a circle

c. the range around a square

25. area

a. the number of circle units inside a 3-dimensional figure
b. the number of triangle units inside a 2-dimensional figure
c. the number of square units inside a 2-dimensional figure

26. volume

a. the number of cubic squared units inside a 2-dimensional figure
b. the number of cubic or circle units inside a 1-dimensional figure
c. the number of cubic units inside a 3-dimensional figure

27. radius

a. a line segment that runs from the center of the circle to somewhere on the circle
b. a line segment that runs from the middle of the circle to end of the circle
c. a line segment that runs from the middle of the square to start of the square

28. chord

a. a circle distance that runs from somewhere on the far left to another place on the circle
b. a line around a circle that runs from somewhere on the right to another place on the circle
c. a line segment that runs from somewhere on the circle to another place on the circle

29. diameter

a. a thin line that passes through the end of the circle
b. a 1/2" line that passes through the top of the circle
c. a chord that passes through the center of the circle

30. mean

a. the sum of the data items added by the number of data items minus 2
b. the sum of the data items divided by the number of data items
c. the sum of the data items divdied by the number of even data items less than 1

31. median

a. the middle data item found after sorting the data items in ascending order
b. the first data item found after sorting the data items in descending order
c. the middle & last data item found after sorting the data items in ascending order

32. mode

a. the data item that occurs less than two times
b. the data item that occurs when two or more numbers equal
c. the data item that occurs most often

33. range

a. the difference between the highest and the lowest data item
b. the difference between the numbers less than 10 and the lowest number item 2
c. the difference between the middle number and the lowest number item

34. outlier

a. a data item that is much higher or much lower than all the other data items
b. a data item that is much lower or less than all the other data items
c. a data item that is always higher than 1 or less than all the other data items

35. ratio

a. a comparison of two quantities by subtraction
b. a comparison of two quantities by multiplication
c. a comparison of two quantities by division

36. rate

a. a ratio that has equal range and distance measured within the first unit set
b. a ratio that has equal quantities measured in the same units
c. a ratio that compares quantities measured in different units

37. proportion

a. a statement (equation) showing two ratios to be equal
b. a statement (property) showing the distance between two variables
c. a statement (ratio) showing five or more ratios to be equal

38. outcomes

a. possible answer when two numbers are the same
b. possible results when the action is by division
c. possible results of action

39. probability

a. a ratio that explains the likelihood of two division problems with equal answers
b. a ratio that explains the likelihood of an event
c. a ratio that explains the likelihood of the distance and miles between to places

40. theoretical probability

a. the probability of the highest favorable number of possible outcomes (based on what is not expected to occur).
b. the ratio of the number of favorable outcomes to the number of possible outcomes (based on what is expected to occur).
c. the probability of the lowest favorable number of possible outcomes (based on what is expected to occur when added by 5).

41. experimental probability

a. the ratio of the number of times multiplied by the number of events that occur to the number of events times 5 (based on real experimental data).
b. the ratio of the number of times by 2 when an event occurs to the number of times times 2 an experiment is done (based on real experimental data).
c. the ratio of the number of times an event occurs to the number of times an experiment is done (based on real experimental data).

42. distributive property

a. a way to simplify an expression that contains a single term being multiplied by a group of terms.
b. a way to simplify an expression that contains a range of like terms being divided by a group of like terms.
c. a way to simplify an expression that contains a equal like term being added by a group of terms.

43. term

a. a number, a variable, or probability of an equal number and a variable(s)
b. a number, a variable, or expression of a range of numbers and a variable(s)
c. a number, a variable, or product of a number and a variable(s)

44. Constant

a. a term with no variable + y part (i.e. 4+y)
b. a term with no variable - x value (i.e. 8-x)
c. a term with no variable part (i.e. a number)

45. Coefficient

a. a number that multiplies a variable
b. a number that divides a variable
c. a number that subtracts a variable

46. Probability is the likelihood of something happening.

a. True
b. False

47. To calculate probability, you need to know how many possible options or _____ there are and how many right combinations you have.

a. outcomes
b. numbers
c. fraction

48. _, _, and _ have two common factors: 2 and 4.

a. 2, 6, and 9
b. 12, 20, and 24
c. 1,4, and 24

49. How do you write a polynomial expression?

a. 3x2 -2x-10
b. 32 -2x-+10y
c. y+3x2 -2x-10

50. How can you simplify rational expression?

a. eliminate all factors that are common of the numerator and the denominator
b. eliminate only 1 factor that are common of the numerator and the denominator
c. eliminate NO factors that are common of the numerator and the denominator

51. The slope intercept form is one of many forms that represents the linear relationship between two variables.

a. True
b. False

52. The slope intercept form equation is written as follows:

a. z = a x + b
b. y = y x + m
c. y = m x + b

53. Simplifying radicals is that we do NOT remove the radicals from the denominator.

a. True
b. False

54. 2 1/3 is a mixed fraction.

a. True
b. False

55. The word ____ literally means 'per hundred.' We use this symbol - %.

a. asterisk
b. percent
c. divide

56. less than or equal to symbol

a. ≤
b. <
c. ≥

57. distance between points x and y

a. |x-y|
b. |x+y|
c. |x-y+x+y|

58. greater than or equal to

a. <
b. ≤
c. ≥

Math:Test Your Knowledge Refresher

Score: ____________________

Date: ____________

1. Addends are numbers_______

a. used in an addition problem.
b. used in an addition or multiplication problem.
c. used in an subtraction problem.

2. What is an example of an Addend?

a. In 9 + 1 = 10, the 9 and the 10 are addends.
b. In 8 - 3 = 5, the 8 and the 3 are addends.
c. In 8 + 3 = 11, the 8 and the 3 are addends.

3. What is a fact family?

a. a group of math facts or equations created using the same set of numbers.
b. is when you take one number and add it together a number of times.
c. is taking away one or more items from a group of items.

4. Which is an example of a fact family?

a. 2, 4, and 6: 2 x 2 = 4, 4 x 2 = 8, 6 − 2 = 4, and 6 − 4 = 2.
b. 1, 2, and 12: 1 + 1 = 2, 2 + 2 = 4, 12 − 12 = 0, and 12 − 2 = 10.
c. 10, 2, and 12: 10 + 2 = 12, 2 + 10 = 12, 12 − 10 = 2, and 12 − 2 = 10.

5. The fact family for 3, 8 and 24 is a set of four multiplication and division facts. Which one is correct?

a. 3 × 8 = 24| 8 × 3 = 24| 24 ÷ 3 = 8| 24 ÷ 8 = 3
b. 3 + 8 = 11| 8 × 3 = 24| 8 ÷ 8 = 0| 24 ÷ 8 = 3
c. 3 × 3 = 9| 8 × 3 = 24| 24 + 3 = 27| 24 ÷ 8 = 3

6. A prime number is________

a. the ways that numbers are combined to make new numbers.
b. any number that is only divisible by itself and 1.
c. the number you are rounding followed by 5, 6, 7, 8, or 9.

7. Examples of prime numbers_____

a. 2, 8 and 15
b. 2, 5 and 17
c. 4, 6 and 10

8. Numbers such as _______ are not prime, because they are divisible by more than just themselves and 1.

a. 2 or 7
b. 5 or 11
c. 15 or 21

9. Prime factor is the factor_______________

a. of the first number which is NOT a prime number.
b. of the smallest to greatest prime number starting with 0..
c. of the given number which is a prime number.

10. The prime factors of 15 _____________

a. are 3 and 5 (because 3×5=15, and 3 and 5 are prime numbers)
b. are 5 and 10 (because 5+10=15, and 10 and 5 are prime numbers)
c. are 25 and 10 (because 25-10=15, and 10 and 5 are prime numbers)

11. A factor tree is a ________

a. natural numbers greater than one that are not products of two smaller natural numbers.

b. diagram that is used to break down a number into its factors until all the numbers left are prime.

c. is divisible by 1, and it's divisible by itself.

12. The greatest common denominator is the _____

a. smallest positive integer that multiplies the numbers without a remainder.

b. largest negative integer that subtracts the numbers without a remainder.

c. largest positive integer that divides the numbers without a remainder.

13. The greatest common factor of 8 and 12 is_____?

a. 12

b. 6

c. 4

14. The lowest common denominator is the ____?

a. lowest common multiple of the denominators of a set of fractions.

b. lowest common multiple of the denominators of a group of numbers divided by 10.

c. lowest common subtraction of the first number of a set of fractions.

15. What is the LCD of 12 and 8?

a. 12 and 8 is 24

b. 12 and 8 is 32

c. 12 and 8 is 20

16. This math concept tells you that to divide means to split fairly.

a. Division

b. Addition

c. Algebra

17. Reduce 48/28 to lowest terms.

a. 12/5

b. 12/7

c. 7/28

18. Which of the following fractions CANNOT be reduced further?

a. 5/3

b. 33/12

c. 16/9

19. It is possible to make a fraction simpler without completely simplifying it.

a. True

b. False

20. Factor 18 into prime factors:

a. 18 = 3 * 3 * 2

b. 18 = 2 * 3 * 3

c. 18 = 1 * 3 * 2

21. An improper fraction is one where the numerator is smaller than the denominator.

a. True

b. False

22. Fractions that have a numerator with a higher value than the denominator

a. simple fractions

b. simplified fractions

c. improper fractions

Reading Comprehension: Social Media Safety

Score: ________________________

Date: _______________

Interactions	policies	relationship	post	pop-ups
incidents	identity	connect	Personal	logins
negative	harmful	restrictive	steal	privacy
passwords	viruses	platform	abuse	security

In the last 20 years, socializing has evolved dramatically. ________________ between people are referred to as socializing. At one time, socializing meant getting together with family and friends. It now frequently refers to accessing the Internet via social media or websites that allow you to ________________ and interact with other people.

One of the first things you can do to protect yourself while online occurs before you even visit a social media website. Ascertain that your computer is outfitted with up-to-date computer ________________ software. This software detects and removes ________________ that are harmful to your computer. When you use your computer, these viruses can sometimes hack into it and ________________ your information, such as ________________. Create strong ________________ for all of your social media accounts. This is necessary to prevent others from accessing your social media account.

Internet security settings are pre-installed on all computers. These can be as loose or as ________________ as you want them to be. To be safe, it is recommended that the Internet security settings be set to medium or higher. This enables your computer to block ________________ and warn you when you are about to visit a potentially harmful website.

Two things to keep in mind

- Don't ________________ anything you wouldn't want broadcast to the entire world.
- The 'Golden Rule' of life is to treat others as you would like to be treated.

________________ information about one's identity should not be posted or shared on social media. Phone numbers, addresses, social security numbers, and family information are all included. This information can be used to recreate your ________________ and should never be made public.

Make use of the ________________ settings on the social media website. These can be used to control who can post information to your wall as well as who can see what is posted on it. Let's face it: there are some things you don't mind if your family and close friends know about, but you don't necessarily want your coworkers to find out about them through online posts.

Be positive.

Be cautious about what you post on any social media ________________. Posting something ________________ about someone hurts their character and opens the door for them, or someone else, to do the same to you. If you are not in a good mood or are upset, think twice. What you post could be ________________ to you or someone else. Once you've made a post, it's always there. Even if you delete the post, this remains true!

If you are in a bad social media ________________ and are being harassed or bullied, you can report it to the social media company. They all have ________________ in place to deal with people who ________________ their websites. Make a note of these ________________ and report them to the company. You may also save the life of another person.

Science: Kinetic Molecular Theory

The Kinetic Molecular Theory (KMT) is a model that explains the behavior of matter based on a set of postulates.

Pour yourself a drink of water. Using a dropper, add a few drops of red food coloring to the mixture. So, what happens next? The red food coloring drops should slowly work their way down the glass of water, spreading out to stain the entire glass crimson in color. What causes this to happen? It happens because both substances are made up of constantly moving molecules. One of the key concepts of the kinetic molecular theory is that these molecules have energy.

Liquids are fluid and can flow, which is one of their most noticeable characteristics. Liquids have a specific volume but no specific shape. Liquids are stated to have low compressibility, which means that packing liquid particles closer together is difficult.

Solids have well-defined shapes and volumes. Solid particles do travel, but just a short distance! Solid particles vibrate in situ because they have minimal kinetic energy. As a result, they are unable to flow like liquids.

Moving Matter

The ability to make changes in matter is defined as energy. When you lift your arm or take a step, for example, your body consumes chemical energy. Energy is utilized to move matter—you—in both circumstances. Any moving matter contains energy simply because it is moving. Kinetic energy is the energy of moving matter.

What are the 4 main points of kinetic molecular theory?

What are the 5 postulates of KMT?

What is the Kelvin scale and how does it relate to kinetic theory?

How does KMT explain Dalton's law?

Does pressure increase kinetic energy?

Extra Credit: Explain how kinetic energy is related to the mass and velocity of a particle.

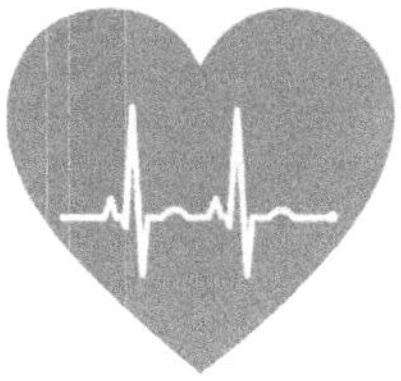

Score: ______________________

Science: Different Blood Types

Date: ______________

compatible	transfusion	recipient's	antibodies	survive
donate	bloodstream	eight	negative	antigens

What comes to mind when you think of blood? It may be the color red, a hospital, or even a horror film! Blood is something that your body requires to ______________, regardless of how you feel about it. Did you realize, though, that not everyone has the same blood type? There are __________ different kinds in total! The letters A, B, and O, as well as positive or ________________ signs, distinguish these blood types. O+, O-, A+, A-, B+, B-, AB+, and AB- are the eight blood types.

What Is the Importance of Blood Types?

Don't be concerned if your blood type differs from that of others! There is no such thing as a better or healthier blood type. The sole reason to know your blood type is in case you need to ____________ or give blood to someone in an emergency. A blood ______________________ is a process of transferring blood from one person to another.

Blood transfusions are only effective when the donor's blood is ____________________ with the ______________________ blood. Some blood types don't mix well because the body produces antibodies to fight off any unfamiliar ________________ that enter the ______________________. Antibodies act as warriors in your blood, guarding you against alien intruders. Assume you have Type A blood, which contains A antigens solely, and someone with Type B blood wishes to donate blood to you. Your body does not recognize B antigens; thus, ____________________ are produced to combat them! This has the potential to make you sick. As a result, people with Type A blood should only receive blood from those with Type A blood or Type O blood, as O blood lacks both A and B antigens.

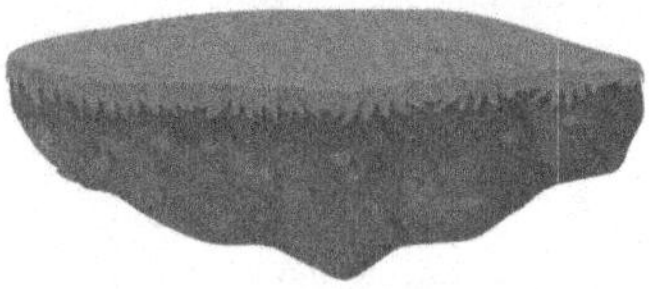

Geography: Landform

Score: ____________________

Date: ____________

A landform is a natural or man-made feature of the Earth's or another planet's solid surface. A given terrain is made up of landforms, and their arrangement in the landscape is known as topography.

1. Lakes are an inland body of water, usually fresh
   a. True
   b. False

2. A sea is the direction from which a river flows
   a. True
   b. False

3. A delta is the land deposited at the mouth of a river
   a. True
   b. False

4. What landform is surrounded by water on three sides?
   a. An island
   b. A peninsula

5. A river is a narrow man-made channel of water that joins other bodies of water
   a. True
   b. False

6. The mouth is where a river flows into a larger body of water.
   a. True
   b. False

7. Which of the following is NOT a landform?
   a. An island
   b. A river

8. Downstream is the direction toward which a river flows.
   a. True
   b. False

9. A sea is a large area of salt water smaller than an ocean.
   a. True
   b. False

10. A bay is land deposited at the mouth of a river.
   a. True
   b. False

11. How are a valley and a canyon alike?
   a. They are both tall landforms.
   b. They are both low landforms.

12. A canal is a man-made channel of water that joins other bodies of water.
   a. True
   b. False

13. A lake is a place where a river begins.
   a. True
   b. False

14. Which types of landforms are always flat?
   a. Plateaus and plains
   b. Hills and peninsulas

Score: ____________________

Science: Organelles

Date: ____________

Organelles are the inside elements of a cell that are responsible for all of the tasks that keep the cell healthy and alive. Each organelle has a distinct function. The word "organelle" means "small organ," and these tiny powerhouses are responsible for everything from defending the cell to repairing/healing, assisting in the development, removing waste products, and even reproduction. The function of each organelle is also influenced by the functions of other organelles. The cell will perish if any organelle fails to perform its function.

Many of the same types of organelles exist in both plant and animal cells, and they function in similar ways. Both plant and animal cells have a total of ten organelles.

Plant-like cells, on the other hand, are built solely for photosynthesis and utilize the rigid wall, as well as organelles that operate to generate energy from sunlight. Organelles in animal-like cells have a lot greater variety and capability.

Match each term with a definition.

1	☐	nucleus	powerhouse of the cell	A
2	☐	lysosomes	lipid synthesis	B
3	☐	Golgi Apparatus	protein synthesis + modifications	C
4	☐	Mitochondria	protein synthesis	D
5	☐	SER	responsible for chromosome segregation	E
6	☐	RER	where DNA is stored	F
7	☐	Microtubules	modification of proteins; "post-office" of the cell	G
8	☐	ribosomes	stores water in plant cells	H
9	☐	peroxysomes	prevents excessive uptake of water, protects the cell (in plants)	I
10	☐	cell wall	degradation of proteins and cellular waste	J
11	☐	chloroplast	degradation of H2O2	K
12	☐	central vacuole	site of photosynthesis	L

Score: ____________________

Science: Space

Date: ____________

No one can hear you scream in space. This is due to the fact that space is devoid of air - it is a vacuum. In a vacuum, sound waves cannot travel. 'Outer space' begins roughly 100 kilometers above the Earth's surface, where the atmosphere that surrounds our planet dissipates. Space appears as a black blanket speckled with stars because there is no air to disperse sunlight and generate a blue sky.

Across

3. The 4 inner planets and 4 outer planets are separated by the _________ Belt.
4. The 4 inner planets are referred to as ____ planets because they are rocky and dense- Earth like
7. only about 1/2 the size of earth- tilted similar to earth- rusty surface- 2 moons
9. Revolves as rapidly as Jupiter- second largest planet- could float in water- Oh yeah...it has rings
10. Sideways rotation- retrograde rotation- has 11 very thin rings
13. ________ Solstice is when we have the longest amount of daylight for that year and the shortest night
16. The way we see the moon as it orbits around the sun and reflects the Sun's light
17. ________ Solstice is when we have the shortest amount of daylight for that year and the longest night

Down

1. The coming apart of an atom that gives off a lot of energy
2. The coming together of 2 atoms that releases a lot of energy - more than fission!
5. smallest planet- slowest rotation- magnetic
6. most like earth size wise- atmospheric pressure able to crush us- retrograde rotation
8. Fastest rotation (a little less than half an earth day)- largest planet- 29 years for 1 trip around the Sun- known also for Great Red Spot
11. Last planet in our solar system- Dark blue and windy-
12. Dwarf planet found just inside the Kuiper Belt- has a few moons- orbit actually crosses Neptune periodically
15. _______ Equinox is an occurrence in the fall where the daylight and nighttime are equivalent
17. the amount of moon that you can see is increasing
18. the amount of moon that you can see is decreasing
19. During a _______ Eclipse the shadow of the earth goes across the face of the moon

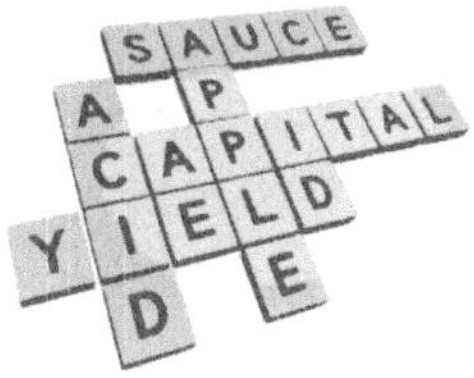

Score: ______________________

Spelling Words Crossword

Date: ______________

Across

1. We will meet at our summer ___ for the wedding
3. My father studied _____.
6. The ______ of the donors came as a surprise.
7. There was a growing ____ between the two sides.
8. The old home was in a ______ state.
9. The ____ between the villages was growing larger.

Down

2. The lamb ____ is nearly done cooking
4. The economic ____ appears to be working.
5. I've always wanted to play the ______.
10. The people were ____ of his motives.
11. Pass the ____ to me so that I can take my medicine.
12. The doctor told my grandma to take only one ____ a day.

VITAMIN RESIDENCE
ANIMOSITY WARY
XYLOPHONE SHANK
CHASM PODIATRY
SYRINGE GENEROSITY
STIMULUS RUINOUS

Score: ____________________

Date: ____________

9th Grade Spelling Words Unscramble

symphony	analysis	agriculture	twelfth	abundant	tendency
souvenir	technique	laborious	ambassador	sophomore	specific
symbol	specimen	aggressive	jealousy	absorption	journal
island	acceptable	syllable	absence	amateur	temperature

1. NECASEB a _ _ _ _ _ e
2. PNSOABROTI _ b _ _ _ _ t _ _ n
3. ABDNUTNA _ _ _ _ d _ _ t
4. BLEATAPCEC _ _ _ _ _ t a _ _ e
5. SLYBLELA _ _ _ _ a _ _ e
6. BLOMYS _ y _ _ _ l
7. OMHYPSYN _ y _ _ _ _ n _
8. ENUTICQHE t _ c _ _ _ _ _ _
9. EPTMERUATRE _ e m _ _ _ _ _ _ _ e
10. EYNNDCET _ _ n _ _ _ c _
11. GEEGSARVIS _ g g _ _ s _ _ _ _
12. ARTEULICRUG _ _ _ i c _ _ _ u _ _
13. UMTEAAR a _ _ _ _ u _
14. AASBOARMSD _ _ _ a _ _ a _ o _
15. LISASNAY a _ _ _ y _ _ _
16. PMREHSOOO _ _ p _ _ _ _ r _
17. VOESINUR _ _ _ v _ n _ _
18. CSPFCIEI _ _ _ c i _ _ _
19. SPCMENEI _ p _ _ _ _ e _
20. DSLINA i _ _ _ _ d
21. JSULYEOA j e _ _ _ _ _ _
22. JRUOLNA _ _ u _ _ a _
23. ASILOBURO _ a b _ _ _ _ _ _
24. TELWTHF _ _ e _ _ _ h

Score: ____________________

English Refresher: 4 Types of Sentences

Date: ____________

Declarative, imperative, interrogative, and exclamatory sentences are all types of sentences. Identifying and classifying sentences is easy once you know why each sort of sentence exists, how many there are, and how they are constructed. Each of these phrases' aims contributes to the uniqueness of the English language. The structure of conversation and written communication would be drastically different if these phrases were not used.

As the name implies, declarative phrases make statements. In most cases, they are expressed in a non-emotional, neutral manner. These sentences are used to state facts, describe things, and explain things.

Imperative sentences are used to express a command or a demand. Rather than being stated directly, the subjects of these sentences are frequently implied to be the listener.

Exclamatory sentences get their name from the fact that they exclaim something. Although exclamatory phrases can be classified in different ways, they are easily distinguished by the presence of intense emotions. An exclamation point marks the end of the sentence.

Interrogative sentences ask questions and are always followed by a question mark. Interrogative sentences frequently begin with "question words" such as who, what, where, when, how, or why. That is not always the case, however.

1. Which type of sentence might have an implied subject?
   a. interrogative
   b. declarative
   c. imperative

2. What end mark is used for interrogative sentences?
   a. period
   b. question mark
   c. exclamation mark

3. Which is an imperative sentence?
   a. What movie do you want to go see?
   b. Can you wash the car today?
   c. Please wash my car.

4. Which type of sentence shows strong emotion?
   a. interrogative
   b. declarative
   c. exclamatory

5. The sunset is beautiful tonight. This is what type of sentence?
   a. declarative
   b. imperative
   c. interrogative

6. Do not touch the stove! This is what type of sentence?
   a. exclamatory
   b. declarative
   c. imperative

7. Do you feel okay? This is what type of sentence?
   a. declarative
   b. Interrogative
   c. exclamatory

8. Declarative sentences make statements and end in ____.
   a. periods
   b. question mark
   c. exclamation mark

9. Imperative sentences make ____or _____.
   a. commands or demand
   b. commands or thoughts
   c. commands or question

10. Interrogative sentences ask ____ and end in ______.
   a. commands and requests
   b. demand and exclamation mark
   c. questions and question marks

Name: ______________________

Date: _____________

Adjectives to Describe People

Adjectives are descriptive or modifying words for nouns or pronouns. For instance, adjectives such as red, quick, happy, and annoying exist to describe things—a red hat, a speedy rabbit, a cheerful duck, and an obnoxious individual.

Unscramble the adjectives to describe people.

polite	friendly	clever	outgoing	good looking	handsome
cute	fat	tall	smart	young	pretty
attractive	rude	easygoing	funny	confident	tidy
old	beautiful	generous	ugly		

1. ulbuefita _ e _ _ t _ _ _ _
2. trpyet _ _ _ _ t y
3. etuc _ u _ _
4. luyg _ g _ _
5. ugnyo _ _ u _ _
6. tleipo _ _ _ i t _
7. nnufy f _ _ _ _
8. riledfny _ _ _ _ n d _ _
9. ohemndsa _ a _ _ _ o _ _
10. rdue _ u _ _
11. dol o _ _
12. aft _ _ t
13. mrtas _ _ _ r _
14. idty _ i _ _
15. yogsgeain _ _ s _ g _ _ _ _
16. cleerv c _ e _ _ _
17. neeugrso g _ n _ _ _ _ _
18. fnitnedoc _ _ n f _ _ _ _ _
19. tngioogu o _ _ g _ _ _ _
20. dgoo oinogkl _ _ _ _ _ o _ _ _ n _
21. vractatite a _ _ _ a _ _ _ _ e
22. tlla t _ _ _

Score: ____________________

Alexander Graham Bell

Date: ____________

It was March 7, 1876, and Alexander Graham Bell, who was 29 years old, was given a patent for his new invention: the telephone.

He worked in London with his father, Melville Bell. His father came up with Visible Speech, a written method for teaching the deaf to speak. The Bells relocated to Boston, Massachusetts, in the 1870s, where the younger Bell obtained work as a teacher at the Pemberton Avenue School for the Deaf.

After moving to Boston, Bell became very interested in transmitting speech over wires. With the introduction of the telegraph by Samuel F.B. Morse in 1843, communication between two distant sites became virtually instantaneous. The disadvantage of the telegraph was that messages had to be delivered by hand between telegraph stations and recipients, and only one message could be transmitted at a time. Bell sought to improve on this by developing the "harmonic telegraph," a gadget that merged the telegraph and record player elements to enable individuals to communicate remotely.

Bell made a prototype with the help of Thomas A. Watson, a worker at a machine shop in Boston. In the original telephone, sound waves altered the amplitude and frequency of an electric current, causing a thin, soft iron plate called the diaphragm to vibrate. These vibrations were sent magnetically to another wire connected to a diaphragm in another, faraway instrument. When that diaphragm moved, the original sound would be played back in the ear of the device that was hearing it. It took three days after Bell filed the patent for the telephone for the first intelligible message to be sent. That message was "Mr. Watson, come here; I need you."

____

Sentence Building: Unscramble the sentences!

1. A ______________ that _____ ____ carried __________ ____ __________ a __________
   ________ ____ ______ _________

   telephone · can · phone. · be · around · mobile · or · cell · is · called · phone

2. ______________ __________ _______ _____ the ________ __________ ____ __________
   the ________________ ____ 1876.

   in · Graham · Alexander · person · Bell · was · first · patent · to · telephone,

3. __________ telephone ____________ _____ ________ ________ to _____ digits ________

   long. · about · ten · are · Today, · numbers · seven

4. In ______ countries, _______ ____ _____ telephone _________ ____ __________ _____
   ______ ________

   number · code. · the · is · the · many · of · area · part · called

5. ______ codes are _______ ____ _______ _______ the ___________ _____ _____ _____
   ______ ____ _____ ______________ places.

   different · make · same · in · used · to · Area · not · two · are · the · numbers · sure

Score: ______________________

Alice & The Rabbit-Hole

Date: ______________

First, read the entire story. After that, go back and fill in the blanks. You can skip the blanks you're unsure about and finish them later.

sister	courageous	tunnel	pictures	hurry
dark	jar	feet	Rabbit	remarkable

ALICE was growing tired of sitting beside her ____________ on the bank and having nothing to do: she had peeped into the book her sister was reading once or twice, but it was lacking ________________ or words; "and what use is a book," Alice argued, "without pictures or conversations?" Thus, she was wondering in her mind (as best she could, given how sleepy and foolish she felt due to the heat) whether the pleasure of creating a cute daisy chain was worth the difficulty of getting up and gathering the daisies when a white ____________ with pink eyes darted nearby her.

There was nothing ____________________ about that; nor did Alice consider it strange to hear the Rabbit exclaim to itself, "Oh no! Oh no! I will arrive too late!" (On reflection, she should have been surprised, but at the time, it seemed perfectly natural). Still, when the Rabbit actually removed a watch from its waistcoat-pocket, examined it, and then hurried on, Alice jumped to her ________, for it flashed across her mind that she had never seen a rabbit with either a waistcoat-pocket or a watch to remove from it, and burning with curiosity, she ran across the field after it. Alice saw the Rabbit go down a hole under the hedge. Alice followed it down in a __________, never once thinking how she would get out again.

The rabbit-hole continued straight ahead like a ____________ for some distance and then suddenly dipped down, so quickly that Alice had no time to think about stopping herself before falling into what appeared to be a very deep well.

Either the well was really deep, or she dropped very slowly, as she had plenty of time to look around her and ponder on what might happen next. She first attempted to glance down and see what she was approaching, but it was too ________ to see anything; then, she discovered the sides of the well were lined with cupboards and bookcases; here and there, she observed maps and images hung on hooks. She removed a ______ from one of the shelves as she passed; it was labeled "ORANGE MARMALADE," but it was empty; she did not want to drop the jar for fear of killing someone beneath, so she managed to stuff it into one of the cupboards as she passed it.

"Perfect!" Alice exclaimed to herself. "After such a tumble, I shall have no worries about falling downstairs! How ____________________ they will all believe I am at home!

Score: ______________________

Alphabetize and Define

Date: ______________

WRITE THE WORDS BELOW IN THE CORRECT ABC ORDER.

meter
irony
personification
denotation
onomatopoeia
alliteration
rhyme
metaphor
theme
symbolism
repetition
simile
stanza
connotation
imagery

1. ______________________
2. ______________________
3. ______________________
4. ______________________
5. ______________________
6. ______________________
7. ______________________
8. ______________________
9. ______________________
10. ______________________
11. ______________________
12. ______________________
13. ______________________
14. ______________________
15. ______________________

After putting the words in alphabetical order, choose 5 and write a definition in the space provided.

____

____

____

____

____

Score: ______________________

Date: _____________

Animal Migrations

At certain times of the year, many mammals, birds, fish, insects, and other animals migrate from one location to another. This is referred to as migration. These animals migrate as part of their life cycle.

Animals migrate for a variety of reasons. Many migrate in order to reproduce or to find food. Some animals migrate to locations where they can hibernate or rest during the winter. Others migrate because the weather is excessively hot, excessively cold, excessively wet, or excessively dry at certain times of the year.

The majority of animals migrate by water, land, or air. Many birds and bats migrate south for the winter in northern parts of the world. Some whales migrate from cold polar regions to warmer waters in the winter. Other types of migration are vertical or up and down. During the winter, mule deer in the western United States migrate from higher to lower elevations of the mountains. Some earthworms move from the top of the soil to the bottom of the ground.

Animals can travel hundreds of miles or thousands of miles. Frogs travel short distances to breed in ponds. On the other hand, the Arctic tern spends the summer in the Arctic and the winter in Antarctica. This journey covers approximately 11,000 miles (18,000 kilometers). Migrations can occur both during the day and at night. During the day, birds such as geese migrate. Sparrows, warblers, and thrushes all migrate at night.

Migrating animals can navigate long and complicated routes. Rivers and mountains help them figure out where they are. Many animals, according to scientists, use the position of the Sun and stars to find their way. Salmon, for example, use their sense of smell.

____

Sentence Building: Unscramble the sentences!

1. _____ ____________ ____________ back ____ the same _________ where ________ ________ ________ ____ ______ _________ _________

beach · Sea · turtles · born · to · were · their · migrate · eggs. · lay · they · to

2. ____________ migrate ________ ______ __________ of ______ ____________ ______ ______ seasons.

the · Animals · change · with · the · the · weather · and

3. ________ ______ __________ walruses ____________ in ______________ __________

and · separate · female · Male · herds. · migrate

4. Different ____________ ________ ____________ different ________ ____ _________________ ______ Earth.

of · have · animals · the · navigating · adapted · ways

5. ________ year Canadian _________ ______ _________ ______ ______ __________ ____ _________ ______ ___________ ___________ of _________ and ponds.

geese · lakes · freeze · the · avoid · fly · for · the · to · south · winter · Each · winter

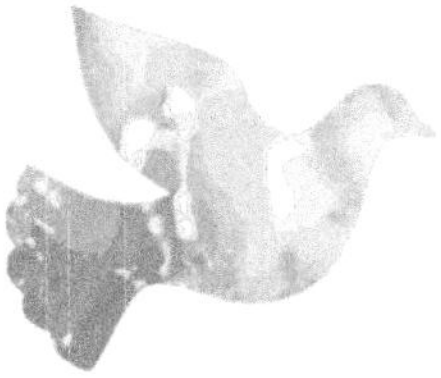

Score: ____________________

Art: Pablo Picasso

Date: ____________

depressed	suicide	features	Carlos	newspapers
blue	historians	circuses	collaborated	sand
painter	Madrid	prestigious	Spanish	French

Pablo Picasso was born on October 25, 1881, in Spain and grew up there. His father was a ______________ who also taught art. Pablo has always enjoyed drawing since he was a child. According to legend, his first word was "piz," which is ______________ for "pencil." Pablo quickly demonstrated that he had little interest in school but was an extremely talented artist. Pablo enrolled in a ______________________ art school in Barcelona when he was fourteen years old. He transferred to another school in ____________ a few years later. Pablo, on the other hand, was dissatisfied with the traditional art school teachings. He didn't want to paint in the manner of people from hundreds of years ago. He wished to invent something new.

Pablo's close friend ____________ Casagemas committed ______________ in 1901. Pablo became __________________. He began painting in Paris around the same time. For the next four years, the color ________ dominated his paintings. Many of the subjects appeared depressed and solemn. He depicted people with elongated ________________ and faces in his paintings. Poor People on the Seashore and The Old Guitarist are two of his paintings from this time.

Pablo eventually recovered from his depression. He also had feelings for a ____________ model. He began to use warmer colors such as pinks, reds, oranges, and beiges in his paintings. The Rose Period is a term used by art ____________________ to describe this period in Pablo's life. He also started painting happier scenes like ________________. The Peasants and Mother and Child are two of his paintings from this time period.

Picasso began experimenting with a new painting style in 1907. He ________________________ with another artist, Georges Braque. By 1909, they had developed a completely new painting style known as Cubism. Cubism analyzes and divides subjects into different sections. The sections are then reassembled and painted from various perspectives and angles.

Picasso began combining Cubism and collage in 1912. He would use ________ or plaster in his paint to give it texture in this area. He would also add dimension to his paintings by using materials such as colored paper, ____________________, and wallpaper. Three Musicians and the Portrait of Ambroise Vollard are two of Picasso's Cubism paintings.

Although Picasso continued to experiment with Cubism, he went through a period of painting more classical-style paintings around 1921. He was influenced by Renaissance painters such as Raphael. He created strong characters that appeared three-dimensional, almost like statues. The Pipes of Pan and Woman in White are two of his works in this style.

Pablo became interested in the Surrealist movement around 1924. Surrealist paintings were never meant to make sense. They frequently resemble something out of a nightmare or dream. Although Picasso did not join the movement, he did incorporate some of its ideas into his paintings. This period was dubbed "Monster Period" by some. Guernica and The Red Armchair are two examples of surrealism's influence on Picasso's art.

Pablo Picasso is widely regarded as the greatest artist of the twentieth century. Many consider him to be one of the greatest artists in all of history. He painted in a variety of styles and made numerous unique contributions to the world of art. He painted several self-portraits near the end of his life. Self-Portrait Facing Death, a self-portrait done with crayons on paper, was one of his final works of art. He died a year later, on April 8, 1973, at the age of 91.

ARTS Vocabulary Terms 6

Score: ______________________

Date: _____________

Choose the best answer to each question.

1. **Select the correct meaning of the word Abstract Art**
   a. A functional object or arrangement whereby the principles of art are applied. Refers to such things as pottery, interior decorating, architecture, furniture, etc
   b. Art created from a realistic situation but represented unrealistically.

2. **Select the correct meaning of the word acrylic paint:**
   a. Use white lead as a base, and are applied in three coats: primer, undercoat and finish coat
   b. A plastic, water soluble pigment used for painting.

3. **A functional object or arrangement whereby the principles of art are applied. Refers to such things as pottery, interior decorating, architecture, furniture, etc.**
   a. applied art
   b. abstract art

4. **A structural support for an object. Particularly used in sculpture to build upon.**
   a. clay object
   b. armature

5. **An image created with a paint brush, typically using India ink or watercolor, that has a linear quality rather than a painterly finish.**
   a. paint brush
   b. brush drawing

6. **A sculpture representing the neck and head only of a person.**
   a. bust
   b. contrapposto

7. **Literally means beautiful line. Typically refers to a type of writing that incorporates the use of a wide pen nib.**
   a. calligraphy
   b. modern cursive

8. **Clay objects that have been fired twice, the second time with a glaze.**
   a. ceramic
   b. pottery

9. **Soft limestone, sometimes used as a drawing material or mixed to make pastels and other crayons.**
   a. watercolor
   b. chalk

10. **Select the correct meaning of the word Charcoal**
    a. A drawing material made from charred wood.
    b. A type of pencil in which a thin graphite core is embedded in a shell of other material

ARTS Vocabulary Terms 7

Score: ____________________

Date: ____________

Choose the best answer to each question.

1. **What is the correct meaning of the word Firing?**
   a. The process of baking clay in a kiln or banked fire outside (such as raku firing). This process hardens the clay and makes it very permanent.
   b. The process of baking clay in a kiln or banked fire outside (such as raku firing). This process softens the clay and makes it very malleable.

2. **Varnish sprayed or painted onto a surface to prevent smudging or smearing. Usually on a charcoal or chalk pastel work.**
   a. spray paint art
   b. fixative

3. **Art made by untrained practitioners. Typically lively, colorful artwork in a somewhat "naive" style**
   a. classical art
   b. folk art

4. **An element of art focused on all three dimensions (height, width and depth).**
   a. form
   b. shape

5. **A surface preparation or primer made of chalk or gypsum for tempura or oil paintings that is painted onto the picture surface.**
   a. gouache
   b. gesso

6. **A transparent or semitransparent coating of a color or stain used over oil paintings, plaster sculpture or ceramics.**
   a. glaze
   b. enamel

7. **A watercolor paint mixed with white pigments making it more opaque and giving it more weight and body.**
   a. gouache
   b. gesso

8. **Select the correct meaning of the word Hue:**
   a. The technical reference to color.
   b. Refers to how strong or weak a color is

9. **An image that accompanies written text and aids in interpreting it.**
   a. diagram
   b. illustration

10. **An element of art used in drawing, painting and sculpture.**
    a. line
    b. shape

ARTS Vocabulary Terms 8

Score: ____________________

Date: ____________

Choose the best answer to each question.

1. **A general purpose drawing and coloring paper. Typically cream color.**
   a. kraft paper
   b. Manila paper

2. **what is the correct meaning of the word Masterpiece?**
   a. An artists finest work, or any particularly fine work.
   b. A principle in art where important elements and ideas are emphasized via composition

3. **Representation, or making sculptural, three-dimensional forms, usually with clay or wax. Also, making two-dimensional surfaces look three-dimensional , by use of light and shade, color and mass.**
   a. modeling
   b. mrototyping

4. **Tints and shades of single hue or color.**
   a. monochrome
   b. monochromatic

5. **Images created using small tesserae arranged and glued into a design or composition; dates back to the Ancient Greeks and Romans, mostly used to decorate walls and floors.**
   a. mosaic
   b. collage

6. **Paint made by mixing ground pigment with oil (usually linseed oil) as a binder.**
   a. oil paint
   b. oil pastel

7. **Art works made with newspaper strips that have been moistened with wallpaper paste or laundry starch.**
   a. mod podge
   b. paper mache

8. **The illusion of a three-dimensional space on a two-dimensional surface through the use of vanishing point, converging lines and diminishing sizes of objects.**
   a. perspective
   b. depth

9. **Uses cut photographs to create a work of art.**
   a. collage
   b. photomontage

10. **An image created with the use of small dots or points.**
    a. cross hatching
    b. pointillism

ARTS Vocabulary Terms 9

Score: ____________________

Date: ____________

Choose the best answer to each question.

1. **Select the correct meaning of the word primary colors:**
    a. The basic colors that can be used to mix other colors. The primary colors are purple, orange and green .
    b. The basic colors that can be used to mix other colors. The primary colors are red, yellow and blue.

2. **A clean, fast drying latex type of adhesive. Excellent for paper projects.**
    a. contact cement
    b. rubber cement

3. **Select the correct Secondary colors:**
    a. orange, green and purple
    b. red, yellow and blue

4. **The element of art that describes a two-dimensional area (height and width).**
    a. shape
    b. form

5. **Refers to the darker values of a color.**
    a. sketch
    b. shade

6. **Dried, crushed clay mixed with water to a creamy consistency. Used as a binder in joining two pieces of clay together.**
    a. carving
    b. slip

7. **The quality of a surface. One of the seven elements of art.**
    a. texture
    b. harmony

8. **Select the correct meaning of the word Tint:**
    a. a mixture with black, which increases darkness
    b. a hue mixed with white to create lighter values.

9. **Pigment with a water-soluble binder. Available in semi-moist cakes or tubes.**
    a. watercolors
    b. acrylic painting

Name: ____________________

Business World Phrases

Date: ____________

Unscramble the words

to learn the ropes	bring to the table	back to the drawing board	from the ground up	up in the air	in a nutshell
to get down to business	back to square one	to get someone up to speed	to go down swinging	the bottom line	hands are tied
a learning curve	to think outside the box	to corner the market	between a rock and a hard place	it's not rocket science	

1. bakc ot hte dairnwg rbdoa   _ _ _ _   _ _   t _ e   d _ _ w _ _ _   _ _ a _ _
2. ot orncre hte tamkre   _ o   c _ _ _ _ _ _   _ _ e   _ _ _ _ _ _ _
3. ahsnd aer idte   _ _ _ _ s   _ _ _   t _ e _
4. pu ni hte iar   _ _   _ _   _ _ e   _ _ r
5. ot enrla hte opers   _ _   l _ _ r _   _ _ _   r _ p _ _
6. a iarngenl vecur   a   _ e _ r _ _ _ _   _ _ r _ _
7. ot og dnow nsggwini   _ _   _ _   _ _ w n   _ _ _ n _ _ n _
8. benweet a okcr nda a hadr calep   _ _ t _ _ e _   _   _ _ _ _ _   _ _ d   _   _ _ _ _ _   _ _ a _ e
9. rofm eth dgonur pu   _ _ _ _   _ h _   _ r _ u _ _   _ _
10. eht ttmoob ilne   _ h e   b o _ _ _ _   _ _ _ _
11. ot egt ndwo ot ssneubsi   _ o   _ _ _   _ _ _ _   _ o   _ u s i _ _ _ _
12. ot tge noeeoms pu ot epdes   _ _   _ _ _   _ _ m _ o _ e   _ _   t o   _ _ _ e _
13. s'ti ont tcorek isecnce   i _ _ _   n _ _   _ o _ _ _ t   _ _ _ e _ _ _
14. ot hnikt dosietu teh oxb   _ _   _ _ i _ k   _ _ _ _ _ _ _ e   _ h _   _ o _
15. ni a elshtlnu   _ _   _   n u _ _ _ _ _ _ _
16. acbk ot aquers eon   _ a _ k   _ _   _ _ _ _ r _   _ n _
17. ribgn ot teh elabt   _ _ _ _ _   _ o   t h _   _ _ _ _ e

Score: ______________________

Civil Rights History: Frederick Douglass

Date: ____________

Frederick Douglass was born in Talbot County, Maryland, into slavery. His grandmother, a slave, was the one who raised him. Douglass was separated from his grandmother in 1826, when he was about 7 or 8 years old, and sent to Baltimore, Maryland. He served as a maid in the home of shipbuilder Hugh Auld while there. His wife, Sophia, began teaching Frederick how to read and write. She was told to stop by her husband, who was displeased. A slave could not be taught to read because it was illegal. On the other hand, Frederick found a way to continue his education. White friends secretly gave him books.

As he grew older, Frederick Douglass developed anti-slavery views. Humans should be treated as equals. That concept was discovered in the Declaration of Independence. At some point, he was returned to his birthplace of Maryland, a plantation. There, he became known for breaking the rules. A big part of this is because he taught other slaves how to read the Bible.

Douglass was soon assigned to work for Edward Covey. Covey was known as a "slave breaker" because of his brutal methods. Douglas spent a year with Covey in 1833, during which he was whipped a lot. Douglass, who had lived much of his life in the city, was unfamiliar with farm tools and procedures. Because he didn't know what to do, he made mistakes and kept getting punished. One day, Douglass decided to fight back physically. It wasn't long before Douglass had the upper hand, and Covey had given up after two hours of wrestling. They went toe-to-toe with each other, and Douglass was never whipped by Covey again after that. Douglass was able to free himself from slavery in 1838. He donned a sailor's hat and set sail for the north. Finally, he arrived in the Big Apple.

Douglass wed Anna Murray in New York City, and they had five children within the first ten years of the marriage. The couple eventually made their home in New Bedford, Massachusetts. They lived in a neighborhood with other free black people. They got involved in the anti-slavery movement. Slavery was something that abolitionists hoped to end. As a storyteller, Douglass was exceptional. William Lloyd Garrison was captivated by his tales of life as a slave. He was the editor of The Liberator, an abolitionist publication. Douglass was encouraged to write by Garrison. An American Slave's Story by Frederick Douglass was the end result. In 1845, the book was published. It quickly became a best-seller in the publishing industry.

Douglass' supporters raised funds to purchase his freedom in 1847. His new home was in Rochester, New York, and he started a newspaper against slavery. The North Star was its name. In 1848, he delivered a speech in Seneca Falls, New York, at a conference on women's rights. He met civil rights activist Elizabeth Cady Stanton there. Elizabeth was an American writer and activist who was a big part of the women's rights movement in the United States.

Frederick Douglass urged President Abraham Lincoln to allow black men to join the Union Army during the Civil War of 1861–1861. Charles and Lewis Douglass, two of Douglass' sons, served in the 54th Massachusetts Infantry Regiment. Douglass heavily promoted the 14th and 15th Amendments to the Constitution after the war. As a result of these, all American men were granted equal rights, including voting. After the 13th Amendment was passed in 1865, slavery was officially abolished.

His career in the United States government went on to include high-ranking positions. He served as the Dominican Republic and Haiti ambassador, respectively. He served as a director of the Freedman's Bank as well. He was an outspoken critic of racial injustice and a human rights activist.

Douglass continued to speak, write, and be an activist until he died on February 20, 1895. After attending a meeting of the National Council of Women, an early women's rights group, in Washington, D.C., he died of a heart attack as he returned home.

1. Which slave owner whipped Douglas a lot?

a. Hugh Auld

b. Edward Covey

2. Who first tried teaching Frederick how to read?

a. Hugh Auld wife Sophia

b. Frederick's grandmother

3. In Rochester, New York, Douglas started a ____ against slavery.

a. newspaper

b. protest

4. Douglas served as the ____ Republic and ____ ambassador.

a. New York, USA

b. Dominican, Haiti

QUANTITATIVE CHEMISTRY

Score: ____________________

Conservation of Mass

Date: ____________

Complete the passage below using the box of words provided - you can use each more than once if you need to.

destroyed	measurements	created	oxygen	1789
escaped	increased	exactly	products	decreased
zinc	same	lead		

In ________, Antoine Lavoisier, a French chemist, first proposed the Law of Conservation of Mass. To do this, he had to carry out thousands of experiments, making very careful ________________________. he found that in any chemical reaction or physical change, the total mass after the reaction was ______________ the ________ as the mass before. His law can be summarised as follows:
"Matter cannot be __________________, or ______________, just changed from one form to another."

If you mix lead nitrate solution with potassium iodide solution a yellow solid is formed called ________ iodide. If you measured the mass of products (the chemicals formed) you would find that it is ______________ the ________ as the mass of the reactants (the chemicals that were mixed).

Mass is never __________________ or __________________ in a chemical reaction - particles cannot just be lost! Sometimes it may look like mass is lost, but in that case it is usually a gas that has been produced and ______________ into the air. The same can happen when the chemicals made have a mass more than the mass of the products started with. You may have guessed, that in this case some gas from the air has been added to the ________________!

For instance, if you heat zinc in the air you get a white powder. The mass of the white powder is greater than the mass of the ________ you started with. The zinc has combined with ____________ from the air to form zinc oxide. The mass of the zinc and the oxygen that reacted would be the same as the mass of the zinc oxide.

Score: ________________

Demonstrative Pronoun

Date: ____________

This, That, These, and Those

Words that point to specific things are known as demonstrative pronouns. "This is a pencil," for example.

These pronouns indicate the relationship between the speaker and the object:

- this / these: an object or objects in close proximity to the person speaking (*often within touching distance*)
- that / those: an object or objects distant from the person speaking (*often out of touching distance*)
- that over there / those over there: object or objects located a long distance away from the person

1. **_____ orange I'm eating is delicious.**
   a. These
   b. That
   c. This

2. **It is better than _____ apples from last week.**
   a. these
   b. that
   c. those

3. **Astronauts don't get fresh fruit like _____ peaches we are eating.**
   a. these
   b. that
   c. this

4. **_____ meals they take into space are freeze-dried.**
   a. Those
   b. This
   c. That

5. **_____ fact means they must add water to them.**
   a. That
   b. This here
   c. These

6. **_____ granola bars are tasty too.**
   a. Them
   b. These
   c. This here

7. **Don't sign me up for _____ next shuttle flight.**
   a. these here
   b. that
   c. that there

8. **_____ book is so heavy I can hardly lift it.**
   a. This here
   b. Those
   c. This

9. **Some believed _____ dream could be a reality.**
   a. that there
   b. these
   c. that

10. **_____ change is due to our astronauts.**
   a. These here
   b. That there
   c. This

Score: ______________________

Date:______________

Different Types of Dangerous Weather

Thunderstorms can form when moist warm air rises quickly. Thunderstorms bring strong winds, heavy rain, lightning, and occasionally hail. Every day, thunderstorms appear all over our planet. They can form at any time of year, but they are most common in the afternoon and evening during the warm seasons.

Thunderstorms are extremely dangerous. Every year, lightning from thunderstorms kills more people than tornadoes.

Lighting is a powerful electrical blast that can form in thunderstorms and strike the earth with great force. Before lightning can strike, high winds within a thunderstorm cause ice and water particles to cross paths at high speeds. This causes a charge to generate. The top of the thunderstorm is positively charged, but the bottom accumulates a negative charge. When the negative charge reaches a certain threshold, it will all discharge at once in the form of a lightning bolt. Because objects on the ground are also positively charged, lighting can frequently strike them.

Lighting will frequently strike the highest point on the land surface when it comes to landing. It is also drawn to metal. If there is a lightning storm, go inside. Don't stand under a tree or carry anything metal, such as a metal umbrella or a golf club. Also, get out of the water as soon as possible. Swimming in a pool during a thunderstorm is not recommended.

Huge and powerful storms that form over the ocean are known as hurricanes. They can stretch for up to 600 miles in width! **Hurricanes** bring high winds, heavy rain, flooding, and an ocean storm surge that can wreak havoc.

In summer and fall, when the ocean water is warm, hurricanes form. Hurricanes are powered by warm ocean water that must be at least 80 degrees Fahrenheit. Hurricanes get their high winds from spinning around the hurricane's center, known as the eye. They spin as a result of the planet's Coriolis force. The wind is usually calm in the center, but steady winds of 80 to 150 miles per hour can be found just outside the center.

Hurricanes can be found in some parts of the world. They form near the Caribbean Sea in the Atlantic Ocean, off the coast of Africa, and in the Gulf of Mexico. They also form in the Indian Ocean and are known as Cyclones. Typhoons are hurricanes that can threaten much of Southeast Asia in the Pacific Ocean.

Tornadoes are extremely fast-spinning columns of wind. They can have winds of up to 300 miles per hour and extend from the bottom of thunderstorms to the ground. Tornadoes are smaller than hurricanes and develop on land rather than at sea. Large thunderstorms provide them with energy. Waterspouts are tornadoes that form over water. A funnel cloud is what happens before a tornado hits the ground.

1. **____ are extremely fast-spinning columns of wind.**
   a. Tornadoes
   b. Hurricanes

2. **______ can form when moist warm air rises quickly.**
   a. Thunderstorms
   b. Lighting

3. **Huge and powerful storms that form over the ocean are known as _____.**
   a. hurricanes
   b. tornadoes

4. **Lighting will frequently strike the ____ point on the land surface when it comes to landing.**
   a. lowest
   b. highest

5. **The top of the thunderstorm is _____ charged, but the bottom accumulates a negative charge.**
   a. positively
   b. steadily

6. **_____ is a powerful electrical blast that can form in thunderstorms and strike the earth with great force.**
   a. Lighting
   b. High winds

The formula for calculating elapsed time is
elapsed time = end time – start time.

Subtract the minutes and hours separately.

Score : ___________

Date : ___________

Complete the Table Below.

Start Time	End Time	Elapsed Time
3:00 P.M.		1 Hours & 32 Minutes
	5:06 A.M.	3 Hours & 46 Minutes
	6:52 P.M.	2 Hours & 12 Minutes
1:20 A.M.	5:18 A.M.	
10:10 P.M.	12:37 A.M.	
5:30 P.M.	9:47 P.M.	
	2:12 A.M.	1 Hours & 52 Minutes
3:50 P.M.		1 Hours & 47 Minutes
3:20 A.M.	4:44 A.M.	
11:00 P.M.		2 Hours & 19 Minutes

Environmental Health: Water Pollution

Score: ____________________

Date: ______________

First, read the entire passage. After that, go back and fill in the blanks. You can skip the blanks you're unsure about and finish them later.

causes	toxic	wastewater	ill	food
Gulf	naturally	Dead	crops	reduce
Acid	herds	spills	streams	planet

Water pollution occurs when waste, chemicals, or other particles cause a body of water (e.g., rivers, oceans, lakes) to become __________ to the fish and animals that rely on it for survival. Water pollution can also disrupt and hurt nature's water cycle.

Water pollution can occur __________________ due to volcanoes, algae blooms, animal waste, and silt from storms and floods.

Human activity contributes significantly to water pollution. Sewage, pesticides, fertilizers from farms, wastewater and chemicals from factories, silt from construction sites, and trash from people littering are some human ____________.

Oil ____________ have been some of the most well-known examples of water pollution. The Exxon Valdez oil spill occurred when an oil tanker collided with a reef off the coast of Alaska, causing over 11 million gallons of oil to spill into the ocean. Another major oil spill was the Deepwater Horizon oil spill, which occurred when an oil well exploded, causing over 200 million gallons of oil to spill into the ________ of Mexico.

Water pollution can be caused directly by air pollution. When sulfur dioxide particles reach high altitudes in the atmosphere, they can combine with rain to form acid rain. ________ rain can cause lakes to become acidic, killing fish and other animals.

The main issue caused by water pollution is the impact on aquatic life. ________ fish, birds, dolphins, and various other animals frequently wash up on beaches, killed by pollutants in their environment. Pollution also has an impact on the natural ________ chain. Small animals consume contaminants like lead and cadmium.

Clean water is one of the most valuable and essential commodities for life on Earth. Clean water is nearly impossible to obtain for over 1 billion people on the ____________. They can become ______ from dirty, polluted water, which is especially difficult for young children. Some bacteria and pathogens in water can make people sick to the point of death.

Water pollution comes from a variety of sources. Here are a few of the main reasons:

Sewage: In many parts of the world, sewage is still flushed directly into ______________ and rivers. Sewage can introduce dangerous bacteria that can make humans and animals very sick.

Farm animal waste: Runoff from large __________ of farm animals such as pigs and cows can enter the water supply due to rain and large storms.

Pesticides: Pesticides and herbicides are frequently sprayed on __________ to kill bugs, while herbicides are sprayed to kill weeds. These potent chemicals can enter the water through rainstorm runoff. They can also contaminate rivers and lakes due to unintentional spills.

Construction, floods, and storms: Silt from construction, earthquakes, and storms can ____________ water oxygen levels and suffocate fish. Factories - Water is frequently used in factories to process chemicals, keep engines cool, and wash things away. Sometimes used ____________________ is dumped into rivers or the ocean. It may contain pollutants.

To estimate means to find an answer that is close to the exact answer. The key to estimation is to use it only when an exact answer is not required. To estimate a sum or difference, the first step is to round the numbers to the nearest power of ten, hundred, thousand, and so on.

- Round down if the number being rounded is less than 5.
- Round up if the number being rounded is 5 or greater.

Score : ____________

Date : ____________

Estimate the sum or difference by rounding each number to the nearest ten.

1) 85 ⟶
- 59 ⟶ - ____

2) 94 ⟶
- 21 ⟶ - ____

3) 23 ⟶
+ 42 ⟶ + ____

4) 71 ⟶
- 53 ⟶ - ____

5) 15 ⟶
+ 74 ⟶ + ____

6) 51 ⟶
+ 26 ⟶ + ____

7) 91 ⟶
- 46 ⟶ - ____

8) 58 ⟶
+ 11 ⟶ + ____

9) 79 ⟶
+ 32 ⟶ + ____

10) 75 ⟶
+ 49 ⟶ + ____

11) 63 ⟶
- 34 ⟶ - ____

12) 33 ⟶
- 22 ⟶ - ____

13) 76 ⟶
+ 12 ⟶ + ____

14) 86 ⟶
- 27 ⟶ - ____

SCORE:__________

Solve the following problems using the order of operations.

DATE:__________

Remember

Step 1: Parenthesis ()	Solve all problems in parenthesis FIRST.
Step 2: Exponents $^{2}, ^{3}, ^{4}$	Next solve any numbers that have exponents.
Step 3: Multiply or Divide ×, ÷	Then solve any multiplication or division problems (going from left to right).
Step 4: Add or Subtract +, -	Finally solve any addition or subtraction problems (going from left to right).

1) 21 ÷ 3 + (3 × 9) × 9 + 5

2) 18 ÷ 6 × (4 - 3) + 6

3) 14 - 8 + 3 + 8 × (24 ÷ 8)

4) 4 × 5 + (14 + 8) - 36 ÷ 9

5) (17 - 7) × 6 + 2 + 56 - 8

6) (28 ÷ 4) + 3 + (10 - 8) × 5

7) 12 - 5 + 6 × 3 + 20 ÷ 4

8) 36 ÷ 9 + 48 - 10 ÷ 2

9) 10 + 8 × 90 ÷ 9 - 4

10) 8 × 3 + 70 ÷ 7 - 7

Using exponents simply means that you want to multiply something by itself a number of times. Say, for instance, you want to do the following: 4 x 4 x 4

This could be written using exponents, as follows: 4^3

They both equal 64, but the exponent method is shorter and easier to remember. This is very useful when you need to multiply something many times.

Score: __________

Date: __________

Exponents

1) $(2)^3$ = ______

2) $(5)^2$ = ______

3) $(12)^3$ = ______

4) $(-8)^2$ = ______

5) $(-4)^2$ = ______

6) $(-2)^2$ = ______

7) $(7)^2$ = ______

8) $(-12)^2$ = ______

9) $(-2)^3$ = ______

10) $(-3)^3$ = ______

11) $(4)^3$ = ______

12) $(3)^3$ = ______

13) $(-5)^3$ = ______

14) $(3)^2$ = ______

15) $(2)^2$ = ______

16) $(-10)^3$ = ______

17) $(-7)^2$ = ______

18) $(-9)^3$ = ______

19) $(-6)^3$ = ______

20) $(10)^2$ = ______

Score: ____________________

Fill-in The Appositive

Date: ____________

Appositives are words or phrases that come before or after other nouns or pronouns to describe them further. The appositives should give the reader additional information about the nouns and pronouns in the sentences. Keep in mind that an appositive can be a single word or a group of words.

Appositives can be either essential or non-essential. If the appositive is required for the sentence to make sense, it is essential. This means it cannot be omitted. If the appositive is not required for the sentence's meaning and could be excluded, it is nonessential.

Commas should be used to separate non-essential appositives from the sentence. Commas are not used to separate essential appositives.

Examples:

Jane, my younger sister, is 27 years old. (Jane renames her younger sister)

My mother, who works as a nurse, has a red automobile. (A nurse renames mother, but this isn't necessary for the meaning of the line.)

Kevin is the name of the young artist that created this painting. (Who painted this image renames boy, which is crucial to the sentence's meaning.)

An insect, a ladybug, has just landed on the rose bush.

meadowlark	fiancé	cousin	valedictorian	Jones
champion	governor	movie	capital	

1. My uncle, the former ________________ of Maine, loves ice cream
2. Sally's ______________ Gerald works at Walmart
3. Providence, the ______________ of RI, is a great city
4. We saw the state bird, the ____________________, at the park
5. My youngest ____________ Caroline goes to Princeton University
6. Muhammad Ali, the three time heavy weight ________________ of the world won a gold medal in 1960
7. Sally Smith, the __________________________, gave a wonderful speech at graduation
8. The vice principal, Mr. __________, suspended my brother
9. My favorite __________, "Stand and Deliver" always makes me cry.

Flamingo Bird Facts

Score: ____________________

Date: ____________

First, read over the entire passage(s). Then go back and fill in the blanks. You can skip the blanks you're unsure about and come back to them later.

females	algae	vivid	coast	diet
prey	theory	top-heavy	wading	mudflats

Flamingos are the show stoppers of the avian world. Their long legs, bending beaks, and __________ orange hue make them a sight to behold. They're a popular attraction at zoos and nature preserves because they are fascinating to see up close.

Phoenicopterus ruber is the scientific name for the American Flamingo. They reach a height of 3 to 5 feet and a weight of 5 to 6 pounds at maturity. Males tend to be larger than ______________ in general. Feathers of the common flamingo are typically pinkish red. Additionally, their pink feet and pink and white bill, which has a black tip, distinguish them.

Central and South America and the Caribbean are home to the American Flamingo. It can also be found in the Bahamas and Cuba, and the Yucatan Peninsula of Mexico's Caribbean coast. As far as Brazil, there are some that can be found on the northern __________. In addition, the Galapagos Islands have a population.

Lagoons and low-lying ________________ or lakes are the preferred environments for the Flamingos. They like seeking food by wading across the water. They form enormous flocks, sometimes numbering in the tens of thousands.

Flamingos come in a variety of colors, including pink and orange. Carotenoids are responsible for the orange hue of several foods, such as carrots. Carrots would turn your skin and eyes orange if you just ate them. Flamingoes appear pink or orange because they eat __________ and small shellfish rich in carotenoids. They would lose their vibrant hue if they switched to a different ________.

Is it possible for flamingoes to fly? Yes. Flamingos can fly, even though we usually associate them with ____________ in the water. Before they can take off, they have to run to build up their speed. They often fly in big groups.

Scientists don't know why Flamingos stand on one leg, but they have a few ideas. There is a rumor that it is to keep one leg warm. Because it's cold outside, they can keep one leg near their body to keep it warm. Another ____________ is that they are drying out one leg at a time. A third idea argues that it aids them in deceiving their ________, as one leg resembles a plant more than two.

It doesn't matter the reason; these __________________ birds can stand on one leg for long periods. They even sleep with one leg balanced on the ground!

Jackie Robinson: The First African-American Player In MLB

Score: ____________________

Date: ____________

First, read over the entire passage(s). Then go back and fill in the blanks. You can skip the blanks you're unsure about and come back to them later.

Roosevelt	general	Pasadena	paved	Dodgers
honorable	Rookie	major	Texas	enthusiast
League	prejudice	batting	military	football

On January 31, 1919, in Cairo, Georgia, Jack ________________ Robinson was born. There were five children in the family, and the youngest one was him. After Jackie was born, Jackie's father left the family, and he never returned. His mother, Millie, took care of him and his three brothers and one sister when they were young.

The family moved to ______________, California, about a year after Jackie was born. Jackie was awed by his older brothers' prowess in sports as a child. Meanwhile, his brother Mack rose to prominence as a track star and Olympic silver medalist in the 200-meter dash.

Jackie was an avid sports __________________. Like his older brother, he competed in track and field and other sports like football, baseball, and tennis. Football and baseball were two of his favorite sports to play. Throughout high school, Jackie was subjected to racism daily. Even though white teammates surrounded him, he felt like a second-class citizen off the field.

After high school, Jackie went to UCLA, where he excelled in track, baseball, ______________, and basketball. To his credit, he was the first player at UCLA to receive all four varsity letters in the same season. The long jump was another event where he excelled at the NCAA level.

With the outbreak of World War II, Robinson's football career was over before it began. He was called up for ______________ service. Jackie made friends with the legendary boxing champion Joe Lewis at basic training. Robinson was accepted into officer training school thanks to Joe's assistance.

After completing his officer training, Jackie was assigned to the 761st Tank Battalion at Fort Hood, _________. Only black soldiers were assigned to this battalion because they could not serve alongside white soldiers. When Jackie refused to move to the back of an army bus one day, he got into trouble. In 1944, he was discharged with an ________________ discharge after nearly being expelled from the military.

Robinson began his professional baseball career with the Kansas City Monarchs soon after he was discharged from the military. The Negro Baseball __________ was home to the Monarchs. Black players were still not allowed to play in Major League Baseball at this time. Jackie performed well on the field. He was an outstanding shortstop, hitting .387 on average.

While playing for the Monarchs, Branch Rickey, the Dodgers' ______________ manager, approached Jackie. Branch hoped that the Dodgers could win the pennant by signing an African-American player. Branch warned Robinson that he would encounter racial __________________ when he first joined the Dodgers. Branch was looking for a person who could take insults without reacting. This famous exchange between Jackie and Branch occurred during their first conversation:

Jackie: "Are you looking for a Negro who is afraid to fight back, Mr. Rickey?"
Jackie: "Are you looking for a Negro who is afraid to fight back, Mr. Rickey?" Robinson, I'm looking for a baseball player who has the guts not to fight back."

For the Montreal Royals, Jackie first played in the minor leagues. He was constantly confronted with racism. Because of Jackie, the opposing team would occasionally fail to show up for games. Then there were the times when people would verbally abuse or throw objects at him. In the midst of all this, Jackie remained calm and focused on the game. He had a .349 batting average and was named the league's most valuable player.

Robinson was called up to play for the Brooklyn ______________ at the start of the 1947 baseball season, and he did. On April 15, 1947, he became the first African-American to play in the sport's major leagues. Racially charged taunts were once again directed at Jackie from both fans and fellow players alike. Death threats were made against him. But Jackie had the courage not to fight back. He kept his word to Branch Rickey and dedicated himself solely to the game of baseball. The Dodgers won the pennant that year, and Jackie was named the team's ____________ of the Year for his achievements.

Jackie Robinson was one of the best __________ league baseball players for the next ten years. During his lengthy career, his ______________ average stood at.311, and he hit 137 home runs while also stealing 197 bases. Six times he was selected to the All-Star team, and in 1949 he was named the National League MVP.

Because of Jackie Robinson's groundbreaking work, other African-American players could play in the major leagues. He also __________ the way for racial integration in different facets of American life. He was inducted into the Baseball Hall of Fame in 1962. On October 24, 1972, Robinson suffered a heart attack and died.

Score: ____________________

Julius Caesar Roman Dictator

Date: ____________

Julius Caesar played a big part in the rise of the Roman Empire and made social and governmental changes. Caesar was not a noble when he was born in Rome, Italy, in July of 100 BC. His parents were not powerful people in politics, and they were not rich. Caesar's story of how he went from being a low-class citizen to becoming a Dictator is one of hard work, inspiration, and personal triumph.

The Rome of Caesar's youth was not stable at all. A few years after leaving Rome and joining the military, Caesar returned to Rome to get involved in politics. This is how it worked: He became a public speaker and advocated for the law. Because of his passionate speech, he was well-known. Most of the time, he spoke out against corrupt politicians. It took a long time, but Caesar was eventually elected to the government office. He started working his way up the political ladder.

He was chosen to be the Chief Priest of the Roman state religion when he was first chosen for the job. Afterward, he was chosen to run Spain in 62 BC. This was a big success. While in Spain, he overthrew two tribes and finished his time there well.

Caesar returned to Rome to run a counsel electoral campaign. During that election, Caesar worked closely with Pompey, a former military officer, and Crassus, one of the wealthiest men in Rome, to help them win. This partnership worked out well for Caesar because it gave him power and money. The First Triumvirate was the name given to the three men because of how close they were.

Caesar was elected easily and made a lot of laws that people liked. He was chosen to run Northern Italy and parts of southeast Europe in the next step.

The 13 Legione led Caesar to conquer Gaul, now France and Belgium. He also punished his enemies by cutting off their hands to show them that they were not welcome in the city. In the end, Caesar was known for the way he treated his enemies.

In 50 BC, the Senate, led by Pompey, told Caesar to go home because his term as governor had ended, so he had to leave. It took Pompey a long time to change his mind about Caesar, but he did.

Caesar went to war with Pompey. Caesar took over Italy and pushed Pompey into Egypt, where Pompey was killed. When Caesar was in Egypt, he had an affair with Cleopatra, who gave birth to Caesar's only known biological son, Caesarion, born after the affair.

Crassus was defeated and killed in a battle in Syria.

They overthrew their king in 509 BC, who had all the power and could rule without the Senate or citizen votes. A system of checks and balances like the US one was put into place to make sure the new government worked well in Rome, which was democratic at one point. However, the Roman founders also included an "emergency clause" that said that the Senate could vote to give absolute power to one man as a dictator when the country was in trouble. This way, the Senate could have strong leaders to help them get through that time. Many people were talking about war and chaos in Rome by 48 BC. Much political corruption took place. Finally, the Senate agreed that Caesar should be made the new ruler.

During Caesar's time as ruler, he made significant progress for Rome. Caesar changed the debt laws in Rome, which freed up a lot of money for the people. In addition, Caesar changed the Senate and election rules.

Most importantly, Caesar made changes to the Roman calendar. The calendar used to be based on the phases of the moon. There were more months in the calendar in this newly updated Julian Calendar. It was set to have 365 days and had a leap day every four years at the end of February. It's almost the same as the Western calendar we use today.

During his time as dictator, Caesar became more and more interested in power. They were worried that Caesar would not step down as dictator when the time came. Then, Marcus Brutus came up with a plan to kill Caesar on the Ides of March (the 15th) in 44 BC. Caesar was going to be killed at a meeting of the Senate at the Theater of Pompey.

It is thought that 60 or more men were involved. Caesar was stabbed 23 times on the Senate floor, and it is thought that there were more than 60 people involved.

During the years following the death of Caesar, there were five civil wars. These wars helped to form the Roman Empire.

Caesar was swiftly martyred and, two years later, became the first Roman to be worshiped.

When Caesar was alive, he was married three times. He married Cornelia Cinnilla for the first time when he was 18. (married 83 BC - 69 BC.) Afterward, Julia married Pompey and gave birth to a child, but she didn't live long enough to see it grow up. She was his second wife (married 67 BC - 61 BC.) His third wife was Calpurnia Pisonis, and they had a daughter together (married 59 BC - 44 BC.) Caesar had an affair with Cleopatra, which led to a son named Caesarion. Since it was an extramarital relationship, Caesarion was never recognized as Caesar's son by the Roman government.

Caesar named his great-nephew Octavian in his will. Octavian became the first Roman emperor, Augustus Caesar, in the end.

1. **Caesar made changes to the Roman ____.**
   a. history
   b. calendar

2. **Julius Caesar parents were the most powerful people in politics.**
   a. True
   b. False

3. **Julius Caesar became a public speaker and advocated for the ____.**
   a. government
   b. law

4. **Julius was chosen to run Spain in ____ BC**
   a. 62
   b. 32

5. **Caesar worked closely with ____, a former military officer, and ____, one of the wealthiest men in Rome**
   a. Crassus, Poindexter
   b. Pompey, Crassus

6. **Caesar changed the debt laws in ___.**
   a. Rome
   b. Egypt

7. **____ came up with a plan to kill Caesar on the Ides of March.**
   a. Marcus Brutus
   b. Mark Buccaning

8. **What wars helped to form the Roman Empire?**
   a. civil wars
   b. World War II

Proofreading Interpersonal Skills: Peer Pressure

Score: ____________________

Date: ____________

In this activity, you'll see lots of grammatical *errors*. Correct all the grammar mistakes you see.

There are **30** mistakes in this passage. 3 capitals missing. 5 unnecessary capitals. 3 unnecessary apostrophes. 6 punctuation marks missing or incorrect. 13 incorrectly spelled words.

Tony is mingling with a large group of what he considers to be the school's cool kids. Suddenly, someone in the group begins mocking Tony's friend Rob, who walks with a limp due to a physical dasability.

They begin to imitate rob's limping and Call him 'lame cripple' and other derogatory terms. Although Tony disapproves of their behavior, he does not want to risk being excluded from the group, and thus joins them in mocking Rob.

Peer pressure is the influence exerted on us by member's of our social group. It can manifest in a variety of ways and can lead to us engaging in behaviors we would not normally consider such as Tony joining in and mocking his friend Rob.

However, peer pressure is not always detrimental. Positive peer pressure can motivate us to make better chioces, such as studying harder, staying in school, or seeking a better job. Whan others influence us to make poor Choices, such as smoking, using illicit drugs, or bullying, we succumb to negative peer pressure. We all desire to belong to a group and fit in, so Developing strategies for resisting peer pressure when necessary can be beneficial.

Tony and his friends are engaging in bullying by moking Rob. Bullying is defined as persistent, unwanted. aggressive behavior directed toward another person. It is moust prevalent in school-aged children but can also aphfect adults. Bullying can take on a variety of forms, including the following:

· Verbil bullying is when someone is called names, threatened, or taunted verbally.
· Bullying is physical in nature - hitting spitting, tripping, or poshing someone.
· Social Bullying is intentionally excluding Someone from activities spreading rumors, or embarrassing sumeone.

· Cyberbullying is the act of verbally or socially bullying someone via the internet, such as through social media sites.

Peer pressure exerts a significant influence on an individual's decision to engage in bullying behavoir. In Tony's case, even though Rob is a friend and tony would never consider mocking his disability, his desire to belong to a group outweighs his willingness to defend his friend

Peer pressure is a strong force that is exerted on us by our social group members. Peer pressure is classified into two types: negative peer pressure, which results in poor decision-making, and positive peer pressure, which influences us to make the correct choices. Adolescents are particularly susceptible to peer pressure because of their desire to fit in

Peer pressure can motivate someone to engage in bullying behaviors such as mocking someone, threatening to harm them, taunting them online, or excluding them from an activity. Each year, bullying affect's an astounding 3.2 million school-aged children. Severil strategies for avoiding peer pressure bullying include the following:

- consider your actions by surrounding yourself with good company.
- Acquiring the ability to say no to someone you trust.

Speak up - bullying is never acceptable and is taken extramely seroiusly in schools and the workplace. If someone is attempting to convince you to bully another person, speaking with a trusted adult such as a teacher, coach, counselor, or coworker can frequently help put thing's into perspective and highlight the issue.

Proofreading Skills: Volunteering

Score: ____________________

Date: ____________

In this activity, you'll see lots of grammatical *errors*. Correct all the grammar mistakes you see.

There are **10** mistakes in this passage. 3 capitals missing. 4 unnecessary capitals. 3 incorrect homophones.

Your own life can be changed and the lives of others, through volunteer work. to cope with the news that there has been a disaster, you can volunteer to help those in need. Even if you can't contribute financially, you can donate you're time instead.

Volunteering is such an integral part of the American culture that many high schools require their students to participate in community service to graduate.

When you volunteer, you have the freedom to choose what you'd like to do and who or what you think is most deserving of your time. Start with these ideas if you need a little inspiration. We've got just a few examples here.

Encourage the growth and development of young people. Volunteer as a Camp counselor, a Big Brother or Big Sister, or an after-school sports program. Special Olympics games and events are excellent opportunities to know children with special needs.

Spend the holidays doing good deeds for others. Volunteer at a food bank or distribute toys to children in need on Thanksgiving Day, and you'll be doing your part to help those in need. your church, temple, mosque, or another place of worship may also require your assistance.

You can visit an animal shelter and play with the Animals. Volunteers are critical to the well-being of shelter animals. (You also get a good workout when you walk rescued dogs.)

Become a member of a political campaign. Its a great way to learn more about the inner workings of politics if your curious about it. If you are not able To cast a ballot, you can still help elect your preferred candidate.

Help save the planet. Join a river preservation group and lend a hand. Participate in a park cleanup day in your community. Not everyone is cut out for the great outdoors; if you can't see yourself hauling trees up a hill, consider working in the park's office or education center instead.

Take an active role in promoting health-related causes. Many of us know someone afflicted with a medical condition (like cancer, HIV, or diabetes, for example). a charity that helps people with a disease, such as delivering meals, raising money, or providing other assistance, can make you Feel good about yourself.

Find a way to combine your favorite things if you have more than one. For example, if you're a fan of kids and have a talent for arts and crafts, consider volunteering at a children's hospital.

Score: ____________________

Science: Titanium (Ti) Element

Date: ____________

Titanium is the first element in the periodic table's fourth column. It is a transition metal. Titanium atoms contain 22 protons and 22 electrons.

Titanium is a complex, light, silvery metal under normal conditions. It can be brittle at room temperature, but it becomes more bendable and pliable as the temperature rises.

Titanium's high strength-to-weight ratio is one of its most desirable properties. This means it is both extremely strong and lightweight. Titanium is double the strength of aluminum but only 60% heavier. It is also as strong as steel but weighs a fraction of the weight.

Compared to other metals, titanium is relatively non-reactive and highly resistant to corrosion caused by different metals and chemicals such as acids and oxygen. As a result, it has relatively low thermal and electrical conductivity.

Titanium is not found in nature as a pure element but rather as a compound found in the Earth's crust as a component of many minerals. According to the International Atomic Energy Agency, it is the ninth most prevalent element in the Earth's crust. Rutile and ilmenite are the two most essential minerals for titanium mining. Australia, South Africa, and Canada are the top producers of these ores.

Titanium is mostly used in the form of titanium dioxide (TiO2). Tio2 is a white powder used in various industrial applications such as white paint, white paper, white polymers, and white cement.

Metals like iron, aluminum, and manganese are combined with titanium to create strong and lightweight alloys that can be utilized in spacecraft, naval vessels, missiles, and armor plating. Due to its corrosion resistance, it is particularly well-suited for seawater applications.

The biocompatibility of titanium is another valuable property of the metal. This indicates that the human body will not reject it. Together with its strength, durability, and lightweight, titanium is a good material for medical applications. It is utilized in various applications, including hip and dental implants. Titanium is also utilized in the manufacture of jewelry, such as rings and watches.

Reverend William Gregor recognized titanium as a new element for the first time in 1791. As a hobby, the English clergyman was fascinated by minerals. He coined the term menachanite for the element. M.H. Kalproth, a German chemist, eventually altered the name to titanium. M. A. Hunter, an American scientist, was the first to create pure titanium in 1910.

Titanium is named after the Greek gods Titans.

Titanium has five stable isotopes: titanium-46, titanium-47, titanium-48, titanium-49, and titanium-50. The isotope titanium-48 accounts for the vast bulk of titanium found in nature.

1. Titanium has five stable ____.

   a. isotopes
   b.

2. Titanium is the first element in the periodic table's ____ column.

   a. 4rd
   b. fourth

3. Titanium is a transition ____.

   a. metal
   b.

4. Titanium is mostly used in the form of ____ (TiO2).

   a. titanium dioxide
   b. dioxide oxygen

Score: ______________________

Reading Storytime: The Frog

Date: _____________

YOU HAVE 15 MINUTES TO COMPLETE

First, read the entire passage. After that, go back and fill in the blanks. You can skip the blanks you're unsure about and finish them later.

Frog	dinner	beautiful	castle	door
ball	cried	companion	fountain	swimming

When wishing was a thing, there was a King whose daughters were all _______________, but the youngest was so stunning that even the sun, which has seen so much, was taken aback whenever it shone in her face.

A large dark forest lay close to the King's _______________, and a fountain was hidden beneath an old lime tree in the woods. When it was a hot day, the King's Child went out into the forest and sat by the cool fountain, and when she was bored, she took a golden ball, threw it up in the air, and caught it. And the ball was her favorite toy.

Now, one day, the King's Daughter's golden _______________ fell onto the ground and rolled straight into the water rather than into the little hand she was holding up for it. The King's Daughter pursued it with her eyes, but it vanished, and the well was deep, so deep that the bottom could not be seen. She began to cry, and she screamed louder and louder, and she could not be consoled.

And as she sobbed, someone asked her, "What ails you, King's Daughter?" You weep so much that even a stone would feel sorry for you."

When she turned around to the side from which the voice had come, she saw a _______________ sticking its thick, ugly head out of the water. "Ah! "Is it you, old water-splasher?" she asked, "I am weeping for my golden ball, which has fallen into the fountain."

"Be quiet and do not weep," the Frog replied, "I can help you." But what will you give me if I bring up your toy again?"

"Whatever you want, dear Frog," she said, "my clothes, my pearls, and jewels, even the golden crown I'm wearing."

"I don't care for your clothes, pearls, and jewels, or your golden crown," the Frog replied, "but if you will love me and let me be your _______________ and playfellow, and sit by you at your little table, and eat off your little golden plate, and drink out of your little cup, and sleep in your little bed-if you promise me this, I will go down below and bring your golden ball up again."

"Oh, yes," she said, "I promise you everything you want if you just bring my ball back." "How the silly

Frog does talk!" she thought. He lives in the water with the other frogs and croaks and can't be a human's companion!"

But, having received this promise, the Frog plunged his head into the water and sank. He quickly came ________________ up with the ball in his mouth, and threw it on the grass. The King's Daughter was thrilled to see her pretty plaything again, and she quickly picked it up and ran away with it.

"Wait, wait," the Frog said. "Bring me along. I can't run as fast as you." But what good did it do him to scream his croak, croak, croak, croak, croak, croak! She ignored it and ran home, quickly forgetting the poor Frog, who was forced to return to his ________________.

The next day, as she sat at the table with the King and all the courtiers, eating from her little golden plate, something crept up the marble staircase, splish splash, splish splash. When it reached the top, it knocked on the ________________ and cried out:

"Youngest King's Daughter."
"Please open the door!"

She dashed outside to see who was there, but when she opened the door, the Frog was standing in front of it. Then she hurriedly slammed the door, sat down to ________________ again, and was terrified.

"My Child, what are you so afraid of?" said the King, seeing her heart beating furiously. Is there a Giant outside looking to take you away?"

"Ah, no," she replied, "it's a disgusting Frog, not a Giant."

"What exactly does the Frog want from you?"

"Ah, dear Father, my golden ball fell into the water yesterday while I was sitting by the fountain in the forest, playing." Because I ________________ so much, the Frog brought it out for me again. And because he insisted, I promised him he could be my companion, but I never imagined he'd be able to get out of the water! And now he's here, wanting to come in."

Meanwhile, it knocked a second time and cried:

"Youngest King's Daughter!"
Allow me to enter!
Don't you remember yesterday and everything you said to me, besides the cooling fountain's spray?
Youngest King's Daughter!
"Let me in!"

Graduated Cylinders DATE:________ SCORE:________

Determine how much liquid is in each graduated cylinder.

1) 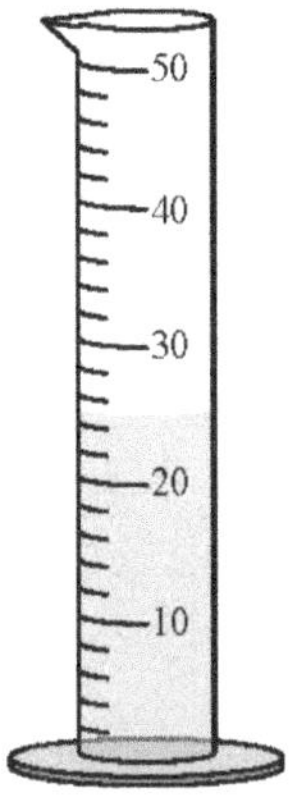

2) 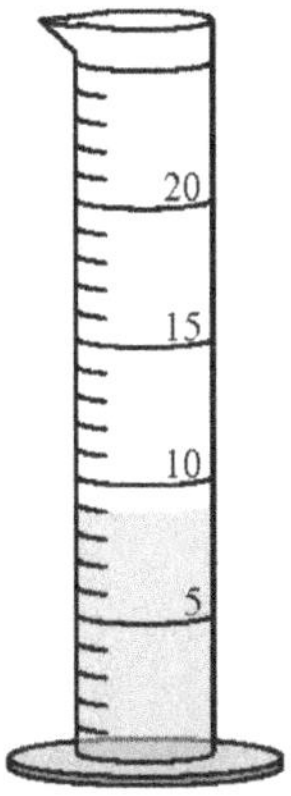

3) 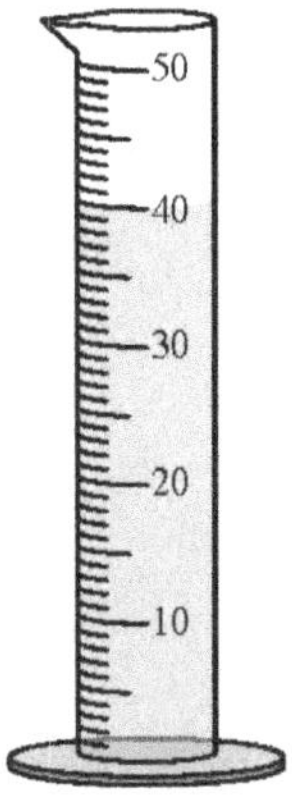

4) 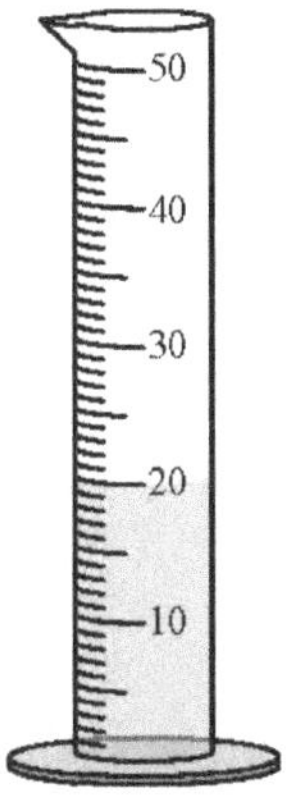

5) 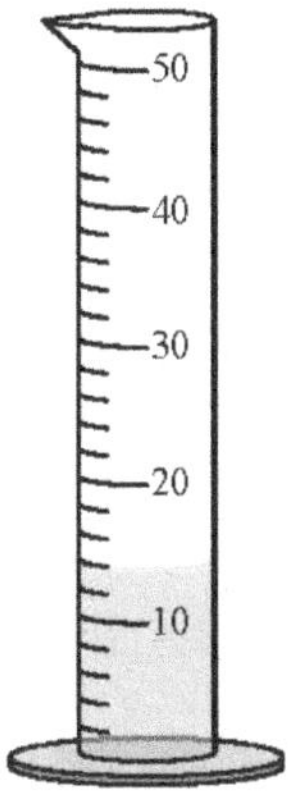

6) 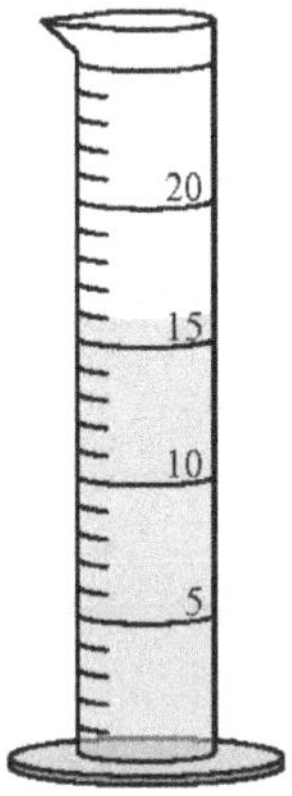

7) 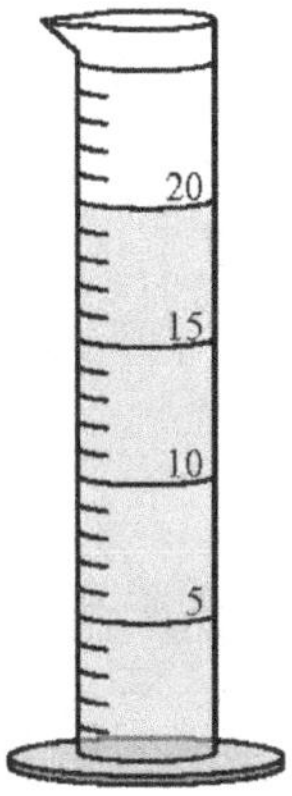

8) 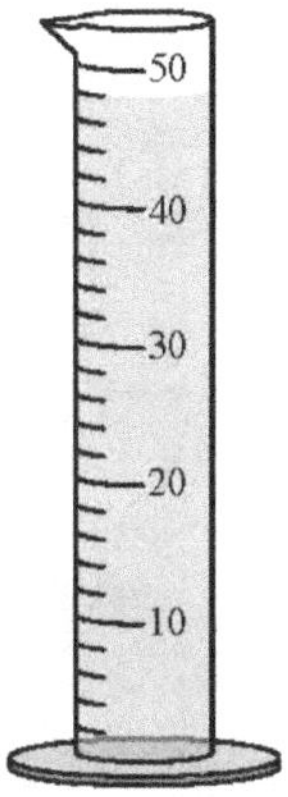

Four different objects were placed in a graduated cylinder 1 at a time:

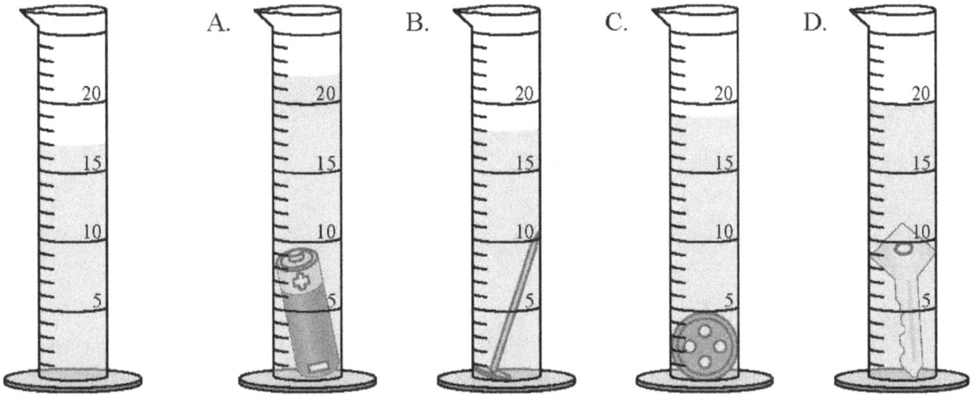

Empty battery nail button key

9) Which object had the greatest volume?

10) Which object had the least volume?

Answers

1. ____________
2. ____________
3. ____________
4. ____________
5. ____________
6. ____________
7. ____________
8. ____________
9. ____________
10. ____________

Determine which letter best matches each microscope piece.

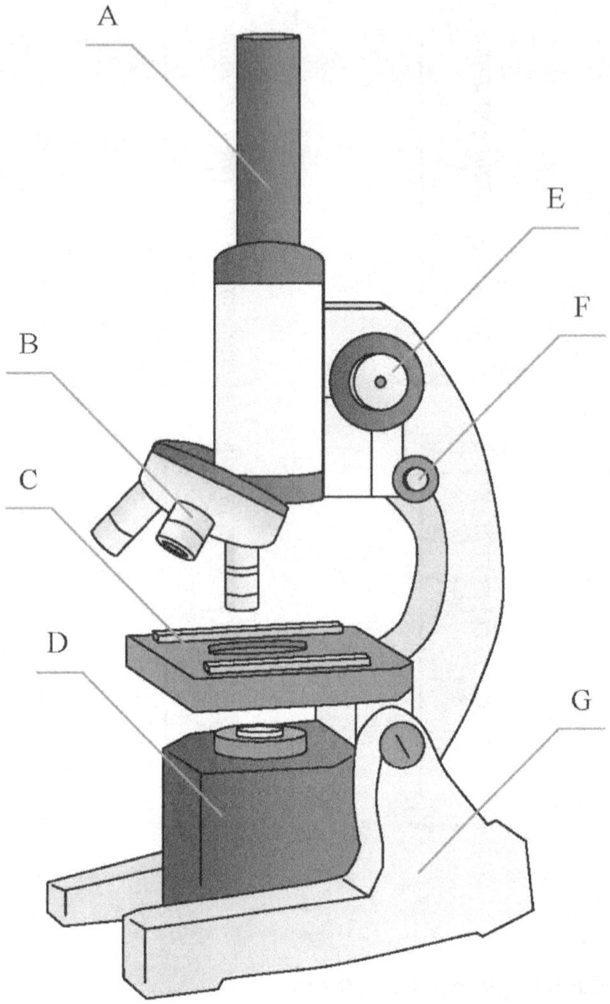

1) Illuminator ______

2) Stage ______

3) Eyepiece ______

4) Focus (Fine) ______

5) Lense ______

6) Focus (Course) ______

7) Base ______

Answers

1. ______
2. ______
3. ______
4. ______
5. ______
6. ______
7. ______

Using Scientific Tools DATE:________ SCORE:________

Determine which scientific tool best answers the question.

A. Thermometer	C. Scale	E. Microscope
B. Ruler	D. Telescope	F. Measuring Cup

1) Will only had enough money to buy 2 pounds of bananas at the grocery store. What tool should he use to make sure he gets exactly 2 pounds?

2) Oliver found a small black dot on his new sweater. What tool should he use to determine what the dot actually is?

3) Adam needed to mix exactly 2 tablespoons of food coloring with 2 quarts of water. What tool should he use to measure the amounts?

4) Maria, while performing an experiment, had to make sure her wires were between 1 and 2 inches. What tool did she use to determine the length?

5) Paige earned $1 dollar for every 3 pounds of cans she recycled. What tool should she use to make sure she recycles at least 3 pounds?

6) Mike wanted to check the water temperature of a hot tub. What tool should he use to see the water temperature?

7) George was trying to view satellites from his backyard. What tool should he use to help find one?

8) Billy needed exactly 6 ounces of cheese. What tool should he use to measure exactly 6 ounces?

9) Paul used a tool to view the Andromeda Galaxy. What tool did he use to see the galaxy?

10) Dave wanted to check the height of his flashlight. What tool should he use?

11) A scientist wanted to view the microbes in a drop of water. What tool should he use?

12) Megan needed to add 500 ml of water to a mixture for an experiment. What tool did she use to measure out 500 ml of water?

13) John wants to compare the cells of an animal and a plant. What tool should he use?

14) Nancy was outside looking at the Crab Nebula. What tool was she using to view the nebula?

15) Tom learned old books needed to stay at around 70° F. What tool should he use to make sure the books don't get too hot?

Answers

1. ________
2. ________
3. ________
4. ________
5. ________
6. ________
7. ________
8. ________
9. ________
10. ________
11. ________
12. ________
13. ________
14. ________
15. ________

Score: ____________________

Science Vocabulary 1

Date: ____________

Choose the best answer to each question.

1. A variable that is intentionally changed to observe its effect on the dependent variable.
   a. Dependent Variable
   b. Independent Variable

2. Choose the correct meaning of the word "Melting Point".
   a. Temperature at which a solid changes state to a liquid.
   b. At normal atmospheric pressure, the temperature at which a liquid solidifies.

3. Temperature at which liquid changes state to gas.
   a. Freezing Point
   b. Boiling Point

4. Anything that takes up space and has mass.
   a. Mass
   b. Matter

5. The event expected to change when the independent variable is changed. Measurable
   a. Dependent Variable
   b. Independent Variable

6. Which word describes the variables that are not changed?
   a. Control Group
   b. Experimental group

7. Select the meaning of the word "Condensation".
   a. Change of matter from a liquid to a gas.
   b. Change of matter from a gas to a liquid state.

8. What is the definition of Freezing Point?
   a. At the temperature at which its vapor pressure is equal to the pressure of the gas above it.
   b. Temperature at which a liquid changes state to solid.

9. Select the meaning of the word "Evaporation".
   a. Change of matter from a gas to a liquid state.
   b. Change of matter from a liquid to a gas.

10. The amount of matter in an object.
   a. Mass
   b. Matter

Score: ______________________

Science Vocabulary 2

Date: _____________

Choose the best answer to each question.

1. Change in which the composition of a substance changes.

a. Physical Change

b. Chemical Change

2. What is the correct definition of the word "Physical Change"?

a. Change in which the composition of a substance changes.

b. Change in which the form or appearance of matter changes, but not its composition.

3. What is the correct definition of the word "Compound"?

a. Two or more substances that are blended without combining chemically.

b. Two or more elements that are chemically combined.

4. Made up of only one kind of atom. Cannot be broken down into a simpler form by chemical reactions.

a. Element

b. Compound

5. What is the correct definition of the word "Chemical Property"?

a. Characteristics that is observable or measureable in a substance without changing the chemical composition of the substance.

b. Characteristic that cannot be observed without altering the sample.

6. Ratio of the mass of a substance to its volume, expressed in g/cm3. Mixture

a. Volume

b. Density

7. What is the correct definition of the word "Mixture"?

a. Two or more substances that are blended without combining chemically.

b. Two or more elements that are chemically combined.

8. What is the correct definition of the word "Volume"?

a. Ratio of the mass of a substance to its volume, expressed in g/cm3. Mixture

b. Amount of space occupied by an object or a substance.

9. Characteristics that is observable or measureable in a substance without changing the chemical composition of the substance.

a. Chemical Property

b. Physical Property

10. What is the correct definition of the word "Solution"?

a. Homogeneous mixture whose elements and/or compounds are evenly mixed at the molecular level but are not bonded together.

b. Two or more substances that are blended without combining chemically.

Science Vocabulary 3

Score: ____________

Date: ____________

Choose the best answer to each question.

1. Type of mixture where the substances are not evenly mixed. Different parts are visible.
   a. Homogeneous Mixture
   b. Heterogeneous Mixture

2. Type of mixture where two or more substances are evenly mixed on a molecular level but are not bonded together.
   a. Homogeneous Mixture
   b. Heterogeneous Mixture

3. Electrically-neutral particle that has the same mass as a proton and is found in an atom's nucleus.
   a. Neutron
   b. Proton

4. Negatively-charged particle that exists in an electron cloud formation around an atom's nucleus.
   a. Neutron
   b. Electron

5. Region surrounding the nucleus of an atom, where electrons are most likely to be found.
   a. Electron Shell
   b. Electron Cloud

6. What is the meaning of the word "Base"?
   a. Substance that releases H+ ions and produces hydronium ions when dissolved in water.
   b. Substance that accepts H+ ions and produces hydroxide ions when dissolved in water.

7. Substance that releases H+ ions and produces hydronium ions when dissolved in water.
   a. Base
   b. Acid

8. What is the meaning of the word "ph"?
   a. a measure of the hydroxide ion (OH-) concentration of a solution.
   b. Measure of how acidic or basic a solution is, ranging in a scale from 0 to 14.

9. What is the meaning of the word "Proton"?
   a. Negatively-charged particle that exists in an electron cloud formation around an atom's nucleus.
   b. Positively-charged particle in the nucleus of an atom.

10. What is the meaning of the word "Nucleus"?
    a. Small region of space at the center of the atom; contains protons and neutrons.
    b. Is a region found within the cell nucleus that is concerned with producing and assembling the cell's ribosomes.

Score: ______________________

Science Vocabulary 4

Date: ______________

Choose the best answer to each question.

1. Family of elements in the periodic table that have similar physical or chemical properties.

a. Group

b. Subgroup

2. Table of elements organized into groups and periods by increasing atomic number.

a. Periodic Table

b. Chemical Elements

3. It is the property of many substances that give the ability to do work; many forms of energy (i.e., light, heat, electricity, sound)

a. Energy

b. Power

4. Number of protons in the nucleus of an atom of a given element.

a. Mass Number

b. Atomic Number

5. The sum of neutrons and protons in the nucleus of an atom.

a. Mass Number

b. Atomic Number

6. Force of attraction between all objects in the universe.

a. Gravity

b. Friction

7. What is the meaning of the word "Isotope"?

a. Atoms of the same element that have different numbers of neutrons.

b. An atom or molecule with a positive or negative charge.

8. What is the meaning of the word "Period"?

a. Vertical row of elements in the periodic table.

b. Horizontal row of elements in the periodic table.

9. What is the meaning of the word "Tides"?

a. Rise and fall of ocean water levels.

b. Ae formed because of the winds blowing over the surface of the ocean.

10. What is the meaning of the word "Kinetic Energy"?

a. Energy an object has due to its motion.

b. A form of energy that has the potential to do work but is not actively doing work or applying any force on any other objects.

Science Vocabulary 5

Score: ____________________

Date: ____________

Choose the best answer to each question.

1. Energy that all objects have that increases as the object's temperature increases.
   a. Thermal Energy
   b. Potential Energy

2. Energy carried by electric current.
   a. Electrical Energy
   b. Radiant Energy

3. Transfer of heat by the flow of material. Heat rises and cool air sinks.
   a. Conduction
   b. Convection

4. What is the meaning of the word "Radiant Energy"?
   a. Energy that all objects have that increases as the object's temperature increases.
   b. Energy carried by light.

5. Transfer of energy that occurs when molecules bump into each other.
   a. Convection
   b. Conduction

6. The crust and the rigid part of Earth's mantle. Divided into tectonic plates.
   a. Lithosphere
   b. Asthenosphere

7. What is the meaning of the word "Potential Energy"?
   a. Energy stored in an object due to its position.
   b. Energy stored in chemical bonds.

8. Energy contained in atomic nuclei; splitting uranium nuclei by nuclear fission.
   a. Nuclear Energy
   b. Thermal Energy

9. States that energy can change its form but is never created or destroyed.
   a. Law of Conservation of Mass
   b. Law of Conservation of Energy

10. What is the meaning of the word "Chemical Energy"?
   a. Energy stored in chemical bonds.
   b. Energy stored in an object due to its position.

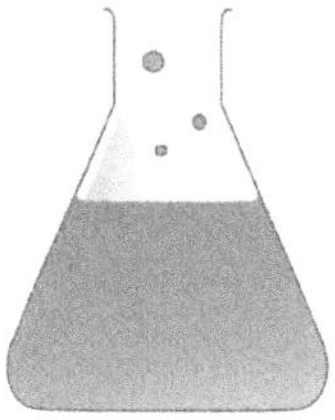

Score: ______________________

Date: ______________

Science Vocabulary 6

Choose the best answer to each question.

1	Precipitation	Earth's solid, rocky surface.	A
2	Inner Core	The movement of the Earth's continents relative to each other by appearing to drift across the ocean bed	B
3	Continental Drift	Process of water vapor changing to liquid water	C
4	Crust	Inner most layer composed of solid iron and nickel. Stays solid due to the pressure of the layers above it.	D
5	Asthenosphere	Continuous movement of water from the air to the earth and back again.	E
6	Condensation	Made up of mostly molten (melted) iron and nickel.	F
7	Mantle	Process of water falling from clouds to earth in the form of rain, sleet, show, or hail	G
8	Core	Solid layer of the mantle beneath lithosphere; made of mantle rock that flows very slowly allowing tectonic plates to move on top of it.	H
9	Plate Tectonics	Scientific theory that describes the large-scale motions of Earth's lithosphere.	I
10	Water Cycle	The layer of Earth beneath the crust.	J

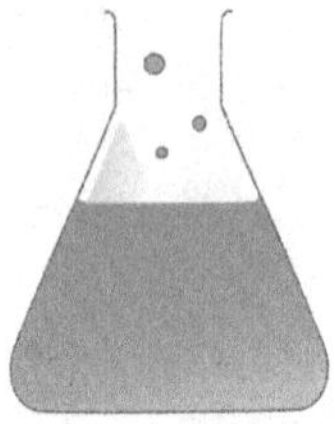

Score: ____________________

Date: ____________

Science Vocabulary 7

Choose the best answer to each question.

1	Mechanical Weathering	Atmospheric layer closest to earth; nearly all weather change occurs here	A
2	Atmosphere	Occurs when the chemical makeup of the rocks changes.	B
3	Mesosphere	Involves only physical changes, such as size and shape. The chemical makeup of the rocks does not change.	C
4	Deposition	Dropping of sediments that occurs when a cause of erosion loses its energy and can no longer carry its load	D
5	Troposphere	Highest layer of the earth's atmosphere; very thin air	E
6	Erosion	Second atmospheric layer above the troposphere; nearly all ozone found here	F
7	Evaporation	Third atmospheric layer above the stratosphere; coldest layer	G
8	Thermosphere	Is the process that wears away surface materials and moves them from one place to another	H
9	Chemical Weathering	Process of liquid water changing to water vapor	I
10	Stratosphere	Thick blanket of gases (nitrogen, oxygen and trace gases) surrounding the earth	J

Score: ____________________

Science Words You Should Know Quiz

Date: ____________

Circle the correct meaning of each word. Need help? Try Google!

1. Bulb
  a. Light producing instrument
  b. Learning by doing

2. Circuit
  a. A representation of data
  b. A path that electricity follows during its flowing

3. Kinetic
  a. An optical instrument
  b. Movement

4. Friction
  a. Resistance due to movement
  b. Making larger

5. Hygrometer
  a. A path that electricity follows during its flowing
  b. Humidity measuring instrument

6. Barometer
  a. The intensity of sound
  b. Pressure measuring instrument

7. Humidity
  a. A quantity expressing water vapor's amount
  b. Movement

8. Pitch
  a. Findings after an investigation
  b. The intensity of sound

9. Neutron
  a. Sub-particle of an atom
  b. Findings after an investigation

10. Proton
  a. Findings after an investigation
  b. A constituent of an atom

11. Dark
  a. Categorization on a common base
  b. Absence of light

12. Practical
  a. Learning by doing
  b. A path that electricity follows during its flowing

13. Classify
  a. Categorization on a common base
  b. Findings after an investigation

14. Analyze
  a. Detail examination
  b. Resistance due to movement

15. Expand
  a. Absence of light
  b. Making larger

16. Graph
  a. A representation of data
  b. A path that electricity follows during its flowing

17. Results
  a. Findings after an investigation
  b. Sub-particle of an atom

18. Microscope
  a. Making larger
  b. An optical instrument

Science: Mollusk

Score: ____________________

Date: ____________

A mollusk is a type of soft-bodied animal. A hard shell protects the body of most mollusks. Mollusks are classified into over 100,000 species or types. Some examples include octopuses, oysters, snails, and squid.

All over the world, mollusks can be found. The majority of them live in the sea, but some are freshwater species. Some prefer the coast's shallow water, and others would rather be in deep water. Many mollusks dig down into muddy or sandy soil, while some cling to rocks.

Snails and slugs can be found on land; they prefer cool, moist environments and can also be found in cold climates and deserts.

Mollusks are invertebrates, which means they lack a backbone. They have a soft body containing the heart, liver, digestive system, and other vital organs. A radula is a mouth structure found in most mollusks; the radula resembles a rough tongue with many tiny teeth.

Many mollusks feed primarily on algae, they scrape algae off rocks with the radula. Larger mollusks, on the other hand, have a big appetite. Snails and slugs eat plants and fruit. Squids can consume fish and shrimp. An octopus is capable of pursuing prey as large as a shark.

Mollusks are usually active at night. Octopuses, for example, spend the day in the deep parts of the ocean. They swim closer to the surface at dawn and dusk, searching for food. Land snails and slugs hide during the day and emerge at night.

Many mollusks hide in their shells from predators. On the other hand, Mollusks without shells must rely on other means of defense. Squid and octopuses change color and pattern to blend in with their surroundings. They also emit an inky liquid to distract and confuse an opponent.

1. Mollusks are invertebrates.

a. True
b. False

2. A mollusk is a kind of animal with a ___.

a. soft body
b. soft shell but hard body

3. Octopuses, oysters, snails, and ___ are a few examples of a mollusk.

a. penguin
b. squid

4. Most mollusks have a mouth structure called a ____.

a. radula
b. reddish

5. Many mollusks eat mostly ____.

a. fish
b. algae

6. Mollusks usually are active during the day.

a. True - they prefer day time to find food
b. False - they are active usually at night

Science: Protists

Score: ____________________

Date: ____________

First, read the entire passage. After that, go back and fill in the blanks. You can skip the blanks you're unsure about and finish them later.

unclassifiable	tiny	consume	enormous	cell
Amoebas	acellular	cellular	tail	color
scoot	reproduce	oxygen	energy	molds

Protists are organisms that are classified under the biological kingdom protista. These are neither plants, animals, bacteria, or fungi, but rather ________________ organisms. Protists are a large group of organisms with a wide variety of characteristics. They are essentially all species that do not fit into any of the other categories.

Protists as a group share very few characteristics. They are eukaryotic microorganisms with eukaryote ________________ structures that are pretty basic. Apart from that, they are defined as any organism that is not a plant, an animal, a bacteria, or a fungus.

Protists can be classified according to their mode of movement.

Cilia - Certain protists move with ________________ hair called cilia. These tiny hairs can flap in unison to assist the creature in moving through water or another liquid.

Other protists have a lengthy ________________ known as flagella. This tail can move back and forth, aiding in the organism's propulsion.

Pseudopodia - When a protist extends a portion of its cell body in order to ________________ or ooze. Amoebas move in this manner.

Different protists collect ________________ in a variety of methods. Certain individuals consume food and digest it internally. Others digest their food through the secretion of enzymes. Then they ________________ the partially digested meal. Other protists, like plants, utilize photosynthesis. They absorb sunlight and convert it to glucose.

Algae is a main form of protist. Algae are photosynthesis-capable protists. Algae are closely related to plants. They contain chlorophyll and utilize ________________ and solar energy to generate food. However, they are not called plants because they lack specialized organs and tissues such as leaves, roots, and stems. Algae are frequently classified according on their ________________, which ranges from red to brown to green.

Slime ________________ are distinct from fungus molds. Slime molds are classified into two types: cellular and plasmodial. Slime molds of Plasmodium are formed from a single big cell. They are also referred to as ________________. Even though these organisms are composed of only one cell, they can grow quite ________________, up to several feet in width. Additionally, they can contain several nuclei inside a single cell. Cellular slime molds are little single-celled protists that can form a single organism when combined. When combined, various ________________ slime molds will perform specific activities.

________________ are single-celled organisms that move with the assistance of pseudopods. Amoebas have no structure and consume their food by engulfing it with their bodies. Amoebas ________________ by dividing in two during a process called mitosis.

Sentence Unscramble

Score: ______________________

Date: ______________

Unscramble the sentences!

1. ____

   5 · the · sun · at · in · rises · morning. · The

2. ____

   get · ready · I · for · school.

3. ____

   a · healthy · breakfast. · I · eat

4. ____

   I · for · leave · school · about · at · 7:30.

5. ____

   prepare. · get · school · I · and · to

6. ____

   friends · my · lunch. · to · talk · before · I

7. ____

   I · lunch. · a · terrible · eat

8. ____

   sleep · lunch. · I · am · after

9. ____

   home. · go · to · prepare · I

10. ____

   I · get · long · after · at · home · a · day · school!

Social Studies Vocabulary 6

Score: ____________________

Date: ____________

Choose the best answer to each question.

1	Primary source	products made in one country and going to another.	A
2	Rural	Two house law-making body.	B
3	Bicameral Legislature	Central government	C
4	Act	group of elected officials that make laws (each state has two).	D
5	Suffrage	Native American word to describe the Iroquois people.	E
6	Tariff	law	F
7	Senate	highly developed level of cultural and technological development.	G
8	Federal	to make a country larger.	H
9	Haudenosaunee	firsthand information about people or events.	I
10	Import	tax	J
11	Civilization	vote	K
12	Exports	country or farmland.	L
13	Expansion	trade product brought into a country.	M

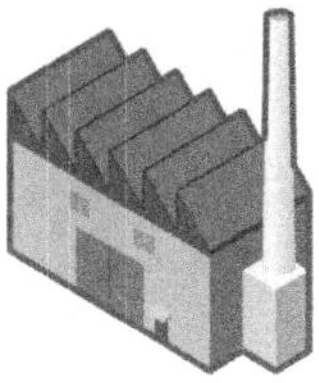

Social Studies Vocabulary 1

Score: ______________________

Date: ____________

Choose the best answer to each question.

1	Abolition	practice of trying to cut costs by using fewer people to do the same work	A
2	Compare	an economic system in which individuals decide for themselves what to produce and sell.	B
3	Concentration Camp	the practice of giv In the Cold War, the policy of trying to prevent the spread of Soviet or communist influence beyond where it already existeding in to an aggressor nation's demands in order to keep the peace (avoid war).	C
4	Containment	increased birth rate in the U.S. after WWII (1940s & 50s).	D
5	Appeasement	rule by the army instead of elected the government characterized by the reduction of civil liberties.	E
6	Industrialization	to state the difference between two or more examples.	F
7	Free Market	In the Cold War, the policy of trying to prevent the spread of Soviet or communist influence beyond where it already existed.	G
8	Fascism	to state the similarities between two or more examples.	H
9	Martial Law	the ending of slavery.	I
10	Baby Boom	The economic transformation of a country marked by the development of new industries, mass production of goods and reduction in its agricultural workforce.	J
11	Contrast	a prison camp for persons who are considered enemies of the state. In WWII, death camps that were run by the German SS at the orders of Adolf Hitler.	K
12	Downsizing	A system of government marked by centralization of authority under a dictator, stringent socioeconomic controls, suppression of political opposition through terror and censorship, and typically a policy of belligerent nationalism and racism.	L

Social Studies Vocabulary 2

Score: ________________

Date: ____________

Choose the best answer to each question.

1	Superpower	exclusive control or ownership of an industry by a single business with the purpose of reducing competition.	A
2	Steerage	agricultural worker who moves with the seasons, planting or harvesting crops.	B
3	Segregation	to present an explanation or assumption that remains to be proved.	C
4	Monopoly	separation of people based on racial, ethnic, or other differences.	D
5	Domino Theory	in the Cold War, belief that if South Vietnam became communist, other countries in Southeast Asia would become communist, too.	E
6	Migrant Worker	a general pardon by an authority such as government.	F
7	Counterculture	On a ship, the cramped quarters for passengers paying the lowest fares.	G
8	Amnesty	rejection of traditional American values and culture associated with the youth movement of the 1960s.	H
9	Balanced Budget	American journalists who wrote investigative reports during the Progressive Era, exposing the ills of society and calling for government reform of political, social and economic institutions.	I
10	Hypothesize	condition that exists when the government spends only as much as it takes in from taxes.	J
11	Freedmen	person who had been slaves but were feed by the Emancipation Proclamation.	K
12	Satellite Nation	a country that is dominated politically and economically by a more powerful nation.	L
13	Muckraker	nation with enough military and economic strength to influence events in many areas around the world.	M

Score: ____________________

Social Studies Vocabulary 3

Date: ____________

Choose the best answer to each question.

1	Renewable Resource	system of social organization (government) in which the most important industries are controlled by the government that often plans and controls the economy. Similar to communism, but some capitalism is allowed.	A
2	Slave Codes	limiting the amount of certain types of goods that people can buy.	B
3	Aggression	condition of spending more money than the amount received in income.	C
4	Illegal Alien	laws controlling the lives of blacks in the south prior to the Civil War.	D
5	Nationalism	an economic system in which all property and resources are owned and controlled by the "community" (in practice, controlled by the government).	E
6	Annex	any warlike act by one country against another without just cause.	F
7	Deficit	to add on, to absorb into a larger body. Example – one nation taking over another and making it part of their own country.	G
8	Communism	pride in one's nation; the idea that the goals of one's nation are more important those of the rest of the world.	H
9	Trade Deficit	someone who enters a country without legal permission.	I
10	Socialism	a ruler who has complete power over government affairs.	J
11	Ration	when a nation buys more goods and services from foreign countries than it sells to them.	K
12	Dictator	a natural resource that can be quickly replaced by nature.	L

Score: ______________________

Social Studies Vocabulary 4

Date: ____________

Choose the best answer to each question.

1	Solar Energy	an idea that supreme governing power belongs to the voters.	A
2	Naturalization	person who works to reduce pollution and protect the natural environment.	B
3	Restate	nonviolent opposition to a government policy or law by refusing to comply with it.	C
4	Totalitarian State	paper money issued by the federal government during the Civil War.	D
5	Inflation	program in areas such as employment and education to provide more opportunities for members of groups that faced discrimination in the past.	E
6	Environmentalist	manufacturing process, developed by Henry Ford in the 1920's, whereby factory workers engage in specific and repetitive tasks.	F
7	Greenbacks	power source derived from the sun.	G
8	Assembly Line	sharp rise in prices and decrease in the value of money.	H
9	Détente	easing of tensions between nations.	I
10	Affirmative Action	a country where a single party controls the government and every aspect of the loves of people.	J
11	Civil Disobedience	to say again in a slightly different way.	K
12	Popular Sovereignty	The process by which an immigrant becomes a citizen.	L

Social Studies Vocabulary 5

Score: ______________________

Date: ______________

Choose the best answer to each question.

1. Political movement of the late 1800's favoring greater government regulation of business, graduated income tax and greater political involvement by the people
   a. Socialism
   b. Populism

2. To arrange in a systematic way.
   a. Manage
   b. Organize

3. Protests in which people sit in a particular place or business and refuse to leave.
   a. Strike
   b. Sit-In

4. An index based on the amount of goods, services, education, and leisure time that a people have.
   a. Standard of Living
   b. Quality of Life

5. Combination of businesses joining together to limit competition within an industry.
   a. Trust
   b. Monopolies

6. The factors that cause people to leave an area. (e.x. famine, war, political upheaval).
   a. Push factors
   b. Pull factors

7. The factors that attract people to a new area (e.x. jobs, freedom, family).
   a. Pull factors
   b. Push factors

8. What is the meaning of the word "Stock"?
   a. a legal entity that holds and manages assets on behalf of another individual or entity
   b. a share in a business

9. What is the meaning of the word "Suburb"?
   a. a community located within commuting distance of a city
   b. a community that's in a city or town

10. What is the meaning of the word "Recession"?
   a. a short term mild depression in which business slows and some workers lose their jobs
   b. an increase in the price of products and services over time in an economy

11. The movement of population from farms to city.
   a. Industrialization
   b. Urbanization

12. A belief that one's own ethnic group is superior to others.
   a. Ethnocentrism
   b. Ethnorelativism

Score: ______________________

Social Studies Vocabulary 6

Date: ______________

Choose the best answer to each question.

1. The workplace where people labor long hours for very low pay.

a. Factory

b. Sweatshop

2. To make plain or understandable; to give reasons for.

a. Explain

b. Interpret

3. What is the meaning of the word "Evaluate"?

a. to examine and judge the significance, worth or condition of or value of

b. to observe or inspect carefully or critically

4. The process by which an immigrant becomes a citizen.

a. Dual Citizenship

b. Naturalization

5. What is the meaning of the word "Draft"?

a. selection of people who would be forced to serve in the military

b. a person who enlists in military service by free will

6. A conference between the highest-ranking officials of different nations.

a. Diplomatic Conference

b. Summit Meeting

7. Select the correct meaning of the word "Identify".

a. to recognize by or divide into classes

b. to establish the essential character of

8. A person who flees his or her homeland to seek safety elsewhere.

a. Immigrant

b. Refugee

9. To make clear or obvious by using the examples or comparisons.

a. Illustrate

b. Demonstrate

10. To investigate closely; to examine critically

a. Scrutinize

b. Analyze

11. Select the correct meaning of the word "Laissez Fair".

a. literally means “hands off”; business principle advocating an economy free of governmental business regulations

b. an economic system whereby monetary goods are owned by individuals or companies.

12. The theory that Earth’s atmosphere is warming up as a result of air pollution, causing ecological problems.

a. Global Warming

b. Climate Change

Social Studies Vocabulary 7

Score: ____________________

Date: ____________

Choose the best answer to each question.

1. To build up, increase, or expand activity.
   a. Escalate
   b. Elevate

2. To conclude or judge from evidence.
   a. Imply
   b. Infer

3. The process of making large quantities of a product quickly and cheaply
   a. Continuous Production
   b. Mass Production

4. Select the correct meaning of the word "Ethnic Group".
   a. a group of people who have in common some visible physical traits, such as skin colour, hair texture, facial features, and eye formation
   b. a group of people that share a similar culture

5. The loyalty to your area or a nation rather then the nation as a whole.
   a. Sectionalism
   b. Nationalism

6. Bringing together people of different races or ethnic groups.
   a. Integration
   b. Inclusion

7. Select the correct meaning of the word "Imply".
   a. to mean or suggest openly without saying
   b. to suppose or come to a conclusion, especially based on an indirect suggestion.

8. The economic system in which businesses are owned by private citizens
   a. Mixed Economy
   b. Free Enterprise System

9. Select the correct meaning of the word "Assimilation".
   a. the process of becoming part of another culture
   b. the retaining of one's own culture within a minority community in a country but adapt to some aspects of the majority culture

10. To reach a broad conclusion avoiding specifics.
    a. Stereotype
    b. Generalize

11. The actions taken against a country in an effort to force a change in its policy.
    a. Sanctions
    b. Penalties

12. Select the correct meaning of the word "Secede".
    a. to give up, give way, give away
    b. to withdraw

Social Studies Vocabulary 8

Score: ______________________

Date: ______________

Choose the best answer to each question.

1. To break an idea into concepts or parts.

a. Analyze

b. Evaluate

2. Select the correct meaning of the word "Fugitive".

a. Runaway

b. Refugee

3. To place into groups or classify.

a. Categorize

b. Classify

4. The settling disagreements by having each side give up some of its demands.

a. Collaboration

b. Compromise

5. Select the correct meaning of the word "Discuss".

a. to explain what something is or what it means

b. to make observations using facts, reasoning or details

6. The persons who led slaves to freedom on the Underground Railroad.

a. Conductors

b. Driver

7. Select the correct meaning of the word "Guerrilla War".

a. a form of warfare conducted by using conventional weapons and battlefield tactics between two or more states in open confrontation.

b. use of hit-and-run tactics to fight a war.

8. The former policy of the South African government of separation of the races enforced by law

a. Apartheid

b. Segregation

9. To determine the importance significance size or value.

a. Assess

b. Evaluate

10. Select the correct meaning of the word "Arsenal".

a. a place where weapons are kept

b. a place where stocks are kept

11. To explain what something is or what it means.

a. Describe

b. Define

12. Select the correct meaning of the word "Corporation".

a. a business owned by a group of people who come together voluntarily for their mutual benefit.

b. a business owned by stockholders.

Identifying Primary and Secondary Sources DATE______ SCORE________

Determine if the source would be a Primary Source(P) or a secondary Source(S).

- A **Primary Source** is information that was created at the same time as an event or by a person directly involved in the event.
  Diaries, speeches, letters, official records, autobiographies.

- A **Secondary Source** is information from somewhere else or by a person not directly involved in the event.
  Encyclopedias, textbooks, book reports.

1) A play showing how Benjamin Franklin flew a kite during a lightning storm.

2) A short story describing Thomas Edison and Nikola Tesla's 'electrical' battle.

3) Anne Frank's diary describing her life during World War 2.

4) A cartoon showing how Pocahontas met John Smith.

5) A text book describing the civil rights movement.

6) A news report about the opening of a power plant.

7) A scientist explaining what it was like for Buzz Aldrin to walk on the moon.

8) A YouTube video describing how the pyramids were built.

9) An interview with Alexander Graham Bell about how he invented the telephone.

10) A radio broadcast from the day the Soviet Union launched Sputnik.

11) An autobiography about the 40th president, Ronald Reagan.

12) A book describing Christopher Columbus sailing to America.

13) A famous artist's painting of what cowboy life was probably like.

14) A journal by a cowboy about the cattle drives from Texas to Kansas.

15) The United States Constitution.

Answers

1. ______
2. ______
3. ______
4. ______
5. ______
6. ______
7. ______
8. ______
9. ______
10. ______
11. ______
12. ______
13. ______
14. ______
15. ______

Reading a Timeline DATE:__________ SCORE:__________

Use the timeline to answer the questions.

Lewis and Clark's Expedition

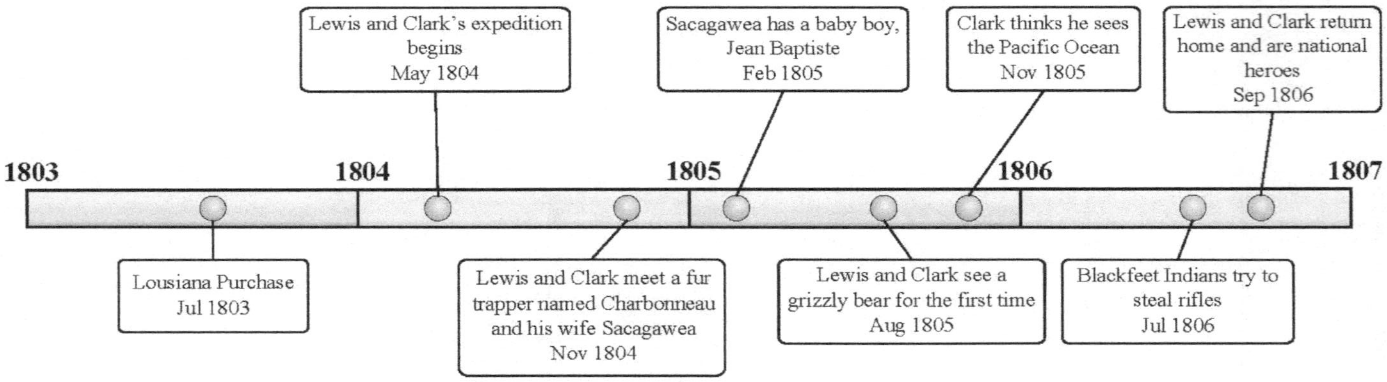

1803
1804
1805
1806
1807
Lousiana Purchase Jul 1803
Lewis and Clark's expedition begins May 1804
Lewis and Clark meet a fur trapper named Charbonneau and his wife Sacagawea Nov 1804
Sacagawea has a baby boy, Jean Baptiste Feb 1805
Lewis and Clark see a grizzly bear for the first time Aug 1805
Clark thinks he sees the Pacific Ocean Nov 1805
Blackfeet Indians try to steal rifles Jul 1806
Lewis and Clark return home and are national heroes Sep 1806

1) How many years did Lewis and Clark's expedition take? ________

2) Which happened earlier? A. Indians try to steal rifles or B. Lewis and Clark see a grizzly bear ________

3) What year was the Louisiana Purchase? ________

4) What year did Sacagawea have her child? ________

5) What is the span (number of years shown) of this timeline? ________

6) What year did Lewis and Clark meet Charbonneau? ________

7) What year did Lewis and Clark return home? ________

8) In September of 1804 Lewis and Clark saw a prairie dog. Could you put this event on the timeline above? (Yes / No)

9) What event happened in Nov 1805? ________________________

10) What is this timeline about? ________________________

Answers

1. ________
2. ________
3. ________
4. ________
5. ________
6. ________
7. ________
8. ________
9. Use Line
10. Use Line

Reading a Timeline DATE:__________ SCORE:__________

Use the timeline to answer the questions.

Major Events of World War 2

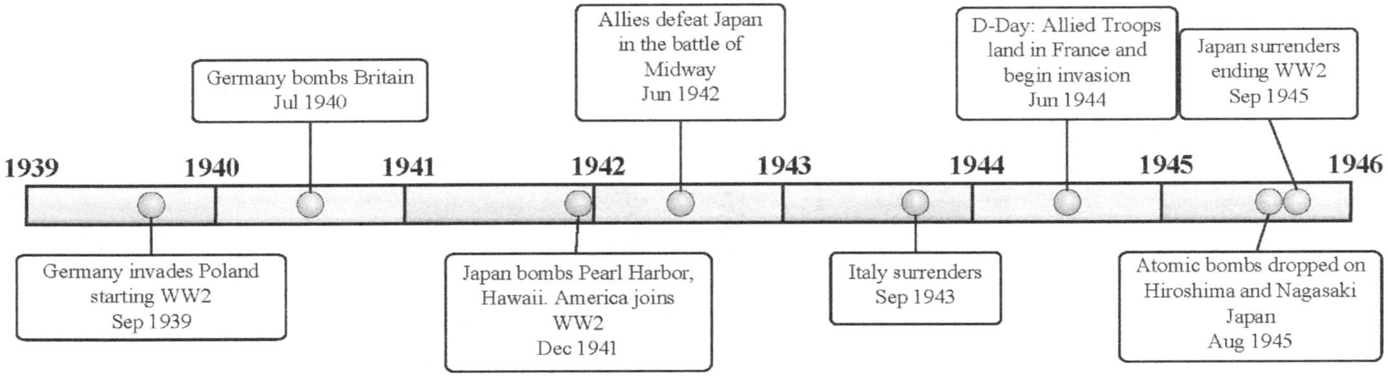
Germany bombs Britain
Jul 1940
Allies defeat Japan in the battle of Midway
Jun 1942
D-Day: Allied Troops land in France and begin invasion
Jun 1944
Japan surrenders ending WW2
Sep 1945
1939
1940
1941
1942
1943
1944
1945
1946
Germany invades Poland starting WW2
Sep 1939
Japan bombs Pearl Harbor, Hawaii. America joins WW2
Dec 1941
Italy surrenders
Sep 1943
Atomic bombs dropped on Hiroshima and Nagasaki Japan
Aug 1945

1) Which happened earlier? A. Italy Surrenders or B. D-Day __________

2) How many months after the atomic bombs were dropped did Japan surrender? __________

3) What year was Britain bombed by Germany? __________

4) What year did World War 2 start? __________

5) What is the span (number of years shown) of this timeline? __________

6) What year was the battle of Midway? __________

7) What year did America join World War 2? __________

8) Japan captured Singapore in February of 1942. Could you put this event on the timeline above? (Yes / No)

9) What is this timeline about? ______________________________

10) What event happened in 1944? ____

Answers

1. __________
2. __________
3. __________
4. __________
5. __________
6. __________
7. __________
8. __________
9. Use Line
10. Use Line

Score: ____________________

State Capitals 1 - 10

Date: ____________

1	Alabama	Montgomery	A
2	Alaska	Little Rock	B
3	Arizona	Denver	C
4	Arkansas	Atlanta	D
5	California	Juneau	E
6	Colorado	Hartford	F
7	Connecticut	Sacramento	G
8	Delaware	Tallahassee	H
9	Florida	Dover	I
10	Georgia	Phoenix	J

Sustainability - Global Warming - Climate Change

Score: ____________________

Date: ____________

This is a spelling worksheet to check your spelling and then your understanding of keywords to do with sustainability, climate change and global warming,

		A	B	C	D
1.	____________	Ozone Layerr	Ozone Leyerr	Ozone Leyer	Ozone Layer
2.	____________	Sustainability	Sustianability	Susstianability	Susstainability
3.	____________	Deforestation	Defforestation	Defforestasion	Deforestasion
4.	____________	Renewablle Resources	Renewablle Resoorces	Renewable Resources	Renewible Resources
5.	____________	Non Renewable Resources	Non Renewablle Resoorces	Non Renewablle Resources	Non Renewible Resources
6.	____________	Cllimate chanje	Climate change	Climate chanje	Cllimate change
7.	____________	Habitat lous	Habitat los	Habitat loss	Habitat louss
8.	____________	Trropical rian forest	Trropical rain forest	Tropical rian forest	Tropical rain forest
9.	____________	Recicling	Reciclling	Recyclling	Recycling
10.	____________	Carbon dioxide	Carrbon dioxide	Carrbon doixide	Carbon doixide
11.	____________	Mathane	Metthane	Matthane	Methane
12.	____________	Grenhouse gas	Grenhoose gas	Greanhouse gas	Greenhouse gas
13.	____________	Hydrroflurocarbons	Hydroflurocarbons	Hydrophlurocarbons	Hydrrophlurocarbons
14.	____________	Sulphur hexophluoride	Sullphur hexofluoride	Sullphur hexophluoride	Sulphur hexofluoride
15.	____________	Nittrous oxide	Nitrous oxide	Nitroos oxide	Nittroos oxide
16.	____________	Foussil Fuels	Fosil Fuels	Fousil Fuels	Fossil Fuels
17.	____________	Trranspurt	Transpurt	Transport	Trransport
18.	____________	Industry	Industry	Indostry	Inducstry
19.	____________	Agrricolture	Agrriculture	Agriculture	Agricolture
20.	____________	Palm Oyl	Palm Oil	Pallm Oil	Pallm Oyl

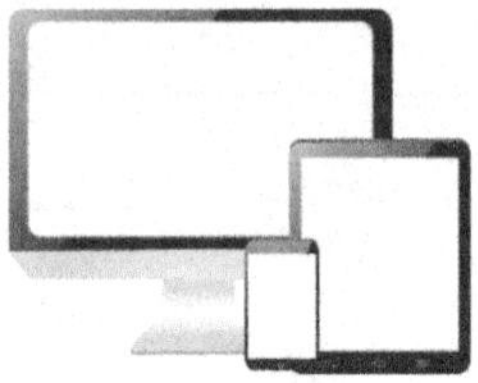

Technology

Score: ____________________

Date: ____________

Match the **English and German** words.

Need help? Try Google translate!

1	☐	mouse		Webseite	A
2	☐	touch		Schreibtischplatte	B
3	☐	screen		App, Anwendung	C
4	☐	Wi-Fi		Bildschirm	D
5	☐	message		Netz	E
6	☐	game		Schoß	F
7	☐	website		Rechner	G
8	☐	mobile		Tastatur	H
9	☐	smart		Handy	I
10	☐	computer		WLAN	J
11	☐	desktop		Maus	K
12	☐	lap		berühren	L
13	☐	net		Spiel	M
14	☐	app(lication)		klug, intelligent	N
15	☐	keyboard		Nachricht	O

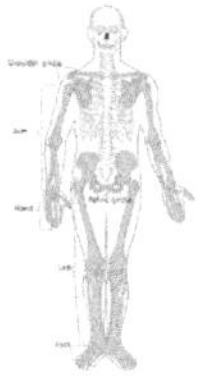

Score: ____________________

Date: ____________

The Lymphatic System Unscramble

There is a part of the immune system called the lymphatic system. It maintains a healthy balance of body fluids and protects the body from illness. Lymphatic (lim-FAT-ik) veins, tissues, organs, and glands collaborate to drain a watery fluid known as lymph from the body.

When there is a lot of extra lymph (LIMF) fluid in the body, the lymphatic system drains it and sends it back to the body's bloodstream. Lymph contains lymphocytes (LIM-fuh-sites), white blood cells, and chyle (KYE-ul), which is made up of fats and proteins from the intestines.

This is critical because water, proteins, and other substances constantly leak out of microscopic blood capillaries and into the surrounding bodily tissues. This additional fluid would build up in the tissues and cause them to bulge if the lymphatic system did not drain it.

lymphatic	antivirals	cytotoxic	leukocyte	phagocyte	immunology
lymphoma	pathogen	lymphedema	tonsillectomy	thymus	capillaries
spleen					

1. yhmtcalpi — l _ _ p _ _ _ _ _
2. muloinmoyg — i _ m _ _ _ l _ _ _
3. tcgayphoe — _ _ _ _ _ _ y t _
4. mehdeaplmy — _ _ m p _ _ _ e _ _
5. ottcyxoci — c _ _ _ t _ _ _ _
6. tvalriinsa — _ _ t _ v _ _ a _ _
7. nymseltooiltc — _ o _ _ _ _ _ _ _ _ _ m y
8. stumyh — _ _ _ _ u s
9. nlsepe — s _ _ e _ _
10. aomlmhyp — l _ _ _ h _ _ _
11. uekloytec — _ _ u k _ _ _ _ _
12. lecasiriapl — _ _ p i _ _ _ _ i _ _
13. hgetpnao — _ a _ _ o _ _ _

Determine the difference in temperatures for the following thermometers.

1)

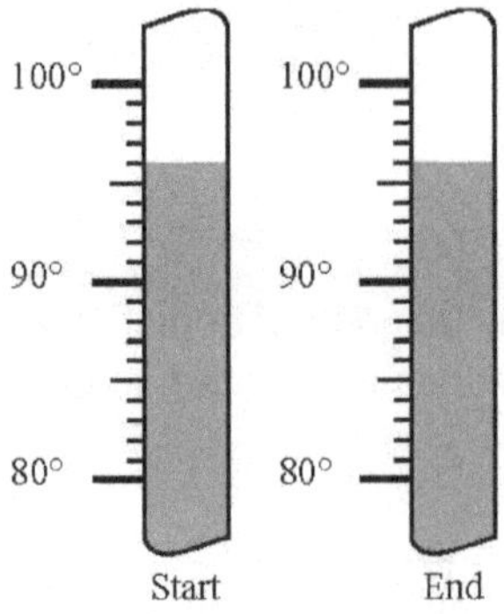

2)

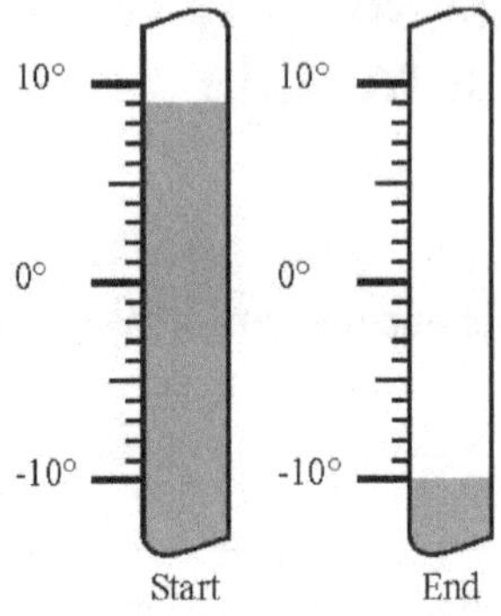

3)

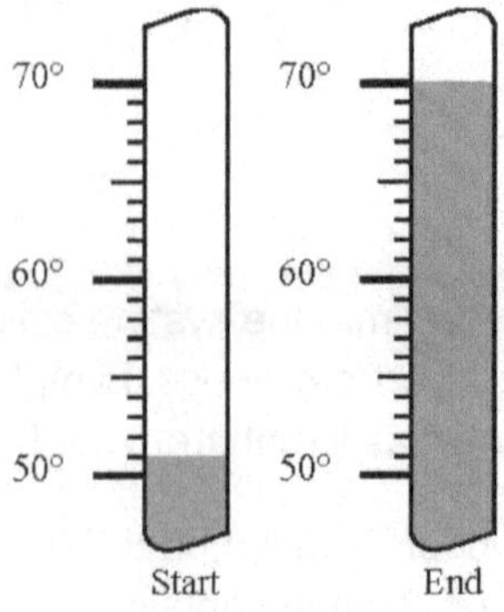

4)

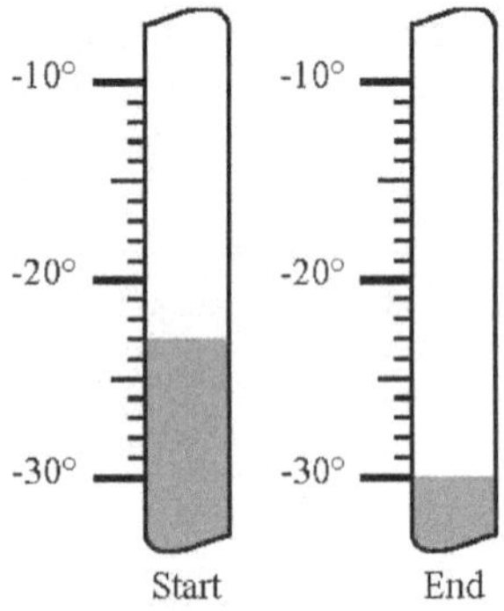

5)

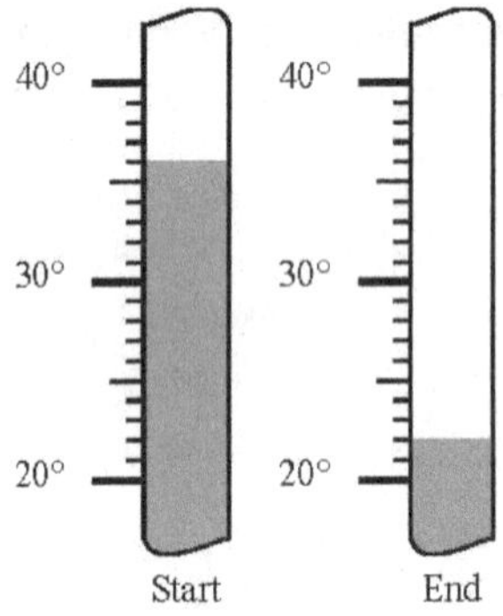

6)

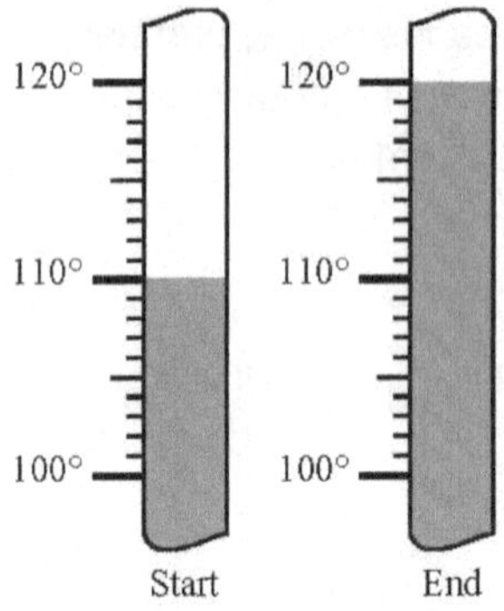

7)

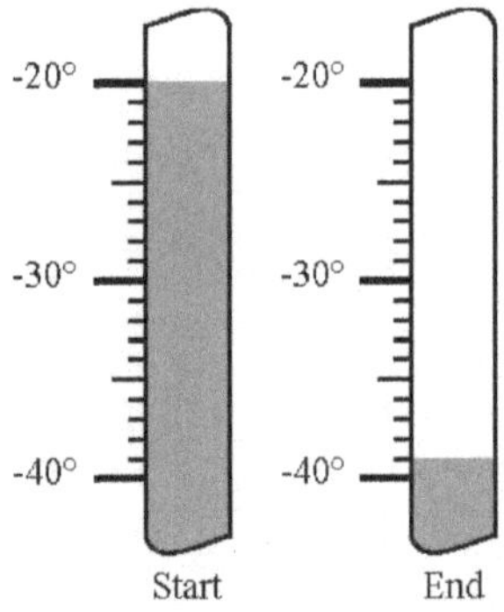

8)

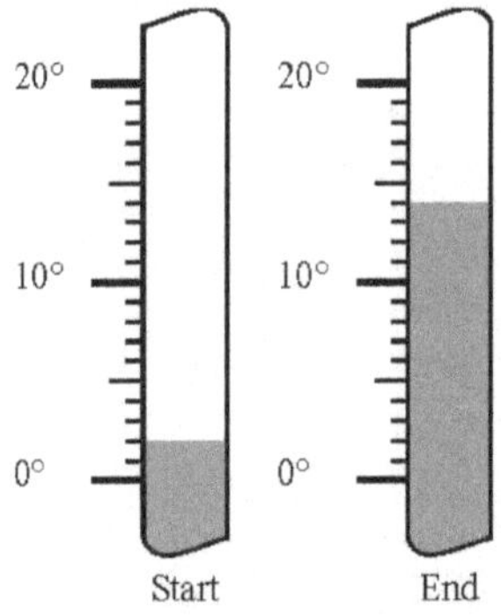

9)

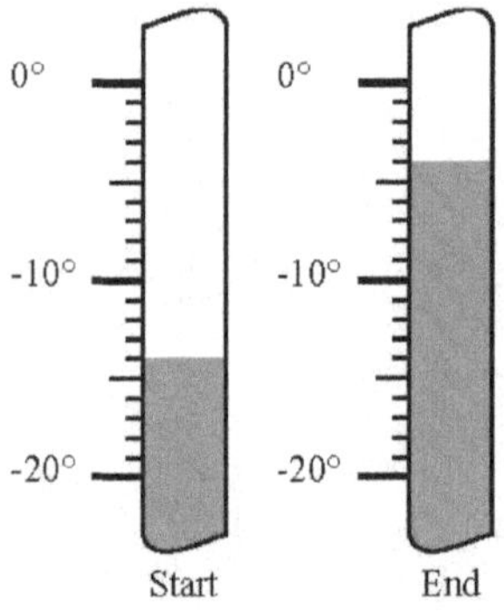

10)

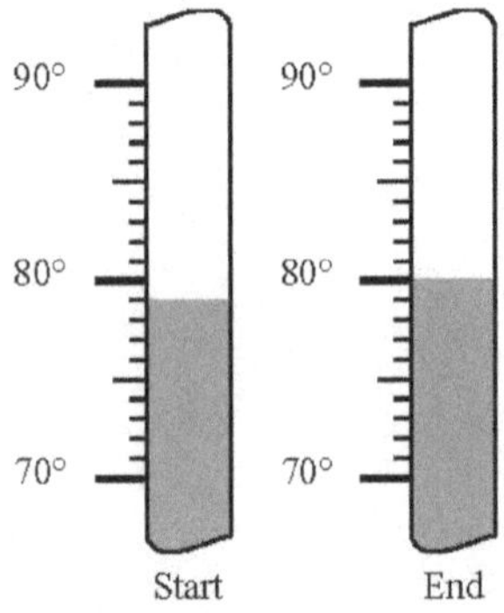

11)

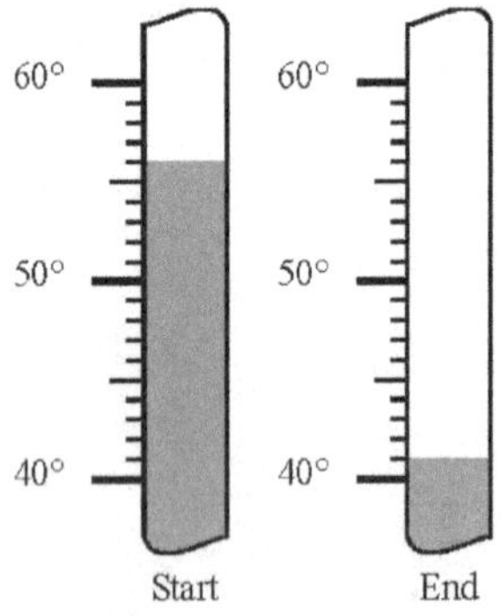

12)

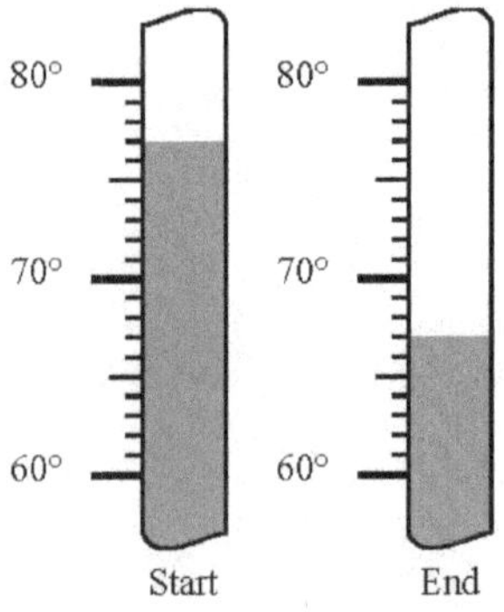

Today Is Know Your Feelings Day!

Score: ____________________

Date: ____________

1	☐		A - cold
2	☐		B - stressed
3	☐		C - happy
4	☐		D - sleepy
5	☐		E - tired
6	☐		F - sad
7	☐		G - angry
8	☐		H - ill
9	☐		I - thirsty
10	☐		J - hot
11	☐		K - worried
12	☐		L - frightened/scared
13	☐		M - surprised
14	☐		N - well
15	☐		O - interested
16	☐		P - bored
17	☐		Q - hungry

Today Is Spelling Words Day!

Score: ______________

Date: ______________

Circle the correctly spelled word then write it on the line.

		A	B	C	D
1.	____________	faitthful	fiathful	faithful	fiatthful
2.	____________	hoorrly	hourly	hoorly	hourrly
3.	____________	forceful	forseful	forrseful	forrceful
4.	____________	thirsty	thirsti	thirrsty	thirrsti
5.	____________	frreqoently	freqoently	frrequently	frequently
6.	____________	misspronoonce	mispronounce	mispronoonce	misspronounce
7.	____________	reinjurre	reinjure	rienjurre	rienjure
8.	____________	reschedule	ressshedule	resshedule	resschedule
9.	____________	disscouragement	disscouragenment	discouragenment	discouragement
10.	____________	rellocating	relucating	rellucating	relocating
11.	____________	disssovery	discovery	dissovery	disscovery
12.	____________	remuvd	removd	removed	remuved
13.	____________	ressaerches	researches	resaerches	ressearches
14.	____________	mystepped	misstepped	miscteppped	mistepped
15.	____________	reffueling	refueling	rephueling	rephfueling
16.	____________	unhaellthy	unhaelthy	unhealthy	unhealthy
17.	____________	disciple	disssiple	dissciple	dissiple
18.	____________	level	levell	lavell	lavel
19.	____________	prromice	promise	promice	prromise
20.	____________	tenys	tenis	tennis	tennys

Score: ____________________

Today Is Spelling Words Puzzle Day!

Date: ____________

S	S	P	P	H	O	T	O	G	R	A	P	H	X	T	V
T	T	L	D	O	P	R	E	S	C	R	I	B	E	R	T
E	R	H	R	M	R	I	Y	T	C	J	M	B	G	A	H
L	A	Z	S	O	C	E	X	P	O	R	T	U	P	N	E
E	N	T	C	G	L	Y	S	I	O	L	I	L	O	S	R
S	S	R	R	R	Z	C	E	F	E	M	J	P	R	F	M
C	P	A	I	A	D	E	S	C	R	I	B	E	T	E	O
O	O	N	B	P	N	N	F	O	Z	Z	W	G	A	R	M
P	R	S	E	H	A	S	F	P	U	M	Y	U	B	S	E
E	T	M	G	R	L	N	P	N	R	N	H	U	L	U	T
I	L	I	T	D	I	C	T	A	T	E	I	A	E	P	E
R	S	T	N	H	M	M	X	H	R	U	D	F	Y	P	R
A	S	C	R	I	P	T	U	R	E	E	W	I	O	O	T
D	I	C	T	I	O	N	A	R	Y	C	N	A	C	R	Q
Y	S	M	I	C	R	O	S	C	O	P	E	T	D	T	M
E	L	L	G	Y	T	R	A	N	S	L	A	T	E	G	S

predict	transfer	support	script	translate
inform	scribe	transform	dictionary	export
Scripture	describe	transmit	dictate	portable
prescribe	transparent	import	uniform	transport
photograph	thermometer	microscope	telescope	homograph

Score: ______________________

Verb Mood

Date: ____________

Let us recap. In a sentence, a verb expresses an action or a state of being.

You're probably aware that the tense of a verb refers to when the event takes place.

The style or attitude in which an action is expressed is referred to as the verb's mood. Verbs, which express actions or states of being, can be articulated as truths, wishes, possibilities, or orders.

1) Indicative Mood—expresses a fact, opinion, claim, or query; most of our verbs are in this mood.

2) Imperative Mood—expresses direct commands and requests.

3) Subjunctive Mood—expresses a desire for something to be true, or expresses something that is not true.

1. I want a chocolate ice cream cone.
  a. imperative mood
  b. indicative mood
  c. subjunctive mood

2. Clean your room, now!
  a. subjunctive mood
  b. indicative mood
  c. imperative mood

3. Coconut tastes funny.
  a. subjunctive mood
  b. imperative mood
  c. indicative mood

4. If only I were at the beach right now.
  a. imperative mood
  b. subjunctive mood
  c. indicative mood

5. Kim, put your paper in the box.
  a. indicative mood
  b. subjunctive mood
  c. imperative mood

6. I wish you had brought your new bike.
  a. subjunctive mood
  b. indicative mood
  c. imperative mood

7. Kick the ball!
  a. imperative mood
  b. subjunctive mood
  c. indicative mood

8. Ostriches cannot fly.
  a. indicative mood
  b. imperative mood
  c. subjunctive mood

9. Be careful!
  a. indicative mood
  b. subjunctive mood
  c. imperative mood

10. If I were you, I would be excited about the play.
  a. indicative mood
  b. imperative mood
  c. subjunctive mood

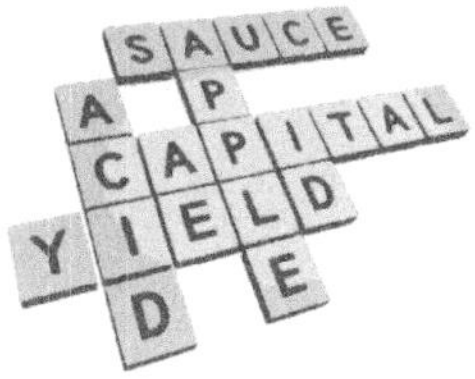

Name: ______________________

Vocab Crossword Puzzle

Date: ______________

Solve the puzzle below with the correct vocabulary word.

Across

1. capability; ability; innate or acquired capacity for something;
3. to seize by or as if by authority; appropriate summarily:
4. to waste time; idle; trifle; loiter: to move slowly
5. the remains of anything broken down or destroyed; ruins; rubble:
6. heroic; majestic; impressively great:
10. something that is not what it purports to be; a spurious imitation; fraud or hoax.

Down

2. violently or destructively frenzied; wild; crazed; deranged:
7. to move or act with haste; proceed with haste; hurry:
8. portending evil or harm; foreboding; threatening; inauspicious:
9. having its original purity; uncorrupted or unsullied.

OMINOUS DEBRIS
APTITUDE BERSERK
SHAM HASTEN PRISTINE
CONFISCATE DAWDLE
EPIC

Score: ____________

Vocabulary: Community Services

Date: ________

Directions: Read the words. Sort the words into the community services in which they belong.

insurance	sick	injured	emergency	firefighter	doctor
driver's license	video	adult education	nurse	ticket	EMS worker
Principal	students	teacher	magazines	officer	return
loan	learning	junior high	borrow	newspapers	librarian
medicine	books	pharmacist	911	high school	pharmacy
elementary school					

Hospital (8)	Library (8)	Police/Fire Department (7)	School (8)

Score: ____________________

WEATHER

Date: ____________

1	☐		A - snowy
2	☐		B - sunny
3	☐		C - rainy
4	☐		D - windy
5	☐		E - stormy
6	☐		F - partly cloudy
7	☐		G - foggy
8	☐		H - cloudy

What is an Adjective?

Score: ____________________

Date: ____________

Adjectives are words that describe a noun in greater detail. It is used to "describe" or "modify" a noun (The **big** *dog* was **hungry**). The adjective is bold in these examples, but the noun it modifies is italicized.

An adjective is frequently used before a noun:
a **blue** *vehicle*

Also, an adjective can appear AFTER a verb: My *truck* is **black**.

However, adjectives can also be used to modify pronouns (*She* is **beautiful**).

____

Unscramble the scrambled adjective words below to find the correct word.

Beautiful	round	large	triangle	sad	yellow
poor	handsome	small	square	happy	elegant
Blue	wealthy	slow			

1. buel _ l _ _
2. auitufbel _ _ _ u _ _ f _ _
3. lamsl _ m _ _ _
4. elrga _ _ _ _ e
5. auersq _ _ u _ r _
6. ndrou _ o _ _ _
7. opor _ o _ _
8. ywaethl w _ _ l _ _ _
9. lwso s _ _ _
10. amshoden _ _ _ _ s _ m _
11. ywlleo y e _ _ _ _
12. tlneega _ _ _ _ _ n t
13. haypp _ _ _ _ y
14. sda s _ _
15. itrngeal _ r _ _ n _ _ _

Score: ____________________

Where is & Where are

Date: ____________

1. ____ Billy?
1. Where are
2. Where's

2. ____ in the bed.
1. He's
2. They're

3. ____ Mom and Dad?
1. Where are
2. Where's

4. _____ in the kitchen.
1. She's
2. They're

5. ____ Grandpa?
1. Where are
2. Where's

6. ____ in the garden.
1. He's
2. She's

7. ____ Lucy and Lilly?
1. Where are
2. Where's

8. ____ in the park.
1. They're
2. She's

9. ____ my sister?
1. Where are
2. Where's

10. ____ in her bedroom.
1. She's
2. He's

11. ____ pupils?
1. Where's
2. Where are

12. ____ at school.
1. He's
2. They're

Which President?

Score: ____________

Date: ________

Match each president to his description

1	☐	Zachary Taylor	"I was a U.S. Army General in the Mexican-American War."	A
2	☐	Jimmy Carter	"I was born in Honolulu, Hawaii. I was elected president in 2008."	B
3	☐	John Adams	"I was the only president to have been elected for four terms. I was in office when Japan attacked Pearl Harbor."	C
4	☐	Ronald Reagan	"I was the first television and movie star to become president."	D
5	☐	Andrew Jackson	"I was a lawyer and the 7th president. People called me 'Old Hickory'."	E
6	☐	Barack Obama	"I was born in New York to wealthy parents. I became president in January 2017."	F
7	☐	Franklin D. Roosevelt	"I was the first Vice-President. I signed the Declaration of Independence."	G
8	☐	Donald Trump	"I was a peanut farmer from Georgia."	H

Score : __________

Date : __________

Numerical Cognition Exercise

Rearranging Digits

Rearrange each set of numbers to produce the largest possible number.

1)	1,182	8,211	6)	7,769	________
2)	1,549	________	7)	7,521	________
3)	5,366	________	8)	8,146	________
4)	3,869	________	9)	8,161	________
5)	2,853	________	10)	7,769	________

Rearrange each set of numbers to make the smallest number possible.

1)	7,816	1,678	6)	6,636	________
2)	3,827	________	7)	8,176	________
3)	4,946	________	8)	9,222	________
4)	5,938	________	9)	2,172	________
5)	1,627	________	10)	5,366	________

Score : ____________

Date : ____________

TIME

What time is on the clock? ____________

What time was it 1 hour ago? ____________

What time was it 3 hours and 40 minutes ago? ____________

What time will it be in 4 hours and 20 minutes? ____________

What time is on the clock? ____________

What time was it 2 hours ago? ____________

What time will it be in 3 hours ? ____________

What time will it be in 4 hours and 20 minutes? ____________

What time is on the clock? ____________

What time was it 1 hour ago? ____________

What time was it 3 hours and 20 minutes ago? ____________

What time will it be in 2 hours ? ____________

What time is on the clock? ____________

What time will it be in 3 hours and 20 minutes? ____________

What time was it 2 hours ago? ____________

What time was it 1 hour ago? ____________

Score : ____________

Date : ____________

Word Problems

1) After eating at the restaurant, Sandy, Melanie, and Jason decided to divide the bill evenly. If each person paid eleven dollars, what was the total of the bill ? ____________

2) There were 17 bales of hay in the barn. Tom stacked more bales in the barn today. There are now 63 bales of hay in the barn. How many bales did he store in the barn ? ____________

3) Mike's high school played twelve soccer games this year. The team won most of their games. They were defeated during four games. How many games did they win ? ____________

4) Jessica is baking a cake. The recipe calls for 7 cups of flour. She already put in 3 cups. How many more cups does she need to add ? ____________

5) How many ink cartridges can you buy with 112 dollars if one cartridge costs 14 dollars ? ____________

6) Joan found ninety - three seashells on the beach, she gave Sam some of her seashells. She has thirty - nine seashell left. How many seashells did she give to Sam ? ____________

7) Dan has twenty - two books in his library. He bought several books at a yard sale over the weekend. He now has seventy - eight books in his library. How many books did he buy at the yard sale ? ____________

8) After paying six dollars for the pie, Sam has fifty - five dollars left. How much money did he have before buying the pie ? ____________

9) There are 38 maple trees currently in the park. Park workers will plant more maple trees today. When the workers are finished there will be 67 maple trees in the park. How many maple trees did the workers plant today ? ____________

10) Fred had 47 peaches left at his roadside fruit stand. He went to the orchard and picked more peaches to stock up the stand. There are now 55 peaches at the stand, how many did he pick ? ____________

Score : ________

Date : ________

Find the Missing Number

1) N÷13 = 35	N = ____	2) 464÷N = 16	N = ____
3) N÷17 = 38	N = ____	4) N÷16 = 27	N = ____
5) 558÷N = 18	N = ____	6) N÷19 = 19	N = ____
7) N÷17 = 27	N = ____	8) N÷20 = 15	N = ____
9) 570÷N = 15	N = ____	10) N÷24 = 30	N = ____
11) N÷15 = 40	N = ____	12) 680÷N = 40	N = ____
13) N÷31 = 40	N = ____	14) 308÷N = 28	N = ____
15) 1482÷N = 39	N = ____	16) 323÷N = 17	N = ____
17) N÷32 = 36	N = ____	18) 1280÷N = 32	N = ____
19) N÷31 = 25	N = ____	20) 1330÷N = 38	N = ____
21) 310÷N = 10	N = ____	22) 532÷N = 38	N = ____
23) N÷40 = 35	N = ____	24) 1520÷N = 38	N = ____
25) N÷33 = 40	N = ____	26) N÷25 = 36	N = ____
27) N÷16 = 27	N = ____	28) 552÷N = 23	N = ____
29) N÷10 = 12	N = ____	30) 272÷N = 16	N = ____

To estimate means to find an answer that is close to the exact answer. The key to estimation is to use it only when an exact answer is not required. To estimate a sum or difference, the first step is to round the numbers to the nearest power of ten, hundred, thousand, and so on.

- Round down if the number being rounded is less than 5.
- Round up if the number being rounded is 5 or greater.

Score : ____________

Date : ____________

Estimate the sum or difference by rounding each number to the nearest ten.

1) 85 ⟶
- 59 ⟶ - ___

2) 94 ⟶
- 21 ⟶ - ___

3) 23 ⟶
+ 42 ⟶ + ___

4) 71 ⟶
- 53 ⟶ - ___

5) 15 ⟶
+ 74 ⟶ + ___

6) 51 ⟶
+ 26 ⟶ + ___

7) 91 ⟶
- 46 ⟶ - ___

8) 58 ⟶
+ 11 ⟶ + ___

9) 79 ⟶
+ 32 ⟶ + ___

10) 75 ⟶
+ 49 ⟶ + ___

11) 63 ⟶
- 34 ⟶ - ___

12) 33 ⟶
- 22 ⟶ - ___

13) 76 ⟶
+ 12 ⟶ + ___

14) 86 ⟶
- 27 ⟶ - ___

SCORE:________

Solve the following problems using the order of operations.

DATE:________

Remember

Step 1: Parenthesis ()	Solve all problems in parenthesis FIRST.
Step 2: Exponents $^{2}, ^{3}, ^{4}$	Next solve any numbers that have exponents.
Step 3: Multiply or Divide ×, ÷	Then solve any multiplication or division problems (going from left to right).
Step 4: Add or Subtract +, -	Finally solve any addition or subtraction problems (going from left to right).

1) $21 \div 3 + (3 \times 9) \times 9 + 5$

2) $18 \div 6 \times (4 - 3) + 6$

3) $14 - 8 + 3 + 8 \times (24 \div 8)$

4) $4 \times 5 + (14 + 8) - 36 \div 9$

5) $(17 - 7) \times 6 + 2 + 56 - 8$

6) $(28 \div 4) + 3 + (10 - 8) \times 5$

7) $12 - 5 + 6 \times 3 + 20 \div 4$

8) $36 \div 9 + 48 - 10 \div 2$

9) $10 + 8 \times 90 \div 9 - 4$

10) $8 \times 3 + 70 \div 7 - 7$

Score: __________

Date: __________

Using exponents simply means that you want to multiply something by itself a number of times. Say, for instance, you want to do the following: 4 x 4 x 4

This could be written using exponents, as follows: 4^3

They both equal 64, but the exponent method is shorter and easier to remember. This is very useful when you need to multiply something many times.

Exponents

1) $(2)^3$ = ______

2) $(5)^2$ = ______

3) $(12)^3$ = ______

4) $(-8)^2$ = ______

5) $(-4)^2$ = ______

6) $(-2)^2$ = ______

7) $(7)^2$ = ______

8) $(-12)^2$ = ______

9) $(-2)^3$ = ______

10) $(-3)^3$ = ______

11) $(4)^3$ = ______

12) $(3)^3$ = ______

13) $(-5)^3$ = ______

14) $(3)^2$ = ______

15) $(2)^2$ = ______

16) $(-10)^3$ = ______

17) $(-7)^2$ = ______

18) $(-9)^3$ = ______

19) $(-6)^3$ = ______

20) $(10)^2$ = ______

In math, the absolute value (or modulus) of a real number is its value as a number, no matter what the sign is. So, the absolute value of 3 and -3 is both 3, and the only absolute value of 0 is 0.

Score : ________

Date : ________

1) Absolute value of 79 is _____

2) Absolute value of 26 is _____

3) Absolute value of 81 is _____

4) Absolute value of 82 is _____

5) Absolute value of -45 is _____

6) Absolute value of 64 is _____

7) Absolute value of -53 is _____

8) Absolute value of 53 is _____

9) Absolute value of -47 is _____

10) Absolute value of 19 is _____

11) Absolute value of -89 is _____

12) Absolute value of 85 is _____

13) Absolute value of 12 is _____

14) Absolute value of 60 is _____

15) Absolute value of -48 is _____

16) Absolute value of 84 is _____

17) Absolute value of 8 is _____

18) Absolute value of 13 is _____

19) Absolute value of 91 is _____

20) Absolute value of 24 is _____

21) Absolute value of 18 is _____

22) Absolute value of -36 is _____

23) Absolute value of 46 is _____

24) Absolute value of -79 is _____

25) Absolute value of 20 is _____

26) Absolute value of 9 is _____

27) Absolute value of -14 is _____

28) Absolute value of 42 is _____

29) Absolute value of -62 is _____

30) Absolute value of 15 is _____

Adding to Multiples of Ten

SCORE:_______
DATE:________

Fill in the blanks for each problem.

_______ + 42 = 50	32 + _______ = 40	_______ + 53 = 60	61 + _______ = 70
_______ + 74 = 80	91 + _______ = 100	_______ + 85 = 90	58 + _______ = 60
_______ + 71 = 80	54 + _______ = 60	_______ + 49 = 50	13 + _______ = 20
_______ + 56 = 60	82 + _______ = 90	_______ + 15 = 20	22 + _______ = 30
_______ + 94 = 100	78 + _______ = 80	_______ + 43 = 50	19 + _______ = 20
_______ + 31 = 40	59 + _______ = 60	_______ + 84 = 90	23 + _______ = 30
_______ + 99 = 100	39 + _______ = 40	_______ + 96 = 100	48 + _______ = 50
_______ + 81 = 90	92 + _______ = 100	_______ + 12 = 20	5 + _______ = 10
_______ + 14 = 20	89 + _______ = 90	_______ + 45 = 50	98 + _______ = 100
_______ + 21 = 30	44 + _______ = 50	_______ + 24 = 30	25 + _______ = 30
_______ + 3 = 10	79 + _______ = 80	_______ + 38 = 40	35 + _______ = 40
_______ + 7 = 10	75 + _______ = 80	_______ + 17 = 20	66 + _______ = 70
_______ + 88 = 90	47 + _______ = 50	_______ + 27 = 30	91 + _______ = 100
_______ + 89 = 90	57 + _______ = 60	_______ + 44 = 50	21 + _______ = 30
_______ + 56 = 60	77 + _______ = 80	_______ + 97 = 100	76 + _______ = 80
_______ + 87 = 90	16 + _______ = 20	_______ + 71 = 80	85 + _______ = 90
_______ + 67 = 70	83 + _______ = 90	_______ + 46 = 50	64 + _______ = 70
_______ + 12 = 20	38 + _______ = 40	_______ + 75 = 80	63 + _______ = 70
_______ + 36 = 40	33 + _______ = 40	_______ + 95 = 100	86 + _______ = 90
_______ + 68 = 70	98 + _______ = 100	_______ + 52 = 60	81 + _______ = 90
_______ + 94 = 100	82 + _______ = 90	_______ + 54 = 60	7 + _______ = 10
_______ + 18 = 20	11 + _______ = 20	_______ + 59 = 60	43 + _______ = 50
_______ + 24 = 30	6 + _______ = 10	_______ + 93 = 100	99 + _______ = 100
_______ + 23 = 30	34 + _______ = 40	_______ + 65 = 70	4 + _______ = 10
_______ + 53 = 60	41 + _______ = 50	_______ + 2 = 10	88 + _______ = 90

Finding Volume

Find the volume of each rectangular prism. Units are in cm (not to scale). Remember V = BH and V=L×W×H

SCORE:________

DATE:________

1) 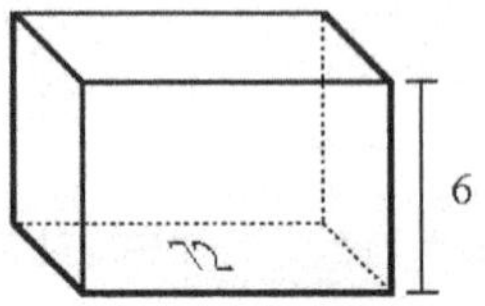

2) 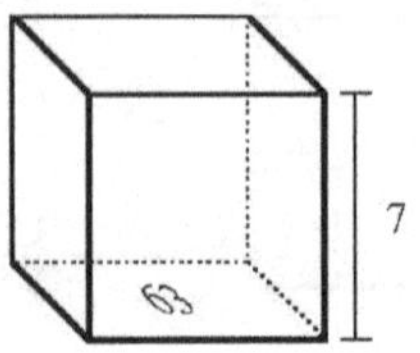

3) 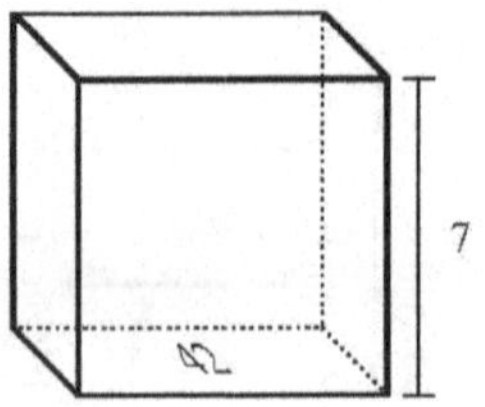

4) 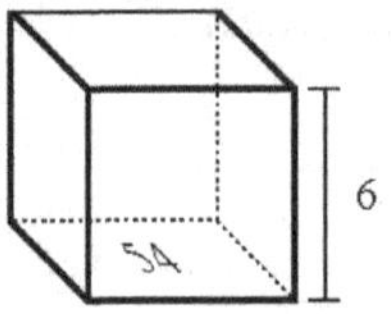

5) 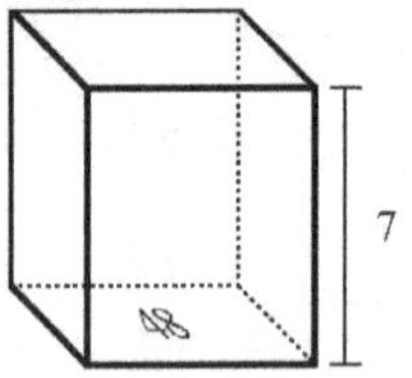

6) 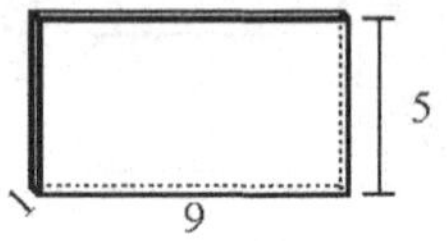

7) 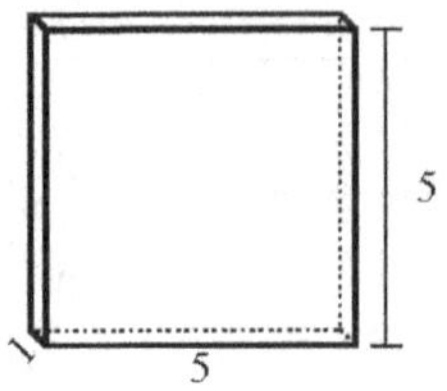

8) 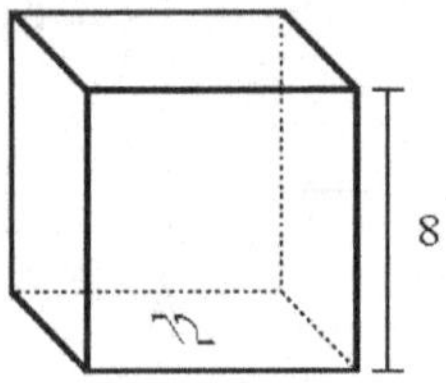

9) 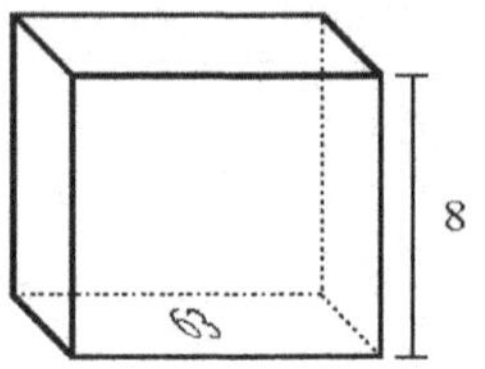

10) 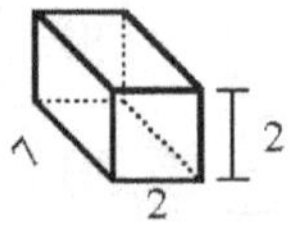

11) 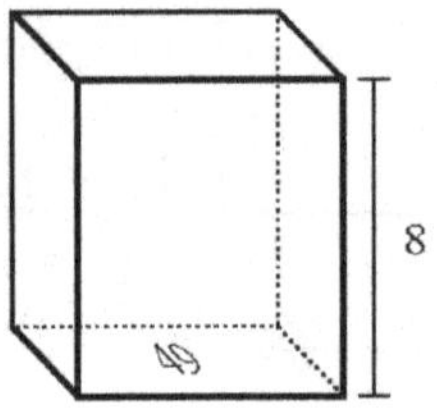

12) 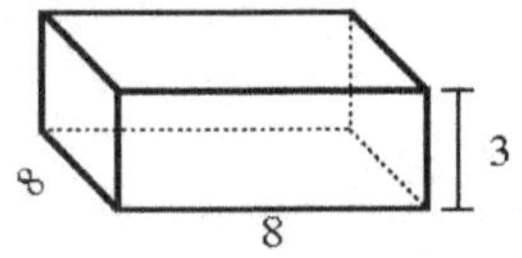

13) 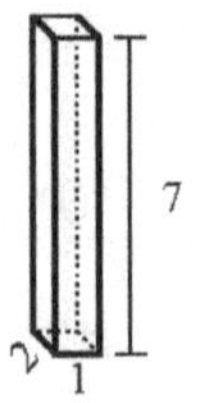

14) 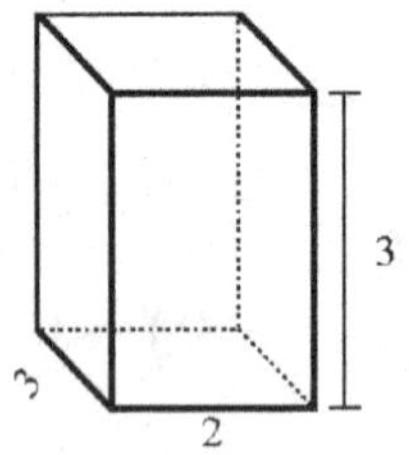

15) 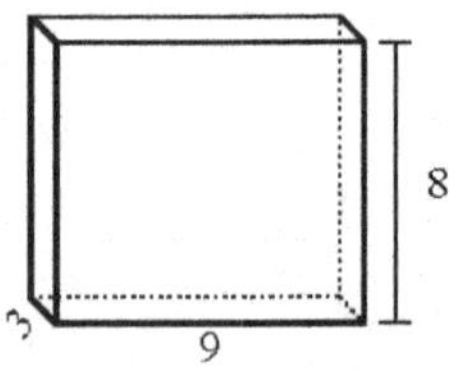

Matching Pictographs to Charts

SCORE:________
DATE:________

Determine which pictograph best represents the information in the chart.

1)

Month	Cats Sold
June	56
July	32
August	24
September	40
October	80

2)

Month	Cats Sold
June	24
July	56
August	8
September	32
October	40

3)

Month	Cats Sold
June	16
July	8
August	56
September	48
October	24

4)

Month	Cats Sold
June	48
July	40
August	24
September	32
October	64

5)

Month	Cats Sold
June	24
July	80
August	48
September	56
October	32

6)

Month	Cats Sold
June	32
July	48
August	80
September	16
October	8

A.

Month	Cats Sold
June	🐈🐈🐈🐈🐈🐈
July	🐈🐈🐈🐈🐈
August	🐈🐈🐈
September	🐈🐈🐈🐈
October	🐈🐈🐈🐈🐈🐈🐈🐈

Each 🐈 = 8 cat

B.

Month	Cats Sold
June	🐈🐈🐈
July	🐈🐈🐈🐈🐈🐈🐈
August	🐈
September	🐈🐈🐈🐈
October	🐈🐈🐈🐈🐈

Each 🐈 = 8 cat

C.

Month	Cats Sold
June	🐈🐈
July	🐈
August	🐈🐈🐈🐈🐈🐈🐈
September	🐈🐈🐈🐈🐈🐈
October	🐈🐈🐈

Each 🐈 = 8 cat

D.

Month	Cats Sold
June	🐈🐈🐈
July	🐈🐈🐈🐈🐈🐈🐈🐈🐈🐈
August	🐈🐈🐈🐈🐈🐈
September	🐈🐈🐈🐈🐈🐈🐈
October	🐈🐈🐈🐈

Each 🐈 = 8 cat

E.

Month	Cats Sold
June	🐈🐈🐈🐈
July	🐈🐈🐈🐈🐈🐈
August	🐈🐈🐈🐈🐈🐈🐈🐈🐈🐈
September	🐈🐈
October	🐈

Each 🐈 = 8 cat

F.

Month	Cats Sold
June	🐈🐈🐈🐈🐈🐈🐈
July	🐈🐈🐈🐈
August	🐈🐈🐈
September	🐈🐈🐈🐈🐈
October	🐈🐈🐈🐈🐈🐈🐈🐈🐈🐈

Each 🐈 = 8 cat

Answers

1. ______
2. ______
3. ______
4. ______
5. ______
6. ______

Examining Number Value by Place Value

SCORE:_______
DATE:_______

Solve each problem.

1) What is the value of the 6 in the number 154,637?

2) What is the value of the 1 in the number 417,298?

3) What is the value of the 9 in the number 97?

4) What is the value of the 3 in the number 9,673,824?

5) What is the value of the 4 in the number 14,697?

6) What is the value of the 4 in the number 42?

7) What is the value of the 1 in the number 29,158?

8) What is the value of the 1 in the number 268,514?

9) What is the value of the 7 in the number 3,576?

10) What is the value of the 5 in the number 3,956,728?

11) What is the value of the 1 in the number 4,781,392?

12) What is the value of the 4 in the number 734,168?

13) What is the value of the 6 in the number 68,435?

14) What is the value of the 2 in the number 51,627?

15) What is the value of the 2 in the number 235?

16) What is the value of the 3 in the number 31,475?

17) What is the value of the 5 in the number 9,536?

18) What is the value of the 7 in the number 37,681?

19) What is the value of the 6 in the number 3,264,871?

20) What is the value of the 1 in the number 76,183?

Finding Ten More & Ten Less

SCORE:______
DATE:_______

Fill in the blanks for each problem.

What is 10 more than 59?______
What is 10 more than 2?______
What is 10 more than 87?______
What is 10 more than 25?______
What is 10 more than 85?______
What is 10 more than 72?______
What is 10 more than 79?______
What is 10 more than 1?______
What is 10 more than 39?______
What is 10 more than 27?______
What is 10 more than 86?______
What is 10 more than 7?______
What is 10 more than 69?______
What is 10 more than 60?______
What is 10 more than 31?______
What is 10 more than 11?______
What is 10 more than 12?______
What is 10 more than 63?______
What is 10 more than 97?______
What is 10 more than 41?______
What is 10 more than 99?______
What is 10 more than 92?______
What is 10 more than 67?______
What is 10 more than 51?______
What is 10 more than 16?______

What is 10 less than 13?______
What is 10 less than 15?______
What is 10 less than 17?______
What is 10 less than 19?______
What is 10 less than 21?______
What is 10 less than 23?______
What is 10 less than 25?______
What is 10 less than 27?______
What is 10 less than 29?______
What is 10 less than 31?______
What is 10 less than 33?______
What is 10 less than 35?______
What is 10 less than 37?______
What is 10 less than 39?______
What is 10 less than 41?______
What is 10 less than 43?______
What is 10 less than 45?______
What is 10 less than 47?______
What is 10 less than 49?______
What is 10 less than 51?______
What is 10 less than 53?______
What is 10 less than 55?______
What is 10 less than 57?______
What is 10 less than 59?______
What is 10 less than 61?______

Score: ____________________

Math Terms Crossword

Date: ____________

Solve the puzzle below with the correct math vocabulary word.

Across

1. A unit of measure equal to 1000 meters.
4. A six-sided and six-angled polygon.
6. Quotient, Goes Into, How Many Times
8. Multiply, Product, By, Times, Lots Of
9. Minus, Less, Difference, Decrease, Take Away, Deduct
10. A value that does not change.

Down

3. The process of breaking numbers down into all of their factors.
4. A graph that uses bars that equal ranges of values.
5. Two rays sharing the same endpoint (called the angle vertex).
7. Sum, Plus, Increase, Total

MULTIPLICATION
HEXAGON KILOMETER
CONSTANT ANGLE
FACTORING DIVISION
SUBTRACTION
HISTOGRAM ADDITION

Math Terms Matching

Score: ____________

Date: ____________

Match each math term to the correct meaning.

1	☐ Rectangle		A parallelogram with four right angles.	A
2	☐ Negative Number		The measure of how heavy something is.	B
3	☐ Triangle		A three-sided polygon.	C
4	☐ X		The Roman numeral for 10.	D
5	☐ X-Axis		A straight infinite path joining an infinite number of points in both directions.	E
6	☐ Weight		The ____ is a list of numbers are the values that occur most frequently.	F
7	☐ Like Fractions		A number less than zero.	G
8	☐ Like Terms		A point that is exactly halfway between two locations.	H
9	☐ Mode		The top number in a fraction.	I
10	☐ Midpoint		The sum of two or more monomials.	J
11	☐ Line		____ with the same variable and same exponents/powers.	K
12	☐ Numerator		The solution to a division problem.	L
13	☐ Octagon		Fractions with the same denominator.	M
14	☐ Logic		Sound reasoning and the formal laws of reasoning.	N
15	☐ Outcome		Used in probability to refer to the result of an event.	O
16	☐ Polynomial		The horizontal axis in a coordinate plane.	P
17	☐ Quotient		A polygon with eight sides.	Q
18	☐ Proper Fraction		A fraction whose denominator is greater than its numerator.	R

- The **mean** is the average, and this is a simple way to remember that. The mean can be calculated by adding all of the numbers in the set and then dividing by the number of numbers in the set.
- The **median** is the middle number of the data set. It is referred to as the "middle number" in a set of data. To calculate the median, the data must first be organized.
- The **mode** is the number that appears the most. All you have to do is figure out which value in a set appears the most.

SCORE:_______

DATE:_______

Mean, Mode, Median

1) 2, 2, 3, 4, 4, 9, 4

Mean ____ Median ____ Mode __________

2) 7, 7, 9, 7, 2, 8, 3, 6, 4, 7

Mean ____ Median ____ Mode __________

3) 8, 4, 2, 7, 5, 6, 2, 3, 4, 9

Mean ____ Median ____ Mode __________

4) 7, 7, 3, 2, 6

Mean ____ Median ____ Mode __________

5) 5, 6, 6, 7, 6, 5, 6, 7, 6

Mean ____ Median ____ Mode __________

6) 9, 7, 4, 4, 4, 2

Mean ____ Median ____ Mode __________

7) 8, 8, 4, 3, 4, 7, 9, 4, 7

Mean ____ Median ____ Mode __________

8) 2, 4, 6, 2, 5, 2, 9, 2

Mean ____ Median ____ Mode __________

9) 6, 5, 8, 2, 9

Mean ____ Median ____ Mode __________

10) 6, 3, 3, 5, 8, 1, 9

Mean ____ Median ____ Mode __________

Score : ____________

Date : ____________

Measure It

Length to measure.

1 in ________

63 mm ________

14.7 cm ________

2.3 cm ________

$2\frac{1}{2}$ in ________

105 mm ________

11.1 cm ________

8.5 cm ________

1.7 cm ________

13.7 cm ________

Score: ______________________

On this day in 1969...

Date: ____________

On this day in 1969...

Cryptogram: You must substitute the code letters for the real letters to reveal the paragraph text.

A	B	C	D	E	F	G	H	I	J	K	L	M	N	O	P	Q	R	S	T	U	V	W	X	Y	Z
			84								67								75		70			77	

_ _ _ _ _   T _ Y L _ _ ,   T _ _
78 76 90 78 89   75 68 77 67 74 69   75 76 83

_ _ _ _ _ T _ _ L L   _ L _ Y _ _   _ _ D
81 68 71 89 83 75 81 68 67 67   85 67 68 77 83 69   68 73 84

_ _ _ _ _   _ _ _   _ _ D _   " _ _ _ _ _ _ "
78 74 68 78 76   86 76 74   72 68 84 83   78 76 90 78 89 71

(_ _ _ V _ _ _ _   _ L L   _ T _ _ _)
78 74 73 70 83 69 71 83   68 67 67   71 75 68 69 71

_ _ _ _ L _ _ ,   _ _ D   _ _ _ _ _   _ _ _ _
85 74 85 90 67 68 69   68 73 84   86 76 74 71 83   73 68 72 83

_ _   _ _   T _ _   _ _ _ L _   _ _ T _ _ ,
66 71   74 73   75 76 83   68 73 89 67 83   85 68 75 78 76

D _ _ D .
84 66 83 84

Score : __________

Date : __________

Converting Between Percents, Decimals, and Fractions

Convert Decimal to Percent

1.22 =	1.83 =	0.353 =
0.19 =	1.23 =	0.432 =

Convert Percent to Decimal

51 % =	94 % =	81.5 % =
29 % =	23.7 % =	189 % =

Convert Decimal to Fraction

1.66 =	1.51 =	0.273 =
0.294 =	0.831 =	0.88 =

Convert Fraction to Decimal

$\frac{2}{20}$ =	$\frac{19}{20}$ =	$\frac{17}{10}$ =
$\frac{15}{20}$ =	$\frac{13}{20}$ =	$\frac{13}{20}$ =

Convert Fraction to Percent

$\frac{1}{10}$ =	$\frac{26}{25}$ =	$\frac{14}{10}$ =
$\frac{38}{25}$ =	$\frac{1}{10}$ =	$\frac{13}{16}$ =

Convert Percent to Fraction

142 % =	76 % =	179 % =
145 % =	48.4 % =	68 % =

Ratio Rule: Find the greatest factor common to both terms of the ratio, and then divide both terms by that factor. In order to simplify a ratio, you divide both terms (both sides of the ratio) by the same number.

Score : ________

Date : ________

Ratios and Rates

Express each ratio as a fraction in the simplest form.

1) 56 beetles out of 84 insects _____

2) 8 blue cars out of 40 cars _____

3) 12 pennies to 15 pennies _____

4) 8 gallons to 36 gallons _____

5) 9 miles out of 33 miles _____

6) 25 dimes to 60 dimes _____

7) 36 cups to 48 cups _____

8) 25 quarts to 45 quarts _____

A rate is a ratio that compares two quantities of DIFFERENT kinds of UNITS. Ex: 2 kilometer in 15 minutes = 2 km/ 15 min

A unit rate is a type of rate written as a fraction with a denominator or 1. To calculate the unit rate, divide the numerator by the denominator. Ex: 8/4 = 2 and 3/6 = 0.5.

Express each phrase as a rate and unit rate. (Round your answer to the nearest hundredth.)	Rate	Unit Rate
9) 8 pencils for 16 dollars	______	______
10) 14 dollars for 6 books	______	______
11) 14 chocolate bars cost 19 dollars	______	______
12) 6 dollars for 3 cans of tuna	______	______
13) 12 batteries cost 17 dollars	______	______
14) 6 calculators cost $125.00	______	______
15) 140 miles on 4 gallons of gas	______	______
16) 7 inches of snow in 7 hours	______	______

The term "prime factorization" refers to the process of determining which prime numbers multiply to produce the original number.

Score : __________

Date : __________

Step 1 : Divide the given number in two factors.

Step 2 : Now divide these two factors into other two multiples.

Step 3 : Repeat the step 2 until we reach all prime factors.

Step 4 : All the prime factors so obtained collectively known as prime factors of given number. In order to cross check; multiply all the prime factors, you must get the given number.

Find the Prime Factors of the Numbers

1)

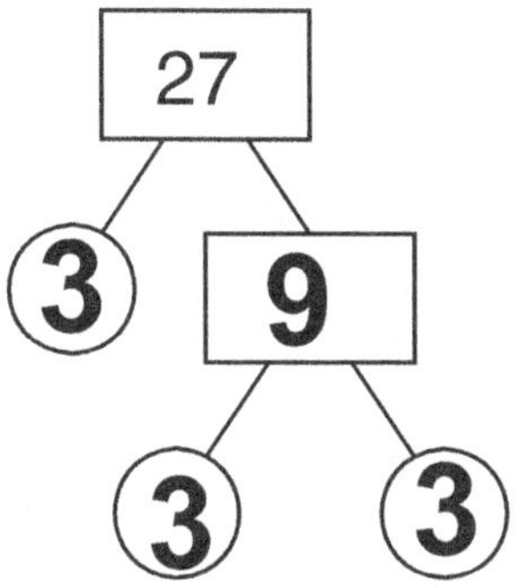

Prime Factors

_ x _ x _ = 27

2)

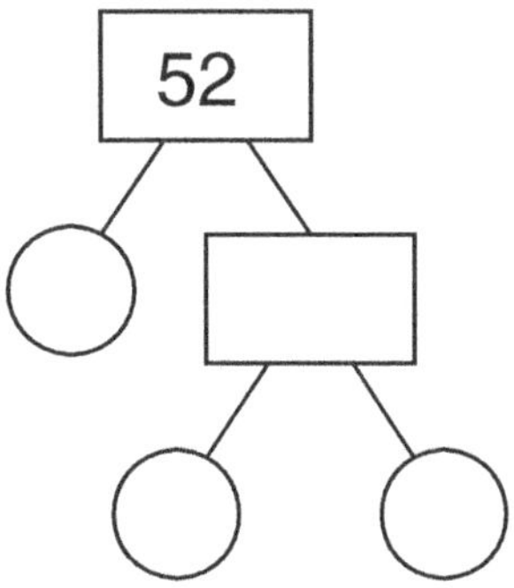

Prime Factors

_ x _ x _ = 52

3)

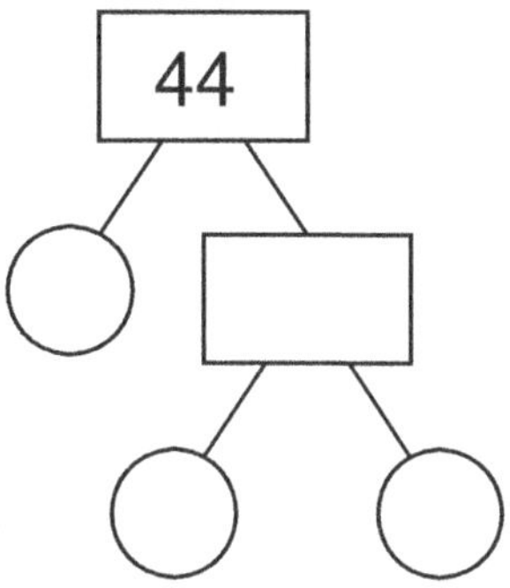

Prime Factors

_ x _ x _ = 44

---

4)

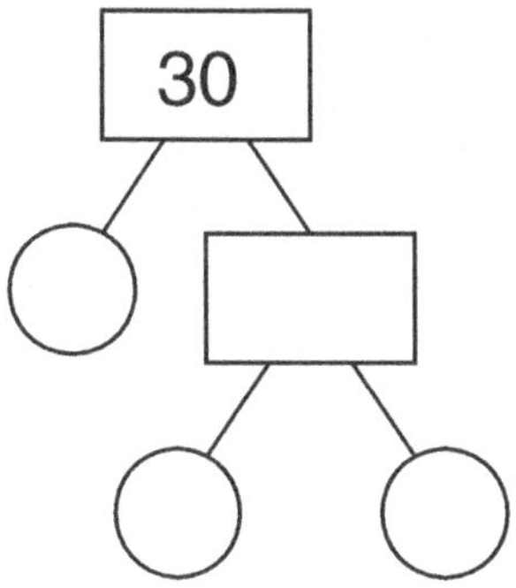

Prime Factors

_ x _ x _ = 30

5)

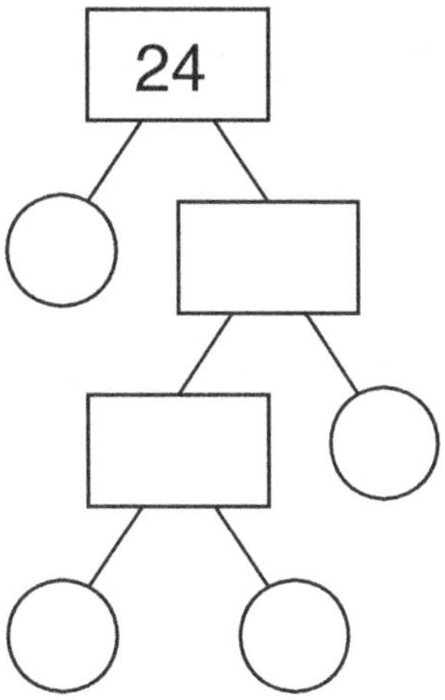

Prime Factors

_ x _ x _ x _ = 24

6)

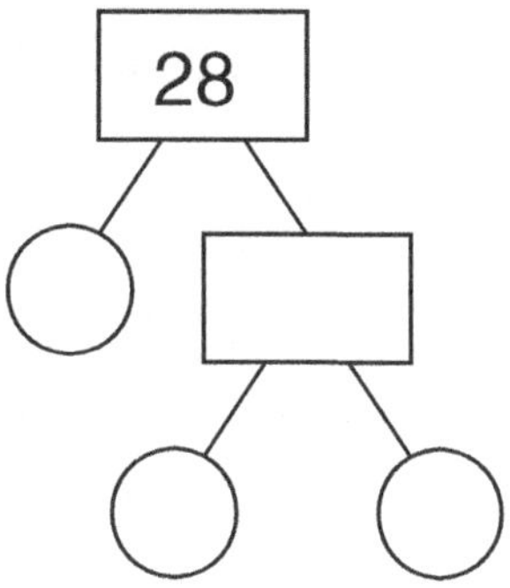

Prime Factors

_ x _ x _ = 28

Score : ________

Date : ________

Reading Pie Graphs

John tracked the time he spent on homework per topic during one week. Answer the questions based on the pie graph below.

1) What percentage of time did John spend on the English and Art homework? ________

2) If John spent 100 minutes on homework, how many minutes were spent on Health? ________

3) Combined, which two topics required the greatest amount of time? ________

4) Was the Math and Spanish work or the History and Health work longer; or were they equally time consuming? ________

5) Between Math and Spanish which topic took longer; or did they require equal time? ________

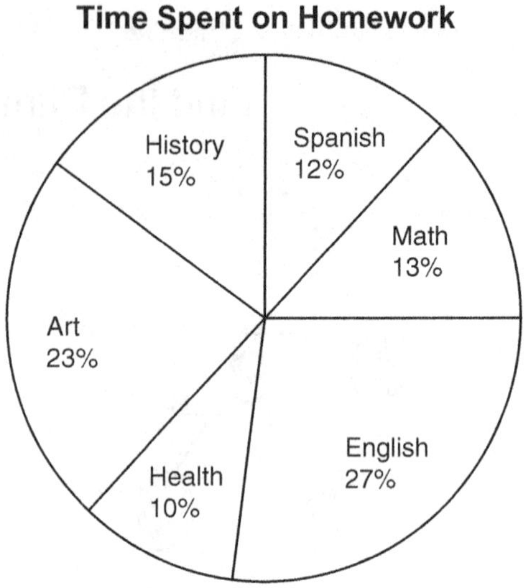

A local pizzeria tracked which pizza toppings customers purchased. Answer the questions based on the pie graph below.

1) Were onion and ham picked more than the bacon and sausage; or were they equally bought? ________

2) Combined, which two toppings did the greatest number of customers choose? ________

3) If there were 200 customers that were tracked, how many bought sausage? ________

4) What percentage of customers chose either the beef or the olives? ________

5) Between onion and ham which topping was more popular; or were they equally popular? ________

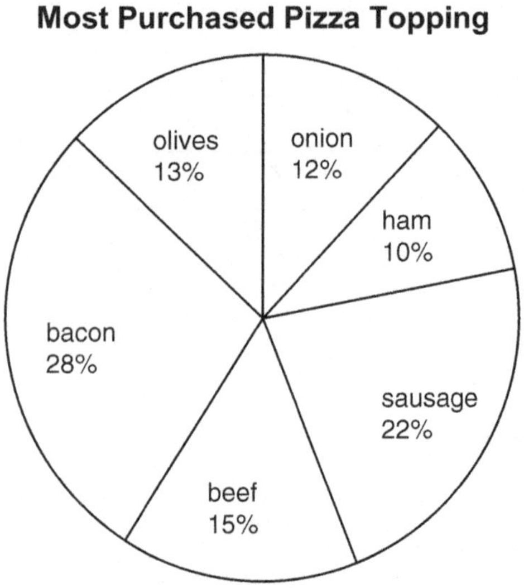

Step 1: Double-check that the bottom numbers (the denominators) are the same.
Step 2: Add the top numbers (the numerators), then place that answer over the denominator
Step 3: Reduce the fraction to its simplest form (if possible)

Score : ___________

Date : ___________

Adding Fractions

1) $\frac{5}{7} + \frac{4}{7} = \frac{9}{7} = 1\frac{2}{7}$

2) $\frac{2}{8} + \frac{5}{8} =$

3) $\frac{6}{7} + \frac{4}{7} =$

4) $\frac{5}{4} + \frac{3}{4} =$

5) $\frac{1}{8} + \frac{3}{8} =$

6) $\frac{2}{6} + \frac{5}{6} =$

7) $\frac{2}{6} + \frac{2}{6} =$

8) $\frac{5}{4} + \frac{3}{4} =$

9) $\frac{8}{8} + \frac{6}{8} =$

10) $\frac{3}{7} + \frac{5}{7} =$

11) $\frac{7}{9} + \frac{1}{9} =$

12) $\frac{3}{9} + \frac{6}{9} =$

13) $\frac{2}{7} + \frac{4}{7} =$

14) $\frac{3}{6} + \frac{2}{6} =$

15) $\frac{3}{6} + \frac{5}{6} =$

- Start by naming the number to the left of the decimal.
- Use the word "and" to indicate the decimal point.
- Then name the number to the right of the decimal point as if it were a whole number.

Score : ________

Date : ________

Write the Names for the Decimal Numbers.

1) 3.48 ____________________

2) 8.20 ____________________

3) 2.19 ____________________

4) 2.38 ____________________

5) 9.47 ____________________

6) 3.51 ____________________

7) 2.25 ____________________

8) 9.47 ____________________

9) 6.76 ____________________

10) 3.28 ____________________

Each digit within a number has a place. The place of a number can be the ones, tens, hundreds, or thousands.

Score : __________

Date : __________

Find the Mystery Numbers

1) **The mystery number has ...**

A 2 in the Thousands place.
A 8 in the Tens place.
A 2 in the Hundreds place.
A 3 in the Ones place.

What is the mystery number ? ____________________

2) **The mystery number has ...**

A 1 in the Tens place.
A 6 in the Hundreds place.
A 1 in the Thousands place.
A 7 in the Ones place.

What is the mystery number ? ____________________

3) **The mystery number has ...**

A 7 in the Thousands place.
A 1 in the Hundreds place.
A 3 in the Tens place.
A 2 in the Ones place.

What is the mystery number ? ____________________

4) **The mystery number has ...**

A 5 in the Ones place.
A 1 in the Thousands place.
A 4 in the Hundreds place.
A 7 in the Tens place.

What is the mystery number ? ____________________

5) **The mystery number has ...**

A 1 in the Ones place.
A 8 in the Hundreds place.
A 8 in the Tens place.
A 6 in the Thousands place.

What is the mystery number ? ____________________

Score : __________

Date : __________

Number Lines

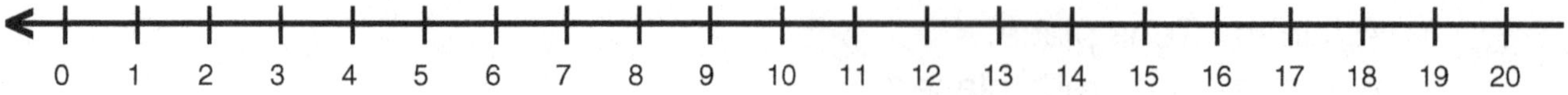

18 + 1 = ____

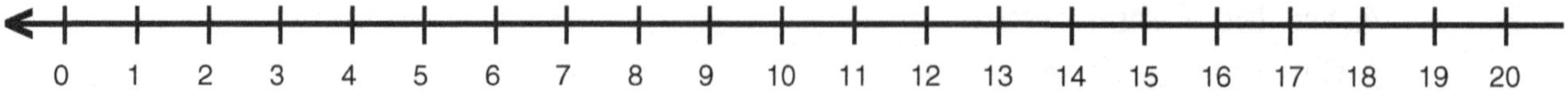

5 + 5 = ____

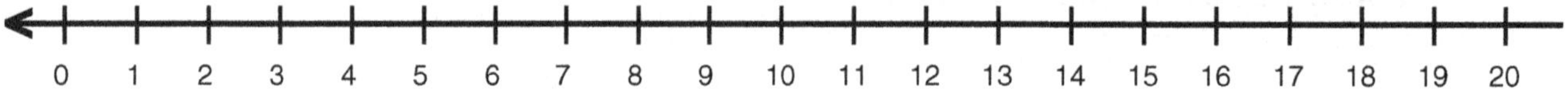

14 + 3 = ____

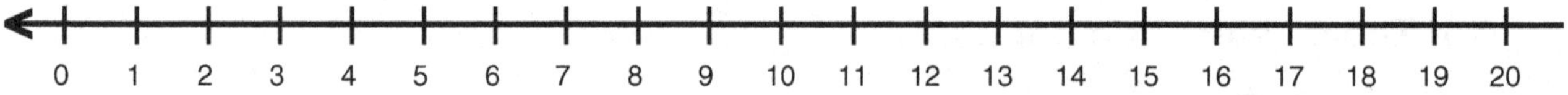

10 + 6 = ____

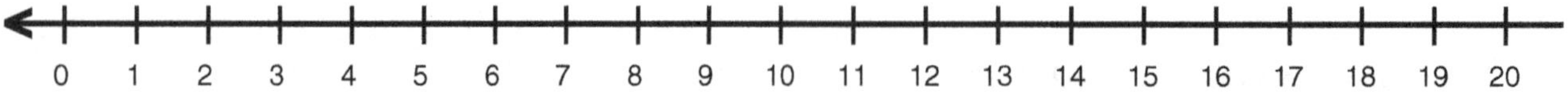

16 + 4 = ____

Score : ___________

Date : ___________

10122 + 86800	265710 + 883815	6900016 + 8967065	94785 + 51037
403123 + 535453	5061847 + 1878336	88389 + 38835	313963 + 824442
2936692 + 7549491	15234 + 29032	512353 + 139827	1923899 + 6762860
93107 + 15816	421331 + 962779	5141586 + 6071731	42257 + 96189

Measure It

Score : ____________

Date : ____________

PLEASE USE A RULER!

Length to measure.

1 in

63 mm

14.7 cm

2.3 cm

$2\frac{1}{2}$ in

105 mm

11.1 cm

8.5 cm

1.7 cm

13.7 cm

"Like terms" are terms whose variables are the same. Terms whose variables (such as x or y) with any exponents (such as the 2 in x^2) are the same.

7m + 14m - 6n - 5n + 2m

Step 1: Organize your like terms. You can use a highlighter, shapes, or just rewrite the problem so that the like terms are next to each other.

7m + 14m - (6n - 5n) + 2m

Step 2: Combine the coefficients.

(7 + 14 + 2)m + (-6 + -5)n

23m - 11n

Score : ____________

Date : ____________

Combining Like Terms

1) 8 + 13y - 15y

2) 14 - 6y + 3

3) -11 + 2 - 14y - 4y

4) -14(5 - 2f) - 8

5) 12n + 6n

6) 13k + k

7) 16(-14z - 4) - 3

8) -19(16 + 13s)

9) 3 + 9r - 7r + 6

10) 14(-19c + 8)

Grammar: Homophones vs Homographs vs. Homonyms

Score: ____________________

Date:______

How do you know which 'there,' 'their,' or 'they're' to use when you're writing? Isn't it a difficult one? These words sound similar but have completely different meanings.

Words with the same sound but different meanings are referred to as **homophones**. Homophones can be spelled differently or the same way. Rose (the flower), rose (the past tense of 'rise,' and rows (a line of items or people) are all homophones.

Homographs are two or more words that have the same spelling but different meanings and it **doesn't have to sound the same**. Because homographs are words with multiple meanings, how can you tell which one is being used? Readers can determine which form of a homograph is being used by looking for context clues, or words surrounding it that provide information about the definition. Take a look at these homograph examples.

A **bat** is either a piece of sporting equipment or an animal.
Bass is either a type of fish or a musical genre.
A **pen** is a writing instrument or a small enclosure in which animals are kept.
Lean is a word that means to be thin or to rest against something.
A **skip** is a fictitious jump or missing out on something.

Homonyms are words that have the same spelling or pronunciation but different meanings. These words can be perplexing at times, especially for students learning to spell them. For example, right means moral, the opposite of left, and a personal freedom. Homonyms can refer to both homophones and homographs. Both a homograph and a homophone are included in the definition of a homonym. For example, the words 'bear,' 'tear,' and 'lead' are all homographs, but they also meet the criteria for homonyms. They simply have to have the same look or sound. Similarly, while the words 'sell,' 'cell,' 'by,' and 'buy' are all homophones, they are also homonyms.

1. **'there,' 'their,' or 'they're' are examples of ______.**
    a. Homophones
    b. Homographs

2. **____ are words that have the same spelling or pronunciation but different meanings.**
    a. Homonyms
    b. Hemograms

3. **Choose the correct homophone for this sentence: Please don't drop and ______that bottle of hand sanitizer!**
    a. brake
    b. break

4. **Homographs are two or more words that have the same spelling but different ____.**
    a. ending sounds
    b. meanings

5. **Current (A flow of water / Up to date) is both homograph and homophone.**
    a. True
    b. False

6. **To, two and too are _____.**
    a. Homagraphs
    b. Homonyms

7. **The candle filled the _____ with a delicious scent.**
    a. heir
    b. air

8. **Kim drove _______ the tunnel.**
    a. threw
    b. through

9. **John wants to go to _____ house for dinner, but they don't like her, so _____ going to say no.**
    a. their, they're
    b. there, they're

10. **We won a $95,000 ________!**
    a. cheque
    b. check

11. **For example, a pencil is not really made with _____.**
    a. led
    b. lead

12. **Choose the correct homophone for this sentence: Timmy was standing _____ in line.**
    a. fourth
    b. forth

13. **Homophones are two words that sound the same but have a different meanings.**
    a. True
    b. False

14. **The word** ring **in the following two sentences is considered what? She wore a ruby** ring**. | We heard the doorbell** ring**.**
    a. hologram
    b. homograph

15. **A Homograph is a word that has more than one meaning and doesn't have to sound the same.**
    a. True
    b. False

16. **Homophones occur when there are multiple ways to spell the same sound.**
    a. True
    b. False

17. **Select the correct homophone: I have very little (patience/patients) when students do not follow directions.**
    a. patients
    b. patience

18. **The correct homophone (s) are used in the sentence: Personally, I hate the smell of read meet.**
    a. True
    b. False

19. **The correct homophone(s) is used in the sentence: We saw a herd of cattle in the farmer's field.**
    a. True
    b. False

20. **What is NOT an example of a homograph?**
    a. or, oar
    b. live, live

Grammar: Singular and Plural

Score: ______________________

Date:______________________

Nouns can take many different forms. Singular and plural are two of these forms. A singular noun refers to a single person, place, thing, or idea. A plural noun is one that refers to two or more people, places, things, or ideas. How do you pluralize a singular noun? Making a singular noun plural is usually as simple as adding a **s** to the end of the word.
Example: Singular toy | Plural toys

Some nouns, however, do not follow this rule and are referred to as irregular nouns. How do I pluralize a singular irregular noun?

We'll start with **singular nouns** that end in s, ss, ch, sh, x, or z. If a singular noun **ends in s, ss, ch, sh, x, or z**, add **es** at the end.
Example: beach--->beaches

If the singular noun **ends in a vowel**, the letters a, e, I o, and u are usually suffixed with an **s**.
Example: video--->videos

If a singular noun **ends with a consonant + o**, it is common to add an **es** at the end. Except for a, e, I o, and u, consonants are all the letters of the alphabet.
Example: potato--->potatoes

Simply add a **s** to the end of the word if the singular noun **ends in a vowel + y** pattern.
Example: day--->days

Now we'll look at singular nouns that **end in f or fe**. If the singular noun ends in a f or fe, **change it to a v and then add es**.
Example: life--->lives

Consonant + y is another unusual noun. If the singular noun **ends with a consonant + y** pattern, **change the y to I before adding es**
Example: bunny---> bunnies

Some nouns are spelled the same way in both the singular and plural forms.

It's now time to make some spelling changes. When you switch from the singular to plural form of a noun, the spelling changes. The following are some examples of common words that change spelling when formed into plurals:
Example: child--->childrens

Select the best answer for each question.

1. **Which word is NOT a plural noun?**
   a. books
   b. hat
   c. toys

2. **Which word is a singular noun?**
   a. bikes
   b. cars
   c. pencil

3. **Which word can be both singular and plural?**
   a. deer
   b. bears
   c. mice

4. **Tommy __________ badminton at the court.**
   a. playing
   b. plays
   c. play's

5. **They _______ to eat at fast food restaurants once in a while.**
   a. likes
   b. like
   c. likies

6. **Everybody _________ Janet Jackson.**
   a. know
   b. known
   c. knows

7. **He ___ very fast. You have to listen carefully.**
   a. spoken
   b. speak
   c. speaks

8. **Which one is the singular form of women?**
   a. womans
   b. woman
   c. women

9. **The plural form of tooth is**
   a. tooths
   b. toothes
   c. teeth

10. **The singular form of mice is _______.**
    a. mouse
    b. mices
    c. mouses

11. **The plural form of glass is _________.**
    a. glassies
    b. glasses
    c. glassy

12. **The plural form of dress is _________.**
    a. dressing
    b. dresses
    c. dressy

13. **Plural means many.**
    a. True
    b. False

14. **Singular means 1.**
    a. True
    b. False

15. **Is this word singular or plural? monsters**
    a. plural
    b. singular

16. **Find the plural noun in the sentence. They gave her a nice vase full of flowers.**
    a. they
    b. flowers
    c. vase

17. **Find the plural noun in the sentence. Her baby brother grabbed the crayons out of the box and drew on the wall.**
    a. crayons
    b. box
    c. brothers

18. **Find the plural noun in the sentence. My friend, Lois, picked enough red strawberries for the whole class.**
    a. strawberries
    b. friends
    c. classes

19. **What is the correct plural form of the noun wish?**
    a. wishes
    b. wishs
    c. wishy

20. **What is the correct plural form of the noun flurry?**
    a. flurrys
    b. flurryies
    c. flurries

21. **What is the correct plural form of the noun box?**
    a. boxs
    b. boxses
    c. boxes

22. **What is the correct plural form of the noun bee?**
    a. beess
    b. beeses
    c. bees

23. **What is the correct plural form of the noun candy?**
    a. candys
    b. candyies
    c. candies

24. **Find the singular noun in the sentence. The boys and girls drew pictures on the sidewalk.**
    a. boys
    b. drew
    c. sidewalk

Spelling: How Do You Spell It? Part I

Score: ____________________

Date: ____________

Write and circle the correct spelling for each word.

		A	B	C	D
1.	____________	grade	grrada	grrade	grada
2.	____________	elementary	elenmentary	ellenmentary	ellementary
3.	____________	marks	marrcks	marrks	marcks
4.	____________	repurt	reporrt	report	repurrt
5.	____________	schedolle	schedule	schedole	schedulle
6.	____________	timetible	timetable	timettable	timettible
7.	____________	highlight	highllight	hyghllight	hyghlight
8.	____________	foell	foel	fuell	fuel
9.	____________	instrucsion	insstruction	instruction	insstrucsion
10.	____________	senttence	sentance	senttance	sentence
11.	____________	vaccination	vacination	vaccinasion	vacinasion
12.	____________	proof	prwf	prouf	proph
13.	____________	mandatury	mandattury	mandatory	mandattory
14.	____________	final	fynall	finall	fynal
15.	____________	envellope	envelope	envellupe	envelupe
16.	____________	equattor	eqauttor	eqautor	equator
17.	____________	bllanks	blanks	blancks	bllancks
18.	____________	honorible	honorrable	honorable	honorrible
19.	____________	scaince	sceince	science	sciance
20.	____________	mussic	mosic	muscic	music
21.	____________	history	hisstory	hisctory	histury
22.	____________	lissten	liscten	lysten	listen
23.	____________	entrence	enttrance	enttrence	entrance
24.	____________	especialy	especailly	especaily	especially
25.	____________	mariage	maraige	marraige	marriage

Spelling: How Do You Spell It? Part II

Score: ____________________

Date: ____________

Write and circle the correct spelling for each word.

		A	B	C	D
1.	________	compllain	complian	complain	compllian
2.	________	negattyve	negatyve	negative	negattive
3.	________	importance	importence	imporrtance	imporrtence
4.	________	encourragement	encouragement	encourragenment	encouragenment
5.	________	shallves	shelves	shellves	shalves
6.	________	mixture	mixttore	mixtore	mixtture
7.	________	honorrable	honorable	honorible	honorrible
8.	________	lagall	legall	lagal	legal
9.	________	manar	mannar	manner	maner
10.	________	encycllopedia	encyclopedia	encycllopedai	encyclopedai
11.	________	repllacement	replacenment	repllacenment	replacement
12.	________	medycie	medycine	medicine	medicie
13.	________	experriance	experience	experiance	experrience
14.	________	hunger	hunjer	hungerr	hunjerr
15.	________	sallote	sallute	salote	salute
16.	________	horrizon	hurizon	hurrizon	horizon
17.	________	sestion	session	setion	sesion
18.	________	shorrten	shurten	shorten	shurrten
19.	________	fuacett	faucett	fuacet	faucet
20.	________	haadache	haadace	haedache	headache
21.	________	further	furrther	forrther	forther
22.	________	injurry	injory	injury	injorry
23.	________	disstance	distence	distance	disstence
24.	________	rattio	ratio	rattoi	ratoi
25.	________	independense	independence	independance	independanse

Spelling: How Do You Spell It? Part III

Score: ____________

Date: ____________

Write and circle the correct spelling for each word.

		A	B	C	D
1.	______	invitation	invittasion	invitasion	invittation
2.	______	denuminator	denominator	denuminattor	denominattor
3.	______	personal	perrsonal	perrsunal	persunal
4.	______	rapkd	rapid	rahid	rapyd
5.	______	oryginal	original	orryginal	orriginal
6.	______	liquvd	liqiod	liqoid	liquid
7.	______	desscendant	descendant	dessendant	desssendant
8.	______	dissastrous	disastrous	dissastroos	disastroos
9.	______	cooperasion	cooperation	coperation	coperasion
10.	______	routine	roottine	routtine	rootine
11.	______	earleist	earrleist	earrliest	earliest
12.	______	acidentally	accidentally	acidentalli	accidentalli
13.	______	rehaerrse	rehearrse	rehaerse	rehearse
14.	______	quotte	qoote	quote	qootte
15.	______	capablla	capablle	capable	capible
16.	______	apointment	appointnment	apointnment	appointment
17.	______	mussician	mussicain	musicain	musician
18.	______	nomerrator	numerrator	numerator	nomerator
19.	______	inquire	inqoire	inquirre	inqoirre
20.	______	remote	remute	remutte	remotte
21.	______	pryncipal	prrincipal	prryncipal	principal
22.	______	sylent	sillent	syllent	silent
23.	______	locatsion	locasion	location	locattion
24.	______	edision	edition	editsion	edittion

Commonly misspelled words that sound alike but are spelled differently

Score: ____________________

Date: ____________

Carefully circle the correct spelling combinations of words.

	A	B	C	D
1.	Sun/Sn	Son/Son	Sun/Son	Son/Sn
2.	Hare/Hiar	Harre/Hair	Hare/Hair	Harre/Hiar
3.	Cache/Cassh	Cache/Cash	Cache/Casch	Cacha/Cash
4.	Cytte/Sight	Cite/Sight	Cyte/Sight	Citte/Sight
5.	Worrn/Warn	Wurn/Warn	Wurrn/Warn	Worn/Warn
6.	Minerr/Minor	Miner/Minur	Miner/Minor	Minerr/Minur
7.	Wratch/Retch	Wretch/Retch	Wrretch/Retch	Wrratch/Retch
8.	Floor/Flower	Flloor/Flower	Flour/Flower	Fllour/Flower
9.	Whille/Wile	While/Wile	Whylle/Wile	Whyle/Wile
10.	Calous/Callus	Caloos/Callus	Callous/Callus	Calloos/Callus
11.	Build/Biled	Build/Billed	Boild/Billed	Boild/Biled
12.	Marrten/Martin	Marten/Martin	Marten/Martyn	Marrten/Martyn
13.	Humerrus/Humorous	Humerus/Humorous	Humerrus/Humoroos	Humerus/Humoroos
14.	Housse/Hoes	Hose/Hoes	House/Hoes	Hosse/Hoes
15.	Mei Be/Maybe	Mai Be/Maybe	May Be/Maybe	Mey Be/Maybe
16.	Matal/Metle/Meddle	Metal/Mettle/Meddle	Matal/Mettle/Meddle	Metal/Metle/Meddle
17.	Halve/Have	Hallva/Have	Hallve/Have	Halva/Have
18.	Wee/We	Wea/We	We/We	Wa/We
19.	Taper/Tapir	Taperr/Tapyr	Taperr/Tapir	Taper/Tapyr
20.	Timberr/Timbre	Tymber/Timbre	Tymberr/Timbre	Timber/Timbre
21.	Minse/Mintts	Mince/Mintts	Minse/Mints	Mince/Mints
22.	Eies/Ayes	Eyesc/Ayes	Eyes/Ayes	Eyess/Ayes
23.	Guesced/Guest	Guessed/Guest	Guesed/Guest	Gueced/Guest
24.	Yore/Your/You'Re	Yore/Yoor/You'Re	Yorre/Your/You'Re	Yorre/Yoor/You'Re
25.	Oarr/Or/Ora	Oarr/Or/Ore	Oar/Or/Ore	Oar/Or/Ora
26.	Bate/Biat	Bate/Bait	Batte/Biat	Batte/Bait
27.	Tax/Tacks	Tax/Taks	Tax/Tacksc	Tax/Tacksс

28.	Bald/Ballad/Bawled	Bald/Baled/Bawled	Bald/Balled/Bawled	Bald/Balad/Bawled
29.	Ewe/Yuo/Yew	Ewe/Yoo/Yew	Ewe/You/Yew	Ewe/Yoo/Yw
30.	Eei/I/Aye	Eie/I/Ae	Eye/I/Aye	Eie/I/Aye
31.	Hoes/Hose	Hoess/Hose	Hoess/House	Hoes/House
32.	Tou/Two/To	Tu/Two/To	To/Two/To	Too/Two/To
33.	Ceres/Series	Cerres/Series	Ceres/Sereis	Cerres/Sereis
34.	Hansom/Handsome	Hansum/Handsome	Hanscom/Handsome	Hanssom/Handsome
35.	Residance/Residents	Residence/Residents	Ressidence/Residents	Ressidance/Residents
36.	Surrf/Serf	Surf/Serf	Surrph/Serf	Surph/Serf
37.	Siall/Sale	Saill/Sale	Sail/Sale	Sial/Sale
38.	Therre's/Thiers	There's/Thiers	There's/Theirs	Therre's/Theirs
39.	Roed/Rode	Roed/Rude	Rued/Rude	Roed/Rue
40.	Aid/Aie	Ayd/Aide	Ayd/Aie	Aid/Aide
41.	Taem/Teem	Taem/Tem	Team/Tem	Team/Teem
42.	Ilusion/Allusion	Ilution/Allusion	Illution/Allusion	Illusion/Allusion
43.	Hi/Hih	Hy/High	Hi/High	Hy/Hih
44.	Barred/Bard	Bared/Bard	Barad/Bard	Barrad/Bard
45.	Mewll/Mule	Mewl/Mule	Mewll/Mole	Mewl/Mole
46.	Rowss/Rose	Rows/Rose	Rowss/Rouse	Rows/Rouse
47.	Chep/Cheap	Cheep/Chaep	Cheep/Cheap	Chep/Chaep
48.	Bah/Ba	Beh/Ba	Bah/Baa	Beh/Baa
49.	Gofer/Gopher	Gopher/Gopher	Gophfer/Gopher	Goffer/Gopher
50.	Don/Doe	Dun/Doe	Dun/Done	Don/Done
51.	Ryte/Write/Right	Ritte/Write/Right	Rytte/Write/Right	Rite/Write/Right
52.	Mite/Might	Mitte/Might	Myte/Might	Mytte/Might
53.	Latter/Ladder	Later/Ladder	Latar/Ladder	Lattar/Ladder
54.	Gorred/Goord	Gored/Gourd	Gored/Goord	Gorred/Gourd
55.	Ball/Belle	Bell/Belle	Bal/Belle	Bel/Belle
56.	Ruscell/Rustle	Russell/Rustle	Rusell/Rustle	Rucell/Rustle
57.	Tuat/Taught	Tautt/Taught	Tuatt/Taught	Taut/Taught
58.	Cozen/Cousin	Cozen/Coosin	Cozen/Coossin	Cozen/Coussin
59.	Morn/Mourn	Morrn/Moorn	Morrn/Mourn	Morn/Moorn
60.	Stare/Stiar	Stare/Stair	Sttare/Stiar	Sttare/Stair
61.	Wrrap/Rap	Wrrep/Rap	Wrap/Rap	Wrep/Rap

62.	Centts/Ssents	Centts/Scents	Cents/Scents	Cents/Ssents
63.	Basste/Based	Baste/Baced	Baste/Based	Bascte/Based
64.	Foorr/Fore/For	Foor/Fore/For	Fourr/Fore/For	Four/Fore/For
65.	Knikers/Nickers	Knickerrs/Nickers	Knikerrs/Nickers	Knickers/Nickers
66.	Marre/Mayor	Mare/Mayor	Mare/Meyor	Marre/Meyor
67.	Surrje/Serge	Surje/Serge	Surrge/Serge	Surge/Serge
68.	Steal/Steel	Steal/Stel	Stael/Steel	Stael/Stel
69.	Haerrt/Hart	Heart/Hart	Hearrt/Hart	Haert/Hart
70.	Holed/Hold	Huled/Hold	Holled/Hold	Hulled/Hold
71.	Way/Wiegh/Whey	Wai/Wiegh/Whey	Wai/Weigh/Whey	Way/Weigh/Whey
72.	Diieng/Dying	Dyieng/Dying	Dieing/Dying	Dyeing/Dying
73.	Holay/Holy/Wholly	Holay/Holy/Wholy	Holey/Holy/Wholy	Holey/Holy/Wholly
74.	Sworrd/Soared	Swurrd/Soared	Swurd/Soared	Sword/Soared
75.	Cane/Cyan	Cane/Cian	Cane/Cayn	Cane/Cain
76.	Arreil/Aerial	Ariel/Aerial	Arriel/Aerial	Areil/Aerial
77.	Brut/Brute	Brrot/Brute	Brot/Brute	Brrut/Brute
78.	Frrays/Phrase	Frays/Phrase	Frreys/Phrase	Freys/Phrase
79.	Throne/Thrown	Thrrune/Thrown	Thrune/Thrown	Thrrone/Thrown
80.	Ha’d/Hed	He’d/Heed	He’d/Hed	He’d/Head
81.	Waerr/Where/Ware	Wear/Where/Ware	Wearr/Where/Ware	Waer/Where/Ware
82.	Brraed/Bred	Bread/Bred	Braed/Bred	Brread/Bred
83.	We’ve/Waeve	We’ve/Weave	Wa’ve/Weave	Wa’ve/Waeve
84.	Hew/Hoe/Huh	Hew/Hue/Hugh	Hew/Hoe/Hugh	Hew/Hoe/Hogh
85.	Nikerrs/Knickers	Nickerrs/Knickers	Nikers/Knickers	Nickers/Knickers
86.	Call/Sell	Cell/Sell	Cal/Sell	Cel/Sell
87.	Isle/I’l/Aisle	Isle/I’ll/Aisle	Isle/I’ll/Aysle	Isle/I’l/Aysle
88.	Brruice/Brews	Bruise/Brews	Brruise/Brews	Bruice/Brews
89.	Except/Accept	Exsept/Accept	Exsept/Acept	Except/Acept

Score : ___________

Date : ___________

MIXED ADDING

1) 1067 + 1078 =

2) 438 + 2611 =

3) -2831 + -2939 =

4) 2330 + -1901 =

5) 935 + 1991 =

6) 603 + 1073 =

7) -2280 + -393 =

8) -230 + -138 =

9) 1368 + 624 =

10) 1143 + -2262 =

11) 1708 + -337 =

12) 2667 + 2849 =

13) 2277 + -466 =

14) -2079 + -2586 =

15) 2966 + 2413 =

16) -1488 + 2557 =

17) 1087 + -2291 =

18) -2005 + 2153 =

19) 2125 + 2919 =

20) -270 + 2104 =

21) 2759 + 592 =

22) -1815 + 2739 =

23) 1956 + -560 =

24) 1569 + 2401 =

25) 2496 + 674 =

26) -2907 + 884 =

27) 1727 + 739 =

28) 125 + 783 =

29) 1602 + -1844 =

30) 2042 + -2763 =

Proofreading Interpersonal Skills: Peer Pressure

Score: ______________________

Date: _____________

In this activity, you'll see lots of grammatical *errors*. Correct all the grammar mistakes you see.

There are **30** mistakes in this passage. 3 capitals missing. 5 unnecessary capitals. 3 unnecessary apostrophes. 6 punctuation marks missing or incorrect. 13 incorrectly spelled words.

Tony is mingling with a large group of what he considers to be the school's cool kids. Suddenly, someone in the group begins mocking Tony's friend Rob, who walks with a limp due to a physical dasability.

They begin to imitate rob's limping and Call him 'lame cripple' and other derogatory terms. Although Tony disapproves of their behavior, he does not want to risk being excluded from the group, and thus joins them in mocking Rob.

Peer pressure is the influence exerted on us by member's of our social group. It can manifest in a variety of ways and can lead to us engaging in behaviors we would not normally consider such as Tony joining in and mocking his friend Rob.

However, peer pressure is not always detrimental. Positive peer pressure can motivate us to make better chioces, such as studying harder, staying in school, or seeking a better job. Whan others influence us to make poor Choices, such as smoking, using illicit drugs, or bullying, we succumb to negative peer pressure. We all desire to belong to a group and fit in, so Developing strategies for resisting peer pressure when necessary can be beneficial.

Tony and his friends are engaging in bullying by moking Rob. Bullying is defined as persistent, unwanted. aggressive behavior directed toward another person. It is moust prevalent in school-aged children but can also aphfect adults. Bullying can take on a variety of forms, including the following:

· Verbil bullying is when someone is called names, threatened, or taunted verbally.
· Bullying is physical in nature - hitting spitting, tripping, or poshing someone.
· Social Bullying is intentionally excluding Someone from activities spreading rumors, or embarrassing sumeone.

· Cyberbullying is the act of verbally or socially bullying someone via the internet, such as through social media sites.

Peer pressure exerts a significant influence on an individual's decision to engage in bullying behavoir. In Tony's case, even though Rob is a friend and tony would never consider mocking his disability, his desire to belong to a group outweighs his willingness to defend his friend

Peer pressure is a strong force that is exerted on us by our social group members. Peer pressure is classified into two types: negative peer pressure, which results in poor decision-making, and positive peer pressure, which influences us to make the correct choices. Adolescents are particularly susceptible to peer pressure because of their desire to fit in

Peer pressure can motivate someone to engage in bullying behaviors such as mocking someone, threatening to harm them, taunting them online, or excluding them from an activity. Each year, bullying affect's an astounding 3.2 million school-aged children. Severil strategies for avoiding peer pressure bullying include the following:

- consider your actions by surrounding yourself with good company.
- Acquiring the ability to say no to someone you trust.

Speak up - bullying is never acceptable and is taken extramely seroiusly in schools and the workplace. If someone is attempting to convince you to bully another person, speaking with a trusted adult such as a teacher, coach, counselor, or coworker can frequently help put thing's into perspective and highlight the issue.

PRACTICE ONLY

Employee Application

Employers use employment applications like this apart of their hiring process. It tells them about the potential employee.

Applicant

Name: Date:

Referral: Phone No.

Fax No. Email:

Address:

Are You…

A U.S. Citizen?	☐ Yes	☐ No
Over 18 years old?	☐ Yes	☐ No
Licensed to drive?	☐ Yes	☐ No

Employment

Position: Department:

Type: ☐ Full-Time ☐ Part-Time ☐ Other (Seasonal/Temp):

Start Date: Starting Salary:

Current Employment: May we contact? ☐ Yes ☐ No

Education History

Education	School	Location	Years	Graduated?	Degree(s)
High School					
College					
Graduate					

Other Training/Classes:

Workshops/Certifications:

Employment History

Employer	Address	Position	Dates	Reason for Leaving

References

Reference	Relationship	Phone	Email	Address

Applicant Signature Date

Social Skill Interests: Things To Do

Score: ____________________

Date: ____________

A **hobby** is something that a person actively pursues relaxation and enjoyment. On the other hand, a person may have an **interest** in something because they are curious or concerned. Hobbies usually do not provide monetary compensation. However, a person's interests can vary and may lead to earning money or making a living from them. Hobbies are typically pursued in one's spare time or when one is not required to work. Interests can be followed in one's spare time or while working, as in the case of using one's passion as a source of income. A hobby can be a recreational activity that is done regularly in one's spare time. It primarily consists of participating in sports, collecting items and objects, engaging in creative and artistic pursuits, etc. The desire to learn or understand something is referred to as interest. If a person has a strong interest in a subject, he or she may pursue it as a hobby. However, an interest is not always a hobby. Hobbies such as stamp and flower collecting may not be a source of income for a person, but the items collected can sometimes be sold. Hobbies frequently lead to discoveries and inventions. Interests could be a source of income or something done for free. If a person is interested in cooking or enjoys creating dishes, he can do so at home or make it a career by becoming a chef.

Put the words in the correct category.

pottery	card making	candle making	reading	weaving	knitting
gym	jewellery	chess	surfing	computer games	collecting
woodwork	Soccer	art	swimming	cooking	skateboarding
embroidery	skiing	gardening	writing	chatting	sewing
netball	stamp collecting	football	music	rugby	basketball

Sport (10)	**Handcrafts** (10)	**Interests** (10)

Dental Health History Form Practice

Dental history reviews the patient's past dental experiences and current dental issues. A look at the dental history can often tell you about past dental problems, previous dental treatment, and how the patient has responded to treatment.

Patient Name: ______________________________ Date: ________________

Email Address: ______________________________ Phone No. ________________

Address: ____

Medications: ____

____

Allergies: ____

____

Pregnant: ☐ Yes ☐ No   Nursing: ☐ Yes ☐ No

Alcohol Use: ☐ Never ☐ Occasionally ☐ Monthly ☐ Weekly ☐ Daily ☐ 4+ per Day

Smoking: ☐ Never ☐ Occasionally ☐ 1 per Day ☐ 1 Pack per Day ☐ 2+ Packs per Day

Illegal Drug Use: ☐ Never ☐ Occasionally ☐ Monthly ☐ Weekly ☐ Daily

Exercise: ☐ Never ☐ Occasionally ☐ Weekly ☐ 2-3 Times per Week ☐ Daily

Dental Symptoms

Pain in teeth	☐ Yes	☐ No
Teeth sensitivity	☐ Yes	☐ No
Teeth sensitivity to heat	☐ Yes	☐ No
Teeth sensitivity to cold	☐ Yes	☐ No
Teeth sensitivity to sour	☐ Yes	☐ No
Teeth sensitivity to sweet	☐ Yes	☐ No
Bleeding gums	☐ Yes	☐ No
Bleeding gums after flossing	☐ Yes	☐ No
Sensitive gums	☐ Yes	☐ No
Swollen gums	☐ Yes	☐ No
Headaches	☐ Yes	☐ No
Earaches	☐ Yes	☐ No
Jaw aching	☐ Yes	☐ No
Tired jaw	☐ Yes	☐ No
Clicking jaw	☐ Yes	☐ No
Jaw gets stuck	☐ Yes	☐ No
Unable to totally open mouth	☐ Yes	☐ No
TMJ	☐ Yes	☐ No
Clenched jaw	☐ Yes	☐ No
Grinding teeth	☐ Yes	☐ No
Food catches in teeth	☐ Yes	☐ No
Tongue pain	☐ Yes	☐ No
Tongue swelling	☐ Yes	☐ No
	☐ Yes	☐ No
	☐ Yes	☐ No
	☐ Yes	☐ No
	☐ Yes	☐ No

Dental History

I gag easily	☐ Yes	☐ No
Dental work makes me nervous	☐ Yes	☐ No
I brush ____________ times per day		
I floss ____________ times per day		
I use mouthwash ____________ times per day		
I chew gum regularly	☐ Yes	☐ No
I chew tobacco regularly	☐ Yes	☐ No
I smoke a pipe regularly	☐ Yes	☐ No
I take pain relievers often	☐ Yes	☐ No
I take muscle relaxants often	☐ Yes	☐ No
I take antidepressants often	☐ Yes	☐ No
I have had trauma to the head	☐ Yes	☐ No
I have had trauma to the face	☐ Yes	☐ No
I have had trauma to the ear	☐ Yes	☐ No
I have had trauma to the mouth	☐ Yes	☐ No
I have had trauma to the throat	☐ Yes	☐ No
I take fluoride supplements	☐ Yes	☐ No
I am dissatisfied with my teeth	☐ Yes	☐ No
I wear dentures	☐ Yes	☐ No
I have braces	☐ Yes	☐ No
I don't like the color of my teeth	☐ Yes	☐ No
I want total dental care	☐ Yes	☐ No
	☐ Yes	☐ No
	☐ Yes	☐ No
	☐ Yes	☐ No
	☐ Yes	☐ No
	☐ Yes	☐ No

RESEARCH WRITING EXAMPLE

Occupation Lawyer, university administrator, writer,

BORN DATE: January 27, 1954 Nationality American

DEATH DATE: still alive and well Education Princeton & Harvard University Children 2 girls

Childhood and Family Background Facts

Born as Mary Robinson in Chicago, Illinois.

Dad's name John Robinson III & mom's name Rose Robinson.

One brother named Malcolm Robinson, he's a college basketball coach.

Her great-great-great-grandmother, Cindy Shields, was born into slavery in South Carolina.

Her childhood home was in New York.

Her great-aunt who was a piano teacher, taught her how to play the piano.

Work and Career Facts

- First job was babysitting.
- Mary majored in sociology at Princeton, where she graduated with honors, and went to Harvard Law School.
- She once worked in public service as an assistant to the mayor.
- She was the Vice President of Community and External Affairs at the University of Chicago Medical Center.

Friends, Social Life and Other Interesting Facts

- When she was a teen, she became friends with Kim Jackson.
- Her college bestie Suzanne Alele died from cancer at a young age in 1990.
- Her two favorite children's books: "Goodnight Moon" and "Where the Wild Things Are."
- Celebrity Crush: Denzel & Will Smith

Children, Marriage or Significant Relationships

- She suffered a heartbreaking miscarriage.
- Gave birth to two beautiful daughters Monica and Jennifer.
- She met her husband Tom when she was assigned to be his mentor when he was a summer associate at the law firm she worked at.

Did you enjoy researching this person?

Rating: ☆ ☆ ☆ ☆ ☆

TODAY IS RESEARCH DAY! GRADE__________

DATE__________ **RESEARCH: Mark Twain**

Occupation ____________________

BORN DATE: ____________________ Nationality ____________________

DEATH DATE: ____________________ Education ____________________ #Children ______

Childhood and Family Background Facts

Work and Career Facts

Children, Marriage and or Significant Relationships

Friends, Social Life and Other Interesting Facts

Did you enjoy researching this person?

Give a Rating: ☆ ☆ ☆ ☆ ☆

TODAY IS RESEARCH DAY! GRADE____________

DATE__________ **RESEARCH: Marie Curie**

Occupation ______________________________

BORN DATE: ______________________ Nationality ______________________

DEATH DATE: ______________________ Education ______________________ #Children ________

Childhood and Family Background Facts

Work and Career Facts

Children, Marriage and or Significant Relationships

Friends, Social Life and Other Interesting Facts

Did you enjoy researching this person?

Give a Rating: ☆ ☆ ☆ ☆ ☆

TODAY IS RESEARCH DAY! GRADE________________

DATE____________ **RESEARCH: Princess Diana**

Occupation ____

BORN DATE: ______________________ Nationality ____________________

DEATH DATE: ____________________ Education ______________________ #Children ________

Childhood and Family Background Facts

Work and Career Facts

Children, Marriage and or Significant Relationships

Friends, Social Life and Other Interesting Facts

Did you enjoy researching this person?

Give a Rating: ☆ ☆ ☆ ☆ ☆

TODAY IS RESEARCH DAY! GRADE________________

DATE____________ **RESEARCH: Andrew Jackson**

Occupation ____

BORN DATE:______________________________ Nationality______________________

DEATH DATE:____________________ Education______________________________ #Children __________

Childhood and Family Background Facts

Work and Career Facts

Children, Marriage and or Significant Relationships

Friends, Social Life and Other Interesting Facts

Did you enjoy researching this person?

Give a Rating: ☆ ☆ ☆ ☆ ☆

TODAY IS RESEARCH DAY!

GRADE________________

DATE____________

RESEARCH: John F. Kennedy

Occupation ____________________

BORN DATE: ____________________ Nationality ____________________

DEATH DATE: ____________________ Education ____________________ #Children __________

Childhood and Family Background Facts

Work and Career Facts

Children, Marriage and or Significant Relationships

Friends, Social Life and Other Interesting Facts

Did you enjoy researching this person?

Give a Rating: ☆ ☆ ☆ ☆ ☆

TODAY IS RESEARCH DAY! GRADE________________

DATE____________ **RESEARCH: King Arthur**

Occupation ____

BORN DATE:____________________ Nationality____________________

DEATH DATE:____________________ Education____________________ #Children ________

Childhood and Family Background Facts

Work and Career Facts

Children, Marriage and or Significant Relationships

Friends, Social Life and Other Interesting Facts

Did you enjoy researching this person?

Give a Rating: ☆ ☆ ☆ ☆ ☆

TODAY IS RESEARCH DAY! GRADE________________

DATE____________ **RESEARCH: Napoleon Bonaparte**

Occupation ________________________________

BORN DATE:________________________ Nationality ________________

DEATH DATE:________________ Education ________________ #Children ________

Childhood and Family Background Facts

Work and Career Facts

Children, Marriage and or Significant Relationships

Friends, Social Life and Other Interesting Facts

Did you enjoy researching this person?

Give a Rating: ☆ ☆ ☆ ☆ ☆

TODAY IS RESEARCH DAY! **GRADE________________**

DATE___________ **RESEARCH: Mother Teresa**

Occupation ______________________________

BORN DATE:______________________ **Nationality**______________________

DEATH DATE:__________________ **Education**______________________ **#Children** ________

Childhood and Family Background Facts

Work and Career Facts

Children, Marriage and or Significant Relationships

Friends, Social Life and Other Interesting Facts

Did you enjoy researching this person?

Give a Rating: ☆ ☆ ☆ ☆ ☆

TODAY IS RESEARCH DAY! GRADE________________

DATE___________ **RESEARCH: Sally Ride**

Occupation ______________________________

BORN DATE: ____________________ Nationality ____________________

DEATH DATE: ____________________ Education ____________________ #Children __________

Childhood and Family Background Facts

Work and Career Facts

Children, Marriage and or Significant Relationships

Friends, Social Life and Other Interesting Facts

Did you enjoy researching this person?

Give a Rating: ☆ ☆ ☆ ☆ ☆

TODAY IS RESEARCH DAY! **GRADE**______________

DATE___________ **RESEARCH: Eli Whitney**

Occupation ____________________

BORN DATE:____________________ **Nationality**____________________

DEATH DATE:______________ **Education**____________________ **#Children** ________

Childhood and Family Background Facts

Work and Career Facts

Children, Marriage and or Significant Relationships

Friends, Social Life and Other Interesting Facts

Did you enjoy researching this person?

Give a Rating: ☆ ☆ ☆ ☆ ☆

TODAY IS RESEARCH DAY! GRADE________________

DATE___________ **RESEARCH: Nellie Bly**

Occupation ____________________

BORN DATE: ____________________ Nationality ____________________

DEATH DATE: ____________________ Education ____________________ #Children __________

Childhood and Family Background Facts

Work and Career Facts

Children, Marriage and or Significant Relationships

Friends, Social Life and Other Interesting Facts

Did you enjoy researching this person?

Give a Rating: ☆ ☆ ☆ ☆ ☆

TODAY IS RESEARCH DAY!

GRADE________________

DATE___________

RESEARCH: Pope John Paul II

Occupation ______________________________

BORN DATE: ______________________ Nationality ______________________

DEATH DATE: ____________________ Education ______________________ #Children ________

Childhood and Family Background Facts

Work and Career Facts

Children, Marriage and or Significant Relationships

Friends, Social Life and Other Interesting Facts

Did you enjoy researching this person?

Give a Rating: ☆ ☆ ☆ ☆ ☆

TODAY IS RESEARCH DAY! GRADE________________

DATE___________ **RESEARCH: Nikola Tesla**

Occupation ______________________________

BORN DATE: ______________________ **Nationality** ______________________

DEATH DATE: ____________________ **Education** ____________________ **#Children** __________

Childhood and Family Background Facts

Work and Career Facts

Children, Marriage and or Significant Relationships

Friends, Social Life and Other Interesting Facts

Did you enjoy researching this person?

Give a Rating: ☆ ☆ ☆ ☆ ☆

TODAY IS RESEARCH DAY! **GRADE**________________

DATE____________ **RESEARCH: Robert E. Lee**

Occupation ______________________________

BORN DATE:______________________ **Nationality**______________________

DEATH DATE:______________________ **Education**______________________ **#Children** ________

Childhood and Family Background Facts

Work and Career Facts

Children, Marriage and or Significant Relationships

Friends, Social Life and Other Interesting Facts

Did you enjoy researching this person?

Give a Rating: ☆ ☆ ☆ ☆ ☆

TODAY IS RESEARCH DAY!

GRADE________________

DATE____________ **RESEARCH: Charles Darwin**

Occupation ____

BORN DATE: ________________________ Nationality ________________

DEATH DATE: ________________ Education ________________________ #Children ________

Childhood and Family Background Facts

Work and Career Facts

Children, Marriage and or Significant Relationships

Friends, Social Life and Other Interesting Facts

Did you enjoy researching this person?

Give a Rating: ☆ ☆ ☆ ☆ ☆

TODAY IS RESEARCH DAY! GRADE________________

DATE____________ **RESEARCH: Ludwig van Beethoven**

Occupation ____________________

BORN DATE:____________________ Nationality____________________

DEATH DATE:____________________ Education____________________ #Children __________

Childhood and Family Background Facts

Work and Career Facts

Children, Marriage and or Significant Relationships

Friends, Social Life and Other Interesting Facts

Did you enjoy researching this person?

Give a Rating: ☆ ☆ ☆ ☆ ☆

TODAY IS RESEARCH DAY! GRADE________________

DATE____________ **RESEARCH:** Harriet Beecher Stowe

Occupation ______________________________

BORN DATE: ______________________ Nationality ______________________

DEATH DATE: ______________________ Education ______________________ #Children __________

Childhood and Family Background Facts

Work and Career Facts

Children, Marriage and or Significant Relationships

Friends, Social Life and Other Interesting Facts

Did you enjoy researching this person?

Give a Rating: ☆ ☆ ☆ ☆ ☆

TODAY IS RESEARCH DAY! GRADE________________

DATE____________ **RESEARCH: Steve Jobs**

Occupation ____

BORN DATE:____________________________ Nationality____________________

DEATH DATE:______________________ Education ______________________ #Children ________

Childhood and Family Background Facts

Work and Career Facts

Children, Marriage and or Significant Relationships

Friends, Social Life and Other Interesting Facts

Did you enjoy researching this person?

Give a Rating: ☆ ☆ ☆ ☆ ☆

TODAY IS RESEARCH DAY! GRADE________________

DATE____________ **RESEARCH: Captain James Cook**

Occupation ______________________________

BORN DATE: ______________________ Nationality ______________________

DEATH DATE: ______________ Education ______________________ #Children ________

Childhood and Family Background Facts

Work and Career Facts

Children, Marriage and or Significant Relationships

Friends, Social Life and Other Interesting Facts

Did you enjoy researching this person?

Give a Rating: ☆ ☆ ☆ ☆ ☆

TODAY IS RESEARCH DAY! GRADE________________

DATE___________ **RESEARCH:** Dmitri Mendeleev

Occupation ______________________________

BORN DATE: ______________________ Nationality ______________________

DEATH DATE: ______________________ Education ______________________ #Children __________

Childhood and Family Background Facts

Work and Career Facts

Children, Marriage and or Significant Relationships

Friends, Social Life and Other Interesting Facts

Did you enjoy researching this person?

Give a Rating: ☆ ☆ ☆ ☆ ☆

TODAY IS RESEARCH DAY! **GRADE**_______________

DATE___________ **RESEARCH: Benedict Arnold**

Occupation ____________________

BORN DATE: ____________________ **Nationality** ____________________

DEATH DATE: ____________________ **Education** ____________________ **#Children** __________

Childhood and Family Background Facts

Work and Career Facts

Children, Marriage and or Significant Relationships

Friends, Social Life and Other Interesting Facts

Did you enjoy researching this person?

Give a Rating: ☆ ☆ ☆ ☆ ☆

TODAY IS RESEARCH DAY! GRADE________________

DATE____________ **RESEARCH: Molly Pitcher**

Occupation ________________________________

BORN DATE:______________________ Nationality________________________

DEATH DATE:____________________ Education________________________ #Children ________

Childhood and Family Background Facts

Work and Career Facts

Children, Marriage and or Significant Relationships

Friends, Social Life and Other Interesting Facts

Did you enjoy researching this person?

Give a Rating: ☆ ☆ ☆ ☆ ☆

TODAY IS RESEARCH DAY! **GRADE**________________

DATE___________ **RESEARCH: Dwight D. Eisenhower**

Occupation ____________________

BORN DATE: ____________________ **Nationality** ____________________

DEATH DATE: ____________________ **Education** ____________________ **#Children** __________

Childhood and Family Background Facts

Work and Career Facts

Children, Marriage and or Significant Relationships

Friends, Social Life and Other Interesting Facts

Did you enjoy researching this person?

Give a Rating: ☆ ☆ ☆ ☆ ☆

TODAY IS RESEARCH DAY! GRADE________________

DATE____________ **RESEARCH: Eleanor Roosevelt**

Occupation ______________________________

BORN DATE:______________________ Nationality ______________________

DEATH DATE:______________________ Education ______________________ #Children __________

Childhood and Family Background Facts

Work and Career Facts

Children, Marriage and or Significant Relationships

Friends, Social Life and Other Interesting Facts

Did you enjoy researching this person?

Give a Rating: ☆ ☆ ☆ ☆ ☆

TODAY IS RESEARCH DAY! GRADE________________

DATE___________ **RESEARCH: Warren Buffett**

Occupation ________________

BORN DATE:________________ Nationality________________

DEATH DATE:________________ Education________________ #Children________

Childhood and Family Background Facts

Work and Career Facts

Children, Marriage and or Significant Relationships

Friends, Social Life and Other Interesting Facts

Did you enjoy researching this person?

Give a Rating: ☆ ☆ ☆ ☆ ☆

TODAY IS RESEARCH DAY! GRADE_______________

DATE____________ **RESEARCH: Nelson Mandela**

Occupation ________________________________

BORN DATE:____________________ Nationality____________________

DEATH DATE:____________________ Education____________________ #Children __________

Childhood and Family Background Facts

Work and Career Facts

Children, Marriage and or Significant Relationships

Friends, Social Life and Other Interesting Facts

Did you enjoy researching this person?

Give a Rating: ☆ ☆ ☆ ☆ ☆

TODAY IS RESEARCH DAY!

GRADE_______________

DATE____________

RESEARCH: Ruth Bader Ginsburg

Occupation ____________________

BORN DATE: ____________________ Nationality ____________________

DEATH DATE: ____________________ Education ____________________ #Children ________

Childhood and Family Background Facts

Work and Career Facts

Children, Marriage and or Significant Relationships

Friends, Social Life and Other Interesting Facts

Did you enjoy researching this person?

Give a Rating: ☆ ☆ ☆ ☆ ☆

TODAY IS RESEARCH DAY! **GRADE**________________

DATE___________ **RESEARCH: Wild Bill Hickok**

Occupation ____________________

BORN DATE:____________________ **Nationality**____________________

DEATH DATE:____________________ **Education**____________________ **#Children** __________

Childhood and Family Background Facts

Work and Career Facts

Children, Marriage and or Significant Relationships

Friends, Social Life and Other Interesting Facts

Did you enjoy researching this person?

Give a Rating: ☆ ☆ ☆ ☆ ☆

TODAY IS RESEARCH DAY!

GRADE________________

DATE____________

RESEARCH: Davy Crockett

Occupation ____________________

BORN DATE:____________________ Nationality____________________

DEATH DATE:____________________ Education____________________ #Children ____________

Childhood and Family Background Facts

Work and Career Facts

Children, Marriage and or Significant Relationships

Friends, Social Life and Other Interesting Facts

Did you enjoy researching this person?

Give a Rating: ☆ ☆ ☆ ☆ ☆

TODAY IS RESEARCH DAY! GRADE____________________

DATE____________ **RESEARCH: William Cullen**

Occupation ______________________________

BORN DATE:______________________ Nationality______________________

DEATH DATE:____________________ Education______________________ #Children ________

Childhood and Family Background Facts

Work and Career Facts

Children, Marriage and or Significant Relationships

Friends, Social Life and Other Interesting Facts

Did you enjoy researching this person?

Give a Rating: ☆ ☆ ☆ ☆ ☆

TODAY IS RESEARCH DAY!

GRADE________________

DATE____________

RESEARCH: Texas Jack Omohundro

Occupation ______________________________

BORN DATE: ______________________ Nationality ______________________

DEATH DATE: ______________________ Education ______________________ #Children __________

Childhood and Family Background Facts

Work and Career Facts

Children, Marriage and or Significant Relationships

Friends, Social Life and Other Interesting Facts

Did you enjoy researching this person?

Give a Rating: ☆ ☆ ☆ ☆ ☆

TODAY IS RESEARCH DAY! GRADE________________

DATE____________ **RESEARCH:** Elizabeth Fries Lummis Ellet

Occupation ______________________________

BORN DATE: ______________________ Nationality ______________________

DEATH DATE: ______________ Education ______________________ #Children ________

Childhood and Family Background Facts

Work and Career Facts

Children, Marriage and or Significant Relationships

Friends, Social Life and Other Interesting Facts

Did you enjoy researching this person?

Give a Rating: ☆ ☆ ☆ ☆ ☆

TODAY IS RESEARCH DAY!

GRADE_______________

DATE___________ **RESEARCH: Susan B. Anthony**

Occupation ______________________________

BORN DATE: ______________________ Nationality ______________________

DEATH DATE: ______________ Education ______________________ #Children ________

Childhood and Family Background Facts

Work and Career Facts

Children, Marriage and or Significant Relationships

Friends, Social Life and Other Interesting Facts

Did you enjoy researching this person?

Give a Rating: ☆ ☆ ☆ ☆ ☆

TODAY IS RESEARCH DAY! GRADE_______________

DATE___________ **RESEARCH: Juliette Gordon Low**

Occupation ____________________

BORN DATE: ____________________ Nationality ____________________

DEATH DATE: ____________________ Education ____________________ #Children ________

Childhood and Family Background Facts

Work and Career Facts

Children, Marriage and or Significant Relationships

Friends, Social Life and Other Interesting Facts

Did you enjoy researching this person?

Give a Rating: ☆ ☆ ☆ ☆ ☆

TODAY IS RESEARCH DAY! GRADE________________

DATE___________ **RESEARCH: Buddha**

Occupation ____________________

BORN DATE: ____________________ Nationality ____________________

DEATH DATE: ____________________ Education ____________________ #Children __________

Childhood and Family Background Facts

Work and Career Facts

Children, Marriage and or Significant Relationships

Friends, Social Life and Other Interesting Facts

Did you enjoy researching this person?

Give a Rating: ☆ ☆ ☆ ☆ ☆

TODAY IS RESEARCH DAY! GRADE________________

DATE___________ **RESEARCH:** Martin Cooper

Occupation ______________________________

BORN DATE:______________________ Nationality ______________________

DEATH DATE:____________________ Education ____________________ #Children __________

Childhood and Family Background Facts

Work and Career Facts

Children, Marriage and or Significant Relationships

Friends, Social Life and Other Interesting Facts

Did you enjoy researching this person?

Give a Rating: ☆ ☆ ☆ ☆ ☆

TODAY IS RESEARCH DAY! GRADE________________

DATE____________ **RESEARCH:** Aristotle

Occupation ____________________

BORN DATE: ____________________ Nationality ____________________

DEATH DATE: ____________________ Education ____________________ #Children ________

Childhood and Family Background Facts

Work and Career Facts

Children, Marriage and or Significant Relationships

Friends, Social Life and Other Interesting Facts

Did you enjoy researching this person?

Give a Rating: ☆ ☆ ☆ ☆ ☆

TODAY IS RESEARCH DAY! GRADE________________

DATE____________ **RESEARCH: Francis Beaufort**

Occupation ______________________________

BORN DATE: ______________________ **Nationality** ______________________

DEATH DATE: ______________ **Education** ______________________ **#Children** ________

Childhood and Family Background Facts

Work and Career Facts

Children, Marriage and or Significant Relationships

Friends, Social Life and Other Interesting Facts

Did you enjoy researching this person?

Give a Rating: ☆ ☆ ☆ ☆ ☆

TODAY IS RESEARCH DAY! GRADE________________

DATE____________ **RESEARCH: Alan Archibald Campbell-Swinton**

Occupation ______________________________

BORN DATE: ______________________ Nationality ______________________

DEATH DATE: ______________________ Education ______________________ #Children __________

Childhood and Family Background Facts

Work and Career Facts

Children, Marriage and or Significant Relationships

Friends, Social Life and Other Interesting Facts

Did you enjoy researching this person?

Give a Rating: ☆ ☆ ☆ ☆ ☆

TODAY IS RESEARCH DAY! GRADE________________

DATE___________ **RESEARCH: Nicolaus Copernicus**

Occupation ______________________________

BORN DATE: ____________________ Nationality ____________________

DEATH DATE: ____________________ Education ____________________ #Children ________

Childhood and Family Background Facts

Work and Career Facts

Children, Marriage and or Significant Relationships

Friends, Social Life and Other Interesting Facts

Did you enjoy researching this person?

Give a Rating: ☆ ☆ ☆ ☆ ☆

TODAY IS RESEARCH DAY! GRADE________________

DATE____________ **RESEARCH: Friedrich Clemens Gerke**

Occupation ______________________________

BORN DATE: ______________________ Nationality ______________________

DEATH DATE: ____________________ Education ____________________ #Children ________

Childhood and Family Background Facts

Work and Career Facts

Children, Marriage and or Significant Relationships

Friends, Social Life and Other Interesting Facts

Did you enjoy researching this person?

Give a Rating: ☆ ☆ ☆ ☆ ☆

TODAY IS RESEARCH DAY! GRADE_______________

DATE____________ **RESEARCH: Ken Kutaragi**

Occupation ____________________

BORN DATE:____________________ Nationality____________________

DEATH DATE:____________________ Education____________________ #Children ________

Childhood and Family Background Facts

Work and Career Facts

Children, Marriage and or Significant Relationships

Friends, Social Life and Other Interesting Facts

Did you enjoy researching this person?

Give a Rating: ☆ ☆ ☆ ☆ ☆

TODAY IS RESEARCH DAY! GRADE________________

DATE____________ **RESEARCH: Charles Macintosh**

Occupation ____________________

BORN DATE: ____________________ Nationality ____________________

DEATH DATE: ____________________ Education ____________________ #Children ________

Childhood and Family Background Facts

Work and Career Facts

Children, Marriage and or Significant Relationships

Friends, Social Life and Other Interesting Facts

Did you enjoy researching this person?

Give a Rating: ☆ ☆ ☆ ☆ ☆

TODAY IS RESEARCH DAY!

GRADE________________

DATE____________ **RESEARCH: Ilya Ilyich Mechnikov**

Occupation ______________________________

BORN DATE:______________________ Nationality______________________

DEATH DATE:____________________ Education______________________ #Children ________

Childhood and Family Background Facts

Work and Career Facts

Children, Marriage and or Significant Relationships

Friends, Social Life and Other Interesting Facts

Did you enjoy researching this person?

Give a Rating: ☆ ☆ ☆ ☆ ☆

TODAY IS RESEARCH DAY! GRADE________________

DATE____________ **RESEARCH: Daniel David Palmer**

Occupation ____________________

BORN DATE: ____________________ Nationality ____________________

DEATH DATE: ____________________ Education ____________________ #Children __________

Childhood and Family Background Facts

Work and Career Facts

Children, Marriage and or Significant Relationships

Friends, Social Life and Other Interesting Facts

Did you enjoy researching this person?

Give a Rating: ☆ ☆ ☆ ☆ ☆

TODAY IS RESEARCH DAY! GRADE______________

DATE___________ **RESEARCH: Adolphe Sax**

Occupation ______________________________

BORN DATE:______________________ Nationality________________

DEATH DATE:_________________ Education ______________________ #Children _______

Childhood and Family Background Facts

Work and Career Facts

Children, Marriage and or Significant Relationships

Friends, Social Life and Other Interesting Facts

Did you enjoy researching this person?

Give a Rating: ☆ ☆ ☆ ☆ ☆

ANSWER SHEET

Your Identity and Reputation Online

Your online identity grows every time you use a social network, send a text, or make a post on a website, for example. Your online persona may be very different from your real-world persona – the way your friends, parents, and teachers see you.

One of the best things about having an online life is trying on different personas. If you want to change how you act and show up to people, you can. You can also learn more about things that you like. Steps to help you maintain control on the internet can be taken just like in real life.

Here are some things to think about to protect your online identity and reputation:

Nothing is temporary online. The worldwide web is full of opportunities to connect and share with other people. It's also a place with no " take-backs " or "temporary" situations. It's easy for other people to copy, save, and forward your information even if you delete it.

Add a "private" option for your profiles. Anyone can copy or screen-grab things that you don't want the world to see using social networking sites. Use caution when using the site's default settings. Each site has its own rules, so read them to ensure you're doing everything you can to keep your information safe.

Keep your passwords safe and change them often. Someone can ruin your reputation by pretending to be you online. The best thing to do is pick passwords that no one can guess. The only people who should know about them are your parents or someone else who you can trust. Your best friend, boyfriend, or girlfriend should not know your passwords.

Don't put up pictures or comments that are inappropriate or sexually provocative. In the future, things that are funny or cool to you now might not be so cool to someone else, like a teacher or admissions officer. If you don't want your grandmother, coach, or best friend's parents to see it, don't post it. Even on a private page, it could be hacked or copied and sent to someone else.

Don't give in to unwanted advances. There are a lot of inappropriate messages and requests for money that teenagers get when they're on the web. These things can be scary, weird, or even embarrassing , but they can also be exciting and fun. Do not keep quiet about being bullied online. Tell an adult you trust right away if a stranger or someone you know is bullying you. It's never a good idea to answer. If you respond, you might say something that makes things even worse.

You can go to www.cybertipline.org to report bad behavior or other problems.

Avoid "flaming" by taking a break now and then. Do you want to send an angry text or comment to someone? Relax for a few minutes and realize that the remarks will be there even if you have cooled off or change your mind about them.

People may feel free to write hurtful, derogatory , or abusive remarks on the internet if they can remain anonymous. We can be painful to others if we share things or make angry comments when we aren't facing someone. If they find out, it could change how they see us. If you wouldn't say it, show it, or do it in person, don't do it online.

Make sure you don't break copyright laws. Don't upload, share, or distribute copyrighted photographs, sounds, or files. Be aware of copyright restrictions. Sharing them is great, but doing so illegally runs the risk of legal repercussions down the road.

It's time for a self-evaluation. Take a look at your "digital footprint," which people can find out about you. When you search for your screen name or email address, see what comes up. That's one way to get a sense of what other people think of you online.

In the same way that your real-life identity is formed, your online identity and reputation are also formed. It's different when you're on the internet because you don't always have the chance to explain how you feel or what you mean. Thinking about what you're going to say and being responsible can help you avoid leaving an online trail that you'll later be sorry about.

ANSWER SHEET

History: Thomas Edison

Thomas Alva Edison was born in Milan, Ohio, on February 11, 1847. He developed **hearing** loss at a young age. He was a creative and inquisitive child. However, he struggled in school, possibly because he couldn't hear his **teacher** . He was then educated at home by his mother.

Because of his numerous important inventions, Thomas Edison was nicknamed the "wizard." On his own or in collaboration with others, he has designed and built more than 1,000 **devices** . The phonograph (record player), the lightbulb, and the motion-picture projector are among his most notable inventions.

Although Thomas did not invent the first electric **light** bulb, he did create the first practical electric light bulb that could be manufactured and used in the home. He also **invented** other items required to make the light bulb usable in homes, such as safety fuses and on/off switches for light sockets.

As a teenager, Thomas worked as a telegraph operator. Telegraphy was one of the most important communication systems in the country at the time. Thomas was skilled at sending and receiving **Morse** code messages. He enjoyed tweaking with telegraphic instruments, and he came up with several improvements to make them even better. By early 1869, he had left his telegraphy job to pursue his **dream** of becoming a full-time inventor.

Edison worked tirelessly with scientists and other collaborators to complete projects. He established **research** facilities in Menlo Park, California, and West Orange, New Jersey. Finally, Edison established companies that manufactured and sold his successful inventions.

Edison's family was essential to him, even though he spent the majority of his life **dedicated** to his work. He had six children from two marriages. Edison **passed** away on October 18, 1931.

ANSWER SHEET

Science: Invertebrates

Invertebrates can be found almost anywhere. Invertebrates account for at least 95% of all animals on the planet! Do you know what one thing they all have in common? Invertebrates lack a backbone.

Your body is supported by a backbone, which protects your organs and connects your other bones. As a result, you are a vertebrate. On the other hand, invertebrates lack the support of bones, so their bodies are often simpler, softer, and smaller. They are also cold-blooded, which means their body temperature fluctuates in response to changes in the air or water around them.

Invertebrates can be found flying, swimming, crawling, or floating and provide essential services to the environment and humans. Nobody knows how many different types of invertebrates there are, but there are millions!

Just because an invertebrate lacks a spinal column does not mean it does not need to eat. Invertebrates, like all other forms of animal life, must obtain nutrients from their surroundings. Invertebrates have evolved two types of digestion to accomplish this. The use of intracellular digestion is common in the most simple organisms. The food is absorbed into the cell and broken down in the cytoplasm at this point. Extracellular digestion, in which cells break down food through the secretion of enzymes and other techniques, is used by more advanced invertebrates. All vertebrates use extracellular digestion.

Still, all animals, invertebrates or not, need a way to get rid of waste. Most invertebrates, especially the simplest ones, use the process of diffusion to eliminate waste. This is merely the opposite of intracellular digestion. However, more advanced invertebrates have more advanced waste disposal mechanisms. Similar to our kidneys, specialized glands in these animals filter and excrete waste. But there is a happy medium. Even though some invertebrates do not have complete digestive tracts like vertebrates, they do not simply flush out waste through diffusion. Instead, the mouth doubles as an exit.

Scientists have classified invertebrates into numerous groups based on what the animals have in common. Arthropods have segmented bodies, which means that they are divided into sections. Consider an ant!

Arthropods are the most numerous group of invertebrates. They can live on land, as spiders and insects do, or in water, as crayfish and crabs do. Because insects are the most numerous group of arthropods, many of them fly, including mosquitoes, bees, locusts, and ladybugs.

They also have jointed legs or limbs to help them walk, similar to how you have knees for your legs and elbows for your arms. The majority of arthropods have an exoskeleton, tough outer skin, or shell that protects their body. Have you ever wondered why when you squish a bug, it makes that crunching sound? That's right; it's the exoskeleton!

Mollusks are the second most numerous group of invertebrates. They have soft bodies and can be found on land or in water. Shells protect the soft bodies of many mollusks, including snails, oysters, clams, and scallops. However, not all, such as octopus, squid, and cuttlefish, have a shell.

1. Invertebrates lack a ______.
   a. backbone
   b. tailbone

2. Invertebrates are also _____.
   a. cold-blooded
   b. warm-blooded

3. _____ can live on land, as spiders and insects do, or in water, as crayfish and crabs do.
   a. Vertebrates
   b. Arthropods

4. All animals, invertebrates or not, need a way to get rid of ____.
   a. their skin
   b. waste

5. _____ have soft bodies and can be found on land or in water.
   a. Arthropods
   b. Mollusks

6. Just because an invertebrate lacks a ______ column does not mean it does not need to eat.
   a. spinal
   b. tissues

7. Your body is supported by a backbone, which protects your ____ and connects your other bones.
   a. organs
   b. muscles

8. Invertebrates lack the support of bones, so their bodies are often simpler, ___, and smaller.
   a. softer and bigger
   b. softer and smaller

ANSWER SHEET

Weather and Climate

The difference between weather and climate is simply a matter of time. Weather refers to the conditions of the atmosphere over a short period of time, whereas climate refers to how the atmosphere "behaves" over a longer period of time.

When we discuss climate change, we are referring to changes in long-term averages of daily weather. Today's children are constantly told by their parents and grandparents about how the snow was always piled up to their waists as they trudged off to school. Most children today have not experienced those kinds of dreadful snow-packed winters. The recent changes in winter snowfall indicate that the climate has changed since their parents were children.

Weather is essentially the atmosphere's behavior, particularly in terms of its effects on life and human activities. The distinction between weather and climate is that weather refers to short-term (minutes to months) changes in the atmosphere, whereas climate refers to long-term changes. Most people associate weather with temperature, humidity, precipitation, cloudiness, brightness, visibility, wind, and atmospheric pressure, as in high and low pressure.

Weather can change from minute to minute, hour to hour, day to day, and season to season in most places. However, the climate is the average of weather over time and space. A simple way to remember the distinction is that climate is what you expect, such as a very hot summer, whereas weather is what you get, such as a hot day with pop-up thunderstorms.

Use the word bank to unscramble the words!

Pressure	Density	Cloudy	Latitude	Elevation	Weather
Absorb	Humid	Precipitation	Windy	Forecast	Climate
Sunshine	Temperature				

1. IUMHD	H u m i d	8. LEICATM	C l i m a t e
2. UDLOYC	C l o u d y	9. SNNIEHUS	S u n s h i n e
3. FSEATOCR	F o r e c a s t	10. OBBASR	A b s o r b
4. UDLTITAE	L a t i t u d e	11. VETIEOANL	E l e v a t i o n
5. IEOCAIIPPTRNT	P r e c i p i t a t i o n	12. EATWRHE	W e a t h e r
6. TEEERPAURMT	T e m p e r a t u r e	13. NDWIY	W i n d y
7. RSEREUPS	P r e s s u r e	14. TYNEIDS	D e n s i t y

ANSWER SHEET

Health: The Food Groups

Eating healthy foods is especially important for children because they are still developing. Children's bodies require nutrition to develop strong, healthy __bones__ and muscles. You will not grow as tall or as strong as you could if you do not get all the __vitamins__ and minerals you require while growing.

Healthy food includes a wide variety of fresh foods from the five healthy food groups:

Dairy: Milk, cheese, and __yogurt__ are the most critical dairy foods, which are necessary for strong and healthy bones. There aren't many other foods in our diet that have as much calcium as these.

Fruit: Fruit contains vitamins, minerals, dietary fiber, and various phytonutrients (nutrients found naturally in plants) that help your body stay healthy. Fruits and vegetables provide you with energy, vitamins, antioxidants, fiber, and __water__. These nutrients help protect you against diseases later in life, such as heart disease, stroke, and some cancers.

Vegetables and legumes/beans: Vegetables should account for a large __portion__ of your daily food intake and should be encouraged at all meals (including snack times). To keep your body healthy, they supply vitamins, minerals, dietary fiber, and phytonutrients (nutrients found naturally in plants).

Grain (cereal) foods: choose wholegrain and/or high __fiber__ bread, cereals, rice, pasta, noodles, and so on. These foods provide you with the energy you require to grow, develop, and learn. Refined grain products (such as cakes and biscuits) can contain added sugar, fat, and sodium.

Protein from lean meats and poultry, fish, eggs, tofu, nuts and seeds, and legumes/beans is used by our bodies to __produce__ specialized chemicals such as hemoglobin and adrenalin. Protein also helps to build, maintain, and __repair__ tissues in our bodies. Protein is the primary component of muscles and organs (such as your heart).

Calories are a unit of measurement for the amount of energy in food. We gain calories when we eat, which gives us the energy to run around and do things. If we __consume__ more calories than we expend while moving, our bodies will store the excess calories as fat. If we burn more calories than we consume, our bodies will begin to burn the previously __stored__ fat.

ANSWER SHEET

Music: The Piano

Bartolomeo Cristofori was the first to successfully develop a hammer-action keyboard instrument and hence deserves to be regarded as the creator of the piano.

Cristofori was dissatisfied with musicians' lack of control over the harpsichord's loudness level. Around 1700, he is credited for replacing the plucking mechanism with a hammer and thus creating the modern piano. Initially, the instrument was dubbed "clavicembalo con piano e forte" (literally, a harpsichord that can play soft and loud noises). This was later abbreviated to the now-common term "piano."

The piano possesses the characteristics of both a string and percussion instrument. A hammer strikes a string inside the piano (much like a percussion instrument). The piano's sounds and notes are produced by the vibration of these strings (like a string instrument).

The piano is commonly referred to as a keyboard instrument. This is because it is performed similarly to several other keyboard instruments, including the organ, harpsichord, electronic keyboards, and synthesizers.

The organ was the first keyboard instrument, dating back to the third century. However, the organ did not begin to use keys until much later. The harpsichord was invented in the 14th century and quickly gained popularity throughout Europe. The harpsichord plucked a string and resembled modern pianos in appearance. However, plucking the string did not allow for the playing of various volumes and expressions.

The term piano is derived from the Italian phrase pianoforte, which translates as "loud and soft." This is because you may now adjust the volume of notes played on the keyboard.

The grand piano and the upright piano are the two primary types of pianos.

Grand piano - a grand piano's strings and primary frame are horizontal. This enables longer strings and also aids in the piano's mechanics. However, grand pianos can consume a significant amount of room.

Upright piano - This piano style is more compact, making it ideal for use in a home. The strings and mainframe are arranged vertically.

Additionally, there are electronic pianos. While the keyboard and playing technique is typically identical to a standard piano, the sound is frequently quite different.

1. This piano style is more compact, making it ideal for use in a home.
   a. Upright piano
   b. Downright piano

2. A ____ strings and primary frame are horizontal.
   a. organ piano's
   b. grand piano's

3. The term piano is derived from the_____phrase pianoforte.
   a. English
   b. Italian

4. The ____ was invented in the 14th century.
   a. pianiochord
   b. harpsichord

5. The piano is commonly referred to as a ____ instrument.
   a. singer
   b. keyboard

6. The organ and harpsichord are keyboard instruments.
   a. organ
   b. guitar

ANSWER SHEET

English: Personal Pronouns

Personal pronouns are words that are used to replace the subject or object of a sentence to make it easier for readers to understand.

To give a brief, personal pronouns are:

1. Replace nouns and other pronouns to make sentences easier to read and understand.

2. A sentence's subject or object can be either. For example, 'I' is the first-person subject pronoun, whereas 'me' is the first-person object pronoun.

3. It is possible to use the singular or plural form.

4. They must agree on gender and number with the words they are substituting.

1. Which of the following sentences has a plural subject pronoun and a plural object pronoun?

a. She wants to live as long as she can, as long as she have someone by her side.

b. While Tom believe everything will be fine, many don't agree with him.

c. Whether we lived or died, it didn't matter to us either way.

2. Which of the following words would make the following sentence grammatically correct? '6th graders should check with their teachers before you leave the classroom.'

a. Replace 'their' with 'they'

b. Replace 'you' with 'they'

c. Replace '6th graders' with 'they'

3. The pronoun 'my' is a . . .

a. 1st person possessive pronoun

b. 3rd person nominative pronoun

c. 2nd person possessive pronoun

4. Which of the following correctly identifies the subjective and objective pronouns in the sentence here? 'Run away from the dinosaurs with the giant feet?' she asked. 'You don't have to tell me twice.'

a. she - subject pronoun; you - subject pronoun; me - object pronoun

b. she - object pronoun; you - object pronoun; me - object pronoun

c. she - object pronoun; you - subject pronoun; me - object pronoun

5. The pronoun 'your' is a . . .

a. 2nd person possessive pronoun

b. 1st person possessive pronoun

c. 2nd person objective pronoun

6. Which pronouns are found in the following sentence? 'I kept telling her that we would go back for John, but I knew we had left him behind. '

a. I, we, knew, we, him

b. I, her, we, I, we, him

c. I, we, I, we, him

7. Kevin likes playing basketball. _________ is a very good player.

a. Him

b. He

c. Their

8. The pronoun 'its' is a . . .

a. 3rd person possessive pronoun

b. 2nd person possessive pronoun

c. 3rd person objective pronoun

9. The pronoun 'their' is a . . .

a. 2nd person possessive pronoun

b. 3rd person objective pronoun

c. 3rd person possessive pronoun

10. Kimmy is a very good cook. _________ can cook any kind of food.

a. She

b. Hey

c. Their

ANSWER SHEET

Reading Comprehension: Law Enforcement Dogs

Police dogs are dogs that assist cops in solving crimes. In recent years, they have grown to be an essential part of law enforcement. With their unique abilities and bravery, police dogs have saved many lives. They are often regarded as an important and irreplaceable part of many police departments because they are loyal, watchful, and protective of their police officer counterparts.

Today, police dogs are trained in specific areas. They could be considered experts in their field. Some of the particular police dog roles are as follows:

Tracking: Tracking police dogs use their keen sense of smell to locate criminal suspects or missing people. Tracking dogs are trained for years and can track down even the most elusive criminal. Without police tracking dogs, many suspects would be able to elude capture.

Substance Detectors: Like tracking dogs, these police dogs use their sense of smell to assist officers. Substance dogs are trained to detect a specific substance. Some dogs are trained to detect bombs or explosives. These brave dogs are trained not only to detect explosives but also to respond (very carefully!) and safely alert their officer partner to the explosive location. Other dogs may be drawn to illegal drugs. By quickly determining whether an illegal substance is nearby, these dogs save officers from searching through luggage, a car, or other areas by hand.

Public Order - These police dogs assist officers in keeping the peace. They may pursue a criminal suspect and hold them until an officer arrives, or they may guard an area (such as a jail or prison) to prevent suspects from fleeing.

Cadaver Dogs: Although it may sound disgusting, these police dogs are trained to locate dead bodies. This is a critical function in a police department, and these dogs perform admirably.

A police dog is not just any dog. Police dogs require very special and specialized training. There are numerous breeds of dogs that have been trained for police work. What breed they are often determined by the type of work they will do. German Shepherds and Belgian Malinois are two of the most popular breeds today, but other dogs such as Bloodhounds (good for tracking) and Beagles (good for drug detection) are also used. Police dogs, regardless of breed, are typically trained to do their job from the time they are puppies.

Typically, police dogs are regarded as heroes. They frequently go to live with their human partner police officer. They've known this person for years and have grown to consider them family, which works out well for both the officer and the dog.

1. Tracking police dogs use their ______ to locate criminal suspects or missing people.

a. keen sense of training
b. keen sense of taste
c. keen sense of smell

2. Some substance dogs are trained to detect _____.

a. runaway children
b. bombs or explosives
c. metal and iron

3. Police dogs are trained in ___ areas.

a. many
b. a few
c. specific

4. Police dogs are dogs that assist cops in solving _____.

a. littering
b. homelessness
c. crimes

5. Substance dogs are trained to detect a specific ____.

a. substance
b. person
c. other police dogs

6. What type of police dog is trained pursue a criminal suspect and hold them until an officer arrives?

a. Crime Fighting dog
b. Tracking dog
c. Public Order dog

7. These police dogs are trained to locate dead bodies

a. Law and Order dogs
b. Cadaver dogs
c. Deadly Substance dogs

8. What are the two most popular police dogs used today?

a. German Shepherds and Belgian Malinois
b. Bloodhounds and German Shepherds
c. Belgian Malinois and Rottweiler

ANSWER SHEET

Spelling: How Do You Spell It?
Part I

	A	B	C	D
1.	**grade**	grrada	grrade	grada
2.	**elementary**	elenmentary	ellenmentary	ellementary
3.	**marks**	marrcks	marrks	marcks
4.	repurt	reporrt	**report**	repurrt
5.	schedolle	**schedule**	schedole	schedulle
6.	timetible	**timetable**	timettable	timettible
7.	**highlight**	highllight	hyghllight	hyghlight
8.	foell	foel	fuell	**fuel**
9.	instrucsion	insstruction	**instruction**	insstrucsion
10.	senttence	sentance	senttance	**sentence**
11.	**vaccination**	vacination	vaccinasion	vacinasion
12.	**proof**	prwf	prouf	proph
13.	mandatury	mandattury	**mandatory**	mandattory
14.	**final**	fynall	finall	fynal
15.	envellope	**envelope**	envellupe	envelupe
16.	equattor	eqauttor	eqautor	**equator**
17.	bllanks	**blanks**	blancks	bllancks
18.	honorible	honorrable	**honorable**	honorrible
19.	scaince	sceince	**science**	sciance
20.	mussic	mosic	muscic	**music**
21.	**history**	hisstory	hisctory	histury
22.	lissten	liscten	lysten	**listen**
23.	entrence	enttrance	enttrence	**entrance**
24.	especialy	especailly	especaily	**especially**
25.	mariage	maraige	marraige	**marriage**

ANSWER SHEET

Spelling: How Do You Spell It? Part II

	A	B	C	D
1.	compllain	complian	**complain**	compllian
2.	negattyve	negatyve	**negative**	negattive
3.	**importance**	importence	imporrtance	imporrtence
4.	encourragement	**encouragement**	encourragenment	encouragenment
5.	shallves	**shelves**	shellves	shalves
6.	**mixture**	mixttore	mixtore	mixtture
7.	honorrable	**honorable**	honorible	honorrible
8.	lagall	legall	lagal	**legal**
9.	manar	mannar	**manner**	maner
10.	encycllopedia	**encyclopedia**	encycllopedai	encyclopedai
11.	repllacement	replacenment	repllacenment	**replacement**
12.	medycie	medycine	**medicine**	medicie
13.	experriance	**experience**	experiance	experrience
14.	**hunger**	hunjer	hungerr	hunjerr
15.	sallote	sallute	salote	**salute**
16.	horrizon	hurizon	hurrizon	**horizon**
17.	sestion	**session**	setion	sesion
18.	shorrten	shurten	**shorten**	shurrten
19.	fuacett	faucett	fuacet	**faucet**
20.	haadache	haadace	haedache	**headache**
21.	**further**	furrther	forrther	forther
22.	injurry	injory	**injury**	injorry
23.	disstance	distence	**distance**	disstence
24.	rattio	**ratio**	rattoi	ratoi
25.	independense	**independence**	independance	independanse

ANSWER SHEET

Spelling: How Do You Spell It?
Part III

Write and circle the correct spelling for each word.

	A	B	C	D
1.	**invitation**	invittasion	invitasion	invittation
2.	denuminator	**denominator**	denuminattor	denominattor
3.	**personal**	perrsonal	perrsunal	persunal
4.	rapkd	**rapid**	rahid	rapyd
5.	oryginal	**original**	orryginal	orriginal
6.	liquvd	liqiod	liqoid	**liquid**
7.	desscendant	**descendant**	dessendant	desssendant
8.	dissastrous	**disastrous**	dissastroos	disastroos
9.	cooperasion	**cooperation**	coperation	coperasion
10.	**routine**	roottine	routtine	rootine
11.	earleist	earrleist	earrliest	**earliest**
12.	acidentally	**accidentally**	acidentalli	accidentalli
13.	rehaerrse	rehearrse	rehaerse	**rehearse**
14.	quotte	qoote	**quote**	qootte
15.	capablla	capablle	**capable**	capible
16.	apointment	appointnment	apointnment	**appointment**
17.	mussician	mussicain	musicain	**musician**
18.	nomerrator	numerrator	**numerator**	nomerator
19.	**inquire**	inqoire	inquirre	inqoirre
20.	**remote**	remute	remutte	remotte
21.	pryncipal	prrincipal	prryncipal	**principal**
22.	sylent	sillent	syllent	**silent**
23.	locatsion	locasion	**location**	locattion
24.	edision	**edition**	editsion	edittion

ANSWER SHEET

Health: Check Your Symptoms

1. **I've got a pain in my head.**
   a. Stiff neck
   b. headache
2. **I was out in the sun too long.**
   a. Sunburn
   b. Fever
3. **I've got a small itchy lump or bump.**
   a. Rash
   b. Insect bite
4. **I might be having a heart attack.**
   a. Cramps
   b. Chest pain
5. **I've lost my voice.**
   a. Laryngitis
   b. Sore throat
6. **I need to blow my nose a lot.**
   a. Runny nose
   b. Blood Nose
7. **I have an allergy. I have a**
   a. Rash
   b. Insect bite
8. **My shoe rubbed my heel. I have a**
   a. Rash
   b. Blister
9. **The doctor gave me antibiotics. I have a/an**
   a. Infection
   b. Cold
10. **I think I want to vomit. I am**
    a. Nauseous
    b. Bloated
11. **My arm is not broken. It is**
    a. Scratched
    b. Sprained
12. **My arm touched the hot stove. It is**
    a. Burned
    b. Bleeding
13. **I have an upset stomach. I might**
    a. Cough
    b. Vomit
14. **The doctor put plaster on my arm. It is**
    a. Sprained
    b. Broken
15. **If you cut your finger it will**
    a. Burn
    b. Bleed
16. **I hit my hip on a desk. It will**
    a. Burn
    b. Bruise
17. **When you have hay-fever you will**
    a. Sneeze
    b. Wheeze
18. **A sharp knife will**
    a. Scratch
    b. Cut

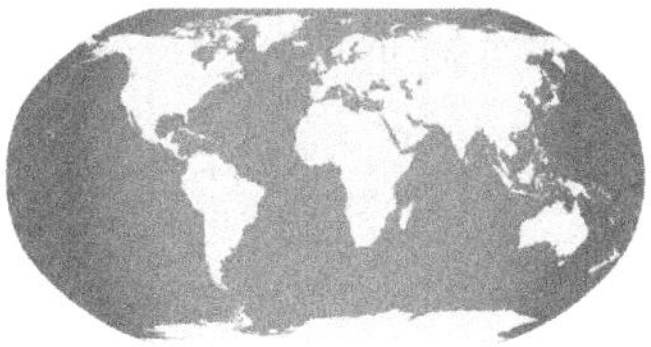

ANSWER SHEET

Geography: Know Your World

Test your knowledge of global, national, and local geography, as well as the environment.

1. Spain can be found in which continent
   a. Europe
   b. New Zealand
   c. Bogota

2. Uganda can be found in which continent
   a. Canberra
   b. Africa
   c. Lake Taupo

3. Uruguay can be found in which continent
   a. South America
   b. Atlantic Ocean
   c. Bogota

4. Beijing is the capital city of
   a. China
   b. Samoa
   c. New York

5. Honshu is an island of what country
   a. Japan
   b. Suva
   c. New York

6. Apia is the capital city of
   a. Bogota
   b. Samoa
   c. Brasilia

7. The Amazon River can be found in which continent
   a. Suva
   b. Buenos Aires
   c. South America

8. The Southern Alps can be found in which country
   a. Portugal
   b. New Zealand
   c. Brasilia

9. The Andes Mountains can be found in which continent
   a. Brasilia
   b. South America
   c. Berlin

10. Lines of longitude run
   a. Vertical - North to South
   b. Wellington
   c. Samoa

11. Lines of latitude run
   a. Horizontal - East to West
   b. Suva
   c. Italy

12. The ocean between the Americas and Europe and Africa is the
   a. Africa
   b. Italy
   c. Atlantic Ocean

13. The capital city of France is
   a. Bogota
   b. Paris
   c. Buenos Aires

14. The capital city of Germany is
   a. Berlin
   b. New Zealand
   c. Moscow

15. The capital city of Russia is

a. Moscow

b. Buenos Aires

c. Paris

16. The capital city of the United States is

a. Brasilia

b. Washington D.C

c. China

17. The capital city of Fiji is

a. Suva

b. Portugal

c. Buenos Aires

18. Mt Everest can be found in what continent

a. Asia

b. Japan

c. Wellington

19. Switzerland is a country in

a. Europe

b. Wellington

c. Portugal

20. The capital city of Brazil is

a. Japan

b. China

c. Brasilia

21. The capital city of Colombia is

a. Spain

b. Bogota

c. Japan

22. The capital city of Argentina is

a. Buenos Aires

b. Portugal

c. Bogota

23. Vietnam can be found in what continent

a. Asia

b. Berlin

c. Vertical - North to South

24. Libya can be found in what continent

a. Africa

b. Bogota

c. New York

25. Rome is the capital city of which European country

a. Buenos Aires

b. Italy

c. Paris

26. Madrid is the capital city of which European country

a. Brasilia

b. Europe

c. Spain

27. Lisbon is the capital city of which European country

a. Samoa

b. Portugal

c. Buenos Aires

28. The Statue of Liberty can be found in what US city

a. Italy

b. New York

c. Paris

29. The capital city of New Zealand is

a. Canberra

b. Wellington

c. Washington D.C

30. The capital city of Australia is

a. China

b. Moscow

c. Canberra

31. What is the largest lake in New Zealand?

a. Spain

b. Lake Taupo

c. Washington D.C

ANSWER SHEET

Grammar: Is vs. Are

Use **is** if the noun is singular. If the noun is plural or there are multiple nouns, use **are**.

1. ____ Billy?
1. Where are
2. Where's

2. ____ in the bed.
1. They're
2. He's

3. ____ Mum and Dad?
1. Where's
2. Where are

4. _____ in the kitchen.
1. She's
2. They're

5. ____ Grandpa?
1. Where are
2. Where's

6. ____ in the garden.
1. He's
2. She's

7. ____ Lucy and Lilly?
1. Where's
2. Where are

8. ____ in the park.
1. She's
2. They're

9. ____ my sister?
1. Where are
2. Where's

10. ____ in her bedroom.
1. He's
2. She's

11. ____ pupils?
1. Where are
2. Where's

12. ____ at school.
1. He's
2. They're

ANSWER SHEET

Grammar: Linking Verbs

A linking verb links the topic of a phrase to a word that describes the subject, such as a condition or a relationship. They don't depict any action; instead, they serve to connect the subject to the rest of the phrase or sentence.

In a sentence, helping verbs always appear before the primary verb. They complete the structure of a phrase by adding information to the main verb. They can also help you understand how time is expressed in a sentence.

To connect nouns, pronouns, and adjectives, both the supporting and linking verb are utilized.

1. Which of the following examples best shows what a linking verb is?

a. Shows action

b. Connects a subject to the predicate

c. Connects a noun and verb

2. How can you determine the difference between a helping verb and a linking verb?

a. There is no difference between a helping verb and a linking verb.

b. The helping verb is combined with an action verb.

c. The helping verb or adverb shows action.

3. Which words belong to the category of state of being verbs?

a. were, am, are, been

b. flow, jump, bounce

c. she, he, they, did

4. Which of the following examples does not connect subject and a predicate?

a. Tiffany is an awesome student.

b. She became the best mom ever!

c. It danced quietly and smoothly.

5. What distinguishes a connecting verb from an action verb?

a. It is an adjective.

b. It shows no action.

c. It shows action and no action.

6. The tomato smells rotten. Which is the linking verb in this sentence?

a. rotten

b. smells

c. tomato

7. My brother is mad when he's hungry.

a. is

b. mad

c. when

8. Identify the linking verb: The girl was frightened.

a. girl

b. was

c. frightened

9. What is the linking verb in the sentence? Rob and Tony were class leaders.

a. were

b. class

c. none

10. The Queen__________ busy laying eggs.

a. is

b. bee

c. are

ANSWER SHEET

History Reading Comprehension: Walt Disney

On December 5, 1901, Walter Elias Disney was born in **Chicago**, Illinois. His family relocated to a farm outside of Marceline, Missouri, when he was **four** years old, thanks to his parents, Elias and Flora. Walt loved growing up on the farm with his three older brothers (Herbert, Raymond, and Roy) and younger **sister** (Ruth). Walt discovered his passion for drawing and art in Marceline.

The Disneys relocated to Kansas City after four years in Marceline. On weekends, Walt continued to draw and attend **art** classes. He even bartered his drawings for free haircuts with a local barber. Walt got a summer job on a train. On the **train**, he walked back and forth, selling **snacks** and newspapers. Walt had a great time on the train and would be fascinated by trains for the rest of his life.

Walt's family relocated to Chicago around the time he started high school. Walt studied at the Chicago Art Institute and worked as a cartoonist for the school **newspaper**. Walt decided at the age of sixteen that he wanted to fight in World War I. Due to the fact that he was still too young to join the army, he decided to drop out of school and join the **Red** Cross instead.

Walt aspired to create his own animated cartoons. He founded his own company, Laugh-O-Gram. He sought the help of some of his **friends**, including Ubbe Iwerks.

Disney, on the other hand, was not going to be deterred by a single setback. In 1923, he relocated to **Hollywood**, California, and founded the Disney Brothers' Studio with his **brother** Roy. He enlisted the services of Ubbe Iwerks and a number of other animators once more.

Walt had to start all over again. This time, he came up with a new character called **Mickey** Mouse.
The movie was a huge success. Disney kept working, creating new characters like **Donald** Duck, Goofy, and Pluto.

In 1932, Walt Disney decided to create a full-length animated film called Snow **White**.

Disney used the proceeds from Snow White to establish a film studio and produce other animated films such as Pinocchio, Fantasia, Dumbo, Bambi, **Alice** in Wonderland, and **Peter** Pan.

Disney's Wonderful World of Color, the Davy Crockett series, and the Mickey Mouse **Club** was among the first Disney television shows to air on network television.

Disney, who is constantly coming up with new ideas, had the idea to build a **theme** park featuring rides and entertainment based on his films. In 1955, Disneyland opened its doors. It cost $17 million to construct. Although it wasn't an immediate success, Disney World has since grown into one of the world's most popular **vacation** destinations.

Every year, millions of people enjoy his films and theme parks. Every year, his company continues to produce fantastic films and **entertainment**.

Reading Comprehension Multiple Choice: Walt Disney

Make sure you go back and read the Disney article through to the very end. If you attempt to complete this assignment solely by scanning for answers, you will almost certainly pick the incorrect answer. Take your time. Ask questions. Get help if you need it. Good Luck!

1. Walter Elias Disney was born in Chicago, ____.
   a. Illinois
   b. Italy

2. Walter's parents names were Elias and Flora.
   a. True
   b. False

3. Walt got a summer job on a _____.
   a. train
   b. boat

4. Walt's younger sister name was ____.
   a. Ruby
   b. Ruth

5. Walt had _____ brothers.
   a. three
   b. two

6. In 1923, walt relocated to Hollywood, ______.
   a. Colorado
   b. California

7. Steamboat ____ was the title of the film, which starred Mickey and Minnie Mouse.
   a. William
   b. Willie

8. Walt spent the next year in France driving _____ for the Red Cross.
   a. taxi cabs
   b. ambulances

9. Walt and his friends created the well-known character Oswald the Lucky _____t.
   a. Dog
   b. Rabbi

10. Walt's first color animated film was____.
   a. Bears and Tigers
   b. Flowers and Trees

11. In ____, Disneyland opened its doors.
   a. 1955
   b. 1995

12. _____ was among the first Disney television shows to air on network television.
   a. Mickey Mouse Club
   b. Mickey and Friends

13. _____ was his first major live-action film.
   a. Treasure Island
   b. Treats Island

14. Walt Disney decided to create a full-length animated film called _____.
   a. Snow White
   b. Robin Hood

ANSWER SHEET

Grammar: some, any, a, an

A is used when the next word starts with a consonant sound.
AN is used when the next word starts with a vowel sound.
Some is generally used in positive sentences.
Any is generally used in negative sentences.

Rewrite the *scrambled words* so they form a complete *sentence.*

1. We don't have any apples.

   We any have don't apples.

2. We can make some sandwiches for lunch.

   make some lunch. for sandwiches We can

3. There isn't any milk in the fridge.

   fridge. in There the isn't any milk

4. I need to buy an onion and some tomatoes.

   buy I to tomatoes. and an onion need some

5. She doesn't need any tomatoes or carrots.

   carrots. need any tomatoes or doesn't She

6. Do we have any potatoes?

   have any we potatoes? Do

7. We have some strawberries but we don't have any grapes.

   some grapes. We have don't but we strawberries any have

8. There isn't any sugar in the bowl.

   There any isn't sugar in bowl. the

9. Can I have a banana, please?

   Can a I banana, have please?

10. Are there any apples on the counter?

on · there · the · any · apples · counter? · Are

11. It wasn't an easy decision.

decision. · an · wasn't · easy · It

12. She forced a smile.

a · She · forced · smile.

13. I have an appointment.

an · I · appointment. · have

14. He is an excellent horseman, you know.

horseman, · you · excellent · He · an · is · know.

15. It's an easy job, like I expected.

I · job, · an · easy · It's · expected. · like

16. That was a no-brainer.

That · was · no-brainer. · a

17. I think you owe me an explanation.

I · an · owe · me · think · you · explanation.

18. Suddenly he stopped at the foot of a tree.

at · the · tree. · foot · of · he · stopped · a · Suddenly

ANSWER SHEET

History Reading Comprehension: John Hanson

1. Hanson served from November 5, 1781 until December 3, 1782
   a. True
   b. False

2. Hanson really LOVED his job.
   a. True
   b. False

3. Under the Articles of Confederation, the United States had no ________.
   a. executive branch
   b. congress office

4. The President of Congress was a _____ position within the Confederation Congress.
   a. senate
   b. ceremonial

5. In November 1781, Hanson became the first President of the United States in Congress Assembled, under the _____.
   a. Articles of Congress
   b. Articles of Confederation

6. ____ men were appointed to serve one year terms as president under the Articles of Confederation.
   a. Eight
   b. Two

7. Hanson was able to remove all _____ troops from American lands.
   a. foreign
   b. USA

8. Hanson is also responsible for establishing _____ as the fourth Thursday in November.
   a. Christmas Day
   b. Thanksgiving Day

9. Instead of the four year term that current Presidents serve, Presidents under the Articles of Confederation served only ___ year.
   a. one
   b. three

10. Hanson died on November 15, 1783 at the age of ____.
    a. 64
    b. sixty-two

11. Both George Washington and Hanson are commemorated with ____ in the United States Capitol in Washington, D.C.
    a. houses
    b. statues

12. George Washington in the military sphere and John Hanson in the ____ sphere.
    a. presidential
    b. political

ANSWER SHEET

Geography: Canada

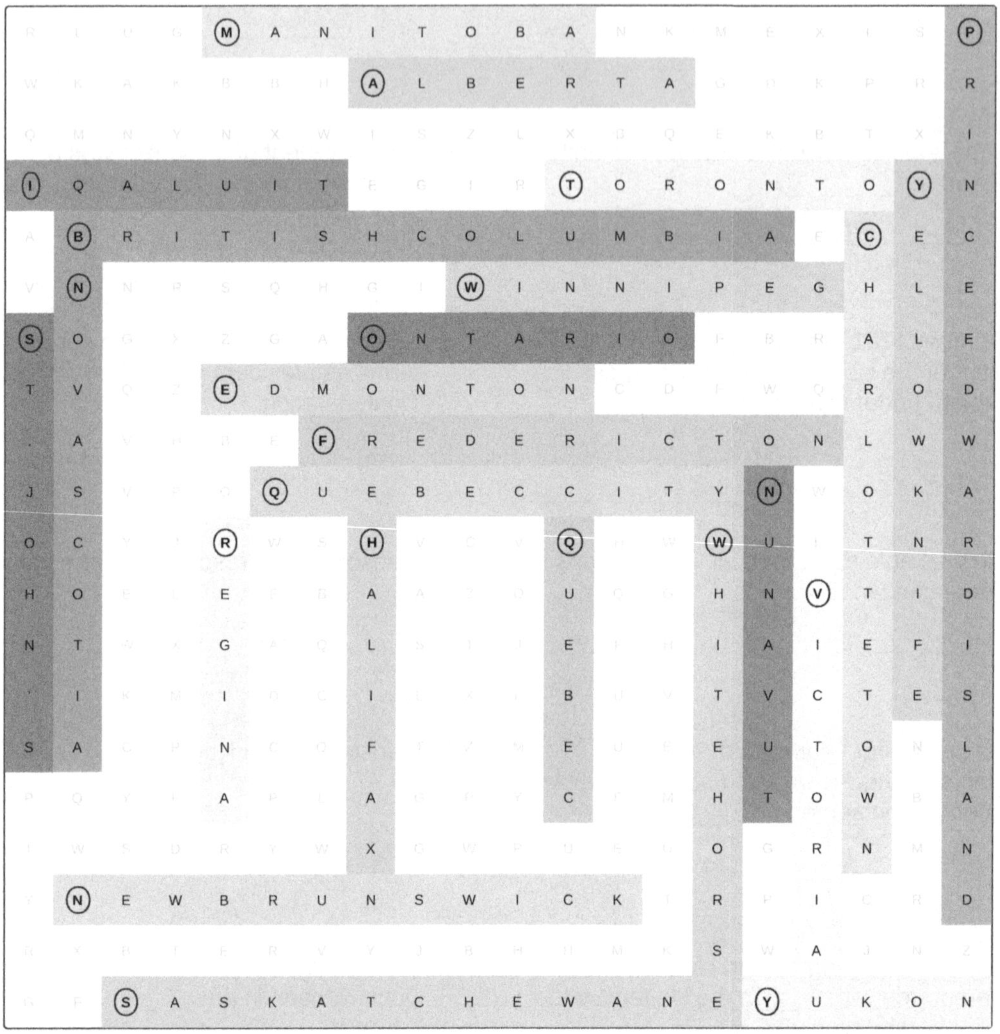

Yukon → | Nunavut ↓ | Nova Scotia ↓ | Prince Edward Island ↓ | New Brunswick → | Quebec ↓ | Ontario → | Manitoba →

Saskatchewan → | Alberta → | British Columbia → | Victoria ↓ | Edmonton → | Regina ↓ | Winnipeg → | Toronto →

Quebec City → | Fredericton → | Charlottetown ↓ | Halifax ↓ | St. John's ↓ | Iqaluit → | Yellowknife ↓ | Whitehorse ↓

24 words in Wordsearch: 11 vertical, 13 horizontal, 0 diagonal. (0 reversed.)

ANSWER SHEET

History: Henry VIII

Read about Henry VIII and answer whatever questions you can.

Read here: https://www.britannica.com/biography/Henry-VIII-king-of-England (or Google "**Britannica.com Henry VIII**")

1. **Henry only became king because his elder brother died young.**
   a. True
   b. False

2. **The Tudors were an English royal dynasty in the 15th century.**
   a. True
   b. False

3. **The young Henry 8th was a weak and sickly young man.**
   a. True
   b. False

4. **His father, Henry 7th, was an unpopular king.**
   a. True
   b. False

5. **Henry tried to emulate his father's way of ruling.**
   a. True
   b. False

6. **Henry married Catherine of Aragon, his brother's wife.**
   a. True
   b. False

7. **Henry had a good relationship with his father-in-law, Ferdinand 2**
   a. True
   b. False

8. **Europe's unity at the time depended on a balance of power between Spain and France.**
   a. True
   b. False

9. **Cardinal Wolsey was a trusted advisor and friend of Henry 8.**
   a. True
   b. False

10. **Many thought that it was actually Wolsey who ruled England.**
    a. True
    b. False

11. **Henry disapproved of Wolsey's ambition of becoming the pope.**
    a. True
    b. False

12. **When Charles 5 came to power, Henry lost influence in Europe.**
    a. True
    b. False

13. **Wolsey lost power when his plans damaged English trade with the Netherlands**
    a. True
    b. False

14. **Ferdinand 2 of Aragon was Queen Catherine's grandfather.**
    a. True
    b. False

15. **By 1523 the English were becoming increasingly dissatisfied with the king.**
   a. True
   b. False

16. **By 1527 Wolsey's policies had brought England to the point of bankruptcy.**
   a. True
   b. False

17. **"The King's Matter" was a plan to break away from the Catholic Church.**
   a. True
   b. False

18. **Henry was a strong believer in the Catholic Church.**
   a. True
   b. False

19. **Both the pope and Henry believed he had been wrong to marry Catherine of Aragon.**
   a. True
   b. False

20. **The pope refused to annul Henry's marriage because a previous pope had allowed it.**
   a. True
   b. False

21. **Henry got rid of Wolsey because he couldn't find a solution to his marital problem.**
   a. True
   b. False

22. **Thomas More promised to help the king divorce.**
   a. True
   b. False

23. **Henry, with Thomas More, tried to preserve Catholicism in England.**
   a. True
   b. False

24. **Thomas More organised the break from Rome in 1532.**
   a. True
   b. False

25. **The split from Rome made the king the leader of the new church.**
   a. True
   b. False

26. **The king converted to protestantism because he no longer believed in the Catholic Church.**
   a. True
   b. False

27. **Henry created a completely new church based on his own religious beliefs.**
   a. True
   b. False

28. **Henry was a great admirer of Luther and used him for inspiration.**
   a. True
   b. False

29. **Henry was excommunicated by the pope.**
   a. True
   b. False

30. **Henry raised money by selling the Catholic Church's lands in England.**
   a. True
   b. False

ANSWER SHEET

Math Vocabulary Quiz

1. algebraic equation

equality of two expressions formulated by applying to a set of variables the algebraic operations

2. direct evidence

evidence that, if believed, directly proves a fact

3. variable

a symbol (usually a letter) standing in for an unknown numerical value in an equation

4. scale factor

the ratio of the lengths of two corresponding sides of two similar polygons or solids

5. computation

Finding an answer by using mathematics or logic

6. equivalent

two meanings, numbers, or quantities that are the same

7. equation

two math expressions are equal (indicated by the sign =)

8. analyze

to study or determine the nature and relationship of the parts of (something) by analysis

9. structure

the way that something is built, arranged, or organized

10. summarize

Express the most important facts or ideas about something or someone in a short and clear form

11. addends

A quantity to be added to another

12. place value

the basis of our entire number system

13. difference

The result of subtracting one number from another.

14. divisor

a number by which another number is to be divided.

15. numerator

number above the line of a fraction, showing the number of parts of the whole

16. quotient

number obtained by dividing one number by another

ANSWER SHEET

Math: Look It Up! Pop Quiz

Learn some basic vocabulary words that you will come across again and again in the course of your studies in algebra. By knowing the definitions of most algebra words, you will be able to construct and solve algebra problems much more easily.

Find the answer to the questions below by *looking up each word. (The wording can be tricky. Take your time.)*

1. improper fraction
  a. a fraction that represents both positive and negative numbers that has a value more than 1
  b. a fraction in which the numerator is greater than the denominator, is always 1 or greater
  c. a fraction that the denominator is equal to the numerator

2. equivalent fraction
  a. a fraction that has a DIFFERENT value as a given fraction
  b. a fraction that has the SAME value as a given fraction
  c. a fraction that has an EQUAL value as a given fraction

3. simplest form of fraction
  a. an equivalent fraction for which the only common factor of the numerator and denominator is 1
  b. an equivalent fraction for which the only least factor of the denominator is -1
  c. an equal value fraction for which the only common factor of the numerator and denominator is -1

4. mixed number
  a. the sum of a positive fraction and a reciprocal
  b. the sum of a whole number and a proper fraction
  c. the sum of a variable and a fraction

5. reciprocal
  a. a number that can be multiplied by another number to make 1
  b. a number that can be divided by another number to make 10
  c. a number that can be subtracted by another number to make -1

6. percent
  a. a ratio that compares a number to 100
  b. a percentage that compares a number to 0.1
  c. a 1/2 ratio that equals a number to 100

7. sequence

a. a set of addition numbers that follow a operation

b. a set of letters & numbers divided by 5 that makes a sequence

c. a set of numbers that follow a pattern

8. arithmetic sequence

a. a sequence where ONE term is found by dividing or subtracting the exact same number to the previous term

b. a sequence where NO term is found by multiplying the exact same number to the previous term

c. a sequence where EACH term is found by adding or subtracting the exact same number to the previous term

9. geometric sequence

a. a sequence where each term is found by multiplying or dividing by the exact same number to the previous term

b. a sequence where each term is divided or subtracted by the same fraction to the previous term

c. a sequence where each term is solved by adding or dividing by a different number to the previous term

10. order of operations

a. the procedure to follow when simplifying a numerical expression

b. the procedure to follow when adding any fraction by 100

c. the procedure to follow when simplifying an equation with the same answer

11. variable expression

a. a mathematical phrase that contains numbers and operation symbols

b. a mathematical phrase that contains variables, addition, and operation sequence

c. a mathematical phrase that contains variables, numbers, and operation symbols

12. absolute value

a. a whole number on the number line from one to zero

b. the distance a number is from zero on the number line

c. the range a number is from one on the number line

13. integers

a. a set of numbers that equal to fractions line variables

b. a set of numbers that includes equal numbers and their difference

c. a set of numbers that includes whole numbers and their opposites

14. x-axis

a. the horizontal number line that, together with the y-axis, establishes the coordinate plane

b. the vertical number line that, together with the y-axis, establishes the coordinate plane

c. both horizontal & vertical number line that, together with the y-axis, establishes the coordinate plane

15. y-axis

a. the horizontal number line that, together with the x-axis, establishes the coordinate plane

b. the vertical number line that, together with the x-axis, establishes the coordinate plane

c. the vertical number line that, together with the x or y-axis, establishes the coordinate plane

16. coordinate plane

a. plane formed by two number lines (the horizontal x-axis and the vertical y-axis) intersecting at their zero points

b. plane formed by three number line (the vertical y-axis and the horizontal x-axis) intersecting at their two points

c. plane formed by one number line (the horizontal y-axis and the vertical x-axis) intersecting at their -1 points

17. quadrant

a. three sections on the axis plane formed by the intersection of the x-axis and the y-axis

b. one of four sections on the coordinate plane formed by the intersection of the x-axis and the y-axis

c. one of two sections on the four plane formed by the intersection of the x-axis

18. ordered pair

a. a pair of integer number sets that gives the range of a point in the axis plane. Also known as the "x-axis" of a point.

b. a pair of equal numbers that gives the range of a point in the axis plane. Also known as the "y-axis" of a point.

c. a pair of numbers that gives the location of a point in the coordinate plane. Also known as the "coordinates" of a point.

19. x-coordinate

a. the number that indicates the position of a point to the left or right of the y-axis

b. the number that indicates the range of a point to the left ONLY of the y-axis

c. the number that indicates the range of a point to both sides of the x-axis

20. y-coordinate

a. the number that indicates the value of a point only above the x-axis

b. the number that indicates the position of a point above or below the x-axis

c. the number that indicates the value or range of a point only above the y-axis

21. inverse operations

a. operations that divide evenly into each other

b. operations that undo each other

c. operations that equals to each other

22. inequality

a. a math sentence that uses a symbol ($<$, $>$, $\leq$, $\geq$, $\neq$) to indicate that the left and right sides of the sentence hold values that are different

b. a math sentence that uses a letter (x or y) to indicate that the left and right sides of the sentence hold values that are different

c. a math sentence that uses both numbers and letters (1=x or 2=y) to indicate that the left and right sides of the sentence hold values that are different

23. perimeter

a. the range around the outside or inside of a figure

b. the distance around the outside of a figure

c. the distance around the inside of a figure

24. circumference

a. the distance around a circle

b. the cube squared value around a circle

c. the range around a square

25. area

a. the number of circle units inside a 3-dimensional figure

b. the number of triangle units inside a 2-dimensional figure

c. the number of square units inside a 2-dimensional figure

26. volume

a. the number of cubic squared units inside a 2-dimensional figure

b. the number of cubic or circle units inside a 1-dimensional figure

c. the number of cubic units inside a 3-dimensional figure

27. radius

a. a line segment that runs from the center of the circle to somewhere on the circle

b. a line segment that runs from the middle of the circle to end of the circle

c. a line segment that runs from the middle of the square to start of the square

28. chord

a. a circle distance that runs from somewhere on the far left to another place on the circle

b. a line around a circle that runs from somewhere on the right to another place on the circle

c. a line segment that runs from somewhere on the circle to another place on the circle

29. diameter

a. a thin line that passes through the end of the circle

b. a 1/2" line that passes through the top of the circle

c. a chord that passes through the center of the circle

30. mean

a. the sum of the data items added by the number of data items minus 2

b. the sum of the data items divided by the number of data items

c. the sum of the data items divdied by the number of even data items less than 1

31. median

a. the middle data item found after sorting the data items in ascending order

b. the first data item found after sorting the data items in descending order

c. the middle & last data item found after sorting the data items in ascending order

32. mode

a. the data item that occurs less than two times

b. the data item that occurs when two or more numbers equal

c. the data item that occurs most often

33. range

a. the difference between the highest and the lowest data item

b. the difference between the numbers less than 10 and the lowest number item 2

c. the difference between the middle number and the lowest number item

34. outlier

a. a data item that is much higher or much lower than all the other data items

b. a data item that is much lower or less than all the other data items

c. a data item that is always higher than 1 or less than all the other data items

35. ratio

a. a comparison of two quantities by subtraction

b. a comparison of two quantities by multiplication

c. a comparison of two quantities by division

36. rate

a. a ratio that has equal range and distance measured within the first unit set

b. a ratio that has equal quantities measured in the same units

c. a ratio that compares quantities measured in different units

37. proportion

a. a statement (equation) showing two ratios to be equal

b. a statement (property) showing the distance between two variables

c. a statement (ratio) showing five or more ratios to be equal

38. outcomes

a. possible answer when two numbers are the same

b. possible results when the action is by division

c. possible results of action

39. probability

a. a ratio that explains the likelihood of two division problems with equal answers

b. a ratio that explains the likelihood of an event

c. a ratio that explains the likelihood of the distance and miles between to places

40. theoretical probability

a. the probability of the highest favorable number of possible outcomes (based on what is not expected to occur).

b. the ratio of the number of favorable outcomes to the number of possible outcomes (based on what is expected to occur).

c. the probability of the lowest favorable number of possible outcomes (based on what is expected to occur when added by 5).

41. experimental probability

a. the ratio of the number of times multiplied by the number of events that occur to the number of events times 5 (based on real experimental data).

b. the ratio of the number of times by 2 when an event occurs to the number of times times 2 an experiment is done (based on real experimental data).

c. the ratio of the number of times an event occurs to the number of times an experiment is done (based on real experimental data).

42. distributive property

a. a way to simplify an expression that contains a single term being multiplied by a group of terms.

b. a way to simplify an expression that contains a range of like terms being divided by a group of like terms.

c. a way to simplify an expression that contains a equal like term being added by a group of terms.

43. term

a. a number, a variable, or probability of an equal number and a variable(s)

b. a number, a variable, or expression of a range of numbers and a variable(s)

c. a number, a variable, or product of a number and a variable(s)

44. Constant

a. a term with no variable + y part (i.e. 4+y)

b. a term with no variable - x value (i.e. 8-x)

c. a term with no variable part (i.e. a number)

45. Coefficient

a. a number that multiplies a variable

b. a number that divides a variable

c. a number that subtracts a variable

46. Probability is the likelihood of something happening.

a. True

b. False

47. To calculate probability, you need to know how many possible options or _____ there are and how many right combinations you have.

a. outcomes

b. numbers

c. fraction

48. _, _, and _ have two common factors: 2 and 4.

a. 2, 6, and 9

b. 12, 20, and 24

c. 1,4, and 24

49. How do you write a polynomial expression?

a. 3x2 -2x-10

b. 32 -2x-+10y

c. y+3x2 -2x-10

50. How can you simplify rational expression?

a. eliminate all factors that are common of the numerator and the denominator

b. eliminate only 1 factor that are common of the numerator and the denominator

c. eliminate NO factors that are common of the numerator and the denominator

51. The slope intercept form is one of many forms that represents the linear relationship between two variables.

a. True

b. False

52. The slope intercept form equation is written as follows:

a. z = a x + b

b. y = y x + m

c. y = m x + b

53. Simplifying radicals is that we do NOT remove the radicals from the denominator.

a. True

b. False

54. 2 1/3 is a mixed fraction.

a. True

b. False

55. The word ____ literally means 'per hundred.' We use this symbol - %.

a. asterisk

b. percent

c. divide

56. less than or equal to symbol

a. ≤

b. <

c. ≥

57. distance between points x and y

a. |x-y|

b. |x+y|

c. |x-y+x+y|

58. greater than or equal to

a. <

b. ≤

c. ≥

Math:Test Your Knowledge Refresher

1. Addends are numbers_______
   a. used in an addition problem.
   b. used in an addition or multiplication problem.
   c. used in an subtraction problem.

2. What is an example of an Addend?
   a. In 9 + 1 = 10, the 9 and the 10 are addends.
   b. In 8 - 3 = 5, the 8 and the 3 are addends.
   c. In 8 + 3 = 11, the 8 and the 3 are addends.

3. What is a fact family?
   a. a group of math facts or equations created using the same set of numbers.
   b. is when you take one number and add it together a number of times.
   c. is taking away one or more items from a group of items.

4. Which is an example of a fact family?
   a. 2, 4, and 6: 2 x 2 = 4, 4 x 2 = 8, 6 − 2 = 4, and 6 − 4 = 2.
   b. 1, 2, and 12: 1 + 1 = 2, 2 + 2 = 4, 12 − 12 = 0, and 12 − 2 = 10.
   c. 10, 2, and 12: 10 + 2 = 12, 2 + 10 = 12, 12 − 10 = 2, and 12 − 2 = 10.

5. The fact family for 3, 8 and 24 is a set of four multiplication and division facts. Which one is correct?
   a. 3 × 8 = 24| 8 × 3 = 24| 24 ÷ 3 = 8| 24 ÷ 8 = 3
   b. 3 + 8 = 11| 8 × 3 = 24| 8 ÷ 8 = 0| 24 ÷ 8 = 3
   c. 3 × 3 = 9| 8 × 3 = 24| 24 + 3 = 27| 24 ÷ 8 = 3

6. A prime number is________
   a. the ways that numbers are combined to make new numbers.
   b. any number that is only divisible by itself and 1.
   c. the number you are rounding followed by 5, 6, 7, 8, or 9.

7. Examples of prime numbers_____
   a. 2, 8 and 15
   b. 2, 5 and 17
   c. 4, 6 and 10

8. Numbers such as _______ are not prime, because they are divisible by more than just themselves and 1.
   a. 2 or 7
   b. 5 or 11
   c. 15 or 21

9. Prime factor is the factor_______________
   a. of the first number which is NOT a prime number.
   b. of the smallest to greatest prime number starting with 0..
   c. of the given number which is a prime number.

10. The prime factors of 15 _____________
    a. are 3 and 5 (because 3×5=15, and 3 and 5 are prime numbers)
    b. are 5 and 10 (because 5+10=15, and 10 and 5 are prime numbers)
    c. are 25 and 10 (because 25-10=15, and 10 and 5 are prime numbers)

11. A factor tree is a ________

a. natural numbers greater than one that are not products of two smaller natural numbers.
b. diagram that is used to break down a number into its factors until all the numbers left are prime.
c. is divisible by 1, and it's divisible by itself.

12. The greatest common denominator is the _____

a. smallest positive integer that multiplies the numbers without a remainder.
b. largest negative integer that subtracts the numbers without a remainder.
c. largest positive integer that divides the numbers without a remainder.

13. The greatest common factor of 8 and 12 is_____?

a. 12
b. 6
c. 4

14. The lowest common denominator is the ____?

a. lowest common multiple of the denominators of a set of fractions.
b. lowest common multiple of the denominators of a group of numbers divided by 10.
c. lowest common subtraction of the first number of a set of fractions.

15. What is the LCD of 12 and 8?

a. 12 and 8 is 24
b. 12 and 8 is 32
c. 12 and 8 is 20

16. This math concept tells you that to divide means to split fairly.

a. Division
b. Addition
c. Algebra

17. Reduce 48/28 to lowest terms.

a. 12/5
b. 12/7
c. 7/28

18. Which of the following fractions CANNOT be reduced further?

a. 5/3
b. 33/12
c. 16/9

19. It is possible to make a fraction simpler without completely simplifying it.

a. True
b. False

20. Factor 18 into prime factors:

a. 18 = 3 * 3 * 2
b. 18 = 2 * 3 * 3
c. 18 = 1 * 3 * 2

21. An improper fraction is one where the numerator is smaller than the denominator.

a. True
b. False

22. Fractions that have a numerator with a higher value than the denominator

a. simple fractions
b. simplified fractions
c. improper fractions

ANSWER SHEET

Reading Comprehension: Social Media Safety

1. In the last 20 years, socializing has evolved dramatically. **Interactions** between people are referred to as socializing.
2. It now frequently refers to accessing the Internet via social media or websites that allow you to **connect** and interact with other people.
3. Ascertain that your computer is outfitted with up-to-date computer **security** software.
4. This software detects and removes **viruses** that are harmful to your computer.
5. When you use your computer, these viruses can sometimes hack into it and **steal** your information, such as **logins** .
6. Create strong **passwords** for all of your social media accounts.
7. These can be as loose or as **restrictive** as you want them to be.
8. This enables your computer to block **pop-ups** and warn you when you are about to visit a potentially harmful website.
9. - Don't **post** anything you wouldn't want broadcast to the entire world.
10. **Personal** information about one's identity should not be posted or shared on social media.
11. This information can be used to recreate your **identity** and should never be made public.
12. Make use of the **privacy** settings on the social media website.
13. Be cautious about what you post on any social media **platform** .
14. Posting something **negative** about someone hurts their character and opens the door for them, or someone else, to do the same to you.
15. If you are not in a good mood or are upset, think twice.
16. What you post could be **harmful** to you or someone else.
17. If you are in a bad social media **relationship** and are being harassed or bullied, you can report it to the social media company.
18. They all have **policies** in place to deal with people who **abuse** their websites.
19. Make a note of these **incidents** and report them to the company. You may also save the life of another person.

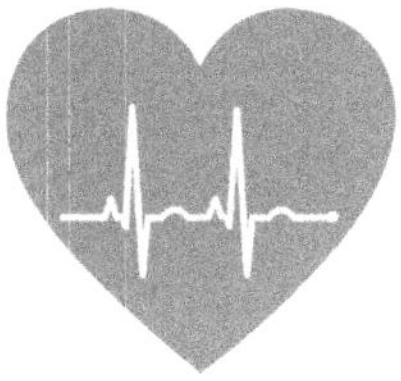

ANSWER SHEET

Science: Different Blood Types

compatible	transfusion	recipient's	antibodies	survive
donate	bloodstream	eight	negative	antigens

What comes to mind when you think of blood? It may be the color red, a hospital, or even a horror film! Blood is something that your body requires to **survive**, regardless of how you feel about it. Did you realize, though, that not everyone has the same blood type? There are **eight** different kinds in total! The letters A, B, and O, as well as positive or **negative** signs, distinguish these blood types. O+, O-, A+, A-, B+, B-, AB+, and AB- are the eight blood types.

What Is the Importance of Blood Types?

Don't be concerned if your blood type differs from that of others! There is no such thing as a better or healthier blood type. The sole reason to know your blood type is in case you need to **donate** or give blood to someone in an emergency. A blood **transfusion** is a process of transferring blood from one person to another.

Blood transfusions are only effective when the donor's blood is **compatible** with the **recipient's** blood. Some blood types don't mix well because the body produces antibodies to fight off any unfamiliar **antigens** that enter the **bloodstream**. Antibodies act as warriors in your blood, guarding you against alien intruders. Assume you have Type A blood, which contains A antigens solely, and someone with Type B blood wishes to donate blood to you. Your body does not recognize B antigens; thus, **antibodies** are produced to combat them! This has the potential to make you sick. As a result, people with Type A blood should only receive blood from those with Type A blood or Type O blood, as O blood lacks both A and B antigens.

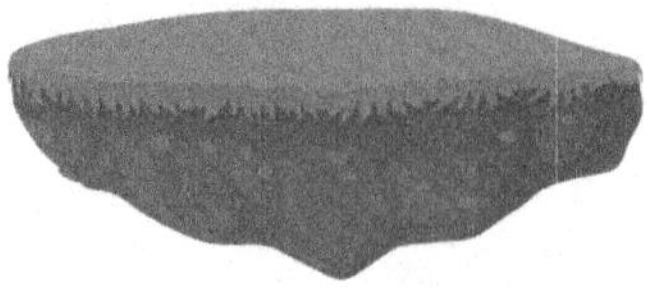

ANSWER SHEET

Geography: Landform

A landform is a natural or man-made feature of the Earth's or another planet's solid surface. A given terrain is made up of landforms, and their arrangement in the landscape is known as topography.

1. Lakes are an inland body of water, usually fresh
   a. True
   b. False

2. A sea is the direction from which a river flows
   a. True
   b. False

3. A delta is the land deposited at the mouth of a river
   a. True
   b. False

4. What landform is surrounded by water on three sides?
   a. An island
   b. A peninsula

5. A river is a narrow man-made channel of water that joins other bodies of water
   a. True
   b. False

6. The mouth is where a river flows into a larger body of water.
   a. True
   b. False

7. Which of the following is NOT a landform?
   a. An island
   b. A river

8. Downstream is the direction toward which a river flows.
   a. True
   b. False

9. A sea is a large area of salt water smaller than an ocean.
   a. True
   b. False

10. A bay is land deposited at the mouth of a river.
   a. True
   b. False

11. How are a valley and a canyon alike?
   a. They are both tall landforms.
   b. They are both low landforms.

12. A canal is a man-made channel of water that joins other bodies of water.
   a. True
   b. False

13. A lake is a place where a river begins.
   a. True
   b. False

14. Which types of landforms are always flat?
   a. Plateaus and plains
   b. Hills and peninsulas

Science: Organelles

Organelles are the inside elements of a cell that are responsible for all of the tasks that keep the cell healthy and alive. Each organelle has a distinct function. The word "organelle" means "small organ," and these tiny powerhouses are responsible for everything from defending the cell to repairing/healing, assisting in the development, removing waste products, and even reproduction. The function of each organelle is also influenced by the functions of other organelles. The cell will perish if any organelle fails to perform its function.

Many of the same types of organelles exist in both plant and animal cells, and they function in similar ways. Both plant and animal cells have a total of ten organelles.

Plant-like cells, on the other hand, are built solely for photosynthesis and utilize the rigid wall, as well as organelles that operate to generate energy from sunlight. Organelles in animal-like cells have a lot greater variety and capability.

Match each term with a definition.

1	F	nucleus	⇢	where DNA is stored
2	J	lysosomes	⇢	degradation of proteins and cellular waste
3	G	Golgi Apparatus	⇢	modification of proteins; "post-office" of the cell
4	A	Mitochondria	⇢	powerhouse of the cell
5	B	SER	⇢	lipid synthesis
6	C	RER	⇢	protein synthesis + modifications
7	E	Microtubules	⇢	responsible for chromosome segregation
8	D	ribosomes	⇢	protein synthesis
9	K	peroxysomes	⇢	degradation of H2O2
10	I	cell wall	⇢	prevents excessive uptake of water, protects the cell (in plants)
11	L	chloroplast	⇢	site of photosynthesis
12	H	central vacuole	⇢	stores water in plant cells

Science: Space

No one can hear you scream in space. This is due to the fact that space is devoid of air - it is a vacuum. In a vacuum, sound waves cannot travel. 'Outer space' begins roughly 100 kilometers above the Earth's surface, where the atmosphere that surrounds our planet dissipates. Space appears as a black blanket speckled with stars because there is no air to disperse sunlight and generate a blue sky.

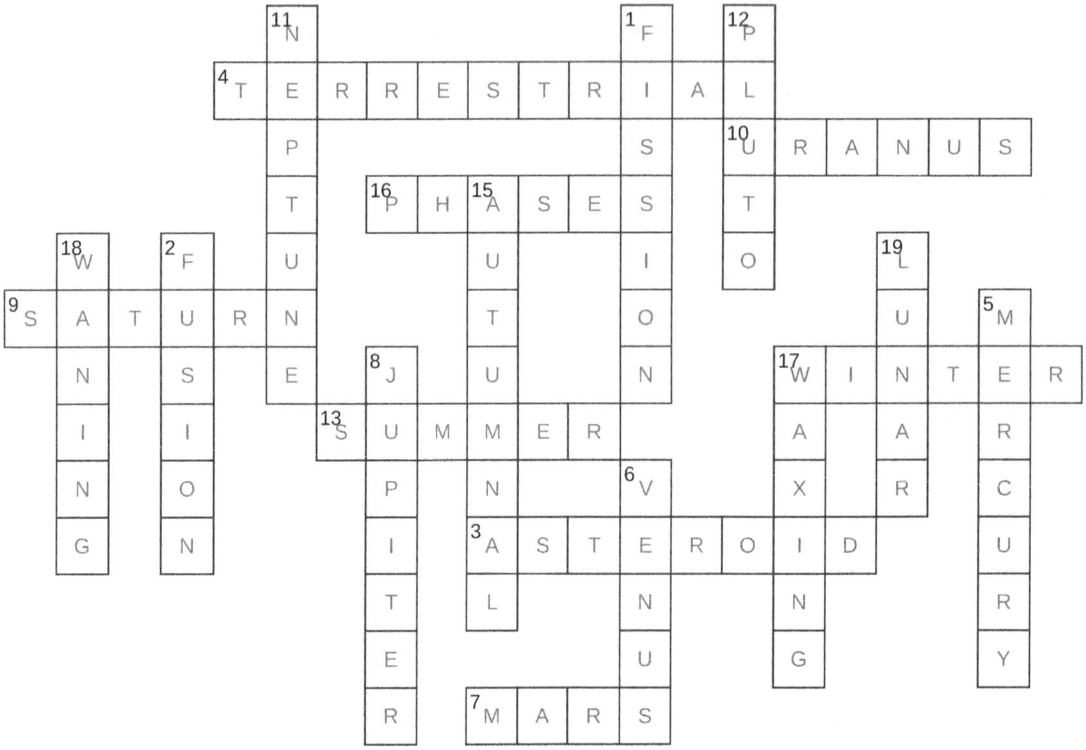

Across

3. The 4 inner planets and 4 outer planets are separated by the _________ Belt.
4. The 4 inner planets are referred to as ____ planets because they are rocky and dense- Earth like
7. only about 1/2 the size of earth- tilted similar to earth- rusty surface- 2 moons
9. Revolves as rapidly as Jupiter- second largest planet- could float in water- Oh yeah...it has rings
10. Sideways rotation- retrograde rotation- has 11 very thin rings
13. ________ Solstice is when we have the longest amount of daylight for that year and the shortest night
16. The way we see the moon as it orbits around the sun and reflects the Sun's light
17. ________ Solstice is when we have the shortest amount of daylight for that year and the longest night

Down

1. The coming apart of an atom that gives off a lot of energy
2. The coming together of 2 atoms that releases a lot of energy - more than fission!
5. smallest planet- slowest rotation- magnetic
6. most like earth size wise- atmospheric pressure able to crush us- retrograde rotation
8. Fastest rotation (a little less than half an earth day)- largest planet- 29 years for 1 trip around the Sun- known also for Great Red Spot
11. Last planet in our solar system- Dark blue and windy-
12. Dwarf planet found just inside the Kuiper Belt- has a few moons- orbit actually crosses Neptune periodically
15. _______ Equinox is an occurrence in the fall where the daylight and nighttime are equivalent
17. the amount of moon that you can see is increasing
18. the amount of moon that you can see is decreasing
19. During a _______ Eclipse the shadow of the earth goes across the face of the moon

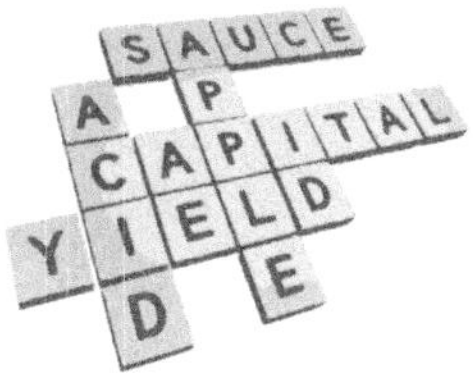

ANSWER SHEET

Spelling Words Crossword

Across

1. We will meet at our summer ___ for the wedding
3. My father studied _____.
6. The ______ of the donors came as a surprise.
7. There was a growing ____ between the two sides.
8. The old home was in a _____ state.
9. The ____ between the villages was growing larger.

Down

2. The lamb ____ is nearly done cooking
4. The economic ____ appears to be working.
5. I've always wanted to play the ______.
10. The people were ____ of his motives.
11. Pass the ____ to me so that I can take my medicine.
12. The doctor told my grandma to take only one ____ a day.

VITAMIN	RESIDENCE
ANIMOSITY	WARY
XYLOPHONE	SHANK
CHASM	PODIATRY
SYRINGE	GENEROSITY
STIMULUS	RUINOUS

ANSWER SHEET

9th Grade Spelling Words Unscramble

symphony	analysis	agriculture	twelfth	abundant	tendency
souvenir	technique	laborious	ambassador	sophomore	specific
symbol	specimen	aggressive	jealousy	absorption	journal
island	acceptable	syllable	absence	amateur	temperature

1. NECASEB a b s e n c e
2. PNSOABROTI a b s o r p t i o n
3. ABDNUTNA a b u n d a n t
4. BLEATAPCEC a c c e p t a b l e
5. SLYBLELA s y l l a b l e
6. BLOMYS s y m b o l
7. OMHYPSYN s y m p h o n y
8. ENUTICQHE t e c h n i q u e
9. EPTMERUATRE t e m p e r a t u r e
10. EYNNDCET t e n d e n c y
11. GEEGSARVIS a g g r e s s i v e
12. ARTEULICRUG a g r i c u l t u r e
13. UMTEAAR a m a t e u r
14. AASBOARMSD a m b a s s a d o r
15. LISASNAY a n a l y s i s
16. PMREHSOOO s o p h o m o r e
17. VOESINUR s o u v e n i r
18. CSPFCIEI s p e c i f i c
19. SPCMENEI s p e c i m e n
20. DSLINA i s l a n d
21. JSULYEOA j e a l o u s y
22. JRUOLNA j o u r n a l
23. ASILOBURO l a b o r i o u s
24. TELWTHF t w e l f t h

ANSWER SHEET

English Refresher: 4 Types of Sentences

Declarative, imperative, interrogative, and exclamatory sentences are all types of sentences. Identifying and classifying sentences is easy once you know why each sort of sentence exists, how many there are, and how they are constructed. Each of these phrases' aims contributes to the uniqueness of the English language. The structure of conversation and written communication would be drastically different if these phrases were not used.

As the name implies, declarative phrases make statements. In most cases, they are expressed in a non-emotional, neutral manner. These sentences are used to state facts, describe things, and explain things.

Imperative sentences are used to express a command or a demand. Rather than being stated directly, the subjects of these sentences are frequently implied to be the listener.

Exclamatory sentences get their name from the fact that they exclaim something. Although exclamatory phrases can be classified in different ways, they are easily distinguished by the presence of intense emotions. An exclamation point marks the end of the sentence.

Interrogative sentences ask questions and are always followed by a question mark. Interrogative sentences frequently begin with "question words" such as who, what, where, when, how, or why. That is not always the case, however.

1. Which type of sentence might have an implied subject?
- a. interrogative
- b. declarative
- c. imperative

2. What end mark is used for interrogative sentences?
- a. period
- b. question mark
- c. exclamation mark

3. Which is an imperative sentence?
- a. What movie do you want to go see?
- b. Can you wash the car today?
- c. Please wash my car.

4. Which type of sentence shows strong emotion?
- a. interrogative
- b. declarative
- c. exclamatory

5. The sunset is beautiful tonight. This is what type of sentence?
- a. declarative
- b. imperative
- c. interrogative

6. Do not touch the stove! This is what type of sentence?
- a. exclamatory
- b. declarative
- c. imperative

7. Do you feel okay? This is what type of sentence?
- a. declarative
- b. Interrogative
- c. exclamatory

8. Declarative sentences make statements and end in ____.
- a. periods
- b. question mark
- c. exclamation mark

9. Imperative sentences make ____or _____.
- a. commands or demand
- b. commands or thoughts
- c. commands or question

10. Interrogative sentences ask ____ and end in ______.
- a. commands and requests
- b. demand and exclamation mark
- c. questions and question marks

ANSWER SHEET

Adjectives to Describe People

Adjectives are descriptive or modifying words for nouns or pronouns. For instance, adjectives such as red, quick, happy, and annoying exist to describe things—a red hat, a speedy rabbit, a cheerful duck, and an obnoxious individual.

Unscramble the adjectives to describe people.

polite	friendly	clever	outgoing	good looking	handsome
cute	fat	tall	smart	young	pretty
attractive	rude	easygoing	funny	confident	tidy
old	beautiful	generous	ugly		

1. ulbuefita b e a u t i f u l
2. trpyet p r e t t y
3. etuc c u t e
4. luyg u g l y
5. ugnyo y o u n g
6. tleipo p o l i t e
7. nnufy f u n n y
8. riledfny f r i e n d l y
9. ohemndsa h a n d s o m e
10. rdue r u d e
11. dol o l d
12. aft f a t
13. mrtas s m a r t
14. idty t i d y
15. yogsgeain e a s y g o i n g
16. cleerv c l e v e r
17. neeugrso g e n e r o u s
18. fnitnedoc c o n f i d e n t
19. tngioogu o u t g o i n g
20. dgoo oinogkl g o o d l o o k i n g
21. vractatite a t t r a c t i v e
22. tlla t a l l

ANSWER SHEET

Alexander Graham Bell

It was March 7, 1876, and Alexander Graham Bell, who was 29 years old, was given a patent for his new invention: the telephone.

He worked in London with his father, Melville Bell. His father came up with Visible Speech, a written method for teaching the deaf to speak. The Bells relocated to Boston, Massachusetts, in the 1870s, where the younger Bell obtained work as a teacher at the Pemberton Avenue School for the Deaf.

After moving to Boston, Bell became very interested in transmitting speech over wires. With the introduction of the telegraph by Samuel F.B. Morse in 1843, communication between two distant sites became virtually instantaneous. The disadvantage of the telegraph was that messages had to be delivered by hand between telegraph stations and recipients, and only one message could be transmitted at a time. Bell sought to improve on this by developing the "harmonic telegraph," a gadget that merged the telegraph and record player elements to enable individuals to communicate remotely.

Bell made a prototype with the help of Thomas A. Watson, a worker at a machine shop in Boston. In the original telephone, sound waves altered the amplitude and frequency of an electric current, causing a thin, soft iron plate called the diaphragm to vibrate. These vibrations were sent magnetically to another wire connected to a diaphragm in another, faraway instrument. When that diaphragm moved, the original sound would be played back in the ear of the device that was hearing it. It took three days after Bell filed the patent for the telephone for the first intelligible message to be sent. That message was "Mr. Watson, come here; I need you."

____

Sentence Building: Unscramble the sentences!

1. A telephone that can be carried around is called a mobile phone or cell phone.

   telephone · can · phone. · be · around · mobile · or · cell · is · called · phone

2. Alexander Graham Bell was the first person to patent the telephone, in 1876.

   in · Graham · Alexander · person · Bell · was · first · patent · to · telephone,

3. Today, telephone numbers are about seven to ten digits long.

   long. · about · ten · are · Today, · numbers · seven

4. In many countries, part of the telephone number is called the area code.

   number · code. · the · is · the · many · of · area · part · called

5. Area codes are used to make sure the numbers are not the same in two different places.

   different · make · same · in · used · to · Area · not · two · are · the · numbers · sure

ANSWER SHEET

Alice & The Rabbit-Hole

ALICE was growing tired of sitting beside her **sister** on the bank and having nothing to do: she had peeped into the book her sister was reading once or twice, but it was lacking **pictures** or words; "and what use is a book," Alice argued, "without pictures or conversations?"
Thus, she was wondering in her mind (as best she could, given how sleepy and foolish she felt due to the heat) whether the pleasure of creating a cute daisy chain was worth the difficulty of getting up and gathering the daisies when a white **Rabbit** with pink eyes darted nearby her.

There was nothing **remarkable** about that; nor did Alice consider it strange to hear the Rabbit exclaim to itself, "Oh no! Oh no! I will arrive too late!" (On reflection, she should have been surprised, but at the time, it seemed perfectly natural). Still, when the Rabbit actually removed a watch from its waistcoat-pocket, examined it, and then hurried on, Alice jumped to her **feet**, for it flashed across her mind that she had never seen a rabbit with either a waistcoat-pocket or a watch to remove from it, and burning with curiosity, she ran across the field after it. Alice saw the Rabbit go down a hole under the hedge. Alice followed it down in a **hurry**, never once thinking how she would get out again.

The rabbit-hole continued straight ahead like a **tunnel** for some distance and then suddenly dipped down, so quickly that Alice had no time to think about stopping herself before falling into what appeared to be a very deep well.

Either the well was really deep, or she dropped very slowly, as she had plenty of time to look around her and ponder on what might happen next. She first attempted to glance down and see what she was approaching, but it was too **dark** to see anything; then, she discovered the sides of the well were lined with cupboards and bookcases; here and there, she observed maps and images hung on hooks. She removed a **jar** from one of the shelves as she passed; it was labeled "ORANGE MARMALADE," but it was empty; she did not want to drop the jar for fear of killing someone beneath, so she managed to stuff it into one of the cupboards as she passed it.

"Perfect!" Alice exclaimed to herself. "After such a tumble, I shall have no worries about falling downstairs! How **courageous** they will all believe I am at home!

ANSWER SHEET

Alphabetize and Define

meter
irony
personification
denotation
onomatopoeia
alliteration
rhyme
metaphor
theme
symbolism
repetition
simile
stanza
connotation
imagery

1. alliteration
2. connotation
3. denotation
4. imagery
5. irony
6. metaphor
7. meter
8. onomatopoeia
9. personification
10. repetition
11. rhyme
12. simile
13. stanza
14. symbolism
15. theme

After putting the words in alphabetical order, choose 5 and write a definition in the space provided.

[Student worksheet has a 5 line writing exercise here.]

ANSWER SHEET

Animal Migrations

At certain times of the year, many mammals, birds, fish, insects, and other animals migrate from one location to another. This is referred to as migration. These animals migrate as part of their life cycle.

Animals migrate for a variety of reasons. Many migrate in order to reproduce or to find food. Some animals migrate to locations where they can hibernate or rest during the winter. Others migrate because the weather is excessively hot, excessively cold, excessively wet, or excessively dry at certain times of the year.

The majority of animals migrate by water, land, or air. Many birds and bats migrate south for the winter in northern parts of the world. Some whales migrate from cold polar regions to warmer waters in the winter. Other types of migration are vertical or up and down. During the winter, mule deer in the western United States migrate from higher to lower elevations of the mountains. Some earthworms move from the top of the soil to the bottom of the ground.

Animals can travel hundreds of miles or thousands of miles. Frogs travel short distances to breed in ponds. On the other hand, the Arctic tern spends the summer in the Arctic and the winter in Antarctica. This journey covers approximately 11,000 miles (18,000 kilometers). Migrations can occur both during the day and at night. During the day, birds such as geese migrate. Sparrows, warblers, and thrushes all migrate at night.

Migrating animals can navigate long and complicated routes. Rivers and mountains help them figure out where they are. Many animals, according to scientists, use the position of the Sun and stars to find their way. Salmon, for example, use their sense of smell.

Sentence Building: Unscramble the sentences!

1. Sea turtles migrate back to the same beach where they were born to lay their eggs.

   beach · Sea · turtles · born · to · were · their · migrate · eggs. · lay · they · to

2. Animals migrate with the change of the weather and the seasons.

   the · Animals · change · with · the · the · weather · and

3. Male and female walruses migrate in separate herds.

   and · separate · female · Male · herds. · migrate

4. Different animals have adapted different ways of navigating the Earth.

   of · have · animals · the · navigating · adapted · ways

5. Each year Canadian geese fly south for the winter to avoid the winter freeze of lakes and ponds.

   geese · lakes · freeze · the · avoid · fly · for · the · to · south · winter · Each · winter

ANSWER SHEET

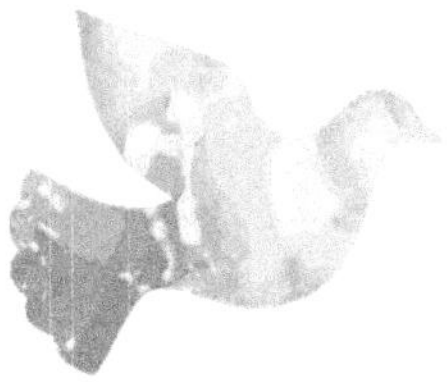

Art: Pablo Picasso

depressed	suicide	features	Carlos	newspapers
blue	historians	circuses	collaborated	sand
painter	Madrid	prestigious	Spanish	French

Pablo Picasso was born on October 25, 1881, in Spain and grew up there. His father was a **painter** who also taught art. Pablo has always enjoyed drawing since he was a child. According to legend, his first word was "piz," which is **Spanish** for "pencil." Pablo quickly demonstrated that he had little interest in school but was an extremely talented artist. Pablo enrolled in a **prestigious** art school in Barcelona when he was fourteen years old. He transferred to another school in **Madrid** a few years later. Pablo, on the other hand, was dissatisfied with the traditional art school teachings. He didn't want to paint in the manner of people from hundreds of years ago. He wished to invent something new.

Pablo's close friend **Carlos** Casagemas committed **suicide** in 1901. Pablo became **depressed**. He began painting in Paris around the same time. For the next four years, the color **blue** dominated his paintings. Many of the subjects appeared depressed and solemn. He depicted people with elongated **features** and faces in his paintings. Poor People on the Seashore and The Old Guitarist are two of his paintings from this time.

Pablo eventually recovered from his depression. He also had feelings for a **French** model. He began to use warmer colors such as pinks, reds, oranges, and beiges in his paintings. The Rose Period is a term used by art **historians** to describe this period in Pablo's life. He also started painting happier scenes like **circuses**. The Peasants and Mother and Child are two of his paintings from this time period.

Picasso began experimenting with a new painting style in 1907. He **collaborated** with another artist, Georges Braque. By 1909, they had developed a completely new painting style known as Cubism. Cubism analyzes and divides subjects into different sections. The sections are then reassembled and painted from various perspectives and angles.

Picasso began combining Cubism and collage in 1912. He would use **sand** or plaster in his paint to give it texture in this area. He would also add dimension to his paintings by using materials such as colored paper, **newspapers**, and wallpaper. Three Musicians and the Portrait of Ambroise Vollard are two of Picasso's Cubism paintings.

Although Picasso continued to experiment with Cubism, he went through a period of painting more classical-style paintings around 1921. He was influenced by Renaissance painters such as Raphael. He created strong characters that appeared three-dimensional, almost like statues. The Pipes of Pan and Woman in White are two of his works in this style.

Pablo became interested in the Surrealist movement around 1924. Surrealist paintings were never meant to make sense. They frequently resemble something out of a nightmare or a dream. Although Picasso did not join the movement, he did incorporate some of its ideas into his paintings. This period was dubbed "Monster Period" by some. Guernica and The Red Armchair are two examples of surrealism's influence on Picasso's art.

Pablo Picasso is widely regarded as the greatest artist of the twentieth century. Many consider him to be one of the greatest artists in all of history. He painted in a variety of styles and made numerous unique contributions to the world of art. He painted several self-portraits near the end of his life. Self-Portrait Facing Death, a self-portrait done with crayons on paper, was one of his final works of art. He died a year later, on April 8, 1973, at the age of 91.

ANSWER SHEET

ARTS Vocabulary Terms 6

Choose the best answer to each question.

1. **Select the correct meaning of the word Abstract Art**
   a. A functional object or arrangement whereby the principles of art are applied. Refers to such things as pottery, interior decorating, architecture, furniture, etc
   b. Art created from a realistic situation but represented unrealistically.

2. **Select the correct meaning of the word acrylic paint:**
   a. Use white lead as a base, and are applied in three coats: primer, undercoat and finish coat
   b. A plastic, water soluble pigment used for painting.

3. **A functional object or arrangement whereby the principles of art are applied. Refers to such things as pottery, interior decorating, architecture, furniture, etc.**
   a. applied art
   b. abstract art

4. **A structural support for an object. Particularly used in sculpture to build upon.**
   a. clay object
   b. armature

5. **An image created with a paint brush, typically using India ink or watercolor, that has a linear quality rather than a painterly finish.**
   a. paint brush
   b. brush drawing

6. **A sculpture representing the neck and head only of a person.**
   a. bust
   b. contrapposto

7. **Literally means beautiful line. Typically refers to a type of writing that incorporates the use of a wide pen nib.**
   a. calligraphy
   b. modern cursive

8. **Clay objects that have been fired twice, the second time with a glaze.**
   a. ceramic
   b. pottery

9. **Soft limestone, sometimes used as a drawing material or mixed to make pastels and other crayons.**
   a. watercolor
   b. chalk

10. **Select the correct meaning of the word Charcoal**
    a. A drawing material made from charred wood.
    b. A type of pencil in which a thin graphite core is embedded in a shell of other material

ARTS Vocabulary Terms 7

Choose the best answer to each question.

1. **What is the correct meaning of the word Firing?**
   a. The process of baking clay in a kiln or banked fire outside (such as raku firing). This process hardens the clay and makes it very permanent.
   b. The process of baking clay in a kiln or banked fire outside (such as raku firing). This process softens the clay and makes it very malleable.

2. **Varnish sprayed or painted onto a surface to prevent smudging or smearing. Usually on a charcoal or chalk pastel work.**
   a. spray paint art
   b. fixative

3. **Art made by untrained practitioners. Typically lively, colorful artwork in a somewhat "naive" style**
   a. classical art
   b. folk art

4. **An element of art focused on all three dimensions (height, width and depth).**
   a. form
   b. shape

5. **A surface preparation or primer made of chalk or gypsum for tempura or oil paintings that is painted onto the picture surface.**
   a. gouache
   b. gesso

6. **A transparent or semitransparent coating of a color or stain used over oil paintings, plaster sculpture or ceramics.**
   a. glaze
   b. enamel

7. **A watercolor paint mixed with white pigments making it more opaque and giving it more weight and body.**
   a. gouache
   b. gesso

8. **Select the correct meaning of the word Hue:**
   a. The technical reference to color.
   b. Refers to how strong or weak a color is.

9. **An image that accompanies written text and aids in interpreting it.**
   a. diagram
   b. illustration

10. **An element of art used in drawing, painting and sculpture.**
    a. line
    b. shape

ANSWER SHEET

ARTS Vocabulary Terms 8

Choose the best answer to each question.

1. **A general purpose drawing and coloring paper. Typically cream color.**
   a. kraft paper
   b. Manila paper

2. **what is the correct meaning of the word Masterpiece?**
   a. An artists finest work, or any particularly fine work.
   b. A principle in art where important elements and ideas are emphasized via composition

3. **Representation, or making sculptural, three-dimensional forms, usually with clay or wax. Also, making two-dimensional surfaces look three-dimensional , by use of light and shade, color and mass.**
   a. modeling
   b. prototyping

4. **Tints and shades of single hue or color.**
   a. monochrome
   b. monochromatic

5. **Images created using small tesserae arranged and glued into a design or composition; dates back to the Ancient Greeks and Romans, mostly used to decorate walls and floors.**
   a. mosaic
   b. collage

6. **Paint made by mixing ground pigment with oil (usually linseed oil) as a binder.**
   a. oil paint
   b. oil pastel

7. **Art works made with newspaper strips that have been moistened with wallpaper paste or laundry starch.**
   a. mod podge
   b. paper mache

8. **The illusion of a three-dimensional space on a two-dimensional surface through the use of vanishing point, converging lines and diminishing sizes of objects.**
   a. perspective
   b. depth

9. **Uses cut photographs to create a work of art.**
   a. collage
   b. photomontage

10. **An image created with the use of small dots or points.**
    a. cross hatching
    b. pointillism

ANSWER SHEET

ARTS Vocabulary Terms 9

Choose the best answer to each question.

1. **Select the correct meaning of the word Primary colors:**
   a. The basic colors that can be used to mix other colors. The primary colors are purple, orange and green .
   b. The basic colors that can be used to mix other colors. The primary colors are red, yellow and blue.

2. **A clean, fast drying latex type of adhesive. Excellent for paper projects.**
   a. contact cement
   b. rubber cement

3. **Select the correct Secondary colors:**
   a. orange, green and purple
   b. red, yellow and blue

4. **The element of art that describes a two-dimensional area (height and width).**
   a. shape
   b. form

5. **Refers to the darker values of a color.**
   a. sketch
   b. shade

6. **Dried, crushed clay mixed with water to a creamy consistency. Used as a binder in joining two pieces of clay together.**
   a. carving
   b. slip

7. **The quality of a surface. One of the seven elements of art.**
   a. texture
   b. harmony

8. **Select the correct meaning of the word Tint:**
   a. a mixture with black, which increases darkness
   b. a hue mixed with white to create lighter values.

9. **Pigment with a water-soluble binder. Available in semi-moist cakes or tubes.**
   a. watercolors
   b. acrylic painting

ANSWER SHEET

Business World Phrases

Unscramble the words

to learn the ropes	bring to the table	back to the drawing board	from the ground up	up in the air	in a nutshell
to get down to business	back to square one	to get someone up to speed	to go down swinging	the bottom line	hands are tied
a learning curve	to think outside the box	to corner the market	between a rock and a hard place	it's not rocket science	

1. bakc ot hte dairnwg rbdoa	back to the drawing board
2. ot orncre hte tamkre	to corner the market
3. ahsnd aer idte	hands are tied
4. pu ni hte iar	up in the air
5. ot enrla hte opers	to learn the ropes
6. a iarngenl vecur	a learning curve
7. ot og dnow nsggwini	to go down swinging
8. benweet a okcr nda a hadr calep	between a rock and a hard place
9. rofm eth dgonur pu	from the ground up
10. eht ttmoob ilne	the bottom line
11. ot egt ndwo ot ssneubsi	to get down to business
12. ot tge noeeoms pu ot epdes	to get someone up to speed
13. s'ti ont tcorek isecnce	it's not rocket science
14. ot hnikt dosietu teh oxb	to think outside the box
15. ni a elshtlnu	in a nutshell
16. acbk ot aquers eon	back to square one
17. ribgn ot teh elabt	bring to the table

ANSWER SHEET

Civil Rights History: Frederick Douglass

Frederick Douglass was born in Talbot County, Maryland, into slavery. His grandmother, a slave, was the one who raised him. Douglass was separated from his grandmother in 1826, when he was about 7 or 8 years old, and sent to Baltimore, Maryland. He served as a maid in the home of shipbuilder Hugh Auld while there. His wife, Sophia, began teaching Frederick how to read and write. She was told to stop by her husband, who was displeased. A slave could not be taught to read because it was illegal. On the other hand, Frederick found a way to continue his education. White friends secretly gave him books.

As he grew older, Frederick Douglass developed anti-slavery views. Humans should be treated as equals. That concept was discovered in the Declaration of Independence. At some point, he was returned to his birthplace of Maryland, a plantation. There, he became known for breaking the rules. A big part of this is because he taught other slaves how to read the Bible.

Douglass was soon assigned to work for Edward Covey. Covey was known as a "slave breaker" because of his brutal methods. Douglas spent a year with Covey in 1833, during which he was whipped a lot. Douglass, who had lived much of his life in the city, was unfamiliar with farm tools and procedures. Because he didn't know what to do, he made mistakes and kept getting punished. One day, Douglass decided to fight back physically. It wasn't long before Douglass had the upper hand, and Covey had given up after two hours of wrestling. They went toe-to-toe with each other, and Douglass was never whipped by Covey again after that. Douglass was able to free himself from slavery in 1838. He donned a sailor's hat and set sail for the north. Finally, he arrived in the Big Apple.

Douglass wed Anna Murray in New York City, and they had five children within the first ten years of the marriage. The couple eventually made their home in New Bedford, Massachusetts. They lived in a neighborhood with other free black people. They got involved in the anti-slavery movement. Slavery was something that abolitionists hoped to end. As a storyteller, Douglass was exceptional. William Lloyd Garrison was captivated by his tales of life as a slave. He was the editor of The Liberator, an abolitionist publication. Douglass was encouraged to write by Garrison. An American Slave's Story by Frederick Douglass was the end result. In 1845, the book was published. It quickly became a best-seller in the publishing industry.

Douglass' supporters raised funds to purchase his freedom in 1847. His new home was in Rochester, New York, and he started a newspaper against slavery. The North Star was its name. In 1848, he delivered a speech in Seneca Falls, New York, at a conference on women's rights. He met civil rights activist Elizabeth Cady Stanton there. Elizabeth was an American writer and activist who was a big part of the women's rights movement in the United States.

Frederick Douglass urged President Abraham Lincoln to allow black men to join the Union Army during the Civil War of 1861–1861. Charles and Lewis Douglass, two of Douglass' sons, served in the 54th Massachusetts Infantry Regiment. Douglass heavily promoted the 14th and 15th Amendments to the Constitution after the war. As a result of these, all American men were granted equal rights, including voting. After the 13th Amendment was passed in 1865, slavery was officially abolished.

His career in the United States government went on to include high-ranking positions. He served as the Dominican Republic and Haiti ambassador, respectively. He served as a director of the Freedman's Bank as well. He was an outspoken critic of racial injustice and a human rights activist.

Douglass continued to speak, write, and be an activist until he died on February 20, 1895. After attending a meeting of the National Council of Women, an early women's rights group, in Washington, D.C., he died of a heart attack as he returned home.

1. Which slave owner whipped Douglas a lot?

a. Hugh Auld

b. Edward Covey

2. Who first tried teaching Frederick how to read?

a. Hugh Auld wife Sophia

b. Frederick's grandmother

3. In Rochester, New York, Douglas started a ____ against slavery.

a. newspaper

b. protest

4. Douglas served as the ____ Republic and ____ ambassador.

a. New York, USA

b. Dominican, Haiti

QUANTITATIVE CHEMISTRY

ANSWER SHEET

Conservation of Mass

In **1789**, Antoine Lavoisier, a French chemist, first proposed the Law of Conservation of Mass. To do this, he had to carry out thousands of experiments, making very careful **measurements**. he found that in any chemical reaction or physical change, the total mass after the reaction was **exactly** the **same** as the mass before. His law can be summarised as follows:
"Matter cannot be **destroyed**, or **created**, just changed from one form to another."

If you mix lead nitrate solution with potassium iodide solution a yellow solid is formed called **lead** iodide. If you measured the mass of products (the chemicals formed) you would find that it is **exactly** the **same** as the mass of the reactants (the chemicals that were mixed).

Mass is never **increased** or **decreased** in a chemical reaction - particles cannot just be lost! Sometimes it may look like mass is lost, but in that case, it is usually a gas that has been produced and **escaped** into the air. The same can happen when the chemicals made have a mass more than the mass of the products started with. You may have guessed, that in this case some gas from the air has been added to the **products**!

For instance, if you heat zinc in the air you get a white powder. The mass of the white powder is greater than the mass of the **zinc** you started with. The zinc has combined with **oxygen** from the air to form zinc oxide. The mass of the zinc and the oxygen that reacted would be the same as the mass of the zinc oxide.

ANSWER SHEET

Demonstrative Pronoun

This, That, These, and Those

1. _____ orange I'm eating is delicious.
    a. These
    b. That
    c. This

2. It is better than _____ apples from last week.
    a. these
    b. that
    c. those

3. Astronauts don't get fresh fruit like _____ peaches we are eating.
    a. these
    b. that
    c. this

4. _____ meals they take into space are freeze-dried.
    a. Those
    b. This
    c. That

5. _____ fact means they must add water to them.
    a. That
    b. This here
    c. These

6. _____ granola bars are tasty too.
    a. Them
    b. These
    c. This here

7. Don't sign me up for _____ next shuttle flight.
    a. these here
    b. that
    c. that there

8. _____ book is so heavy I can hardly lift it.
    a. This here
    b. Those
    c. This

9. Some believed _____ dream could be a reality.
    a. that there
    b. these
    c. that

10. _____ change is due to our astronauts.
    a. These here
    b. That there
    c. This

ANSWER SHEET

Different Types of Dangerous Weather

1. ____ are extremely fast-spinning columns of wind.
   a. Tornadoes
   b. Hurricanes

2. ______ can form when moist warm air rises quickly.
   a. Thunderstorms
   b. Lighting

3. Huge and powerful storms that form over the ocean are known as _____.
   a. hurricanes
   b. tornadoes

4. Lighting will frequently strike the ____ point on the land surface when it comes to landing.
   a. lowest
   b. highest

5. The top of the thunderstorm is _____ charged, but the bottom accumulates a negative charge.
   a. positively
   b. steadily

6. _____ is a powerful electrical blast that can form in thunderstorms and strike the earth with great force.
   a. Lighting
   b. High winds

Complete the Table Below.

Start Time	End Time	Elapsed Time
3:00 P.M.	4:32 P.M.	1 Hours & 32 Minutes
1:20 A.M.	5:06 A.M.	3 Hours & 46 Minutes
4:40 P.M.	6:52 P.M.	2 Hours & 12 Minutes
1:20 A.M.	5:18 A.M.	3 Hours & 58 Minutes
10:10 P.M.	12:37 A.M.	2 Hours & 27 Minutes
5:30 P.M.	9:47 P.M.	4 Hours & 17 Minutes
12:20 A.M.	2:12 A.M.	1 Hours & 52 Minutes
3:50 P.M.	5:37 P.M.	1 Hours & 47 Minutes
3:20 A.M.	4:44 A.M.	1 Hours & 24 Minutes
11:00 P.M.	1:19 A.M.	2 Hours & 19 Minutes

ANSWER SHEET

Environmental Health: Water Pollution

Water pollution occurs when waste, chemicals, or other particles cause a body of water (e.g., rivers, oceans, lakes) to become toxic to the fish and animals that rely on it for survival. Water pollution can also disrupt and hurt nature's water cycle.

Water pollution can occur naturally due to volcanoes, algae blooms, animal waste, and silt from storms and floods.

Human activity contributes significantly to water pollution. Sewage, pesticides, fertilizers from farms, wastewater and chemicals from factories, silt from construction sites, and trash from people littering are some human causes .

Oil spills have been some of the most well-known examples of water pollution. The Exxon Valdez oil spill occurred when an oil tanker collided with a reef off the coast of Alaska, causing over 11 million gallons of oil to spill into the ocean. Another major oil spill was the Deepwater Horizon oil spill, which occurred when an oil well exploded, causing over 200 million gallons of oil to spill into the Gulf of Mexico.

Water pollution can be caused directly by air pollution. When sulfur dioxide particles reach high altitudes in the atmosphere, they can combine with rain to form acid rain. Acid rain can cause lakes to become acidic, killing fish and other animals.

The main issue caused by water pollution is the impact on aquatic life. Dead fish, birds, dolphins, and various other animals frequently wash up on beaches, killed by pollutants in their environment. Pollution also has an impact on the natural food chain. Small animals consume contaminants like lead and cadmium.

Clean water is one of the most valuable and essential commodities for life on Earth. Clean water is nearly impossible to obtain for over 1 billion people on the planet . They can become ill from dirty, polluted water, which is especially difficult for young children. Some bacteria and pathogens in water can make people sick to the point of death.

Water pollution comes from a variety of sources. Here are a few of the main reasons:

Sewage: In many parts of the world, sewage is still flushed directly into streams and rivers. Sewage can introduce dangerous bacteria that can make humans and animals very sick.

Farm animal waste: Runoff from large herds of farm animals such as pigs and cows can enter the water supply due to rain and large storms.

Pesticides: Pesticides and herbicides are frequently sprayed on crops to kill bugs, while herbicides are sprayed to kill weeds. These potent chemicals can enter the water through rainstorm runoff. They can also contaminate rivers and lakes due to unintentional spills.

Construction, floods, and storms: Silt from construction, earthquakes, and storms can reduce water oxygen levels and suffocate fish. Factories - Water is frequently used in factories to process chemicals, keep engines cool, and wash things away. Sometimes used wastewater is dumped into rivers or the ocean. It may contain pollutants.

Estimate the sum or difference by rounding each number to the nearest ten.

1) 85 → 90; − 59 → − 60; 26 | 30

Problem	Original		Rounded
1)	85	→	90
	- 59	→	- 60
	26		30
2)	94	→	90
	- 21	→	- 20
	73		70
3)	23	→	20
	+ 42	→	+ 40
	65		60
4)	71	→	70
	- 53	→	- 50
	18		20
5)	15	→	20
	+ 74	→	+ 70
	89		90
6)	51	→	50
	+ 26	→	+ 30
	77		80
7)	91	→	90
	- 46	→	- 50
	45		40
8)	58	→	60
	+ 11	→	+ 10
	69		70
9)	79	→	80
	+ 32	→	+ 30
	111		110
10)	75	→	80
	+ 49	→	+ 50
	124		130
11)	63	→	60
	- 34	→	- 30
	29		30
12)	33	→	30
	- 22	→	- 20
	11		10
13)	76	→	80
	+ 12	→	+ 10
	88		90
14)	86	→	90
	- 27	→	- 30
	59		60

Answer Key

Order of Operations

Answers

1. 255
2. 9
3. 33
4. 38
5. 110
6. 20
7. 30
8. 47
9. 86
10. 27

1) $21 \div 3 + (3 \times 9) \times 9 + 5$

Step 1:	$(3 \times 9) = 27$	$21 \div 3 + 27 \times 9 + 5$
Step 2:	$21 \div 3 = 7$	$7 + 27 \times 9 + 5$
Step 3:	$27 \times 9 = 243$	$7 + 243 + 5$
Step 4:	$7 + 243 = 250$	$250 + 5$
Step 5:	$250 + 5 = 255$	255

2) $18 \div 6 \times (4 - 3) + 6$

Step 1:	$(4 - 3) = 1$	$18 \div 6 \times 1 + 6$
Step 2:	$18 \div 6 = 3$	$3 \times 1 + 6$
Step 3:	$3 \times 1 = 3$	$3 + 6$
Step 4:	$3 + 6 = 9$	9

3) $14 - 8 + 3 + 8 \times (24 \div 8)$

Step 1:	$(24 \div 8) = 3$	$14 - 8 + 3 + 8 \times 3$
Step 2:	$8 \times 3 = 24$	$14 - 8 + 3 + 24$
Step 3:	$14 - 8 = 6$	$6 + 3 + 24$
Step 4:	$6 + 3 = 9$	$9 + 24$
Step 5:	$9 + 24 = 33$	33

4) $4 \times 5 + (14 + 8) - 36 \div 9$

Step 1:	$(14 + 8) = 22$	$4 \times 5 + 22 - 36 \div 9$
Step 2:	$4 \times 5 = 20$	$20 + 22 - 36 \div 9$
Step 3:	$36 \div 9 = 4$	$20 + 22 - 4$
Step 4:	$20 + 22 = 42$	$42 - 4$
Step 5:	$42 - 4 = 38$	38

5) $(17 - 7) \times 6 + 2 + 56 - 8$

Step 1:	$(17 - 7) = 10$	$10 \times 6 + 2 + 56 - 8$
Step 2:	$10 \times 6 = 60$	$60 + 2 + 56 - 8$
Step 3:	$60 + 2 = 62$	$62 + 56 - 8$
Step 4:	$62 + 56 = 118$	$118 - 8$
Step 5:	$118 - 8 = 110$	110

6) $(28 \div 4) + 3 + (10 - 8) \times 5$

Step 1:	$(28 \div 4) = 7$	$7 + 3 + (10 - 8) \times 5$
Step 2:	$(10 - 8) = 2$	$7 + 3 + 2 \times 5$
Step 3:	$2 \times 5 = 10$	$7 + 3 + 10$
Step 4:	$7 + 3 = 10$	$10 + 10$
Step 5:	$10 + 10 = 20$	20

7) $12 - 5 + 6 \times 3 + 20 \div 4$

Step 1:	$6 \times 3 = 18$	$12 - 5 + 18 + 20 \div 4$
Step 2:	$20 \div 4 = 5$	$12 - 5 + 18 + 5$
Step 3:	$12 - 5 = 7$	$7 + 18 + 5$
Step 4:	$7 + 18 = 25$	$25 + 5$
Step 5:	$25 + 5 = 30$	30

8) $36 \div 9 + 48 - 10 \div 2$

Step 1:	$36 \div 9 = 4$	$4 + 48 - 10 \div 2$
Step 2:	$10 \div 2 = 5$	$4 + 48 - 5$
Step 3:	$4 + 48 = 52$	$52 - 5$
Step 4:	$52 - 5 = 47$	47

9) $10 + 8 \times 90 \div 9 - 4$

Step 1:	$8 \times 90 = 720$	$10 + 720 \div 9 - 4$
Step 2:	$720 \div 9 = 80$	$10 + 80 - 4$
Step 3:	$10 + 80 = 90$	$90 - 4$
Step 4:	$90 - 4 = 86$	86

10) $8 \times 3 + 70 \div 7 - 7$

Step 1:	$8 \times 3 = 24$	$24 + 70 \div 7 - 7$
Step 2:	$70 \div 7 = 10$	$24 + 10 - 7$
Step 3:	$24 + 10 = 34$	$34 - 7$
Step 4:	$34 - 7 = 27$	27

Exponents

1) $(2)^3$ = 8

2) $(5)^2$ = 25

3) $(12)^3$ = 1728

4) $(-8)^2$ = 64

5) $(-4)^2$ = 16

6) $(-2)^2$ = 4

7) $(7)^2$ = 49

8) $(-12)^2$ = 144

9) $(-2)^3$ = -8

10) $(-3)^3$ = -27

11) $(4)^3$ = 64

12) $(3)^3$ = 27

13) $(-5)^3$ = -125

14) $(3)^2$ = 9

15) $(2)^2$ = 4

16) $(-10)^3$ = -1000

17) $(-7)^2$ = 49

18) $(-9)^3$ = -729

19) $(-6)^3$ = -216

20) $(10)^2$ = 100

ANSWER SHEET

Fill-in The Appositive

Appositives are words or phrases that come before or after other nouns or pronouns to describe them further. The appositives should give the reader additional information about the nouns and pronouns in the sentences. Keep in mind that an appositive can be a single word or a group of words.

Appositives can be either essential or non-essential. If the appositive is required for the sentence to make sense, it is essential. This means it cannot be omitted. If the appositive is not required for the sentence's meaning and could be excluded, it is nonessential.

Commas should be used to separate non-essential appositives from the sentence. Commas are not used to separate essential appositives.

Examples:

Jane, my younger sister, is 27 years old. (Jane renames her younger sister)

My mother, who works as a nurse, has a red automobile. (A nurse renames mother, but this isn't necessary for the meaning of the line.)

Kevin is the name of the young artist that created this painting. (Who painted this image renames boy, which is crucial to the sentence's meaning.)

An insect, a ladybug, has just landed on the rose bush.

meadowlark	fiancé	cousin	valedictorian	Jones
champion	governor	movie	capital	

1. My uncle, the former **governor** of Maine, loves ice cream
2. Sally's **fiancé** Gerald works at Walmart
3. Providence, the **capital** of RI, is a great city
4. We saw the state bird, the **meadowlark**, at the park
5. My youngest **cousin** Caroline goes to Princeton University
6. Muhammad Ali, the three time heavy weight **champion** of the world won a gold medal in 1960
7. Sally Smith, the **valedictorian**, gave a wonderful speech at graduation
8. The vice principal, Mr. **Jones**, suspended my brother
9. My favorite **movie**, "Stand and Deliver" always makes me cry.

ANSWER SHEET

Flamingos Bird Facts

Flamingos are the show stoppers of the avian world. Their long legs, bending beaks, and **vivid** orange hue make them a sight to behold. They're a popular attraction at zoos and nature preserves because they are fascinating to see up close.

Phoenicopterus ruber is the scientific name for the American Flamingo. They reach a height of 3 to 5 feet and a weight of 5 to 6 pounds at maturity. Males tend to be larger than **females** in general. Feathers of the common flamingo are typically pinkish red. Additionally, their pink feet and pink and white bill, which has a black tip, distinguish them.

Central and South America and the Caribbean are home to the American Flamingo. It can also be found in the Bahamas and Cuba, and the Yucatan Peninsula of Mexico's Caribbean coast. As far as Brazil, there are some that can be found on the northern **coast**. In addition, the Galapagos Islands have a population.

Lagoons and low-lying **mudflats** or lakes are the preferred environments for the Flamingos. They like seeking food by wading across the water. They form enormous flocks, sometimes numbering in the tens of thousands.

Flamingos come in a variety of colors, including pink and orange. Carotenoids are responsible for the orange hue of several foods, such as carrots. Carrots would turn your skin and eyes orange if you just ate them. Flamingoes appear pink or orange because they eat **algae** and small shellfish rich in carotenoids. They would lose their vibrant hue if they switched to a different **diet**.

Is it possible for flamingoes to fly? Yes. Flamingos can fly, even though we usually associate them with **wading** in the water. Before they can take off, they have to run to build up their speed. They often fly in big groups.

Scientists don't know why Flamingos stand on one leg, but they have a few ideas. There is a rumor that it is to keep one leg warm. Because it's cold outside, they can keep one leg near their body to keep it warm. Another **theory** is that they are drying out one leg at a time. A third idea argues that it aids them in deceiving their **prey**, as one leg resembles a plant more than two.

It doesn't matter the reason; these **top-heavy** birds can stand on one leg for long periods. They even sleep with one leg balanced on the ground!

ANSWER SHEET

Jackie Robinson: The First African-American Player In MLB

On January 31, 1919, in Cairo, Georgia, Jack Roosevelt Robinson was born. There were five children in the family, and the youngest one was him. After Jackie was born, Jackie's father left the family, and he never returned. His mother, Millie, took care of him and his three brothers and one sister when they were young.

The family moved to Pasadena, California, about a year after Jackie was born. Jackie was awed by his older brothers' prowess in sports as a child. Meanwhile, his brother Mack rose to prominence as a track star and Olympic silver medalist in the 200-meter dash.

Jackie was an avid sports enthusiast. Like his older brother, he competed in track and field and other sports like football, baseball, and tennis. Football and baseball were two of his favorite sports to play. Throughout high school, Jackie was subjected to racism daily. Even though white teammates surrounded him, he felt like a second-class citizen off the field.

After high school, Jackie went to UCLA, where he excelled in track, baseball, football, and basketball. To his credit, he was the first player at UCLA to receive all four varsity letters in the same season. The long jump was another event where he excelled at the NCAA level.

With the outbreak of World War II, Robinson's football career was over before it began. He was called up for military service. Jackie made friends with the legendary boxing champion Joe Lewis at basic training. Robinson was accepted into officer training school thanks to Joe's assistance.

After completing his officer training, Jackie was assigned to the 761st Tank Battalion at Fort Hood, Texas. Only black soldiers were assigned to this battalion because they could not serve alongside white soldiers. When Jackie refused to move to the back of an army bus one day, he got into trouble. In 1944, he was discharged with an honorable discharge after nearly being expelled from the military.

Robinson began his professional baseball career with the Kansas City Monarchs soon after he was discharged from the military. The Negro Baseball League was home to the Monarchs. Black players were still not allowed to play in Major League Baseball at this time. Jackie performed well on the field. He was an outstanding shortstop, hitting .387 on average.

While playing for the Monarchs, Branch Rickey, the Dodgers' general manager, approached Jackie. Branch hoped that the Dodgers could win the pennant by signing an African-American player. Branch warned Robinson that he would encounter racial prejudice when he first joined the Dodgers. Branch was looking for a person who could take insults without reacting. This famous exchange between Jackie and Branch occurred during their first conversation:

Jackie: "Are you looking for a Negro who is afraid to fight back, Mr. Rickey?"
Jackie: "Are you looking for a Negro who is afraid to fight back, Mr. Rickey?" Robinson, I'm looking for a baseball player who has the guts not to fight back."

For the Montreal Royals, Jackie first played in the minor leagues. He was constantly confronted with racism. Because of Jackie, the opposing team would occasionally fail to show up for games. Then there were the times when people would verbally abuse or throw objects at him. In the midst of all this, Jackie remained calm and focused on the game. He had a .349 batting average and was named the league's most valuable player.

Robinson was called up to play for the Brooklyn Dodgers at the start of the 1947 baseball season, and he did. On April 15, 1947, he became the first African-American to play in the sport's major leagues. Racially charged taunts were once again directed at Jackie from both fans and fellow players alike. Death threats were made against him. But Jackie had the courage not to fight back. He kept his word to Branch Rickey and dedicated himself solely to the game of baseball. The Dodgers won the pennant that year, and Jackie was named the team's Rookie of the Year for his achievements.

Jackie Robinson was one of the best major league baseball players for the next ten years. During his lengthy career, his batting average stood at.311, and he hit 137 home runs while also stealing 197 bases. Six times he was selected to the All-Star team, and in 1949 he was named the National League MVP.

Because of Jackie Robinson's groundbreaking work, other African-American players could play in the major leagues. He also paved the way for racial integration in different facets of American life. He was inducted into the Baseball Hall of Fame in 1962. On October 24, 1972, Robinson suffered a heart attack and died.

Julius Caesar Roman Dictator

1. **Caesar made changes to the Roman ____.**
   a. history
   b. calendar

2. **Julius Caesar parents were the most powerful people in politics.**
   a. True
   b. False

3. **Julius Caesar became a public speaker and advocated for the ____.**
   a. government
   b. law

4. **Julius was chosen to run Spain in ____ BC**
   a. 62
   b. 32

5. **Caesar worked closely with ____, a former military officer, and ____, one of the wealthiest men in Rome**
   a. Crassus, Poindexter
   b. Pompey, Crassus

6. **Caesar changed the debt laws in ___.**
   a. Rome
   b. Egypt

7. **____ came up with a plan to kill Caesar on the Ides of March.**
   a. Marcus Brutus
   b. Mark Buccaning

8. **What wars helped to form the Roman Empire?**
   a. civil wars
   b. World War II

ANSWER SHEET

Proofreading Interpersonal Skills: Peer Pressure

Tony is mingling with a large group of what he considers to be the school's cool kids. Suddenly, someone in the group begins mocking Tony's friend Rob, who walks with a limp due to a physical ~~dasability.~~ **disability.**

They begin to imitate ~~rob's~~ **Rob's** limping and ~~Call~~ **call** him 'lame cripple' and other derogatory terms. Although Tony disapproves of their behavior, he does not want to risk being excluded from the group, and thus joins them in mocking Rob.

Peer pressure is the influence exerted on us by ~~member's~~ **members** of our social group. It can manifest in a variety of ways and can lead to us engaging in behaviors we would not normally ~~consider~~ **consider,** such as Tony joining in and mocking his friend Rob.

However, peer pressure is not always detrimental. Positive peer pressure can motivate us to make better ~~chioces,~~ **choices,** such as studying harder, staying in school, or seeking a better job. ~~Whan~~ **When** others influence us to make poor ~~Choices,~~ **choices,** such as smoking, using illicit drugs, or bullying, we succumb to negative peer pressure. We all desire to belong to a group and fit in, so ~~Developing~~ **developing** strategies for resisting peer pressure when necessary can be beneficial.

Tony and his friends are engaging in bullying by ~~moking~~ **mocking** Rob. Bullying is defined as persistent, ~~unwanted.~~ **unwanted,** aggressive behavior directed toward another person. It is ~~moust~~ **most** prevalent in school-aged children but can also ~~aphfect~~ **affect** adults. Bullying can take on a variety of forms, including the following:

~~· Verbil~~
· **Verbal** bullying is when someone is called names, threatened, or taunted verbally.
· Bullying is physical in nature - ~~hitting~~ **hitting,** spitting, tripping, or ~~poshing~~ **pushing** someone.
· Social ~~Bullying~~ **bullying** is intentionally excluding ~~Someone~~ **someone** from ~~activities~~ **activities,** spreading rumors, or embarrassing ~~sumeone.~~ **someone.**
· Cyberbullying is the act of verbally or socially bullying someone via the internet, such as through social media sites.

Peer pressure exerts a significant influence on an individual's decision to engage in bullying ~~behavoir.~~ **behavior.** In Tony's case, even though Rob is a friend and ~~tony~~ **Tony** would never consider mocking his disability, his desire to belong to a group outweighs his willingness to defend his ~~friend~~ **friend.**

Peer pressure is a strong force that is exerted on us by our social group members. Peer pressure is classified into two types: negative peer pressure, which results in poor decision-making, and positive peer pressure, which influences us to make the correct choices. Adolescents are particularly susceptible to peer pressure because of their desire to fit ~~in~~ **in.**

Peer pressure can motivate someone to engage in bullying behaviors such as mocking someone, threatening to harm them, taunting them online, or excluding them from an activity. Each year, bullying ~~affect's~~ **affects** an astounding 3.2 million school-aged children. ~~Severil~~ **Several** strategies for avoiding peer pressure bullying include the following:

- ~~consider~~ **Consider** your actions by surrounding yourself with good company.
- Acquiring the ability to say no to someone you trust.

Speak up - bullying is never acceptable and is taken ~~extramely~~ **extremely** ~~seroiusly~~ **seriously** in schools and the workplace. If someone is attempting to convince you to bully another person, speaking with a trusted adult such as a teacher, coach, counselor, or coworker can frequently help put ~~thing's~~ **things** into perspective and highlight the issue.

ANSWER SHEET

Proofreading Skills: Volunteering

There are **10** mistakes in this passage. 3 capitals missing. 4 unnecessary capitals. 3 incorrect homophones.

Your own life can be changed and the lives of others, through volunteer work. ~~to~~ **To** cope with the news that there has been a disaster, you can volunteer to help those in need. Even if you can't contribute financially, you can donate ~~you're~~ **your** time instead.

Volunteering is such an integral part of the American culture that many high schools require their students to participate in community service to graduate.

When you volunteer, you have the freedom to choose what you'd like to do and who or what you think is most deserving of your time. Start with these ideas if you need a little inspiration. We've got just a few examples here.

Encourage the growth and development of young people. Volunteer as a ~~Camp~~ **camp** counselor, a Big Brother or Big Sister, or an after-school sports program. Special Olympics games and events are excellent opportunities to know children with special needs.

Spend the holidays doing good deeds for others. Volunteer at a food bank or distribute toys to children in need on Thanksgiving Day, and you'll be doing your part to help those in need. ~~your~~ **Your** church, temple, mosque, or another place of worship may also require your assistance.

You can visit an animal shelter and play with the ~~Animals.~~ **animals.** Volunteers are critical to the well-being of shelter animals. (You also get a good workout when you walk rescued dogs.)

Become a member of a political campaign. ~~Its~~ **It's** a great way to learn more about the inner workings of politics if ~~your~~ **you're** curious about it. If you are not able ~~To~~ **to** cast a ballot, you can still help elect your preferred candidate.

Help save the planet. Join a river preservation group and lend a hand. Participate in a park cleanup day in your community. Not everyone is cut out for the great outdoors; if you can't see yourself hauling trees up a hill, consider working in the park's office or education center instead.

Take an active role in promoting health-related causes. Many of us know someone afflicted with a medical condition (like cancer, HIV, or diabetes, for example). ~~a~~ **A** charity that helps people with a disease, such as delivering meals, raising money, or providing other assistance, can make you ~~Feel~~ **feel** good about yourself.

Find a way to combine your favorite things if you have more than one. For example, if you're a fan of kids and have a talent for arts and crafts, consider volunteering at a children's hospital.

Science: Titanium (Ti) Element

Titanium is the first element in the periodic table's fourth column. It is a transition metal. Titanium atoms contain 22 protons and 22 electrons.

Titanium is a complex, light, silvery metal under normal conditions. It can be brittle at room temperature, but it becomes more bendable and pliable as the temperature rises.

Titanium's high strength-to-weight ratio is one of its most desirable properties. This means it is both extremely strong and lightweight. Titanium is double the strength of aluminum but only 60% heavier. It is also as strong as steel but weighs a fraction of the weight.

Compared to other metals, titanium is relatively non-reactive and highly resistant to corrosion caused by different metals and chemicals such as acids and oxygen. As a result, it has relatively low thermal and electrical conductivity.

Titanium is not found in nature as a pure element but rather as a compound found in the Earth's crust as a component of many minerals. According to the International Atomic Energy Agency, it is the ninth most prevalent element in the Earth's crust. Rutile and ilmenite are the two most essential minerals for titanium mining. Australia, South Africa, and Canada are the top producers of these ores.

Titanium is mostly used in the form of titanium dioxide (TiO_2). TiO_2 is a white powder used in various industrial applications such as white paint, white paper, white polymers, and white cement.

Metals like iron, aluminum, and manganese are combined with titanium to create strong and lightweight alloys that can be utilized in spacecraft, naval vessels, missiles, and armor plating. Due to its corrosion resistance, it is particularly well-suited for seawater applications.

The biocompatibility of titanium is another valuable property of the metal. This indicates that the human body will not reject it. Together with its strength, durability, and lightweight, titanium is a good material for medical applications. It is utilized in various applications, including hip and dental implants. Titanium is also utilized in the manufacture of jewelry, such as rings and watches.

Reverend William Gregor recognized titanium as a new element for the first time in 1791. As a hobby, the English clergyman was fascinated by minerals. He coined the term menachanite for the element. M.H. Kalproth, a German chemist, eventually altered the name to titanium. M. A. Hunter, an American scientist, was the first to create pure titanium in 1910.

Titanium is named after the Greek gods Titans.

Titanium has five stable isotopes: titanium-46, titanium-47, titanium-48, titanium-49, and titanium-50. The isotope titanium-48 accounts for the vast bulk of titanium found in nature.

1. Titanium has five stable ____.

a. isotopes
b.

2. Titanium is the first element in the periodic table's ____ column.

a. 4rd
b. fourth

3. Titanium is a transition ____.

a. metal
b.

4. Titanium is mostly used in the form of ____ (TiO_2).

a. titanium dioxide
b. dioxide oxygen

ANSWER SHEET

Reading Storytime: The Frog

When wishing was a thing, there was a King whose daughters were all **beautiful**, but the youngest was so stunning that even the sun, which has seen so much, was taken aback whenever it shone in her face.

A large dark forest lay close to the King's **castle**, and a fountain was hidden beneath an old lime tree in the woods. When it was a hot day, the King's Child went out into the forest and sat by the cool fountain, and when she was bored, she took a golden ball, threw it up in the air, and caught it. And the ball was her favorite toy.

Now, one day, the King's Daughter's golden **ball** fell onto the ground and rolled straight into the water rather than into the little hand she was holding up for it. The King's Daughter pursued it with her eyes, but it vanished, and the well was deep, so deep that the bottom could not be seen. She began to cry, and she screamed louder and louder, and she could not be consoled.

And as she sobbed, someone asked her, "What ails you, King's Daughter?" You weep so much that even a stone would feel sorry for you."

When she turned around to the side from which the voice had come, she saw a **Frog** sticking its thick, ugly head out of the water. "Ah! "Is it you, old water-splasher?" she asked, "I am weeping for my golden ball, which has fallen into the fountain."

"Be quiet and do not weep," the Frog replied, "I can help you." But what will you give me if I bring up your toy again?"

"Whatever you want, dear Frog," she said, "my clothes, my pearls, and jewels, even the golden crown I'm wearing."

"I don't care for your clothes, pearls, and jewels, or your golden crown," the Frog replied, "but if you will love me and let me be your **companion** and playfellow, and sit by you at your little table, and eat off your little golden plate, and drink out of your little cup, and sleep in your little bed-if you promise me this, I will go down below and bring your golden ball up again."

"Oh, yes," she said, "I promise you everything you want if you just bring my ball back." "How the silly Frog does talk!" she thought. He lives in the water with the other frogs and croaks and can't be a human's companion!"

But, having received this promise, the Frog plunged his head into the water and sank. He quickly came **swimming** up with the ball in his mouth, and threw it on the grass. The King's Daughter was thrilled to see her pretty plaything again, and she quickly picked it up and ran away with it.

"Wait, wait," the Frog said. "Bring me along. I can't run as fast as you." But what good did it do him to scream his croak, croak, croak, croak, croak, croak! She ignored it and ran home, quickly forgetting the poor Frog, who was forced to return to his **fountain**.

The next day, as she sat at the table with the King and all the courtiers, eating from her little golden plate, something crept up the marble staircase, splish splash, splish splash. When it reached the top, it knocked on the **door** and cried out:

"Youngest King's Daughter."
"Please open the door!"

She dashed outside to see who was there, but when she opened the door, the Frog was standing in front of it. Then she hurriedly slammed the door, sat down to **dinner** again, and was terrified.

"My Child, what are you so afraid of?" said the King, seeing her heart beating furiously. Is there a Giant outside looking to take you away?"

"Ah, no," she replied, "it's a disgusting Frog, not a Giant."

"What exactly does the Frog want from you?"

"Ah, dear Father, my golden ball fell into the water yesterday while I was sitting by the fountain in the forest, playing." Because I **cried** so much, the Frog brought it out for me again. And because he insisted, I promised him he could be my companion, but I never imagined he'd be able to get out of the water! And now he's here, wanting to come in."

Meanwhile, it knocked a second time and cried:

"Youngest King's Daughter!"
Allow me to enter!
Don't you remember yesterday and everything you said to me, besides the cooling fountain's spray?
Youngest King's Daughter!
"Let me in!"

Determine how much liquid is in each graduated cylinder.

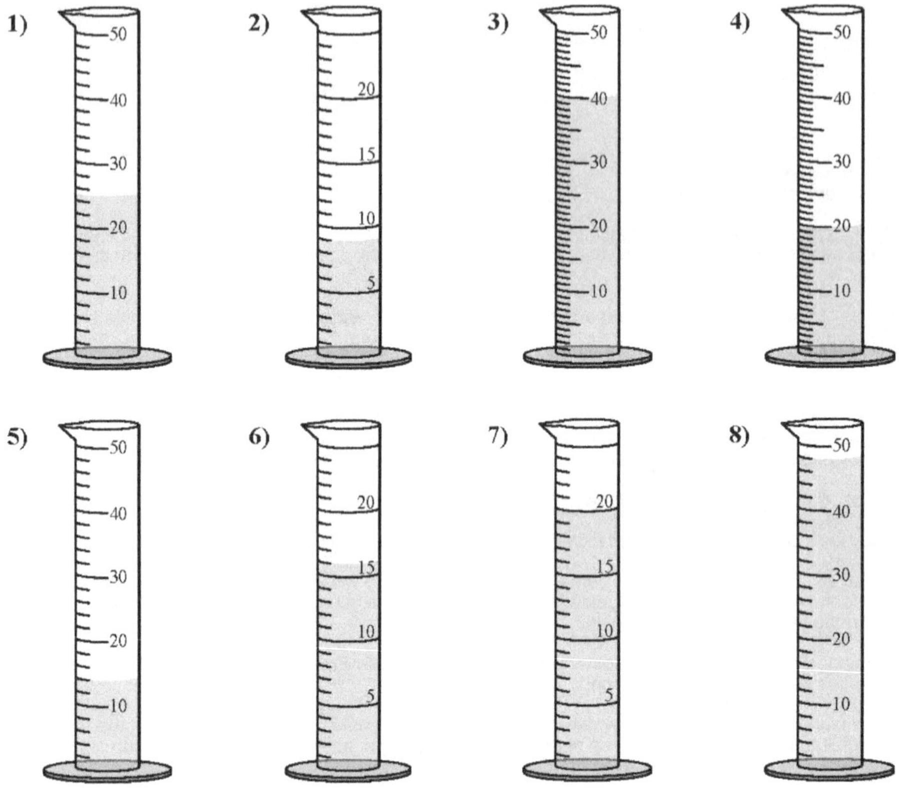

Four different objects were placed in a graduated cylinder 1 at a time:

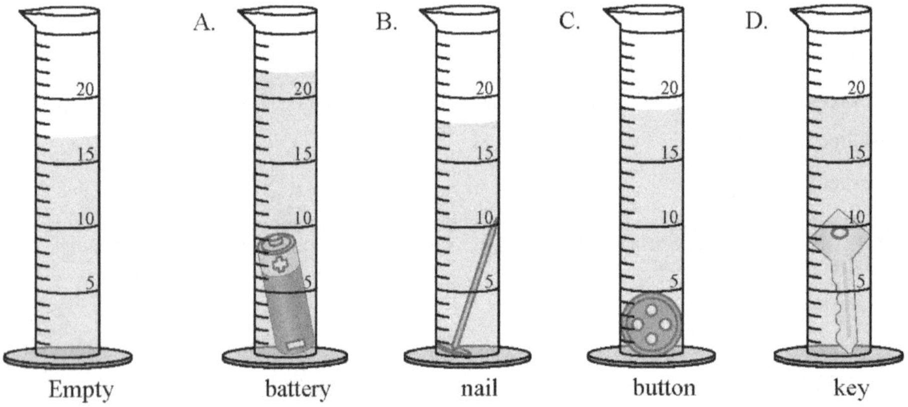

9) Which object had the greatest volume?

10) Which object had the least volume?

Answers

1. 25
2. 9
3. 40
4. 20
5. 14
6. 16
7. 20
8. 48
9. A
10. B

Labeling Scientific Tools (Microscope) **Answer Key**

Determine which letter best matches each microscope piece.

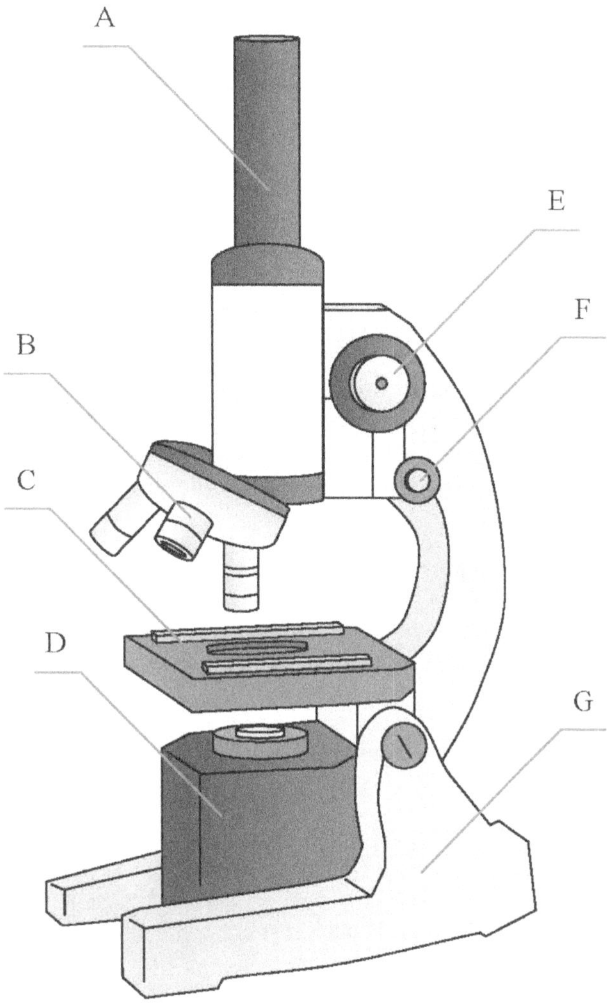

1) Illuminator ______

2) Stage ______

3) Eyepiece ______

4) Focus (Fine) ______

5) Lense ______

6) Focus (Course) ______

7) Base ______

Answers

1. D
2. C
3. A
4. F
5. B
6. E
7. G

Using Scientific Tools **Answer Key**

Determine which scientific tool best answers the question.

A. Thermometer	C. Scale	E. Microscope
B. Ruler	D. Telescope	F. Measuring Cup

1) Will only had enough money to buy 2 pounds of bananas at the grocery store. What tool should he use to make sure he gets exactly 2 pounds?

2) Oliver found a small black dot on his new sweater. What tool should he use to determine what the dot actually is?

3) Adam needed to mix exactly 2 tablespoons of food coloring with 2 quarts of water. What tool should he use to measure the amounts?

4) Maria, while performing an experiment, had to make sure her wires were between 1 and 2 inches. What tool did she use to determine the length?

5) Paige earned $1 dollar for every 3 pounds of cans she recycled. What tool should she use to make sure she recycles at least 3 pounds?

6) Mike wanted to check the water temperature of a hot tub. What tool should he use to see the water temperature?

7) George was trying to view satellites from his backyard. What tool should he use to help find one?

8) Billy needed exactly 6 ounces of cheese. What tool should he use to measure exactly 6 ounces?

9) Paul used a tool to view the Andromeda Galaxy. What tool did he use to see the galaxy?

10) Dave wanted to check the height of his flashlight. What tool should he use?

11) A scientist wanted to view the microbes in a drop of water. What tool should he use?

12) Megan needed to add 500 ml of water to a mixture for an experiment. What tool did she use to measure out 500 ml of water?

13) John wants to compare the cells of an animal and a plant. What tool should he use?

14) Nancy was outside looking at the Crab Nebula. What tool was she using to view the nebula?

15) Tom learned old books needed to stay at around 70° F. What tool should he use to make sure the books don't get too hot?

Answers

1. C
2. E
3. F
4. B
5. C
6. A
7. D
8. C
9. D
10. B
11. E
12. F
13. E
14. D
15. A

ANSWER SHEET

Science Vocabulary 1

Choose the best answer to each question.

1. A variable that is intentionally changed to observe its effect on the dependent variable.

a. Dependent Variable

b. Independent Variable

2. Choose the correct meaning of the word "Melting Point".

a. Temperature at which a solid changes state to a liquid.

b. At normal atmospheric pressure, the temperature at which a liquid solidifies.

3. Temperature at which liquid changes state to gas.

a. Freezing Point

b. Boiling Point

4. Anything that takes up space and has mass.

a. Mass

b. Matter

5. The event expected to change when the independent variable is changed. Measurable

a. Dependent Variable

b. Independent Variable

6. Which word describes the variables that are not changed?

a. Control Group

b. Experimental group

7. Select the meaning of the word "Condensation".

a. Change of matter from a liquid to a gas.

b. Change of matter from a gas to a liquid state.

8. What is the definition of Freezing Point?

a. At the temperature at which its vapor pressure is equal to the pressure of the gas above it.

b. Temperature at which a liquid changes state to solid.

9. Select the meaning of the word "Evaporation".

a. Change of matter from a gas to a liquid state.

b. Change of matter from a liquid to a gas.

10. The amount of matter in an object.

a. Mass

b. Matter

ANSWER SHEET

Science Vocabulary 2

Choose the best answer to each question.

1. **Change in which the composition of a substance changes.**
   a. Physical Change
   b. Chemical Change

2. **What is the correct definition of the word "Physical Change"?**
   a. Change in which the composition of a substance changes.
   b. Change in which the form or appearance of matter changes, but not its composition.

3. **What is the correct definition of the word "Compound"?**
   a. Two or more substances that are blended without combining chemically.
   b. Two or more elements that are chemically combined.

4. **Made up of only one kind of atom. Cannot be broken down into a simpler form by chemical reactions.**
   a. Element
   b. Compound

5. **What is the correct definition of the word "Chemical Property"?**
   a. Characteristics that is observable or measureable in a substance without changing the chemical composition of the substance.
   b. Characteristic that cannot be observed without altering the sample.

6. **Ratio of the mass of a substance to its volume, expressed in g/cm3. Mixture**
   a. Volume
   b. Density

7. **What is the correct definition of the word "Mixture"?**
   a. Two or more substances that are blended without combining chemically.
   b. Two or more elements that are chemically combined.

8. **What is the correct definition of the word "Volume"?**
   a. Ratio of the mass of a substance to its volume, expressed in g/cm3. Mixture
   b. Amount of space occupied by an object or a substance.

9. **Characteristics that is observable or measureable in a substance without changing the chemical composition of the substance.**
   a. Chemical Property
   b. Physical Property

10. **What is the correct definition of the word "Solution"?**
    a. Homogeneous mixture whose elements and/or compounds are evenly mixed at the molecular level but are not bonded together.
    b. Two or more substances that are blended without combining chemically.

ANSWER SHEET

Science Vocabulary 3

Choose the best answer to each question.

1. Type of mixture where the substances are not evenly mixed. Different parts are visible.
   a. Homogeneous Mixture
   b. Heterogeneous Mixture

2. Type of mixture where two or more substances are evenly mixed on a molecular level but are not bonded together.
   a. Homogeneous Mixture
   b. Heterogeneous Mixture

3. Electrically-neutral particle that has the same mass as a proton and is found in an atom's nucleus.
   a. Neutron
   b. Proton

4. Negatively-charged particle that exists in an electron cloud formation around an atom's nucleus.
   a. Neutron
   b. Electron

5. Region surrounding the nucleus of an atom, where electrons are most likely to be found.
   a. Electron Shell
   b. Electron Cloud

6. What is the meaning of the word "Base"?
   a. Substance that releases H+ ions and produces hydronium ions when dissolved in water.
   b. Substance that accepts H+ ions and produces hydroxide ions when dissolved in water.

7. Substance that releases H+ ions and produces hydronium ions when dissolved in water.
   a. Base
   b. Acid

8. What is the meaning of the word "ph"?
   a. a measure of the hydroxide ion (OH-) concentration of a solution.
   b. Measure of how acidic or basic a solution is, ranging in a scale from 0 to 14.

9. What is the meaning of the word "Proton"?
   a. Negatively-charged particle that exists in an electron cloud formation around an atom's nucleus.
   b. Positively-charged particle in the nucleus of an atom.

10. What is the meaning of the word "Nucleus"?
   a. Small region of space at the center of the atom; contains protons and neutrons.
   b. Is a region found within the cell nucleus that is concerned with producing and assembling the cell's ribosomes.

Science Vocabulary 4

Choose the best answer to each question.

1. Family of elements in the periodic table that have similar physical or chemical properties.

a. Group

b. Subgroup

2. Table of elements organized into groups and periods by increasing atomic number.

a. Periodic Table

b. Chemical Elements

3. It is the property of many substances that give the ability to do work; many forms of energy (i.e., light, heat, electricity, sound)

a. Energy

b. Power

4. Number of protons in the nucleus of an atom of a given element.

a. Mass Number

b. Atomic Number

5. The sum of neutrons and protons in the nucleus of an atom.

a. Mass Number

b. Atomic Number

6. Force of attraction between all objects in the universe.

a. Gravity

b. Friction

7. What is the meaning of the word "Isotope"?

a. Atoms of the same element that have different numbers of neutrons.

b. An atom or molecule with a positive or negative charge.

8. What is the meaning of the word "Period"?

a. Vertical row of elements in the periodic table.

b. Horizontal row of elements in the periodic table.

9. What is the meaning of the word "Tides"?

a. Rise and fall of ocean water levels.

b. Ae formed because of the winds blowing over the surface of the ocean.

10. What is the meaning of the word "Kinetic Energy"?

a. Energy an object has due to its motion.

b. A form of energy that has the potential to do work but is not actively doing work or applying any force on any other objects.

ANSWER SHEET

Science Vocabulary 5

Choose the best answer to each question.

1. Energy that all objects have that increases as the object's temperature increases.
   a. Thermal Energy
   b. Potential Energy

2. Energy carried by electric current.
   a. Electrical Energy
   b. Radiant Energy

3. Transfer of heat by the flow of material. Heat rises and cool air sinks.
   a. Conduction
   b. Convection

4. What is the meaning of the word "Radiant Energy"?
   a. Energy that all objects have that increases as the object's temperature increases.
   b. Energy carried by light.

5. Transfer of energy that occurs when molecules bump into each other.
   a. Convection
   b. Conduction

6. The crust and the rigid part of Earth's mantle. Divided into tectonic plates.
   a. Lithosphere
   b. Asthenosphere

7. What is the meaning of the word "Potential Energy"?
   a. Energy stored in an object due to its position.
   b. Energy stored in chemical bonds.

8. Energy contained in atomic nuclei; splitting uranium nuclei by nuclear fission.
   a. Nuclear Energy
   b. Thermal Energy

9. States that energy can change its form but is never created or destroyed.
   a. Law of Conservation of Mass
   b. Law of Conservation of Energy

10. What is the meaning of the word "Chemical Energy"?
   a. Energy stored in chemical bonds.
   b. Energy stored in an object due to its position.

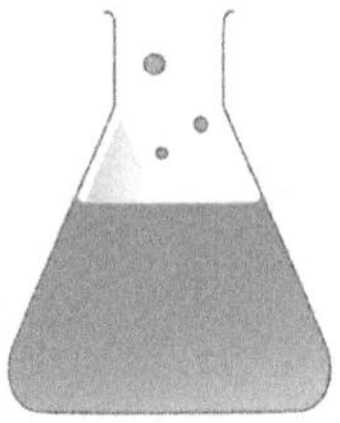

ANSWER SHEET

Science Vocabulary 6

Choose the best answer to each question.

1	G	Precipitation	⇢	Process of water falling from clouds to earth in the form of rain, sleet, show, or hail
2	D	Inner Core	⇢	Inner most layer composed of solid iron and nickel. Stays solid due to the pressure of the layers above it.
3	B	Continental Drift	⇢	The movement of the Earth's continents relative to each other by appearing to drift across the ocean bed
4	A	Crust	⇢	Earth's solid, rocky surface.
5	H	Asthenosphere	⇢	Solid layer of the mantle beneath lithosphere; made of mantle rock that flows very slowly allowing tectonic plates to move on top of it.
6	C	Condensation	⇢	Process of water vapor changing to liquid water
7	J	Mantle	⇢	The layer of Earth beneath the crust.
8	F	Core	⇢	Made up of mostly molten (melted) iron and nickel.
9	I	Plate Tectonics	⇢	Scientific theory that describes the large-scale motions of Earth's lithosphere.
10	E	Water Cycle	⇢	Continuous movement of water from the air to the earth and back again.

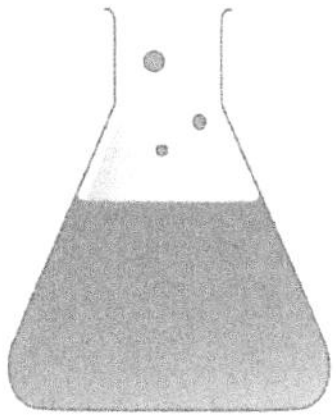

ANSWER SHEET

Science Vocabulary 7

Choose the best answer to each question.

1	C	Mechanical Weathering	⇢	Involves only physical changes, such as size and shape. The chemical makeup of the rocks does not change.
2	J	Atmosphere	⇢	Thick blanket of gases (nitrogen, oxygen and trace gases) surrounding the earth
3	G	Mesosphere	⇢	Third atmospheric layer above the stratosphere; coldest layer
4	D	Deposition	⇢	Dropping of sediments that occurs when a cause of erosion loses its energy and can no longer carry its load
5	A	Troposphere	⇢	Atmospheric layer closest to earth; nearly all weather change occurs here
6	H	Erosion	⇢	Is the process that wears away surface materials and moves them from one place to another
7	I	Evaporation	⇢	Process of liquid water changing to water vapor
8	E	Thermosphere	⇢	Highest layer of the earth's atmosphere; very thin air
9	B	Chemical Weathering	⇢	Occurs when the chemical makeup of the rocks changes.
10	F	Stratosphere	⇢	Second atmospheric layer above the troposphere; nearly all ozone found here

ANSWER SHEET

Science Words You Should Know Quiz

Circle the correct meaning of each word. Need help? Try Google!

1. Bulb
a. Light producing instrument
b. Learning by doing

2. Circuit
a. A representation of data
b. A path that electricity follows during its flowing

3. Kinetic
a. An optical instrument
b. Movement

4. Friction
a. Resistance due to movement
b. Making larger

5. Hygrometer
a. A path that electricity follows during its flowing
b. Humidity measuring instrument

6. Barometer
a. The intensity of sound
b. Pressure measuring instrument

7. Humidity
a. A quantity expressing water vapor's amount
b. Movement

8. Pitch
a. Findings after an investigation
b. The intensity of sound

9. Neutron
a. Sub-particle of an atom
b. Findings after an investigation

10. Proton
a. Findings after an investigation
b. A constituent of an atom

11. Dark
a. Categorization on a common base
b. Absence of light

12. Practical
a. Learning by doing
b. A path that electricity follows during its flowing

13. Classify
a. Categorization on a common base
b. Findings after an investigation

14. Analyze
a. Detail examination
b. Resistance due to movement

15. Expand
a. Absence of light
b. Making larger

16. Graph
a. A representation of data
b. A path that electricity follows during its flowing

17. Results
a. Findings after an investigation
b. Sub-particle of an atom

18. Microscope
a. Making larger
b. An optical instrument

ANSWER SHEET

Science: Mollusk

A mollusk is a type of soft-bodied animal. A hard shell protects the body of most mollusks. Mollusks are classified into over 100,000 species or types. Some examples include octopuses, oysters, snails, and squid.

All over the world, mollusks can be found. The majority of them live in the sea, but some are freshwater species. Some prefer the coast's shallow water, and others would rather be in deep water. Many mollusks dig down into muddy or sandy soil, while some cling to rocks.

Snails and slugs can be found on land; they prefer cool, moist environments and can also be found in cold climates and deserts.

Mollusks are invertebrates, which means they lack a backbone. They have a soft body containing the heart, liver, digestive system, and other vital organs. A radula is a mouth structure found in most mollusks; the radula resembles a rough tongue with many tiny teeth.

Many mollusks feed primarily on algae, they scrape algae off rocks with the radula. Larger mollusks, on the other hand, have a big appetite. Snails and slugs eat plants and fruit. Squids can consume fish and shrimp. An octopus is capable of pursuing prey as large as a shark.

Mollusks are usually active at night. Octopuses, for example, spend the day in the deep parts of the ocean. They swim closer to the surface at dawn and dusk, searching for food. Land snails and slugs hide during the day and emerge at night.

Many mollusks hide in their shells from predators. On the other hand, Mollusks without shells must rely on other means of defense. Squid and octopuses change color and pattern to blend in with their surroundings. They also emit an inky liquid to distract and confuse an opponent.

1. Mollusks are invertebrates.
   a. True
   b. False

2. A mollusk is a kind of animal with a ___.
   a. soft body
   b. soft shell but hard body

3. Octopuses, oysters, snails, and ___ are a few examples of a mollusk.
   a. penguin
   b. squid

4. Most mollusks have a mouth structure called a ____.
   a. radula
   b. reddish

5. Many mollusks eat mostly ____.
   a. fish
   b. algae

6. Mollusks usually are active during the day.
   a. True - they prefer day time to find food
   b. False - they are active usually at night

Science: Protists

Protists are organisms that are classified under the biological kingdom protista. These are neither plants, animals, bacteria, or fungi, but rather **unclassifiable** organisms. Protists are a large group of organisms with a wide variety of characteristics. They are essentially all species that do not fit into any of the other categories.

Protists as a group share very few characteristics. They are eukaryotic microorganisms with eukaryote **cell** structures that are pretty basic. Apart from that, they are defined as any organism that is not a plant, an animal, a bacteria, or a fungus.

Protists can be classified according to their mode of movement.

Cilia - Certain protists move with **tiny** hair called cilia. These tiny hairs can flap in unison to assist the creature in moving through water or another liquid.

Other protists have a lengthy **tail** known as flagella. This tail can move back and forth, aiding in the organism's propulsion.

Pseudopodia - When a protist extends a portion of its cell body in order to **scoot** or ooze. Amoebas move in this manner.

Different protists collect **energy** in a variety of methods. Certain individuals consume food and digest it internally. Others digest their food through the secretion of enzymes. Then they **consume** the partially digested meal. Other protists, like plants, utilize photosynthesis. They absorb sunlight and convert it to glucose.

Algae is a main form of protist. Algae are photosynthesis-capable protists. Algae are closely related to plants. They contain chlorophyll and utilize **oxygen** and solar energy to generate food. However, they are not called plants because they lack specialized organs and tissues such as leaves, roots, and stems. Algae are frequently classified according on their **color**, which ranges from red to brown to green.

Slime **molds** are distinct from fungus molds. Slime molds are classified into two types: cellular and plasmodial. Slime molds of Plasmodium are formed from a single big cell. They are also referred to as **acellular**. Even though these organisms are composed of only one cell, they can grow quite **enormous**, up to several feet in width. Additionally, they can contain several nuclei inside a single cell. Cellular slime molds are little single-celled protists that can form a single organism when combined. When combined, various **cellular** slime molds will perform specific activities.

Amoebas are single-celled organisms that move with the assistance of pseudopods. Amoebas have no structure and consume their food by engulfing it with their bodies. Amoebas **reproduce** by dividing in two during a process called mitosis.

ANSWER SHEET

Sentence Unscramble

Unscramble the sentences!

1. The sun rises at 5 in the morning.

   5 · the · sun · at · in · rises · morning. · The

2. I get ready for school.

   get · ready · I · for · school.

3. I eat a healthy breakfast.

   a · healthy · breakfast. · I · eat

4. I leave for school at about 7:30.

   I · for · leave · school · about · at · 7:30.

5. I get to school and prepare.

   prepare. · get · school · I · and · to

6. I talk to my friends before lunch.

   friends · my · lunch. · to · talk · before · I

7. I eat a terrible lunch.

   I · lunch. · a · terrible · eat

8. I am sleep after lunch.

   sleep · lunch. · I · am · after

9. I prepare to go home.

   home. · go · to · prepare · I

10. I get home after a long day at school!

    I · get · long · after · at · home · a · day · school!

ANSWER SHEET

Social Studies Vocabulary 6

Choose the best answer to each question.

1	I	Primary source	⇢	firsthand information about people or events.
2	L	Rural	⇢	country or farmland.
3	B	Bicameral Legislature	⇢	Two house law-making body.
4	F	Act	⇢	law
5	K	Suffrage	⇢	vote
6	J	Tariff	⇢	tax
7	D	Senate	⇢	group of elected officials that make laws (each state has two).
8	C	Federal	⇢	Central government
9	E	Haudenosaunee	⇢	Native American word to describe the Iroquois people.
10	M	Import	⇢	trade product brought into a country.
11	G	Civilization	⇢	highly developed level of cultural and technological development.
12	A	Exports	⇢	products made in one country and going to another.
13	H	Expansion	⇢	to make a country larger.

ANSWER SHEET

Social Studies Vocabulary 1

Choose the best answer to each question.

1	I	Abolition	⇢	the ending of slavery.
2	H	Compare	⇢	to state the similarities between two or more examples.
3	K	Concentration Camp	⇢	a prison camp for persons who are considered enemies of the state. In WWII, death camps that were run by the German SS at the orders of Adolf Hitler.
4	G	Containment	⇢	In the Cold War, the policy of trying to prevent the spread of Soviet or communist influence beyond where it already existed.
5	C	Appeasement	⇢	the practice of giv In the Cold War, the policy of trying to prevent the spread of Soviet or communist influence beyond where it already existeding in to an aggressor nation's demands in order to keep the peace (avoid war).
6	J	Industrialization	⇢	The economic transformation of a country marked by the development of new industries, mass production of goods and reduction in its agricultural workforce.
7	B	Free Market	⇢	an economic system in which individuals decide for themselves what to produce and sell.
8	L	Fascism	⇢	A system of government marked by centralization of authority under a dictator, stringent socioeconomic controls, suppression of political opposition through terror and censorship, and typically a policy of belligerent nationalism and racism.
9	E	Martial Law	⇢	rule by the army instead of elected the government characterized by the reduction of civil liberties.
10	D	Baby Boom	⇢	increased birth rate in the U.S. after WWII (1940s & 50s).
11	F	Contrast	⇢	to state the difference between two or more examples.
12	A	Downsizing	⇢	practice of trying to cut costs by using fewer people to do the same work

ANSWER SHEET

Social Studies Vocabulary 2

Choose the best answer to each question.

1	M	Superpower	⇢	nation with enough military and economic strength to influence events in many areas around the world.
2	G	Steerage	⇢	On a ship, the cramped quarters for passengers paying the lowest fares.
3	D	Segregation	⇢	separation of people based on racial, ethnic, or other differences.
4	A	Monopoly	⇢	exclusive control or ownership of an industry by a single business with the purpose of reducing competition.
5	E	Domino Theory	⇢	in the Cold War, belief that if South Vietnam became communist, other countries in Southeast Asia would become communist, too.
6	B	Migrant Worker	⇢	agricultural worker who moves with the seasons, planting or harvesting crops.
7	H	Counterculture	⇢	rejection of traditional American values and culture associated with the youth movement of the 1960s.
8	F	Amnesty	⇢	a general pardon by an authority such as government.
9	J	Balanced Budget	⇢	condition that exists when the government spends only as much as it takes in from taxes.
10	C	Hypothesize	⇢	to present an explanation or assumption that remains to be proved.
11	K	Freedmen	⇢	person who had been slaves but were feed by the Emancipation Proclamation.
12	L	Satellite Nation	⇢	a country that is dominated politically and economically by a more powerful nation.
13	I	Muckraker	⇢	American journalists who wrote investigative reports during the Progressive Era, exposing the ills of society and calling for government reform of political, social and economic institutions.

ANSWER SHEET

Social Studies Vocabulary 3

Choose the best answer to each question.

1	L	Renewable Resource	⇢	a natural resource that can be quickly replaced by nature.
2	D	Slave Codes	⇢	laws controlling the lives of blacks in the south prior to the Civil War.
3	F	Aggression	⇢	any warlike act by one country against another without just cause.
4	I	Illegal Alien	⇢	someone who enters a country without legal permission.
5	H	Nationalism	⇢	pride in one's nation; the idea that the goals of one's nation are more important those of the rest of the world.
6	G	Annex	⇢	to add on, to absorb into a larger body. Example – one nation taking over another and making it part of their own country.
7	C	Deficit	⇢	condition of spending more money than the amount received in income.
8	E	Communism	⇢	an economic system in which all property and resources are owned and controlled by the "community" (in practice, controlled by the government).
9	K	Trade Deficit	⇢	when a nation buys more goods and services from foreign countries than it sells to them.
10	A	Socialism	⇢	system of social organization (government) in which the most important industries are controlled by the government that often plans and controls the economy. Similar to communism, but some capitalism is allowed.
11	B	Ration	⇢	limiting the amount of certain types of goods that people can buy.
12	J	Dictator	⇢	a ruler who has complete power over government affairs.

ANSWER SHEET

Social Studies Vocabulary 4

Choose the best answer to each question.

1	G	Solar Energy	⇢	power source derived from the sun.
2	L	Naturalization	⇢	The process by which an immigrant becomes a citizen.
3	K	Restate	⇢	to say again in a slightly different way.
4	J	Totalitarian State	⇢	a country where a single party controls the government and every aspect of the loves of people.
5	H	Inflation	⇢	sharp rise in prices and decrease in the value of money.
6	B	Environmentalist	⇢	person who works to reduce pollution and protect the natural environment.
7	D	Greenbacks	⇢	paper money issued by the federal government during the Civil War.
8	F	Assembly Line	⇢	manufacturing process, developed by Henry Ford in the 1920's, whereby factory workers engage in specific and repetitive tasks.
9	I	Détente	⇢	easing of tensions between nations.
10	E	Affirmative Action	⇢	program in areas such as employment and education to provide more opportunities for members of groups that faced discrimination in the past.
11	C	Civil Disobedience	⇢	nonviolent opposition to a government policy or law by refusing to comply with it.
12	A	Popular Sovereignty	⇢	an idea that supreme governing power belongs to the voters.

Social Studies Vocabulary 5

Choose the best answer to each question.

1. Political movement of the late 1800's favoring greater government regulation of business, graduated income tax and greater political involvement by the people

a. Socialism

b. Populism

2. To arrange in a systematic way.

a. Manage

b. Organize

3. Protests in which people sit in a particular place or business and refuse to leave.

a. Strike

b. Sit-In

4. An index based on the amount of goods, services, education, and leisure time that a people have.

a. Standard of Living

b. Quality of Life

5. Combination of businesses joining together to limit competition within an industry.

a. Trust

b. Monopolies

6. The factors that cause people to leave an area. (e.x. famine, war, political upheaval).

a. Push factors

b. Pull factors

7. The factors that attract people to a new area (e.x. jobs, freedom, family).

a. Pull factors

b. Push factors

8. What is the meaning of the word "Stock"?

a. a legal entity that holds and manages assets on behalf of another individual or entity

b. a share in a business

9. What is the meaning of the word "Suburb"?

a. a community located within commuting distance of a city

b. a community that's in a city or town

10. What is the meaning of the word "Recession"?

a. a short term mild depression in which business slows and some workers lose their jobs

b. an increase in the price of products and services over time in an economy

11. The movement of population from farms to city.

a. Industrialization

b. Urbanization

12. A belief that one's own ethnic group is superior to others.

a. Ethnocentrism

b. Ethnorelativism

Social Studies Vocabulary 6

Choose the best answer to each question.

1. The workplace where people labor long hours for very low pay.
   a. Factory
   b. Sweatshop

2. To make plain or understandable; to give reasons for.
   a. Explain
   b. Interpret

3. What is the meaning of the word "Evaluate"?
   a. to examine and judge the significance, worth or condition of or value of
   b. to observe or inspect carefully or critically

4. The process by which an immigrant becomes a citizen.
   a. Dual Citizenship
   b. Naturalization

5. What is the meaning of the word "Draft"?
   a. selection of people who would be forced to serve in the military
   b. a person who enlists in military service by free will

6. A conference between the highest-ranking officials of different nations.
   a. Diplomatic Conference
   b. Summit Meeting

7. Select the correct meaning of the word "Identify".
   a. to recognize by or divide into classes
   b. to establish the essential character of

8. A person who flees his or her homeland to seek safety elsewhere.
   a. Immigrant
   b. Refugee

9. To make clear or obvious by using the examples or comparisons.
   a. Illustrate
   b. Demonstrate

10. To investigate closely; to examine critically
    a. Scrutinize
    b. Analyze

11. Select the correct meaning of the word "Laissez Fair".
    a. literally means “hands off”; business principle advocating an economy free of governmental business regulations
    b. an economic system whereby monetary goods are owned by individuals or companies.

12. The theory that Earth’s atmosphere is warming up as a result of air pollution, causing ecological problems.
    a. Global Warming
    b. Climate Change

Social Studies Vocabulary 7

Choose the best answer to each question.

1. To build up, increase, or expand activity.
a. Escalate
b. Elevate

2. To conclude or judge from evidence.
a. Imply
b. Infer

3. The process of making large quantities of a product quickly and cheaply
a. Continuous Production
b. Mass Production

4. Select the correct meaning of the word "Ethnic Group".
a. a group of people who have in common some visible physical traits, such as skin colour, hair texture, facial features, and eye formation
b. a group of people that share a similar culture

5. The loyalty to your area or a nation rather then the nation as a whole.
a. Sectionalism
b. Nationalism

6. Bringing together people of different races or ethnic groups.
a. Integration
b. Inclusion

7. Select the correct meaning of the word "Imply".
a. to mean or suggest openly without saying
b. to suppose or come to a conclusion, especially based on an indirect suggestion.

8. The economic system in which businesses are owned by private citizens
a. Mixed Economy
b. Free Enterprise System

9. Select the correct meaning of the word "Assimilation".
a. the process of becoming part of another culture
b. the retaining of one's own culture within a minority community in a country but adapt to some aspects of the majority culture

10. To reach a broad conclusion avoiding specifics.
a. Stereotype
b. Generalize

11. The actions taken against a country in an effort to force a change in its policy.
a. Sanctions
b. Penalties

12. Select the correct meaning of the word "Secede".
a. to give up, give way, give away
b. to withdraw

Social Studies Vocabulary 8

Choose the best answer to each question.

1. To break an idea into concepts or parts.
   a. Analyze
   b. Evaluate

2. Select the correct meaning of the word "Fugitive".
   a. Runaway
   b. Refugee

3. To place into groups or classify.
   a. Categorize
   b. Classify

4. The settling disagreements by having each side give up some of its demands.
   a. Collaboration
   b. Compromise

5. Select the correct meaning of the word "Discuss".
   a. to explain what something is or what it means
   b. to make observations using facts, reasoning or details

6. The persons who led slaves to freedom on the Underground Railroad.
   a. Conductors
   b. Driver

7. Select the correct meaning of the word "Guerrilla War".
   a. a form of warfare conducted by using conventional weapons and battlefield tactics between two or more states in open confrontation.
   b. use of hit-and-run tactics to fight a war.

8. The former policy of the South African government of separation of the races enforced by law
   a. Apartheid
   b. Segregation

9. To determine the importance significance size or value.
   a. Assess
   b. Evaluate

10. Select the correct meaning of the word "Arsenal".
    a. a place where weapons are kept
    b. a place where stocks are kept

11. To explain what something is or what it means.
    a. Describe
    b. Define

12. Select the correct meaning of the word "Corporation".
    a. a business owned by a group of people who come together voluntarily for their mutual benefit.
    b. a business owned by stockholders.

Identifying Primary and Secondary Sources

Name: Answer Key

Determine if the source would be a Primary Source(P) or a secondary Source(S).

- A **Primary Source** is information that was created at the same time as an event or by a person directly involved in the event.
  Diaries, speeches, letters, official records, autobiographies.

- A **Secondary Source** is information from somewhere else or by a person not directly involved in the event.
  Encyclopedias, textbooks, book reports.

1) A play showing how Benjamin Franklin flew a kite during a lightning storm.

2) A short story describing Thomas Edison and Nikola Tesla's 'electrical' battle.

3) Anne Frank's diary describing her life during World War 2.

4) A cartoon showing how Pocahontas met John Smith.

5) A text book describing the civil rights movement.

6) A news report about the opening of a power plant.

7) A scientist explaining what it was like for Buzz Aldrin to walk on the moon.

8) A YouTube video describing how the pyramids were built.

9) An interview with Alexander Graham Bell about how he invented the telephone.

10) A radio broadcast from the day the Soviet Union launched Sputnik.

11) An autobiography about the 40th president, Ronald Reagan.

12) A book describing Christopher Columbus sailing to America.

13) A famous artist's painting of what cowboy life was probably like.

14) A journal by a cowboy about the cattle drives from Texas to Kansas.

15) The United States Constitution.

Answers

1. S
2. S
3. P
4. S
5. S
6. P
7. S
8. S
9. P
10. P
11. P
12. S
13. S
14. P
15. P

Use the timeline to answer the questions.

Lewis and Clark's Expedition

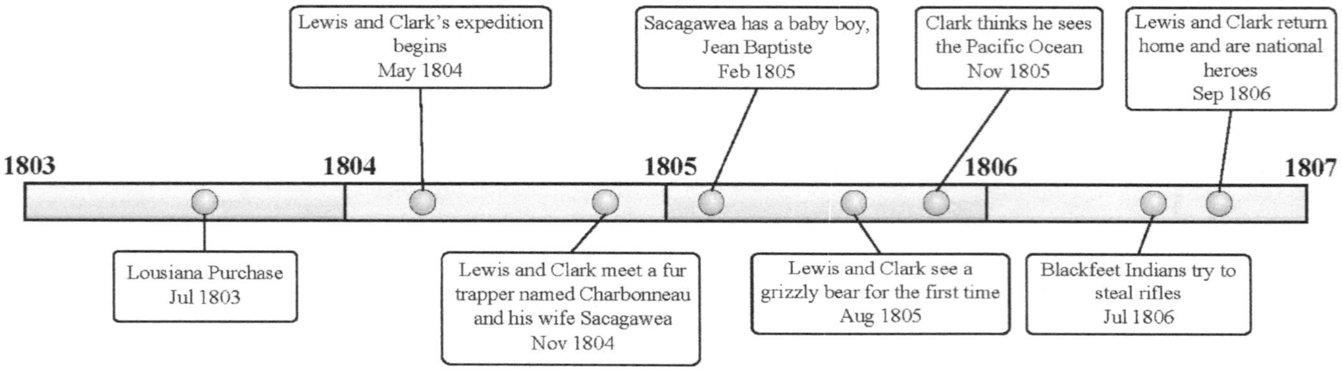
Lewis and Clark's expedition begins May 1804
Sacagawea has a baby boy, Jean Baptiste Feb 1805
Clark thinks he sees the Pacific Ocean Nov 1805
Lewis and Clark return home and are national heroes Sep 1806
1803
1804
1805
1806
1807
Lousiana Purchase Jul 1803
Lewis and Clark meet a fur trapper named Charbonneau and his wife Sacagawea Nov 1804
Lewis and Clark see a grizzly bear for the first time Aug 1805
Blackfeet Indians try to steal rifles Jul 1806

1) How many years did Lewis and Clark's expedition take? 2

2) Which happened earlier? A. Indians try to steal rifles or B. Lewis and Clark see a grizzly bear B

3) What year was the Louisiana Purchase? 1803

4) What year did Sacagawea have her child? 1805

5) What is the span (number of years shown) of this timeline? 4

6) What year did Lewis and Clark meet Charbonneau? 1804

7) What year did Lewis and Clark return home? 1806

8) In September of 1804 Lewis and Clark saw a prairie dog. Could you put this event on the timeline above? (Yes / No)

9) What event happened in Nov 1805? Clark thinks he sees the Pacific Ocean

10) What is this timeline about? Lewis and Clark's Expedition

Answers

1. 2
2. B
3. 1803
4. 1805
5. 4
6. 1804
7. 1806
8. Yes
9. Use Line
10. Use Line

Reading a Timeline — Name: Answer Key

Use the timeline to answer the questions.

Major Events of World War 2

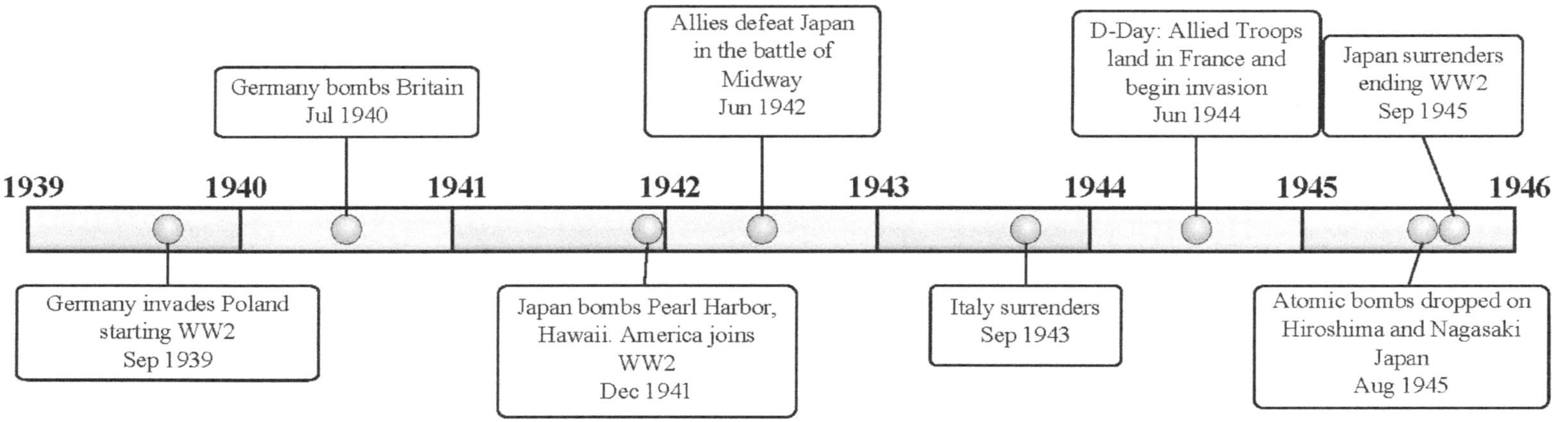

Germany bombs Britain
Jul 1940
Allies defeat Japan in the battle of Midway
Jun 1942
D-Day: Allied Troops land in France and begin invasion
Jun 1944
Japan surrenders ending WW2
Sep 1945
1939
1940
1941
1942
1943
1944
1945
1946
Germany invades Poland starting WW2
Sep 1939
Japan bombs Pearl Harbor, Hawaii. America joins WW2
Dec 1941
Italy surrenders
Sep 1943
Atomic bombs dropped on Hiroshima and Nagasaki Japan
Aug 1945

1) Which happened earlier? A. Italy Surrenders or B. D-Day A

2) How many months after the atomic bombs were dropped did Japan surrender? 1

3) What year was Britain bombed by Germany? 1940

4) What year did World War 2 start? 1939

5) What is the span (number of years shown) of this timeline? 7

6) What year was the battle of Midway? 1942

7) What year did America join World War 2? 1941

8) Japan captured Singapore in February of 1942. Could you put this event on the timeline above? (Yes / No)

9) What is this timeline about? Major Events of World War 2

10) What event happened in 1944? D-Day: Allied Troops land in France and begin invasion

Answers

1. A
2. 1
3. 1940
4. 1939
5. 7
6. 1942
7. 1941
8. Yes
9. Use Line
10. Use Line

ANSWER SHEET

State Capitals 1 - 10

1	A	Alabama	⇢	Montgomery
2	E	Alaska	⇢	Juneau
3	J	Arizona	⇢	Phoenix
4	B	Arkansas	⇢	Little Rock
5	G	California	⇢	Sacramento
6	C	Colorado	⇢	Denver
7	F	Connecticut	⇢	Hartford
8	I	Delaware	⇢	Dover
9	H	Florida	⇢	Tallahassee
10	D	Georgia	⇢	Atlanta

ANSWER SHEET

Sustainability - Global Warming - Climate Change

This is a spelling worksheet to check your spelling and then your understanding of keywords to do with sustainability, climate change and global warming,

	A	B	C	D
1.	Ozone Layerr	Ozone Leyerr	Ozone Leyer	**Ozone Layer**
2.	**Sustainability**	Sustianability	Susstianability	Susstainability
3.	**Deforestation**	Defforestation	Defforestasion	Deforestasion
4.	Renewablle Resources	Renewablle Resoorces	**Renewable Resources**	Renewible Resources
5.	**Non Renewable Resources**	Non Renewablle Resoorces	Non Renewablle Resources	Non Renewible Resources
6.	Cllimate chanje	**Climate change**	Climate chanje	Cllimate change
7.	Habitat lous	Habitat los	**Habitat loss**	Habitat louss
8.	Trropical rian forest	Trropical rain forest	Tropical rian forest	**Tropical rain forest**
9.	Recicling	Reciclling	Recyclling	**Recycling**
10.	**Carbon dioxide**	Carrbon dioxide	Carrbon doixide	Carbon doixide
11.	Mathane	Metthane	Matthane	**Methane**
12.	Grenhouse gas	Grenhoose gas	Greanhouse gas	**Greenhouse gas**
13.	Hydrroflurocarbons	**Hydroflurocarbons**	Hydrophlurocarbons	Hydrrophlurocarbons
14.	Sulphur hexophluoride	Sullphur hexofluoride	Sullphur hexophluoride	**Sulphur hexofluoride**
15.	Nittrous oxide	**Nitrous oxide**	Nitroos oxide	Nittroos oxide
16.	Foussil Fuels	Fosil Fuels	Fousil Fuels	**Fossil Fuels**
17.	Trranspurt	Transpurt	**Transport**	Trransport
18.	Industry	**Industry**	Indostry	Inducstry
19.	Agrricolture	Agrriculture	**Agriculture**	Agricolture
20.	Palm Oyl	**Palm Oil**	Pallm Oil	Pallm Oyl

ANSWER SHEET

Technology

Match the **English and German** words.

Need help? Try Google translate!

1	K	mouse	⇢	Maus
2	L	touch	⇢	berühren
3	D	screen	⇢	Bildschirm
4	J	Wi-Fi	⇢	WLAN
5	O	message	⇢	Nachricht
6	M	game	⇢	Spiel
7	A	website	⇢	Webseite
8	I	mobile	⇢	Handy
9	N	smart	⇢	klug, intelligent
10	G	computer	⇢	Rechner
11	B	desktop	⇢	Schreibtischplatte
12	F	lap	⇢	Schoß
13	E	net	⇢	Netz
14	C	app(lication)	⇢	App, Anwendung
15	H	keyboard	⇢	Tastatur

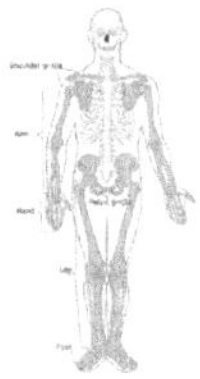

ANSWER SHEET

The Lymphatic System Unscramble

There is a part of the immune system called the lymphatic system. It maintains a healthy balance of body fluids and protects the body from illness. Lymphatic (lim-FAT-ik) veins, tissues, organs, and glands collaborate to drain a watery fluid known as lymph from the body.

When there is a lot of extra lymph (LIMF) fluid in the body, the lymphatic system drains it and sends it back to the body's bloodstream. Lymph contains lymphocytes (LIM-fuh-sites), white blood cells, and chyle (KYE-ul), which is made up of fats and proteins from the intestines.

This is critical because water, proteins, and other substances constantly leak out of microscopic blood capillaries and into the surrounding bodily tissues. This additional fluid would build up in the tissues and cause them to bulge if the lymphatic system did not drain it.

lymphatic	antivirals	cytotoxic	leukocyte	phagocyte	immunology
lymphoma	pathogen	lymphedema	tonsillectomy	thymus	capillaries
spleen					

1. yhmtcalpi — l y m p h a t i c
2. muloinmoyg — i m m u n o l o g y
3. tcgayphoe — p h a g o c y t e
4. mehdeaplmy — l y m p h e d e m a
5. ottcyxoci — c y t o t o x i c
6. tvalriinsa — a n t i v i r a l s
7. nymseltooiltc — t o n s i l l e c t o m y
8. stumyh — t h y m u s
9. nlsepe — s p l e e n
10. aomlmhyp — l y m p h o m a
11. uekloytec — l e u k o c y t e
12. lecasiriapl — c a p i l l a r i e s
13. hgetpnao — p a t h o g e n

Determine the difference in temperatures for the following thermometers.

1)

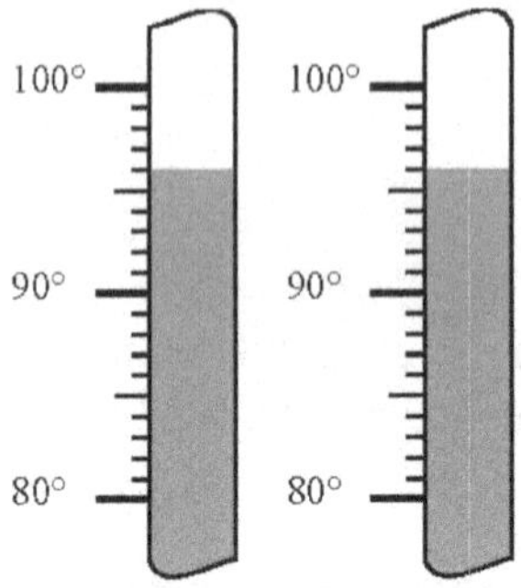

Start 96 | End 96

2)

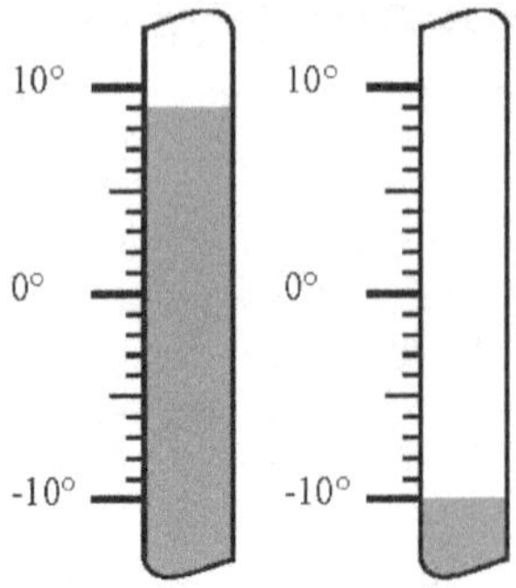

Start 9 | End -10

3)

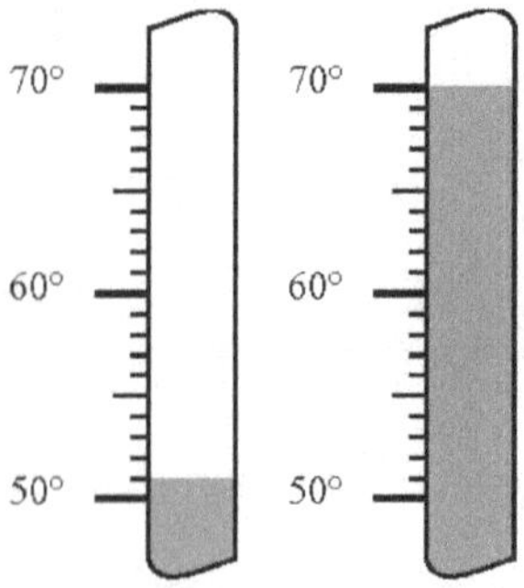

Start 51 | End 70

4)

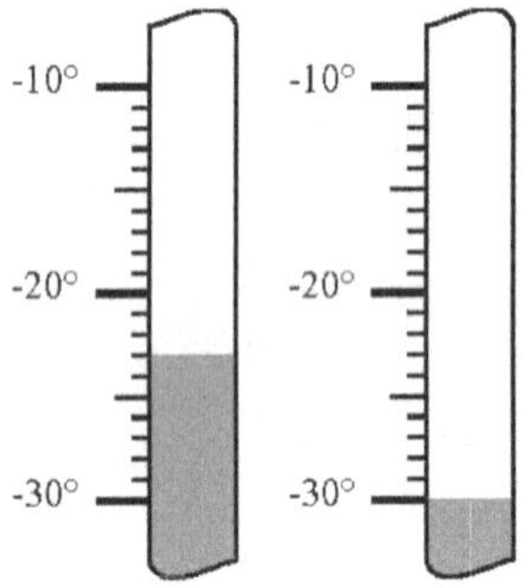

Start -23 | End -30

5)

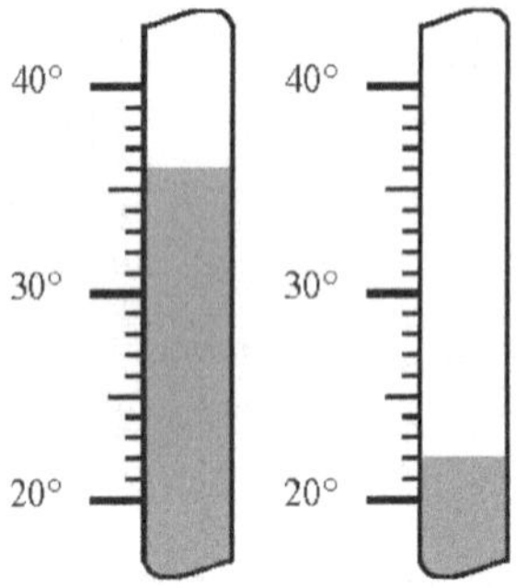

Start 36 | End 22

6)

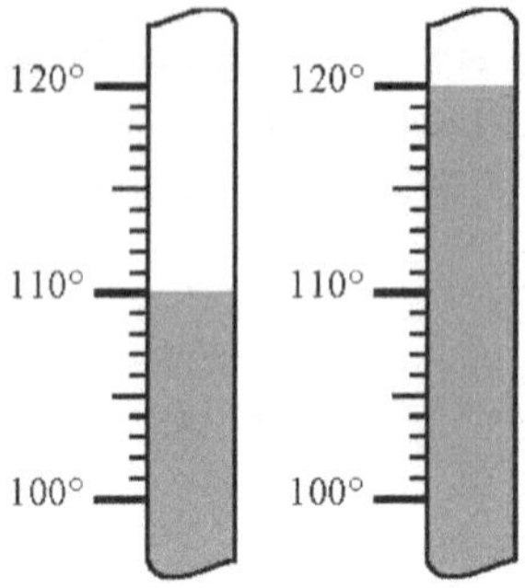

Start 110 | End 120

7)

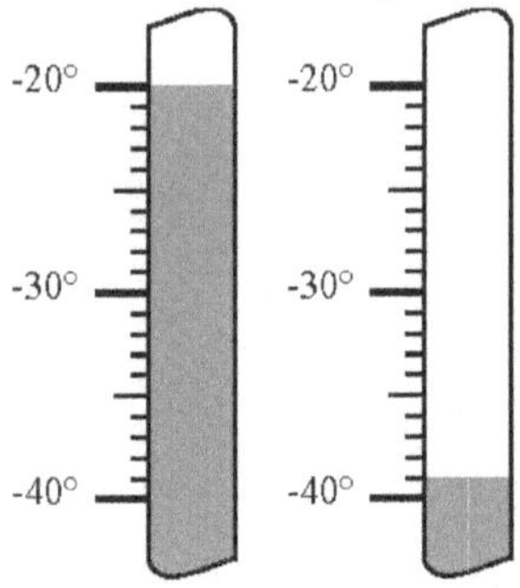

Start -20 | End -39

8)

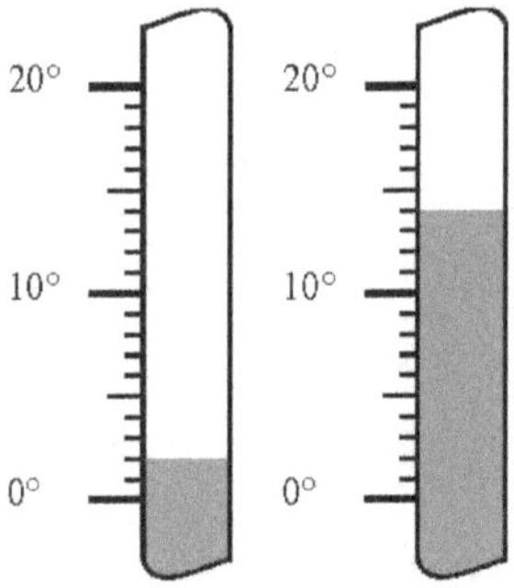

Start 2 | End 14

9)

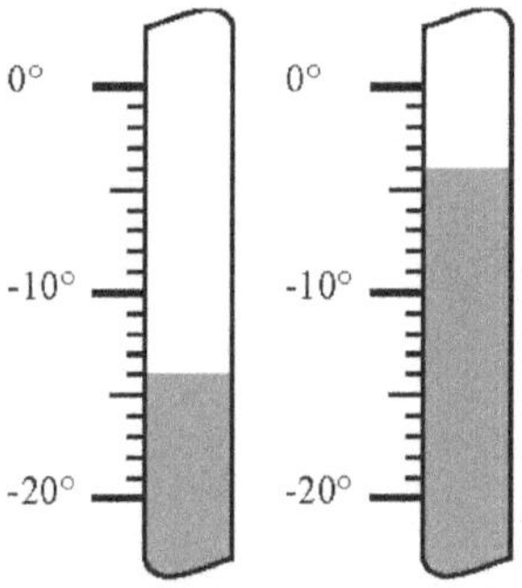

Start -14 | End -4

10)

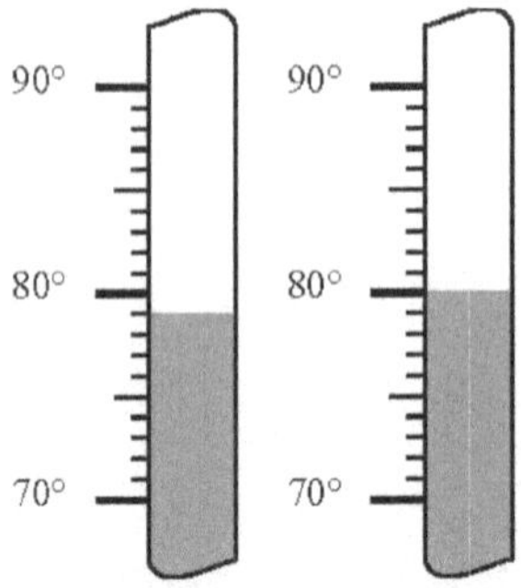

Start 79 | End 80

11)

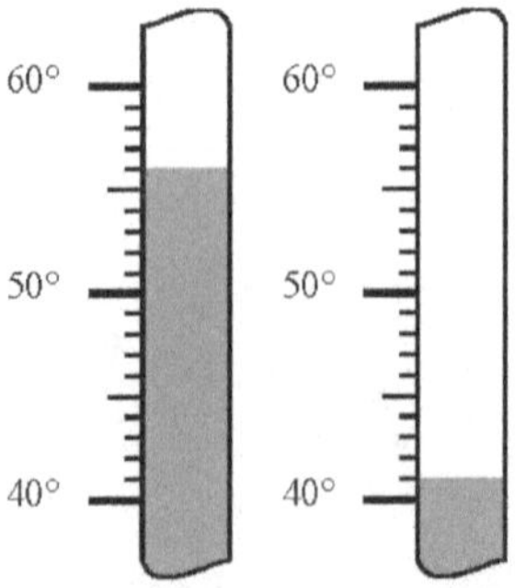

Start 56 | End 41

12)

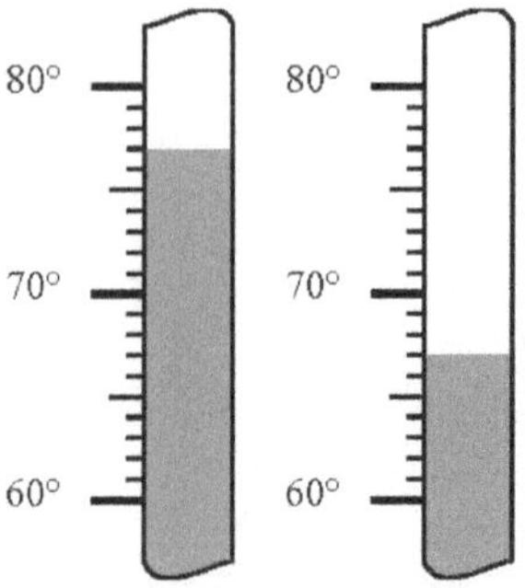

Start 77 | End 67

Answers

1. 0°
2. 19°
3. 19°
4. 7°
5. 14°
6. 10°
7. 19°
8. 12°
9. 10°
10. 1°
11. 15°
12. 10°

FEELINGS

1	Q		⇢	hungry
2	G		⇢	angry
3	J		⇢	hot
4	E		⇢	tired
5	F		⇢	sad
6	I		⇢	thirsty
7	A		⇢	cold
8	K		⇢	worried
9	P		⇢	bored
10	C		⇢	happy
11	B		⇢	stressed
12	L		⇢	frightened/scared
13	H		⇢	ill
14	N		⇢	well
15	M		⇢	surprised
16	O		⇢	interested
17	D		⇢	sleepy

ANSWER SHEET

Today Is Spelling Words Day!

Circle the correctly spelled word then write it on the line.

	A	B	C	D
1.	faitthful	fiathful	**faithful**	fiatthful
2.	hoorrly	**hourly**	hoorly	hourrly
3.	**forceful**	forseful	forrseful	forrceful
4.	**thirsty**	thirsti	thirrsty	thirrsti
5.	frreqoently	freqoently	frrequently	**frequently**
6.	misspronoonce	**mispronounce**	mispronoonce	misspronounce
7.	reinjurre	**reinjure**	rienjurre	rienjure
8.	**reschedule**	ressshedule	resshedule	resschedule
9.	disscouragement	disscouragenment	discouragenment	**discouragement**
10.	rellocating	relucating	rellucating	**relocating**
11.	disssovery	**discovery**	dissovery	disscovery
12.	remuvd	removd	**removed**	remuved
13.	ressaerches	**researches**	resaerches	ressearches
14.	mystepped	**misstepped**	misctepped	mistepped
15.	reffueling	**refueling**	rephueling	rephfueling
16.	unhaellthy	unhaelthy	unheallthy	**unhealthy**
17.	**disciple**	dissiple	dissciple	dissiple
18.	**level**	levell	lavell	lavel
19.	prromice	**promise**	promice	prromise
20.	tenys	tenis	**tennis**	tennys

ANSWER SHEET

Today Is Spelling Words Puzzle Day!

S	S	H	P	H	O	T	O	G	R	A	P	H	X	T	V
T	T	I	U	O	P	R	E	S	C	R	I	B	E	R	T
E	R	H	R	M	R	I	Y	F	C	J	M	B	G	A	H
L	A	Z	S	O	C	E	X	P	O	R	T	U	P	N	E
E	N	T	C	G	I	Y	S	I	O	L	I	L	O	S	R
S	S	R	R	R	Z	C	E	F	E	M	J	P	R	F	M
C	P	A	I	A	D	E	S	C	R	I	B	E	T	E	O
O	O	N	B	P	N	N	F	O	Z	Z	W	G	A	R	M
P	R	S	E	H	A	S	F	P	U	M	Y	U	B	S	E
E	T	M	G	R	L	N	P	N	R	N	H	U	L	U	T
I	L	I	T	D	I	C	T	A	T	E	I	A	E	P	E
R	S	T	N	H	M	M	X	H	R	U	D	F	Y	P	R
A	S	C	R	I	P	T	U	R	E	E	W	I	O	O	T
D	I	C	T	I	O	N	A	R	Y	C	N	A	C	R	Q
Y	S	M	I	C	R	O	S	C	O	P	E	T	D	T	M
E	L	L	G	Y	T	R	A	N	S	L	A	T	E	G	S

predict ↘ transfer ↓ support ↓ script ↘ translate → inform ↗ scribe ↓ transform ↗ dictionary →

export → Scripture → describe → transmit ↓ dictate → portable ↓ prescribe → transparent ↘

import ↓ uniform ↘ transport ↓ photograph → thermometer ↓ microscope → telescope ↓

homograph ↓

25 words in Wordsearch: 10 vertical, 9 horizontal, 6 diagonal. (0 reversed.)

Verb Mood

Let us recap. In a sentence, a verb expresses an action or a state of being.

You're probably aware that the tense of a verb refers to when the event takes place.

The style or attitude in which an action is expressed is referred to as the verb's mood. Verbs, which express actions or states of being, can be articulated as truths, wishes, possibilities, or orders.

1) Indicative Mood—expresses a fact, opinion, claim, or query; most of our verbs are in this mood.

2) Imperative Mood—expresses direct commands and requests.

3) Subjunctive Mood—expresses a desire for something to be true, or expresses something that is not true.

1. I want a chocolate ice cream cone.

a. imperative mood
b. indicative mood
c. subjunctive mood

2. Clean your room, now!

a. subjunctive mood
b. indicative mood
c. imperative mood

3. Coconut tastes funny.

a. subjunctive mood
b. imperative mood
c. indicative mood

4. If only I were at the beach right now.

a. imperative mood
b. subjunctive mood
c. indicative mood

5. Kim, put your paper in the box.

a. indicative mood
b. subjunctive mood
c. imperative mood

6. I wish you had brought your new bike.

a. subjunctive mood
b. indicative mood
c. imperative mood

7. Kick the ball!

a. imperative mood
b. subjunctive mood
c. indicative mood

8. Ostriches cannot fly.

a. indicative mood
b. imperative mood
c. subjunctive mood

9. Be careful!

a. indicative mood
b. subjunctive mood
c. imperative mood

10. If I were you, I would be excited about the play.

a. indicative mood
b. imperative mood
c. subjunctive mood

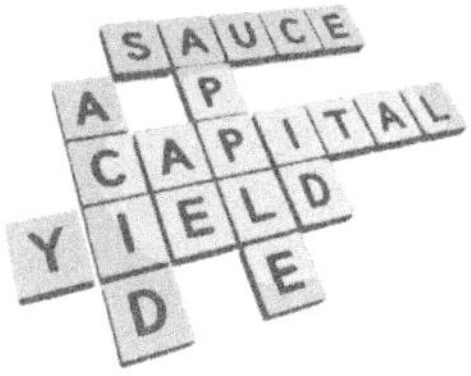

ANSWER SHEET

Vocab Crossword Puzzle

Solve the puzzle below with the correct vocabulary word.

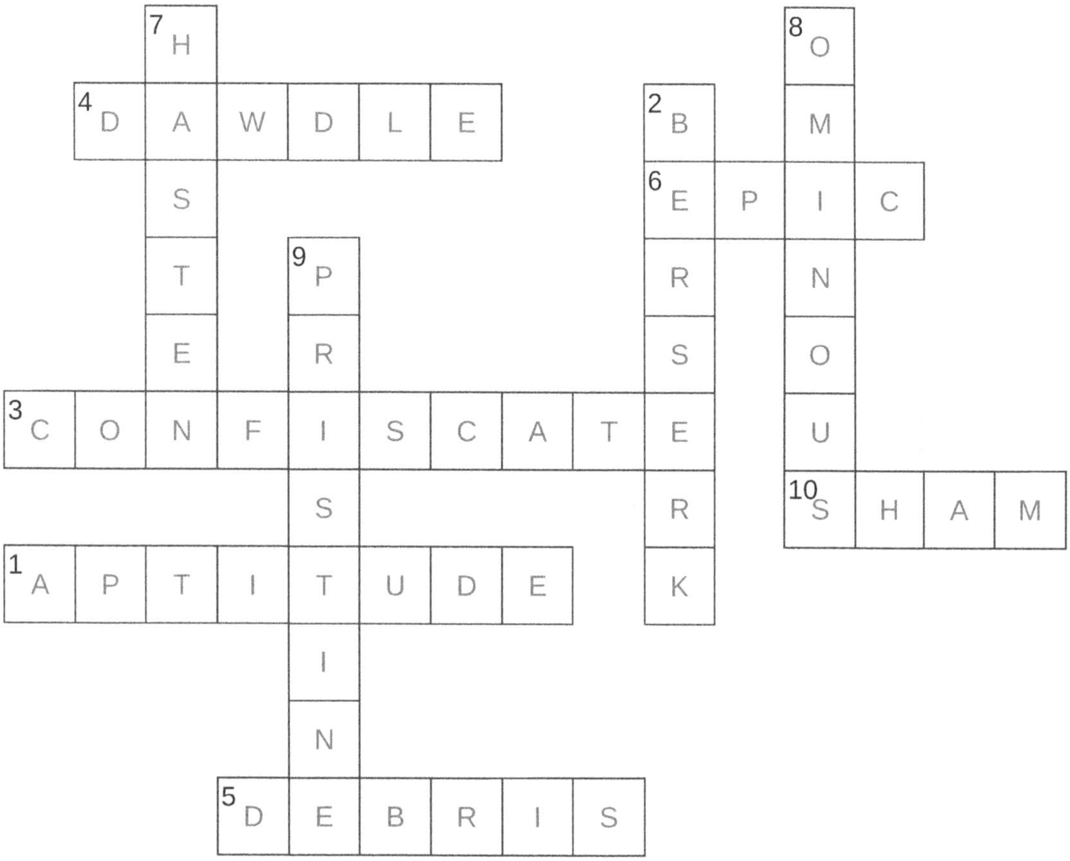

Across

1. capability; ability; innate or acquired capacity for something;
3. to seize by or as if by authority; appropriate summarily:
4. to waste time; idle; trifle; loiter: to move slowly
5. the remains of anything broken down or destroyed; ruins; rubble:
6. heroic; majestic; impressively great:
10. something that is not what it purports to be; a spurious imitation; fraud or hoax.

Down

2. violently or destructively frenzied; wild; crazed; deranged:
7. to move or act with haste; proceed with haste; hurry:
8. portending evil or harm; foreboding; threatening; inauspicious:
9. having its original purity; uncorrupted or unsullied.

OMINOUS DEBRIS APTITUDE BERSERK SHAM HASTEN PRISTINE CONFISCATE DAWDLE EPIC

ANSWER SHEET

Vocabulary: Community Services

Directions: Read the words. Sort the words into the community services in which they belong.

insurance	sick	injured	emergency	firefighter	doctor
driver's license	video	adult education	nurse	ticket	EMS worker
Principal	students	teacher	magazines	officer	return
loan	learning	junior high	borrow	newspapers	librarian
medicine	books	pharmacist	911	high school	pharmacy
elementary school					

Hospital (8)	**Library** (8)	**Police/Fire Department** (7)	**School** (8)
doctor	librarian	officer	teacher
nurse	books	firefighter	Principal
pharmacy	video	EMS worker	students
pharmacist	magazines	911	elementary school
sick	newspapers	ticket	junior high
injured	borrow	emergency	high school
medicine	loan	driver's license	adult education
insurance	return		learning

ANSWER SHEET

WEATHER

1 C  ⇢ rainy

2 E  ⇢ stormy

3 B  ⇢ sunny

4 F  ⇢ partly cloudy

5 D 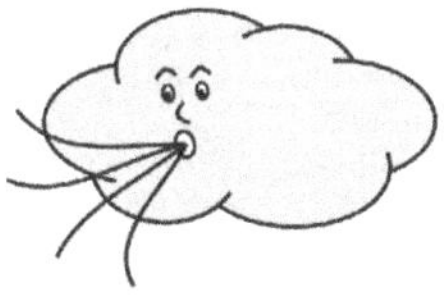 ⇢ windy

6 H  ⇢ cloudy

7 A  ⇢ snowy

8 G  ⇢ foggy

ANSWER SHEET

What is an Adjective?

Adjectives are words that describe a noun in greater detail. It is used to "describe" or "modify" a noun (The **big** *dog* was **hungry**). The adjective is bold in these examples, but the noun it modifies is italicized.

An adjective is frequently used before a noun:
a **blue** *vehicle*

Also, an adjective can appear AFTER a verb: My *truck* is **black**.

However, adjectives can also be used to modify pronouns (*She* is **beautiful**).

Unscramble the scrambled adjective words below to find the correct word.

Beautiful	round	large	triangle	sad	yellow
poor	handsome	small	square	happy	elegant
Blue	wealthy	slow			

1. buel B l u e
2. auitufbel B e a u t i f u l
3. lamsl s m a l l
4. elrga l a r g e
5. auersq s q u a r e
6. ndrou r o u n d
7. opor p o o r
8. ywaethl w e a l t h y
9. lwso s l o w
10. amshoden h a n d s o m e
11. ywlleo y e l l o w
12. tlneega e l e g a n t
13. haypp h a p p y
14. sda s a d
15. itrngeal t r i a n g l e

Where is & Where are

1. ____ Billy?
1. Where are
2. Where's

2. ____ in the bed.
1. He's
2. They're

3. ____ Mom and Dad?
1. Where are
2. Where's

4. _____ in the kitchen.
1. She's
2. They're

5. ____ Grandpa?
1. Where are
2. Where's

6. ____ in the garden.
1. He's
2. She's

7. ____ Lucy and Lilly?
1. Where are
2. Where's

8. ____ in the park.
1. They're
2. She's

9. ____ my sister?
1. Where are
2. Where's

10. ____ in her bedroom.
1. She's
2. He's

11. ____ pupils?
1. Where's
2. Where are

12. ____ at school.
1. He's
2. They're

ANSWER SHEET

Which President?

Match each president to his description

1	A	Zachary Taylor	⇢	"I was a U.S. Army General in the Mexican-American War."
2	H	Jimmy Carter	⇢	"I was a peanut farmer from Georgia."
3	G	John Adams	⇢	"I was the first Vice-President. I signed the Declaration of Independence."
4	D	Ronald Reagan	⇢	"I was the first television and movie star to become president."
5	E	Andrew Jackson	⇢	"I was a lawyer and the 7th president. People called me 'Old Hickory'."
6	B	Barack Obama	⇢	"I was born in Honolulu, Hawaii. I was elected president in 2008."
7	C	Franklin D. Roosevelt	⇢	"I was the only president to have been elected for four terms. I was in office when Japan attacked Pearl Harbor."
8	F	Donald Trump	⇢	"I was born in New York to wealthy parents. I became president in January 2017."

ANSWERS

Rearranging Digits

1)	1,182	8,211	6)	7,769	9,776
2)	1,549	9,541	7)	7,521	7,521
3)	5,366	6,653	8)	8,146	8,641
4)	3,869	9,863	9)	8,161	8,611
5)	2,853	8,532	10)	7,769	9,776

1)	7,816	1,678	6)	6,636	3,666
2)	3,827	2,378	7)	8,176	1,678
3)	4,946	4,469	8)	9,222	2,229
4)	5,938	3,589	9)	2,172	1,227
5)	1,627	1,267	10)	5,366	3,566

TIME ANSWERS

What time is on the clock?	6:00
What time was it 1 hour ago?	5:00
What time was it 3 hours and 40 minutes ago?	2:20
What time will it be in 4 hours and 20 minutes?	10:20

What time is on the clock?	7:40
What time was it 2 hours ago?	5:40
What time will it be in 3 hours ?	10:40
What time will it be in 4 hours and 20 minutes?	12:00

What time is on the clock?	10:20
What time was it 1 hour ago?	9:20
What time was it 3 hours and 20 minutes ago?	7:00
What time will it be in 2 hours ?	12:20

What time is on the clock?	10:00
What time will it be in 3 hours and 20 minutes?	1:20
What time was it 2 hours ago?	8:00
What time was it 1 hour ago?	9:00

ANSWER SHEET
Word Problems

1) After eating at the restaurant, Sandy, Melanie, and Jason decided to divide the bill evenly. If each person paid eleven dollars, what was the total of the bill ? 33 dollars

2) There were 17 bales of hay in the barn. Tom stacked more bales in the barn today. There are now 63 bales of hay in the barn. How many bales did he store in the barn ? 46 bales of hay

3) Mike's high school played twelve soccer games this year. The team won most of their games. They were defeated during four games. How many games did they win ? 8 games

4) Jessica is baking a cake. The recipe calls for 7 cups of flour. She already put in 3 cups. How many more cups does she need to add ? 4 cups of flour

5) How many ink cartridges can you buy with 112 dollars if one cartridge costs 14 dollars ? 8 cartridges

6) Joan found ninety - three seashells on the beach, she gave Sam some of her seashells. She has thirty - nine seashell left. How many seashells did she give to Sam ? 54 seashells

7) Dan has twenty - two books in his library. He bought several books at a yard sale over the weekend. He now has seventy - eight books in his library. How many books did he buy at the yard sale ? 56 books

8) After paying six dollars for the pie, Sam has fifty - five dollars left. How much money did he have before buying the pie ? 61 dollars

9) There are 38 maple trees currently in the park. Park workers will plant more maple trees today. When the workers are finished there will be 67 maple trees in the park. How many maple trees did the workers plant today ? 29 maple trees

10) Fred had 47 peaches left at his roadside fruit stand. He went to the orchard and picked more peaches to stock up the stand. There are now 55 peaches at the stand, how many did he pick ? 8 peaches

ANSWER SHEET

1) N÷13 = 35	N = 455	2) 464÷N = 16	N = 29
3) N÷17 = 38	N = 646	4) N÷16 = 27	N = 432
5) 558÷N = 18	N = 31	6) N÷19 = 19	N = 361
7) N÷17 = 27	N = 459	8) N÷20 = 15	N = 300
9) 570÷N = 15	N = 38	10) N÷24 = 30	N = 720
11) N÷15 = 40	N = 600	12) 680÷N = 40	N = 17
13) N÷31 = 40	N = 1240	14) 308÷N = 28	N = 11
15) 1482÷N = 39	N = 38	16) 323÷N = 17	N = 19
17) N÷32 = 36	N = 1152	18) 1280÷N = 32	N = 40
19) N÷31 = 25	N = 775	20) 1330÷N = 38	N = 35
21) 310÷N = 10	N = 31	22) 532÷N = 38	N = 14
23) N÷40 = 35	N = 1400	24) 1520÷N = 38	N = 40
25) N÷33 = 40	N = 1320	26) N÷25 = 36	N = 900
27) N÷16 = 27	N = 432	28) 552÷N = 23	N = 24
29) N÷10 = 12	N = 120	30) 272÷N = 16	N = 17

Estimate the sum or difference by rounding each number to the nearest ten.

1)	85	⟶	90
	- 59	⟶	- 60
	26		30
2)	94	⟶	90
	- 21	⟶	- 20
	73		70
3)	23	⟶	20
	+ 42	⟶	+ 40
	65		60
4)	71	⟶	70
	- 53	⟶	- 50
	18		20
5)	15	⟶	20
	+ 74	⟶	+ 70
	89		90
6)	51	⟶	50
	+ 26	⟶	+ 30
	77		80
7)	91	⟶	90
	- 46	⟶	- 50
	45		40
8)	58	⟶	60
	+ 11	⟶	+ 10
	69		70
9)	79	⟶	80
	+ 32	⟶	+ 30
	111		110
10)	75	⟶	80
	+ 49	⟶	+ 50
	124		130
11)	63	⟶	60
	- 34	⟶	- 30
	29		30
12)	33	⟶	30
	- 22	⟶	- 20
	11		10
13)	76	⟶	80
	+ 12	⟶	+ 10
	88		90
14)	86	⟶	90
	- 27	⟶	- 30
	59		60

Answer Key

Answers

1. 255
2. 9
3. 33
4. 38
5. 110
6. 20
7. 30
8. 47
9. 86
10. 27

Order of Operations

1) $21 \div 3 + (3 \times 9) \times 9 + 5$

Step 1: $(3 \times 9) = 27$ — $21 \div 3 + 27 \times 9 + 5$
Step 2: $21 \div 3 = 7$ — $7 + 27 \times 9 + 5$
Step 3: $27 \times 9 = 243$ — $7 + 243 + 5$
Step 4: $7 + 243 = 250$ — $250 + 5$
Step 5: $250 + 5 = 255$ — 255

2) $18 \div 6 \times (4 - 3) + 6$

Step 1: $(4 - 3) = 1$ — $18 \div 6 \times 1 + 6$
Step 2: $18 \div 6 = 3$ — $3 \times 1 + 6$
Step 3: $3 \times 1 = 3$ — $3 + 6$
Step 4: $3 + 6 = 9$ — 9

3) $14 - 8 + 3 + 8 \times (24 \div 8)$

Step 1: $(24 \div 8) = 3$ — $14 - 8 + 3 + 8 \times 3$
Step 2: $8 \times 3 = 24$ — $14 - 8 + 3 + 24$
Step 3: $14 - 8 = 6$ — $6 + 3 + 24$
Step 4: $6 + 3 = 9$ — $9 + 24$
Step 5: $9 + 24 = 33$ — 33

4) $4 \times 5 + (14 + 8) - 36 \div 9$

Step 1: $(14 + 8) = 22$ — $4 \times 5 + 22 - 36 \div 9$
Step 2: $4 \times 5 = 20$ — $20 + 22 - 36 \div 9$
Step 3: $36 \div 9 = 4$ — $20 + 22 - 4$
Step 4: $20 + 22 = 42$ — $42 - 4$
Step 5: $42 - 4 = 38$ — 38

5) $(17 - 7) \times 6 + 2 + 56 - 8$

Step 1: $(17 - 7) = 10$ — $10 \times 6 + 2 + 56 - 8$
Step 2: $10 \times 6 = 60$ — $60 + 2 + 56 - 8$
Step 3: $60 + 2 = 62$ — $62 + 56 - 8$
Step 4: $62 + 56 = 118$ — $118 - 8$
Step 5: $118 - 8 = 110$ — 110

6) $(28 \div 4) + 3 + (10 - 8) \times 5$

Step 1: $(28 \div 4) = 7$ — $7 + 3 + (10 - 8) \times 5$
Step 2: $(10 - 8) = 2$ — $7 + 3 + 2 \times 5$
Step 3: $2 \times 5 = 10$ — $7 + 3 + 10$
Step 4: $7 + 3 = 10$ — $10 + 10$
Step 5: $10 + 10 = 20$ — 20

7) $12 - 5 + 6 \times 3 + 20 \div 4$

Step 1: $6 \times 3 = 18$ — $12 - 5 + 18 + 20 \div 4$
Step 2: $20 \div 4 = 5$ — $12 - 5 + 18 + 5$
Step 3: $12 - 5 = 7$ — $7 + 18 + 5$
Step 4: $7 + 18 = 25$ — $25 + 5$
Step 5: $25 + 5 = 30$ — 30

8) $36 \div 9 + 48 - 10 \div 2$

Step 1: $36 \div 9 = 4$ — $4 + 48 - 10 \div 2$
Step 2: $10 \div 2 = 5$ — $4 + 48 - 5$
Step 3: $4 + 48 = 52$ — $52 - 5$
Step 4: $52 - 5 = 47$ — 47

9) $10 + 8 \times 90 \div 9 - 4$

Step 1: $8 \times 90 = 720$ — $10 + 720 \div 9 - 4$
Step 2: $720 \div 9 = 80$ — $10 + 80 - 4$
Step 3: $10 + 80 = 90$ — $90 - 4$
Step 4: $90 - 4 = 86$ — 86

10) $8 \times 3 + 70 \div 7 - 7$

Step 1: $8 \times 3 = 24$ — $24 + 70 \div 7 - 7$
Step 2: $70 \div 7 = 10$ — $24 + 10 - 7$
Step 3: $24 + 10 = 34$ — $34 - 7$
Step 4: $34 - 7 = 27$ — 27

Exponents

1) $(2)^3$ = 8

2) $(5)^2$ = 25

3) $(12)^3$ = 1728

4) $(-8)^2$ = 64

5) $(-4)^2$ = 16

6) $(-2)^2$ = 4

7) $(7)^2$ = 49

8) $(-12)^2$ = 144

9) $(-2)^3$ = -8

10) $(-3)^3$ = -27

11) $(4)^3$ = 64

12) $(3)^3$ = 27

13) $(-5)^3$ = -125

14) $(3)^2$ = 9

15) $(2)^2$ = 4

16) $(-10)^3$ = -1000

17) $(-7)^2$ = 49

18) $(-9)^3$ = -729

19) $(-6)^3$ = -216

20) $(10)^2$ = 100

ABSOLUTE VALUE ANSWERS

1) Absolute value of 79 is 79

2) Absolute value of 26 is 26

3) Absolute value of 81 is 81

4) Absolute value of 82 is 82

5) Absolute value of -45 is 45

6) Absolute value of 64 is 64

7) Absolute value of -53 is 53

8) Absolute value of 53 is 53

9) Absolute value of -47 is 47

10) Absolute value of 19 is 19

11) Absolute value of -89 is 89

12) Absolute value of 85 is 85

13) Absolute value of 12 is 12

14) Absolute value of 60 is 60

15) Absolute value of -48 is 48

16) Absolute value of 84 is 84

17) Absolute value of 8 is 8

18) Absolute value of 13 is 13

19) Absolute value of 91 is 91

20) Absolute value of 24 is 24

21) Absolute value of 18 is 18

22) Absolute value of -36 is 36

23) Absolute value of 46 is 46

24) Absolute value of -79 is 79

25) Absolute value of 20 is 20

26) Absolute value of 9 is 9

27) Absolute value of -14 is 14

28) Absolute value of 42 is 42

29) Absolute value of -62 is 62

30) Absolute value of 15 is 15

Adding to Multiples of Ten — Answer Key

Fill in the blanks for each problem.

8 + 42 = 50	32 + 8 = 40	7 + 53 = 60	61 + 9 = 70
6 + 74 = 80	91 + 9 = 100	5 + 85 = 90	58 + 2 = 60
9 + 71 = 80	54 + 6 = 60	1 + 49 = 50	13 + 7 = 20
4 + 56 = 60	82 + 8 = 90	5 + 15 = 20	22 + 8 = 30
6 + 94 = 100	78 + 2 = 80	7 + 43 = 50	19 + 1 = 20
9 + 31 = 40	59 + 1 = 60	6 + 84 = 90	23 + 7 = 30
1 + 99 = 100	39 + 1 = 40	4 + 96 = 100	48 + 2 = 50
9 + 81 = 90	92 + 8 = 100	8 + 12 = 20	5 + 5 = 10
6 + 14 = 20	89 + 1 = 90	5 + 45 = 50	98 + 2 = 100
9 + 21 = 30	44 + 6 = 50	6 + 24 = 30	25 + 5 = 30
7 + 3 = 10	79 + 1 = 80	2 + 38 = 40	35 + 5 = 40
3 + 7 = 10	75 + 5 = 80	3 + 17 = 20	66 + 4 = 70
2 + 88 = 90	47 + 3 = 50	3 + 27 = 30	91 + 9 = 100
1 + 89 = 90	57 + 3 = 60	6 + 44 = 50	21 + 9 = 30
4 + 56 = 60	77 + 3 = 80	3 + 97 = 100	76 + 4 = 80
3 + 87 = 90	16 + 4 = 20	9 + 71 = 80	85 + 5 = 90
3 + 67 = 70	83 + 7 = 90	4 + 46 = 50	64 + 6 = 70
8 + 12 = 20	38 + 2 = 40	5 + 75 = 80	63 + 7 = 70
4 + 36 = 40	33 + 7 = 40	5 + 95 = 100	86 + 4 = 90
2 + 68 = 70	98 + 2 = 100	8 + 52 = 60	81 + 9 = 90
6 + 94 = 100	82 + 8 = 90	6 + 54 = 60	7 + 3 = 10
2 + 18 = 20	11 + 9 = 20	1 + 59 = 60	43 + 7 = 50
6 + 24 = 30	6 + 4 = 10	7 + 93 = 100	99 + 1 = 100
7 + 23 = 30	34 + 6 = 40	5 + 65 = 70	4 + 6 = 10
7 + 53 = 60	41 + 9 = 50	8 + 2 = 10	88 + 2 = 90

Finding Volume

Answer Key

Find the volume of each rectangular prism. Units are in cm (not to scale). Remember V = BH and V=L×W×H

1)

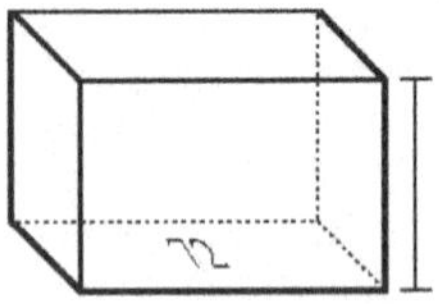

2)

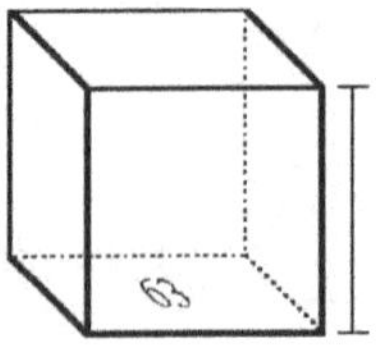

3)

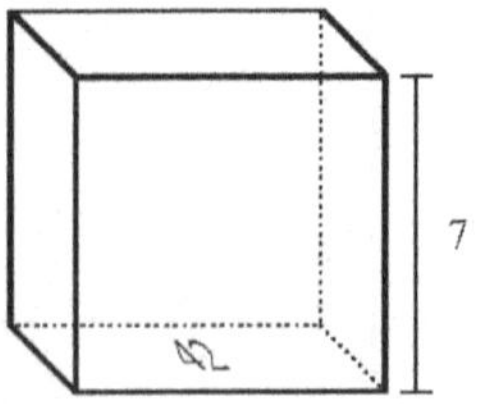

4)

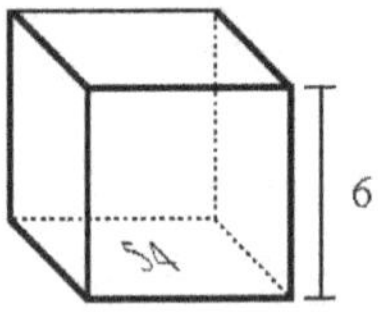

5)

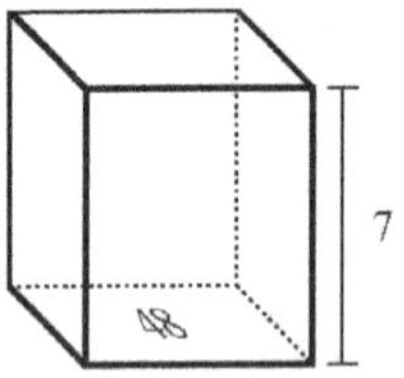

6)

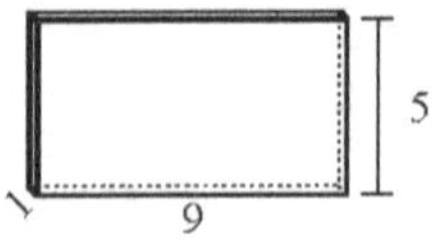

7)

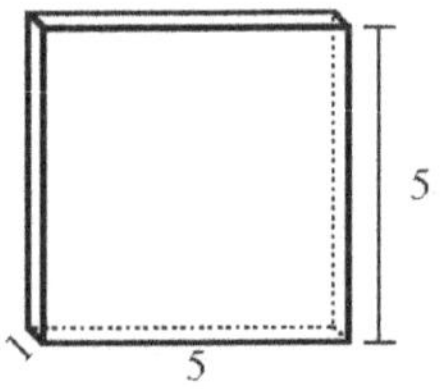

8)

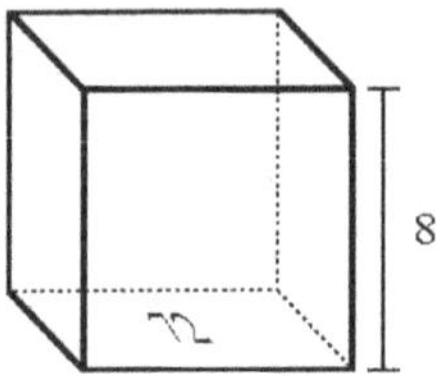

9)

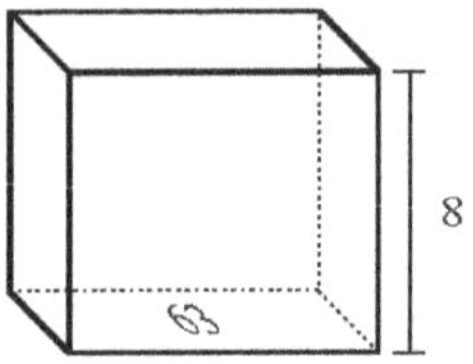

10)

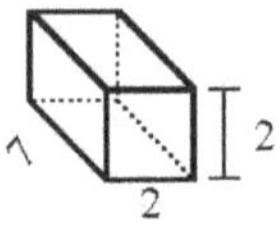

11)

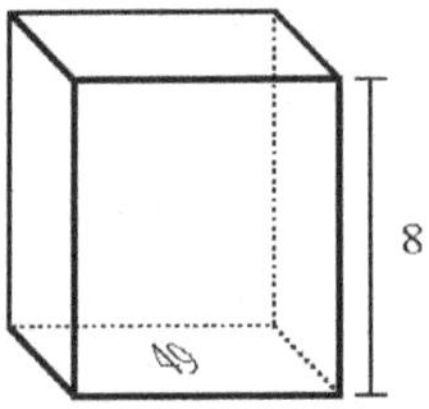

12)

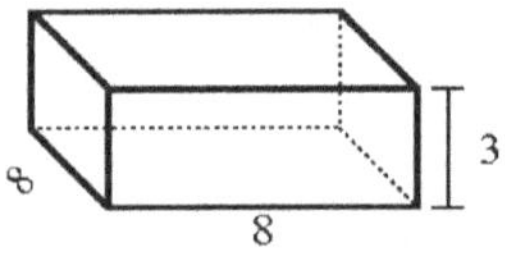

13)

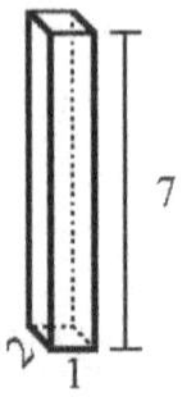

14)

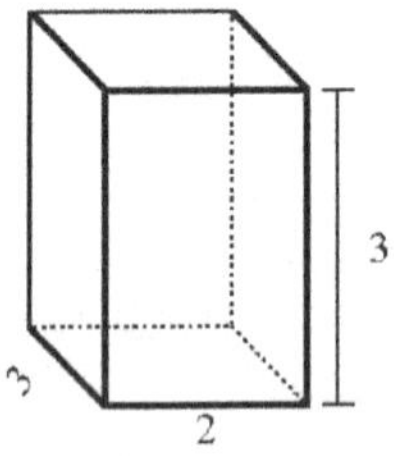

15)

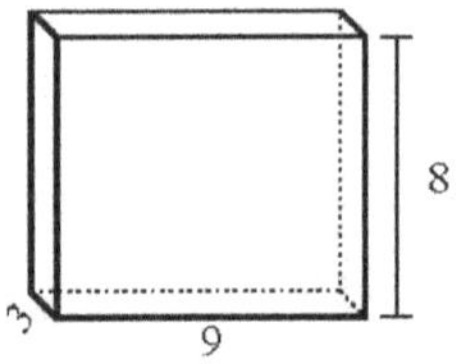

Answers

1. $432\ cm^3$
2. $441\ cm^3$
3. $294\ cm^3$
4. $324\ cm^3$
5. $336\ cm^3$
6. $45\ cm^3$
7. $25\ cm^3$
8. $576\ cm^3$
9. $504\ cm^3$
10. $28\ cm^3$
11. $392\ cm^3$
12. $192\ cm^3$
13. $14\ cm^3$
14. $18\ cm^3$
15. $216\ cm^3$

Matching Pictographs to Charts

Answer Key

Determine which pictograph best represents the information in the chart.

1)

Month	Cats Sold
June	56
July	32
August	24
September	40
October	80

2)

Month	Cats Sold
June	24
July	56
August	8
September	32
October	40

3)

Month	Cats Sold
June	16
July	8
August	56
September	48
October	24

4)

Month	Cats Sold
June	48
July	40
August	24
September	32
October	64

5)

Month	Cats Sold
June	24
July	80
August	48
September	56
October	32

6)

Month	Cats Sold
June	32
July	48
August	80
September	16
October	8

A.

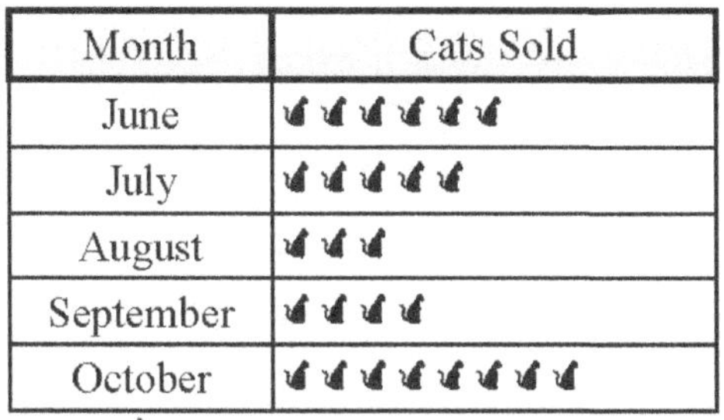

Each = 8 cat

B.

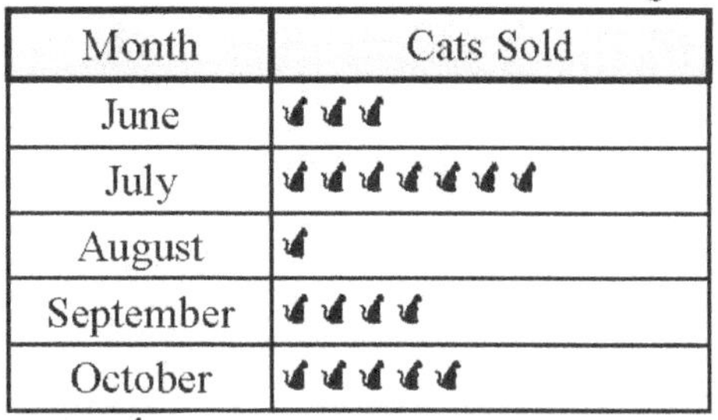

Each = 8 cat

C.

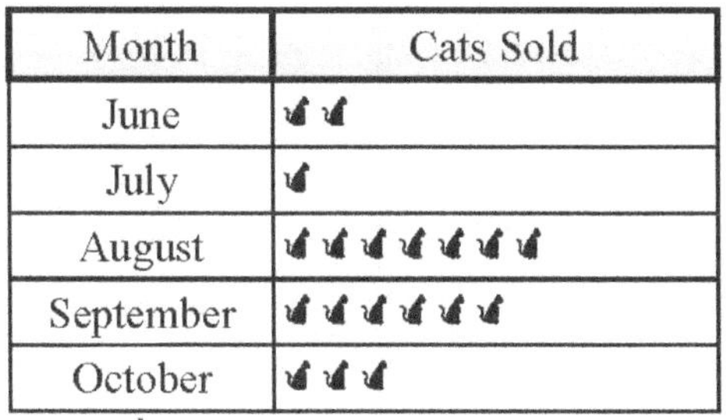

Each = 8 cat

D.

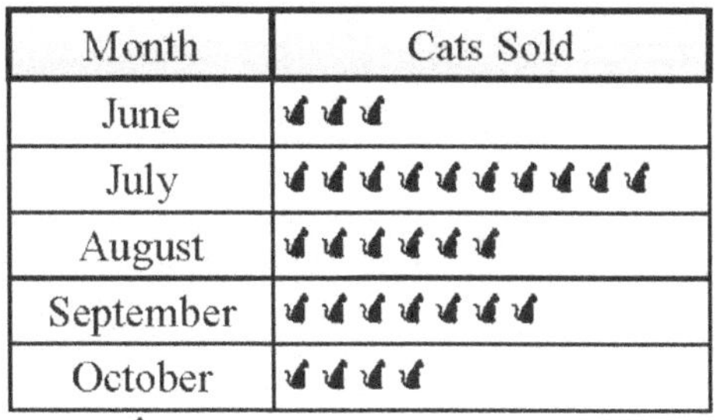

Each = 8 cat

E.

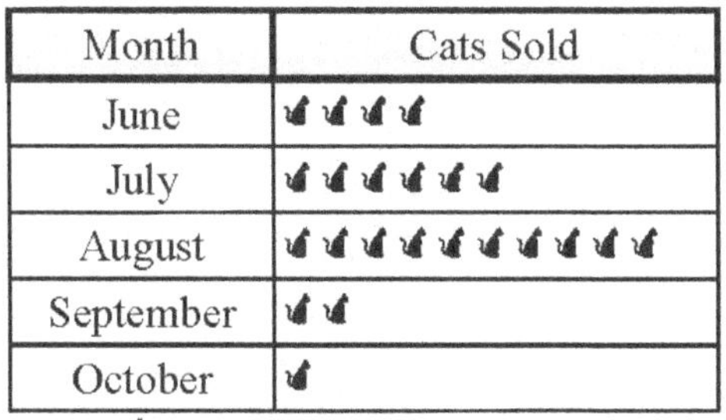

Each = 8 cat

F.

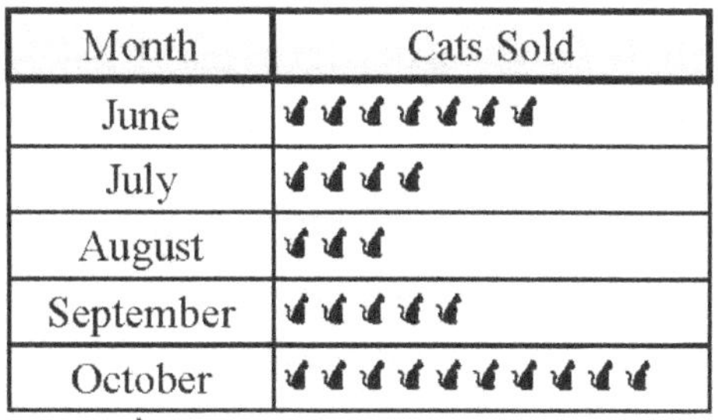

Each = 8 cat

Answers

1. F
2. B
3. C
4. A
5. D
6. E

Examining Number Value by Place Value

Solve each problem.

1) What is the value of the 6 in the number 154,637?
2) What is the value of the 1 in the number 417,298?
3) What is the value of the 9 in the number 97?
4) What is the value of the 3 in the number 9,673,824?
5) What is the value of the 4 in the number 14,697?
6) What is the value of the 4 in the number 42?
7) What is the value of the 1 in the number 29,158?
8) What is the value of the 1 in the number 268,514?
9) What is the value of the 7 in the number 3,576?
10) What is the value of the 5 in the number 3,956,728?
11) What is the value of the 1 in the number 4,781,392?
12) What is the value of the 4 in the number 734,168?
13) What is the value of the 6 in the number 68,435?
14) What is the value of the 2 in the number 51,627?
15) What is the value of the 2 in the number 235?
16) What is the value of the 3 in the number 31,475?
17) What is the value of the 5 in the number 9,536?
18) What is the value of the 7 in the number 37,681?
19) What is the value of the 6 in the number 3,264,871?
20) What is the value of the 1 in the number 76,183?

Answer Key

Answers

1. **600**
2. **10,000**
3. **90**
4. **3,000**
5. **4,000**
6. **40**
7. **100**
8. **10**
9. **70**
10. **50,000**
11. **1,000**
12. **4,000**
13. **60,000**
14. **20**
15. **200**
16. **30,000**
17. **500**
18. **7,000**
19. **60,000**
20. **100**

Finding Ten More & Ten Less Name: Answer Key

Fill in the blanks for each problem.

What is 10 more than 59? 69

What is 10 more than 2? 12

What is 10 more than 87? 97

What is 10 more than 25? 35

What is 10 more than 85? 95

What is 10 more than 72? 82

What is 10 more than 79? 89

What is 10 more than 1? 11

What is 10 more than 39? 49

What is 10 more than 27? 37

What is 10 more than 86? 96

What is 10 more than 7? 17

What is 10 more than 69? 79

What is 10 more than 60? 70

What is 10 more than 31? 41

What is 10 more than 11? 21

What is 10 more than 12? 22

What is 10 more than 63? 73

What is 10 more than 97? 107

What is 10 more than 41? 51

What is 10 more than 99? 109

What is 10 more than 92? 102

What is 10 more than 67? 77

What is 10 more than 51? 61

What is 10 more than 16? 26

What is 10 less than 13? 3

What is 10 less than 15? 5

What is 10 less than 17? 7

What is 10 less than 19? 9

What is 10 less than 21? 11

What is 10 less than 23? 13

What is 10 less than 25? 15

What is 10 less than 27? 17

What is 10 less than 29? 19

What is 10 less than 31? 21

What is 10 less than 33? 23

What is 10 less than 35? 25

What is 10 less than 37? 27

What is 10 less than 39? 29

What is 10 less than 41? 31

What is 10 less than 43? 33

What is 10 less than 45? 35

What is 10 less than 47? 37

What is 10 less than 49? 39

What is 10 less than 51? 41

What is 10 less than 53? 43

What is 10 less than 55? 45

What is 10 less than 57? 47

What is 10 less than 59? 49

What is 10 less than 61? 51

Math Terms Crossword

Solve the puzzle below with the correct math vocabulary word.

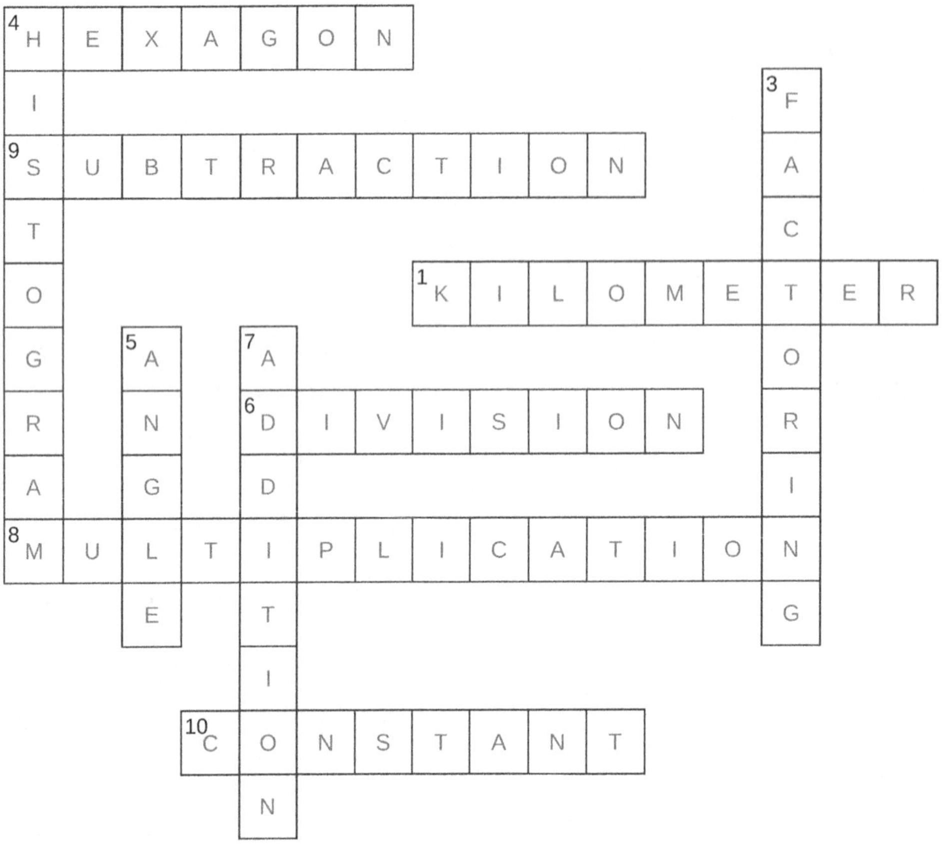

Across

1. A unit of measure equal to 1000 meters.
4. A six-sided and six-angled polygon.
6. Quotient, Goes Into, How Many Times
8. Multiply, Product, By, Times, Lots Of
9. Minus, Less, Difference, Decrease, Take Away, Deduct
10. A value that does not change.

Down

3. The process of breaking numbers down into all of their factors.
4. A graph that uses bars that equal ranges of values.
5. Two rays sharing the same endpoint (called the angle vertex).
7. Sum, Plus, Increase, Total

MULTIPLICATION
HEXAGON KILOMETER
CONSTANT ANGLE
FACTORING DIVISION
SUBTRACTION
HISTOGRAM ADDITION

ANSWER SHEET

Math Terms Matching

Match each math term to the correct meaning.

1	A	Rectangle	⇢	A parallelogram with four right angles.
2	G	Negative Number	⇢	A number less than zero.
3	C	Triangle	⇢	A three-sided polygon.
4	D	X	⇢	The Roman numeral for 10.
5	P	X-Axis	⇢	The horizontal axis in a coordinate plane.
6	B	Weight	⇢	The measure of how heavy something is.
7	M	Like Fractions	⇢	Fractions with the same denominator.
8	K	Like Terms	⇢	_____ with the same variable and same exponents/powers.
9	F	Mode	⇢	The _____ is a list of numbers are the values that occur most frequently.
10	H	Midpoint	⇢	A point that is exactly halfway between two locations.
11	E	Line	⇢	A straight infinite path joining an infinite number of points in both directions.
12	I	Numerator	⇢	The top number in a fraction.
13	Q	Octagon	⇢	A polygon with eight sides.
14	N	Logic	⇢	Sound reasoning and the formal laws of reasoning.
15	O	Outcome	⇢	Used in probability to refer to the result of an event.
16	J	Polynomial	⇢	The sum of two or more monomials.
17	L	Quotient	⇢	The solution to a division problem.
18	R	Proper Fraction	⇢	A fraction whose denominator is greater than its numerator.

Mean, Mode, Median

1) 2, 2, 3, 4, 4, 9, 4
2, 2, 3, 4, 4, 4, 9

Mean 4 Median 4 Mode 4

2) 7, 7, 9, 7, 2, 8, 3, 6, 4, 7
2, 3, 4, 6, 7, 7, 7, 7, 8, 9

Mean 6 Median 7 Mode 7

3) 8, 4, 2, 7, 5, 6, 2, 3, 4, 9
2, 2, 3, 4, 4, 5, 6, 7, 8, 9

Mean 5 Median 4.5 Mode 2, 4

4) 7, 7, 3, 2, 6
2, 3, 6, 7, 7

Mean 5 Median 6 Mode 7

5) 5, 6, 6, 7, 6, 5, 6, 7, 6
5, 5, 6, 6, 6, 6, 6, 7, 7

Mean 6 Median 6 Mode 6

6) 9, 7, 4, 4, 4, 2
2, 4, 4, 4, 7, 9

Mean 5 Median 4 Mode 4

7) 8, 8, 4, 3, 4, 7, 9, 4, 7
3, 4, 4, 4, 7, 7, 8, 8, 9

Mean 6 Median 7 Mode 4

8) 2, 4, 6, 2, 5, 2, 9, 2
2, 2, 2, 2, 4, 5, 6, 9

Mean 4 Median 3 Mode 2

9) 6, 5, 8, 2, 9
2, 5, 6, 8, 9

Mean 6 Median 6 Mode None

10) 6, 3, 3, 5, 8, 1, 9
1, 3, 3, 5, 6, 8, 9

Mean 5 Median 5 Mode 3

Measure It

Length to measure.

1 in

63 mm

14.7 cm

2.3 cm

$2\frac{1}{2}$ in

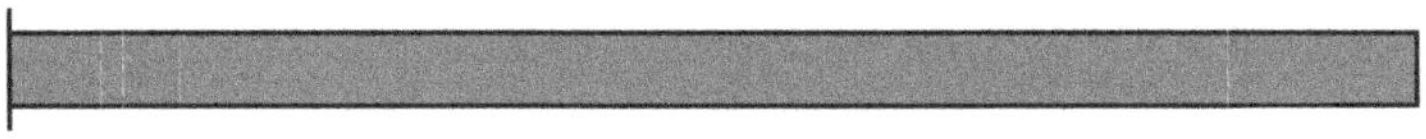

105 mm

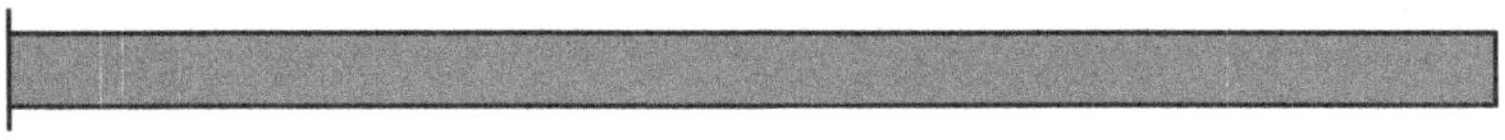

11.1 cm

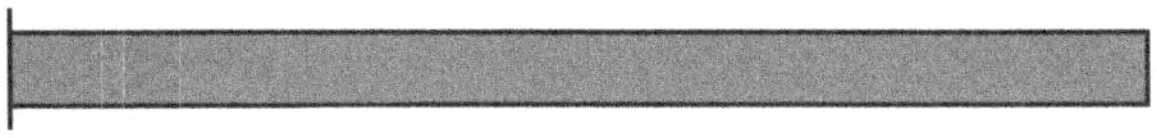

8.5 cm

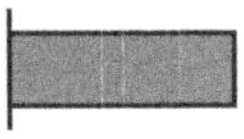

1.7 cm

13.7 cm

ANSWER SHEET

On this day in 1969...

On this day in 1969...

Cryptogram: You must substitute the code letters for the real letters to reveal the paragraph text.

A	B	C	D	E	F	G	H	I	J	K	L	M	N	O	P	Q	R	S	T	U	V	W	X	Y	Z
68	81	78	84	83	87	88	76	66	65	89	67	72	73	74	85	80	69	71	75	90	70	86	82	77	79

C H U C K   T A Y L O R ,   T H E
78 76 90 78 89   75 68 77 67 74 69   75 76 83

B A S K E T B A L L   P L A Y E R   A N D
81 68 71 89 83 75 81 68 67 67   85 67 68 77 83 69   68 73 84

C O A C H   W H O   M A D E   " C H U C K S "
78 74 68 78 76   86 76 74   72 68 84 83   78 76 90 78 89 71

(C O N V E R S E   A L L   S T A R S)
78 74 73 70 83 69 71 83   68 67 67   71 75 68 69 71

P O P U L A R ,   A N D   W H O S E   N A M E
85 74 85 90 67 68 69   68 73 84   86 76 74 71 83   73 68 72 83

I S   O N   T H E   A N K L E   P A T C H ,
66 71   74 73   75 76 83   68 73 89 67 83   85 68 75 78 76

D I E D .
84 66 83 84

Converting Between Percents, Decimals, and Fractions

Convert Decimal to Percent

1.22 = 122 %

1.83 = 183 %

0.353 = 35.3 %

0.19 = 19 %

1.23 = 123 %

0.432 = 43.2 %

Convert Percent to Decimal

51 % = 0.51

94 % = 0.94

81.5 % = 0.815

29 % = 0.29

23.7 % = 0.237

189 % = 1.89

Convert Decimal to Fraction

$1.66 = \frac{166}{100} = \frac{83}{50}$

$1.51 = \frac{151}{100}$

$0.273 = \frac{273}{1000}$

$0.294 = \frac{294}{1000} = \frac{147}{500}$

$0.831 = \frac{831}{1000}$

$0.88 = \frac{88}{100} = \frac{22}{25}$

Convert Fraction to Decimal

$\frac{2}{20} = 0.1$

$\frac{19}{20} = 0.95$

$\frac{17}{10} = 1.7$

$\frac{15}{20} = 0.75$

$\frac{13}{20} = 0.65$

$\frac{13}{20} = 0.65$

Convert Fraction to Percent

$\frac{1}{10} = 10\ \%$

$\frac{26}{25} = 104\ \%$

$\frac{14}{10} = 140\ \%$

$\frac{38}{25} = 152\ \%$

$\frac{1}{10} = 10\ \%$

$\frac{13}{16} = 81.25\ \%$

Convert Percent to Fraction

$142\ \% = \frac{142}{100} = \frac{71}{50}$

$76\ \% = \frac{76}{100} = \frac{19}{25}$

$179\ \% = \frac{179}{100}$

$145\ \% = \frac{145}{100} = \frac{29}{20}$

$48.4\ \% = \frac{484}{1000} = \frac{121}{250}$

$68\ \% = \frac{68}{100} = \frac{17}{25}$

Ratios and Rates

Express each ratio as a fraction in the simplest form.

1) 56 beetles out of 84 insects $\frac{2}{3}$

2) 8 blue cars out of 40 cars $\frac{1}{5}$

3) 12 pennies to 15 pennies $\frac{4}{5}$

4) 8 gallons to 36 gallons $\frac{2}{9}$

5) 9 miles out of 33 miles $\frac{3}{11}$

6) 25 dimes to 60 dimes $\frac{5}{12}$

7) 36 cups to 48 cups $\frac{3}{4}$

8) 25 quarts to 45 quarts $\frac{5}{9}$

Express each phrase as a rate and unit rate.
(Round your answer to the nearest hundredth.)

	Rate	Unit Rate
9) 8 pencils for 16 dollars	$\frac{\text{16 dollars}}{\text{8 pencils}}$	2.00 dollars per pencil
10) 14 dollars for 6 books	$\frac{\text{14 dollars}}{\text{6 books}}$	2.33 dollars per book
11) 14 chocolate bars cost 19 dollars	$\frac{\text{19 dollars}}{\text{14 chocolate bars}}$	1.36 dollars per chocolate bar
12) 6 dollars for 3 cans of tuna	$\frac{\text{6 dollars}}{\text{3 cans}}$	2.00 dollars per can
13) 12 batteries cost 17 dollars	$\frac{\text{17 dollars}}{\text{12 batteries}}$	1.42 dollars per battery
14) 6 calculators cost $125.00	$\frac{\text{125 dollars}}{\text{6 calculators}}$	20.83 dollars per calculator
15) 140 miles on 4 gallons of gas	$\frac{\text{140 miles}}{\text{4 gallons}}$	35.00 miles per gallon
16) 7 inches of snow in 7 hours	$\frac{\text{7" of snow}}{\text{7 hours}}$	1.00" of snow per hour

ANSWERS

Find the Prime Factors of the Numbers

1)

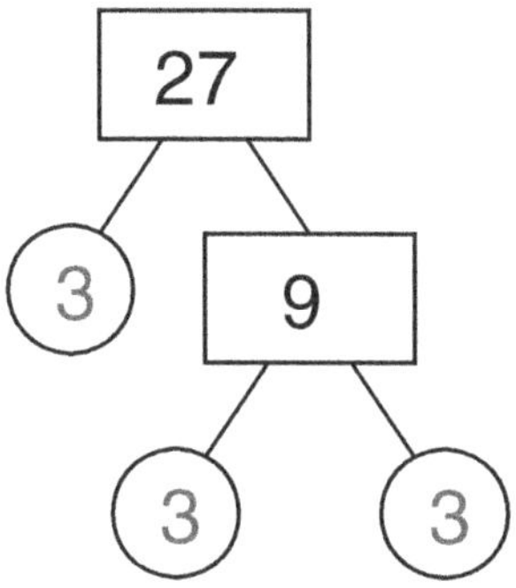

2)

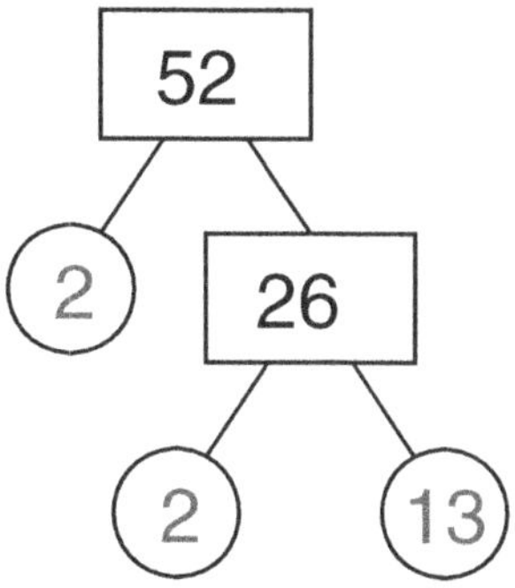

3)

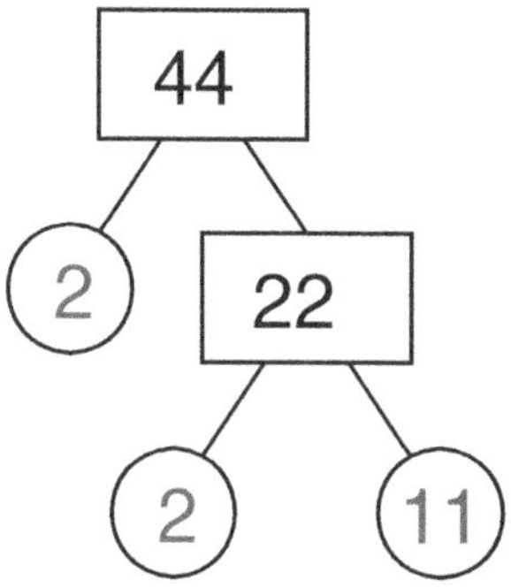

Factors
3 x 3 x 3 = 27

Factors
2 x 2 x 13 = 52

Factors
2 x 2 x 11 = 44

---

4)

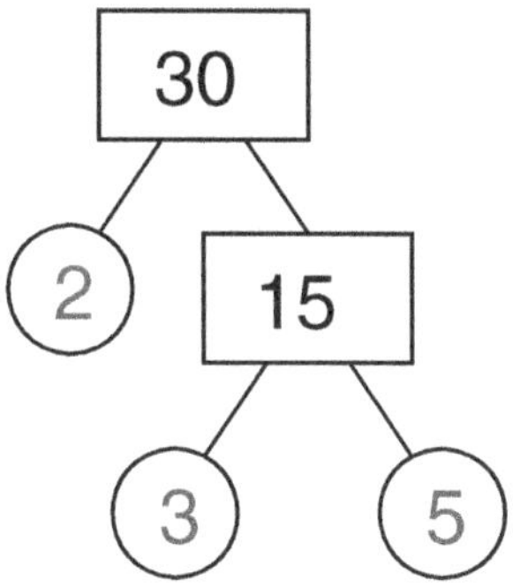

5)

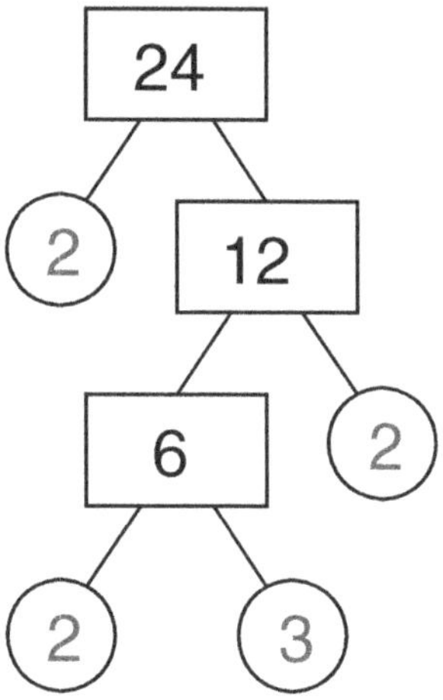

6)

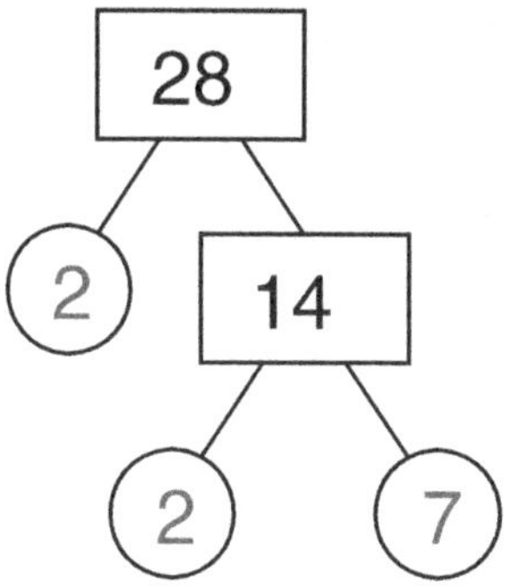

Factors
2 x 3 x 5 = 30

Factors
2 x 2 x 2 x 3 = 24

Factors
2 x 2 x 7 = 28

ANSWER SHEET

Reading Pie Graphs

**John tracked the time he spent on homework per topic during one week.
Answer the questions based on the pie graph below.**

1) What percentage of time did John spend on the English and Art homework? 50%

2) If John spent 100 minutes on homework, how many minutes were spent on Health? 10

3) Combined, which two topics required the greatest amount of time? English & Art

4) Was the Math and Spanish work or the History and Health work longer; or were they equally time consuming? Equal Amounts

5) Between Math and Spanish which topic took longer; or did they require equal time? Math

Time Spent on Homework

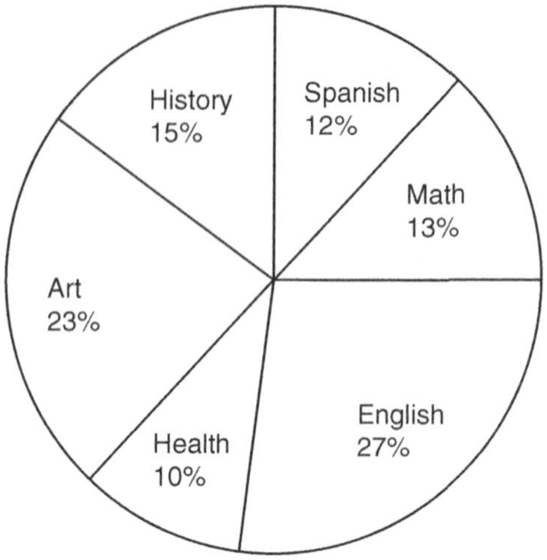

**A local pizzeria tracked which pizza toppings customers purchased.
Answer the questions based on the pie graph below.**

1) Were onion and ham picked more than the bacon and sausage; or were they equally bought? bacon & sausage

2) Combined, which two toppings did the greatest number of customers choose? bacon & sausage

3) If there were 200 customers that were tracked, how many bought sausage? 44

4) What percentage of customers chose either the beef or the olives? 28%

5) Between onion and ham which topping was more popular; or were they equally popular? onion

Most Purchased Pizza Topping

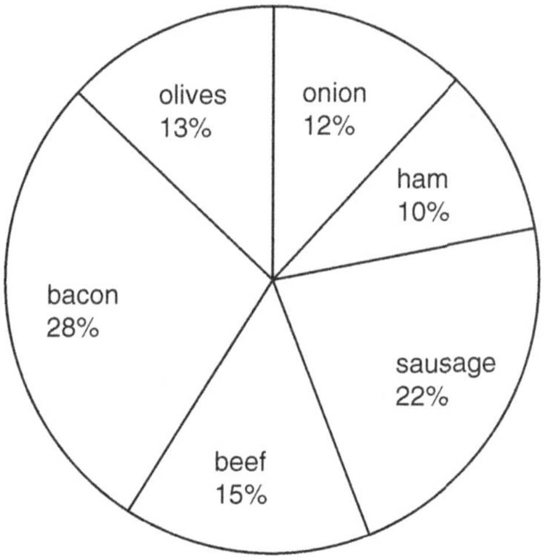

ANSWERS

Adding Fractions

1) $\frac{5}{7} + \frac{4}{7} = \frac{5}{7} + \frac{4}{7} = \frac{9}{7} = 1\frac{2}{7}$

2) $\frac{2}{8} + \frac{5}{8} = \frac{2}{8} + \frac{5}{8} = \frac{7}{8}$

3) $\frac{6}{7} + \frac{4}{7} = \frac{6}{7} + \frac{4}{7} = \frac{10}{7} = 1\frac{3}{7}$

4) $\frac{5}{4} + \frac{3}{4} = \frac{5}{4} + \frac{3}{4} = \frac{8}{4} = \frac{2}{1} = 2\frac{0}{1}$

5) $\frac{1}{8} + \frac{3}{8} = \frac{1}{8} + \frac{3}{8} = \frac{4}{8} = \frac{1}{2}$

6) $\frac{2}{6} + \frac{5}{6} = \frac{2}{6} + \frac{5}{6} = \frac{7}{6} = 1\frac{1}{6}$

7) $\frac{2}{6} + \frac{2}{6} = \frac{2}{6} + \frac{2}{6} = \frac{4}{6} = \frac{2}{3}$

8) $\frac{5}{4} + \frac{3}{4} = \frac{5}{4} + \frac{3}{4} = \frac{8}{4} = \frac{2}{1} = 2\frac{0}{1}$

9) $\frac{8}{8} + \frac{6}{8} = \frac{8}{8} + \frac{6}{8} = \frac{14}{8} = \frac{7}{4} = 1\frac{3}{4}$

10) $\frac{3}{7} + \frac{5}{7} = \frac{3}{7} + \frac{5}{7} = \frac{8}{7} = 1\frac{1}{7}$

11) $\frac{7}{9} + \frac{1}{9} = \frac{7}{9} + \frac{1}{9} = \frac{8}{9}$

12) $\frac{3}{9} + \frac{6}{9} = \frac{3}{9} + \frac{6}{9} = \frac{9}{9} = 1$

13) $\frac{2}{7} + \frac{4}{7} = \frac{2}{7} + \frac{4}{7} = \frac{6}{7}$

14) $\frac{3}{6} + \frac{2}{6} = \frac{3}{6} + \frac{2}{6} = \frac{5}{6}$

15) $\frac{3}{6} + \frac{5}{6} = \frac{3}{6} + \frac{5}{6} = \frac{8}{6} = \frac{4}{3} = 1\frac{1}{3}$

Write the Names for the Decimal Numbers.

1) 3.48 Three and Forty Eight Hundredths

2) 8.20 Eight and Two Tenths

3) 2.19 Two and Nineteen Hundredths

4) 2.38 Two and Thirty Eight Hundredths

5) 9.47 Nine and Forty Seven Hundredths

6) 3.51 Three and Fifty One Hundredths

7) 2.25 Two and Twenty Five Hundredths

8) 9.47 Nine and Forty Seven Hundredths

9) 6.76 Six and Seventy Six Hundredths

10) 3.28 Three and Twenty Eight Hundredths

Find the Mystery Numbers

1) **The mystery number has ...**

A 2 in the Thousands place.
A 8 in the Tens place.
A 2 in the Hundreds place.
A 3 in the Ones place.

What is the mystery number ? 2,283

2) **The mystery number has ...**

A 1 in the Tens place.
A 6 in the Hundreds place.
A 1 in the Thousands place.
A 7 in the Ones place.

What is the mystery number ? 1,617

3) **The mystery number has ...**

A 7 in the Thousands place.
A 1 in the Hundreds place.
A 3 in the Tens place.
A 2 in the Ones place.

What is the mystery number ? 7,132

4) **The mystery number has ...**

A 5 in the Ones place.
A 1 in the Thousands place.
A 4 in the Hundreds place.
A 7 in the Tens place.

What is the mystery number ? 1,475

5) **The mystery number has ...**

A 1 in the Ones place.
A 8 in the Hundreds place.
A 8 in the Tens place.
A 6 in the Thousands place.

What is the mystery number ? 6,881

ANSWER SHEET

Number Lines

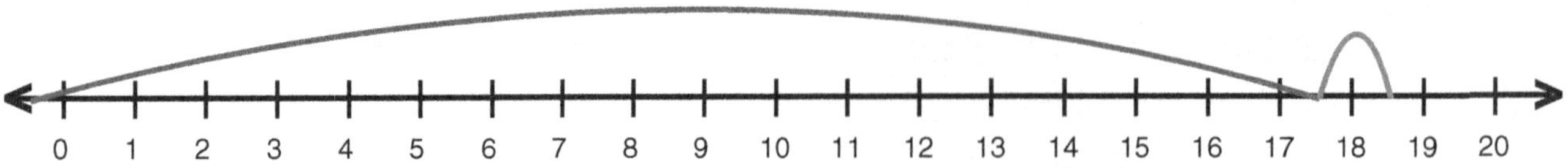

18 + 1 = 19

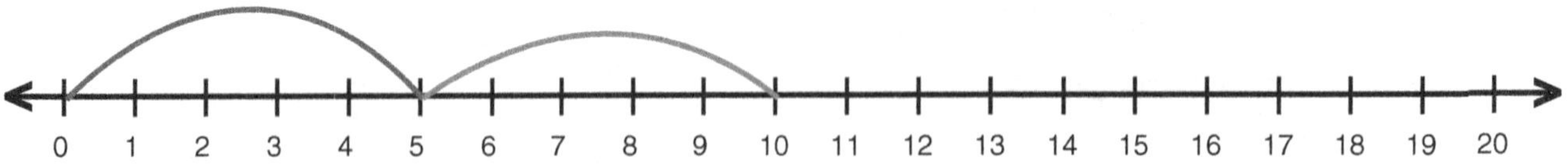

5 + 5 = 10

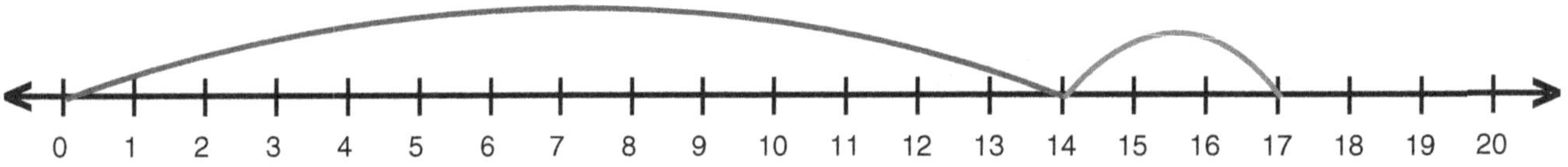

14 + 3 = 17

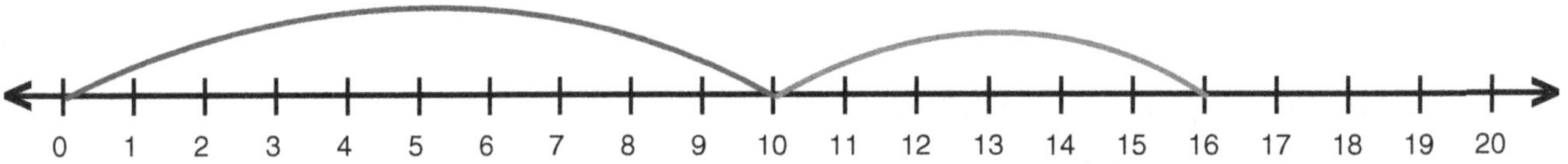

10 + 6 = 16

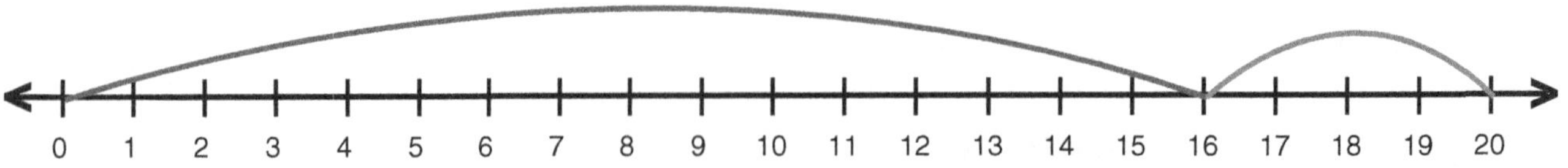

16 + 4 = 20

ANSWER SHEET

10122	265710	6900016	94785
+ 86800	+ 883815	+ 8967065	+ 51037
96922	1149525	15867081	145822

403123	5061847	88389	313963
+ 535453	+ 1878336	+ 38835	+ 824442
938576	6940183	127224	1138405

2936692	15234	512353	1923899
+ 7549491	+ 29032	+ 139827	+ 6762860
10486183	44266	652180	8686759

93107	421331	5141586	42257
+ 15816	+ 962779	+ 6071731	+ 96189
108923	1384110	11213317	138446

Measure It

Length to measure.

1 in

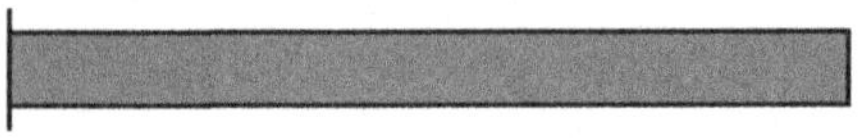

63 mm

14.7 cm

2.3 cm

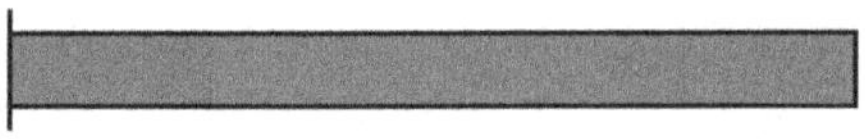

$2\frac{1}{2}$ in

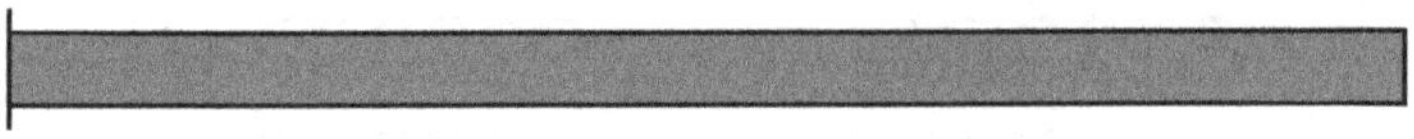

105 mm

11.1 cm

8.5 cm

1.7 cm

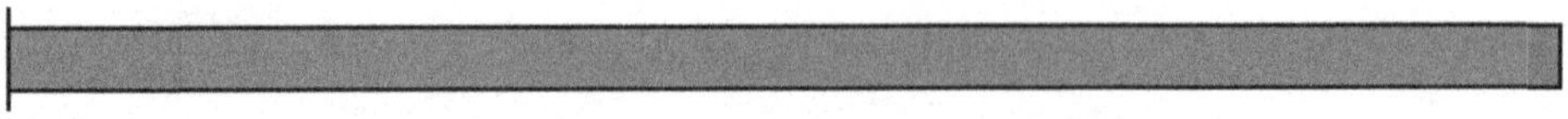

13.7 cm

Combining Like Terms

1) 8 + 13y - 15y

   -2y + 8

2) 14 - 6y + 3

   -6y + 17

3) -11 + 2 - 14y - 4y

   -18y -9

4) -14(5 - 2f) - 8

   28f -78

5) 12n + 6n

   18n

6) 13k + k

   14k

7) 16(-14z - 4) - 3

   -224z -67

8) -19(16 + 13s)

   -247s -304

9) 3 + 9r - 7r + 6

   2r +9

10) 14(-19c + 8)

   -266c +112

Grammar: Homophones vs Homographs vs. Homonyms

ANSWER SHEET

1. 'there,' 'their,' or 'they're' are examples of ______.
   a. Homophones
   b. Homographs

2. ____ are words that have the same spelling or pronunciation but different meanings.
   a. Homonyms
   b. Hemograms

3. Choose the correct homophone for this sentence: Please don't drop and ______that bottle of hand sanitizer!
   a. brake
   b. break

4. Homographs are two or more words that have the same spelling but different ____.
   a. ending sounds
   b. meanings

5. Current (A flow of water / Up to date) is both homograph and homophone.
   a. True
   b. False

6. To, two and too are _____.
   a. Homagraphs
   b. Homonyms

7. The candle filled the _____ with a delicious scent.
   a. heir
   b. air

8. Kim drove _______ the tunnel.
   a. threw
   b. through

9. John wants to go to _____ house for dinner, but they don't like her, so _____ going to say no.
   a. their, they're
   b. there, they're

10. We won a $95,000 ________!
    a. cheque
    b. check

11. For example, a pencil is not really made with _____.
    a. led
    b. lead

12. Choose the correct homophone for this sentence: Timmy was standing _____ in line.
    a. fourth
    b. forth

13. Homophones are two words that sound the same but have a different meanings.
    a. True
    b. False

14. The word ring in the following two sentences is considered what? She wore a ruby ring. | We heard the doorbell ring.
    a. hologram
    b. homograph

15. A Homograph is a word that has more than one meaning and doesn't have to sound the same.
    a. True
    b. False

16. Homophones occur when there are multiple ways to spell the same sound.
    a. True
    b. False

17. Select the correct homophone: I have very little (patience/patients) when students do not follow directions.
    a. patients
    b. patience

18. The correct homophone (s) are used in the sentence: Personally, I hate the smell of read meet.
    a. True
    b. False

19. The correct homophone(s) is used in the sentence: We saw a herd of cattle in the farmer's field.
    a. True
    b. False

20. What is NOT an example of a homograph?
    a. or, oar
    b. live, live

ANSWER SHEET

Grammar: Singular and Plural

1. **Which word is NOT a plural noun?**
   a. books
   b. hat
   c. toys

2. **Which word is a singular noun?**
   a. bikes
   b. cars
   c. pencil

3. **Which word can be both singular and plural?**
   a. deer
   b. bears
   c. mice

4. **Tommy _________ badminton at the court.**
   a. playing
   b. plays
   c. play's

5. **They _______ to eat at fast food restaurants once in a while.**
   a. likes
   b. like
   c. likies

6. **Everybody _________ Janet Jackson.**
   a. know
   b. known
   c. knows

7. **He ___ very fast. You have to listen carefully.**
   a. spoken
   b. speak
   c. speaks

8. **Which one is the singular form of women?**
   a. womans
   b. woman
   c. women

9. **The plural form of tooth is**
   a. tooths
   b. toothes
   c. teeth

10. **The singular form of mice is _______.**
    a. mouse
    b. mices
    c. mouses

11. **The plural form of glass is _________.**
    a. glassies
    b. glasses
    c. glassy

12. **The plural form of dress is _________.**
    a. dressing
    b. dresses
    c. dressy

13. **Plural means many.**
    a. True
    b. False

14. **Singular means 1.**
    a. True
    b. False

15. **Is this word singular or plural? monsters**
    a. plural
    b. singular

16. **Find the plural noun in the sentence. They gave her a nice vase full of flowers.**
    a. they
    b. flowers
    c. vase

17. Find the plural noun in the sentence. Her baby brother grabbed the crayons out of the box and drew on the wall.

a. crayons
b. box
c. brothers

18. Find the plural noun in the sentence. My friend, Lois, picked enough red strawberries for the whole class.

a. strawberries
b. friends
c. classes

19. What is the correct plural form of the noun wish?

a. wishes
b. wishs
c. wishy

20. What is the correct plural form of the noun flurry?

a. flurrys
b. flurryies
c. flurries

21. What is the correct plural form of the noun box?

a. boxs
b. boxses
c. boxes

22. What is the correct plural form of the noun bee?

a. beess
b. beeses
c. bees

23. What is the correct plural form of the noun candy?

a. candys
b. candyies
c. candies

24. Find the singular noun in the sentence. The boys and girls drew pictures on the sidewalk.

a. boys
b. drew
c. sidewalk

ANSWER SHEET

Spelling: How Do You Spell It? Part I

	A	B	C	D
1.	**grade**	grrada	grrade	grada
2.	**elementary**	elenmentary	ellenmentary	ellementary
3.	**marks**	marrcks	marrks	marcks
4.	repurt	reporrt	**report**	repurrt
5.	schedolle	**schedule**	schedole	schedulle
6.	timetible	**timetable**	timettable	timettible
7.	**highlight**	highllight	hyghllight	hyghlight
8.	foell	foel	fuell	**fuel**
9.	instrucsion	insstruction	**instruction**	insstrucsion
10.	senttence	sentance	senttance	**sentence**
11.	**vaccination**	vacination	vaccinasion	vacinasion
12.	**proof**	prwf	prouf	proph
13.	mandatury	mandattury	**mandatory**	mandattory
14.	**final**	fynall	finall	fynal
15.	envellope	**envelope**	envellupe	envelupe
16.	equattor	eqauttor	eqautor	**equator**
17.	bllanks	**blanks**	blancks	bllancks
18.	honorible	honorrable	**honorable**	honorrible
19.	scaince	sceince	**science**	sciance
20.	mussic	mosic	muscic	**music**
21.	**history**	hisstory	hisctory	histury
22.	lissten	liscten	lysten	**listen**
23.	entrence	enttrance	enttrence	**entrance**
24.	especialy	especailly	especaily	**especially**
25.	mariage	maraige	marraige	**marriage**

ANSWER SHEET

Spelling: How Do You Spell It?
Part II

	A	B	C	D
1.	compllain	complian	**complain**	compllian
2.	negattyve	negatyve	**negative**	negattive
3.	**importance**	importence	imporrtance	imporrtence
4.	encourragement	**encouragement**	encourragenment	encouragenment
5.	shallves	**shelves**	shellves	shalves
6.	**mixture**	mixttore	mixtore	mixtture
7.	honorrable	**honorable**	honorible	honorrible
8.	lagall	legall	lagal	**legal**
9.	manar	mannar	**manner**	maner
10.	encycllopedia	**encyclopedia**	encycllopedai	encyclopedai
11.	repllacement	replacenment	repllacenment	**replacement**
12.	medycie	medycine	**medicine**	medicie
13.	experriance	**experience**	experiance	experrience
14.	**hunger**	hunjer	hungerr	hunjerr
15.	sallote	sallute	salote	**salute**
16.	horrizon	hurizon	hurrizon	**horizon**
17.	sestion	**session**	setion	sesion
18.	shorrten	shurten	**shorten**	shurrten
19.	fuacett	faucett	fuacet	**faucet**
20.	haadache	haadace	haedache	**headache**
21.	**further**	furrther	forrther	forther
22.	injurry	injory	**injury**	injorry
23.	disstance	distence	**distance**	disstence
24.	rattio	**ratio**	rattoi	ratoi
25.	independense	**independence**	independance	independanse

ANSWER SHEET

Spelling: How Do You Spell It? Part III

Write and circle the correct spelling for each word.

	A	B	C	D
1.	**invitation**	invittasion	invitasion	invittation
2.	denuminator	**denominator**	denuminattor	denominattor
3.	**personal**	perrsonal	perrsunal	persunal
4.	rapkd	**rapid**	rahid	rapyd
5.	oryginal	**original**	orryginal	orriginal
6.	liquvd	liqiod	liqoid	**liquid**
7.	desscendant	**descendant**	dessendant	desssendant
8.	dissastrous	**disastrous**	dissastroos	disastroos
9.	cooperasion	**cooperation**	coperation	coperasion
10.	**routine**	roottine	routtine	rootine
11.	earleist	earrleist	earrliest	**earliest**
12.	acidentally	**accidentally**	acidentalli	accidentalli
13.	rehaerrse	rehearrse	rehaerse	**rehearse**
14.	quotte	qoote	**quote**	qootte
15.	capablla	capablle	**capable**	capible
16.	apointment	appointnment	apointnment	**appointment**
17.	mussician	mussicain	musicain	**musician**
18.	nomerrator	numerrator	**numerator**	nomerator
19.	**inquire**	inqoire	inquirre	inqoirre
20.	**remote**	remute	remutte	remotte
21.	pryncipal	prrincipal	prryncipal	**principal**
22.	sylent	sillent	syllent	**silent**
23.	locatsion	locasion	**location**	locattion
24.	edision	**edition**	editsion	edittion

ANSWER SHEET

Commonly misspelled words that sound alike but are spelled differently

Carefully circle the correct spelling combinations of words.

	A	B	C	D
1.	Sun/Sn	Son/Son	**Sun/Son**	Son/Sn
2.	Hare/Hiar	Harre/Hair	**Hare/Hair**	Harre/Hiar
3.	Cache/Cassh	**Cache/Cash**	Cache/Casch	Cacha/Cash
4.	Cytte/Sight	**Cite/Sight**	Cyte/Sight	Citte/Sight
5.	Worrn/Warn	Wurn/Warn	Wurrn/Warn	**Worn/Warn**
6.	Minerr/Minor	Miner/Minur	**Miner/Minor**	Minerr/Minur
7.	Wratch/Retch	**Wretch/Retch**	Wrretch/Retch	Wrratch/Retch
8.	Floor/Flower	Flloor/Flower	**Flour/Flower**	Fllour/Flower
9.	Whille/Wile	**While/Wile**	Whyle/Wile	Whyle/Wile
10.	Calous/Callus	Caloos/Callus	**Callous/Callus**	Calloos/Callus
11.	Build/Biled	**Build/Billed**	Boild/Billed	Boild/Biled
12.	Marrten/Martin	**Marten/Martin**	Marten/Martyn	Marrten/Martyn
13.	Humerrus/Humorous	**Humerus/Humorous**	Humerrus/Humoroos	Humerus/Humoroos
14.	Housse/Hoes	**Hose/Hoes**	House/Hoes	Hosse/Hoes
15.	Mei Be/Maybe	Mai Be/Maybe	**May Be/Maybe**	Mey Be/Maybe
16.	Matal/Metle/Meddle	**Metal/Mettle/Meddle**	Matal/Mettle/Meddle	Metal/Metle/Meddle
17.	**Halve/Have**	Hallva/Have	Hallve/Have	Halva/Have
18.	**Wee/We**	Wea/We	We/We	Wa/We
19.	**Taper/Tapir**	Taperr/Tapyr	Taperr/Tapir	Taper/Tapyr
20.	Timberr/Timbre	Tymber/Timbre	Tymberr/Timbre	**Timber/Timbre**
21.	Minse/Mintts	Mince/Mintts	Minse/Mints	**Mince/Mints**
22.	Eies/Ayes	Eyesc/Ayes	**Eyes/Ayes**	Eyess/Ayes
23.	Guesced/Guest	**Guessed/Guest**	Guesed/Guest	Gueced/Guest
24.	**Yore/Your/You'Re**	Yore/Yoor/You'Re	Yorre/Your/You'Re	Yorre/Yoor/You'Re
25.	Oarr/Or/Ora	Oarr/Or/Ore	**Oar/Or/Ore**	Oar/Or/Ora

26.	Bate/Biat	**Bate/Bait**	Batte/Biat	Batte/Bait
27.	**Tax/Tacks**	Tax/Taks	Tax/Tacksc	Tax/Tackss
28.	Bald/Ballad/Bawled	Bald/Baled/Bawled	**Bald/Balled/Bawled**	Bald/Balad/Bawled
29.	Ewe/Yuo/Yew	Ewe/Yoo/Yew	**Ewe/You/Yew**	Ewe/Yoo/Yw
30.	Eei/I/Aye	Eie/I/Ae	**Eye/I/Aye**	Eie/I/Aye
31.	**Hoes/Hose**	Hoess/Hose	Hoess/House	Hoes/House
32.	Tou/Two/To	Tu/Two/To	To/Two/To	**Too/Two/To**
33.	**Ceres/Series**	Cerres/Series	Ceres/Sereis	Cerres/Sereis
34.	**Hansom/Handsome**	Hansum/Handsome	Hanscom/Handsome	Hanssom/Handsome
35.	Residance/Residents	**Residence/Residents**	Ressidence/Residents	Ressidance/Residents
36.	Surrf/Serf	**Surf/Serf**	Surrph/Serf	Surph/Serf
37.	Siall/Sale	Saill/Sale	**Sail/Sale**	Sial/Sale
38.	Therre's/Thiers	There's/Thiers	**There's/Theirs**	Therre's/Theirs
39.	Roed/Rode	Roed/Rude	**Rued/Rude**	Roed/Rue
40.	Aid/Aie	Ayd/Aide	Ayd/Aie	**Aid/Aide**
41.	Taem/Teem	Taem/Tem	Team/Tem	**Team/Teem**
42.	Ilusion/Allusion	Ilution/Allusion	Illution/Allusion	**Illusion/Allusion**
43.	Hi/Hih	Hy/High	**Hi/High**	Hy/Hih
44.	**Barred/Bard**	Bared/Bard	Barad/Bard	Barrad/Bard
45.	Mewll/Mule	**Mewl/Mule**	Mewll/Mole	Mewl/Mole
46.	Rowss/Rose	**Rows/Rose**	Rowss/Rouse	Rows/Rouse
47.	Chep/Cheap	Cheep/Chaep	**Cheep/Cheap**	Chep/Chaep
48.	Bah/Ba	Beh/Ba	**Bah/Baa**	Beh/Baa
49.	**Gofer/Gopher**	Gopher/Gopher	Gophfer/Gopher	Goffer/Gopher
50.	Don/Doe	Dun/Doe	**Dun/Done**	Don/Done
51.	Ryte/Write/Right	Ritte/Write/Right	Rytte/Write/Right	**Rite/Write/Right**
52.	**Mite/Might**	Mitte/Might	Myte/Might	Mytte/Might
53.	**Latter/Ladder**	Later/Ladder	Latar/Ladder	Lattar/Ladder
54.	Gorred/Goord	**Gored/Gourd**	Gored/Goord	Gorred/Gourd
55.	Ball/Belle	**Bell/Belle**	Bal/Belle	Bel/Belle
56.	Ruscell/Rustle	**Russell/Rustle**	Rusell/Rustle	Rucell/Rustle
57.	Tuat/Taught	Tautt/Taught	Tuatt/Taught	**Taut/Taught**

58.	**Cozen/Cousin**	Cozen/Coosin	Cozen/Coossin	Cozen/Coussin
59.	**Morn/Mourn**	Morrn/Moorn	Morrn/Mourn	Morn/Moorn
60.	Stare/Stiar	**Stare/Stair**	Sttare/Stiar	Sttare/Stair
61.	Wrrap/Rap	Wrrep/Rap	**Wrap/Rap**	Wrep/Rap
62.	Centts/Ssents	Centts/Scents	**Cents/Scents**	Cents/Ssents
63.	Basste/Based	Baste/Baced	**Baste/Based**	Bascte/Based
64.	Foorr/Fore/For	Foor/Fore/For	Fourr/Fore/For	**Four/Fore/For**
65.	Knikers/Nickers	Knickerrs/Nickers	Knikerrs/Nickers	**Knickers/Nickers**
66.	Marre/Mayor	**Mare/Mayor**	Mare/Meyor	Marre/Meyor
67.	Surrje/Serge	Surje/Serge	Surrge/Serge	**Surge/Serge**
68.	**Steal/Steel**	Steal/Stel	Stael/Steel	Stael/Stel
69.	Haerrt/Hart	**Heart/Hart**	Hearrt/Hart	Haert/Hart
70.	**Holed/Hold**	Huled/Hold	Holled/Hold	Hulled/Hold
71.	Way/Wiegh/Whey	Wai/Wiegh/Whey	Wai/Weigh/Whey	**Way/Weigh/Whey**
72.	Diieng/Dying	Dyieng/Dying	Dieing/Dying	**Dyeing/Dying**
73.	Holay/Holy/Wholly	Holay/Holy/Wholy	Holey/Holy/Wholy	**Holey/Holy/Wholly**
74.	Sworrd/Soared	Swurrd/Soared	Swurd/Soared	**Sword/Soared**
75.	Cane/Cyan	Cane/Cian	Cane/Cayn	**Cane/Cain**
76.	Arreil/Aerial	**Ariel/Aerial**	Arriel/Aerial	Areil/Aerial
77.	**Brut/Brute**	Brrot/Brute	Brot/Brute	Brrut/Brute
78.	Frrays/Phrase	**Frays/Phrase**	Frreys/Phrase	Freys/Phrase
79.	**Throne/Thrown**	Thrrune/Thrown	Thrune/Thrown	Thrrone/Thrown
80.	Ha'd/Hed	**He'd/Heed**	He'd/Hed	He'd/Head
81.	Waerr/Where/Ware	**Wear/Where/Ware**	Wearr/Where/Ware	Waer/Where/Ware
82.	Brraed/Bred	**Bread/Bred**	Braed/Bred	Brread/Bred
83.	We've/Waeve	**We've/Weave**	Wa've/Weave	Wa've/Waeve
84.	Hew/Hoe/Huh	**Hew/Hue/Hugh**	Hew/Hoe/Hugh	Hew/Hoe/Hogh
85.	Nikerrs/Knickers	Nickerrs/Knickers	Nikers/Knickers	**Nickers/Knickers**
86.	Call/Sell	**Cell/Sell**	Cal/Sell	Cel/Sell
87.	Isle/I'l/Aisle	**Isle/I'll/Aisle**	Isle/I'll/Aysle	Isle/I'l/Aysle
88.	Brruice/Brews	**Bruise/Brews**	Brruise/Brews	Bruice/Brews
89.	**Except/Accept**	Exsept/Accept	Exsept/Acept	Except/Acept

MIXED ADDING

ANSWER SHEET

1) 1067 + 1078 = 2145

2) 438 + 2611 = 3049

3) -2831 + -2939 = -5770

4) 2330 + -1901 = 429

5) 935 + 1991 = 2926

6) 603 + 1073 = 1676

7) -2280 + -393 = -2673

8) -230 + -138 = -368

9) 1368 + 624 = 1992

10) 1143 + -2262 = -1119

11) 1708 + -337 = 1371

12) 2667 + 2849 = 5516

13) 2277 + -466 = 1811

14) -2079 + -2586 = -4665

15) 2966 + 2413 = 5379

16) -1488 + 2557 = 1069

17) 1087 + -2291 = -1204

18) -2005 + 2153 = 148

19) 2125 + 2919 = 5044

20) -270 + 2104 = 1834

21) 2759 + 592 = 3351

22) -1815 + 2739 = 924

23) 1956 + -560 = 1396

24) 1569 + 2401 = 3970

25) 2496 + 674 = 3170

26) -2907 + 884 = -2023

27) 1727 + 739 = 2466

28) 125 + 783 = 908

29) 1602 + -1844 = -242

30) 2042 + -2763 = -721

ANSWER SHEET

Proofreading Interpersonal Skills: Peer Pressure

Tony is mingling with a large group of what he considers to be the school's cool kids. Suddenly, someone in the group begins mocking Tony's friend Rob, who walks with a limp due to a physical ~~dasability.~~ **disability.**

They begin to imitate ~~rob's~~ **Rob's** limping and ~~Call~~ **call** him 'lame cripple' and other derogatory terms. Although Tony disapproves of their behavior, he does not want to risk being excluded from the group, and thus joins them in mocking Rob.

Peer pressure is the influence exerted on us by ~~member's~~ **members** of our social group. It can manifest in a variety of ways and can lead to us engaging in behaviors we would not normally ~~consider~~ **consider,** such as Tony joining in and mocking his friend Rob.

However, peer pressure is not always detrimental. Positive peer pressure can motivate us to make better ~~chioces,~~ **choices,** such as studying harder, staying in school, or seeking a better job. ~~Whan~~ **When** others influence us to make poor ~~Choices,~~ **choices,** such as smoking, using illicit drugs, or bullying, we succumb to negative peer pressure. We all desire to belong to a group and fit in, so ~~Developing~~ **developing** strategies for resisting peer pressure when necessary can be beneficial.

Tony and his friends are engaging in bullying by ~~moking~~ **mocking** Rob. Bullying is defined as persistent, ~~unwanted.~~ **unwanted,** aggressive behavior directed toward another person. It is ~~moust~~ **most** prevalent in school-aged children but can also ~~aphfect~~ **affect** adults. Bullying can take on a variety of forms, including the following:

~~· Verbil~~
· **Verbal** bullying is when someone is called names, threatened, or taunted verbally.
· Bullying is physical in nature - ~~hitting~~ **hitting,** spitting, tripping, or ~~poshing~~ **pushing** someone.
· Social ~~Bullying~~ **bullying** is intentionally excluding ~~Someone~~ **someone** from ~~activities~~ **activities,** spreading rumors, or embarrassing ~~sumeone.~~ **someone.**
· Cyberbullying is the act of verbally or socially bullying someone via the internet, such as through social media sites.

Peer pressure exerts a significant influence on an individual's decision to engage in bullying ~~behavoir.~~ **behavior.** In Tony's case, even though Rob is a friend and ~~tony~~ **Tony** would never consider mocking his disability, his desire to belong to a group outweighs his willingness to defend his ~~friend~~ **friend.**

Peer pressure is a strong force that is exerted on us by our social group members. Peer pressure is classified into two types: negative peer pressure, which results in poor decision-making, and positive peer pressure, which influences us to make the correct choices. Adolescents are particularly susceptible to peer pressure because of their desire to fit ~~in~~ **in.**

Peer pressure can motivate someone to engage in bullying behaviors such as mocking someone, threatening to harm them, taunting them online, or excluding them from an activity. Each year, bullying ~~affect's~~ **affects** an astounding 3.2 million school-aged children. ~~Severil~~ **Several** strategies for avoiding peer pressure bullying include the following:

- ~~consider~~ **Consider** your actions by surrounding yourself with good company.
- Acquiring the ability to say no to someone you trust.

Speak up - bullying is never acceptable and is taken ~~extramely~~ **extremely** ~~seroiusly~~ **seriously** in schools and the workplace. If someone is attempting to convince you to bully another person, speaking with a trusted adult such as a teacher, coach, counselor, or coworker can frequently help put ~~thing's~~ **things** into perspective and highlight the issue.

ANSWER SHEET

Social Skill Interests: Things To Do

A **hobby** is something that a person actively pursues relaxation and enjoyment. On the other hand, a person may have an **interest** in something because they are curious or concerned. Hobbies usually do not provide monetary compensation. However, a person's interests can vary and may lead to earning money or making a living from them. Hobbies are typically pursued in one's spare time or when one is not required to work. Interests can be followed in one's spare time or while working, as in the case of using one's passion as a source of income. A hobby can be a recreational activity that is done regularly in one's spare time. It primarily consists of participating in sports, collecting items and objects, engaging in creative and artistic pursuits, etc. The desire to learn or understand something is referred to as interest. If a person has a strong interest in a subject, he or she may pursue it as a hobby. However, an interest is not always a hobby. Hobbies such as stamp and flower collecting may not be a source of income for a person, but the items collected can sometimes be sold. Hobbies frequently lead to discoveries and inventions. Interests could be a source of income or something done for free. If a person is interested in cooking or enjoys creating dishes, he can do so at home or make it a career by becoming a chef.

Put the words in the correct category.

pottery	card making	candle making	reading	weaving	knitting
gym	jewellery	chess	surfing	computer games	collecting
woodwork	Soccer	art	swimming	cooking	skateboarding
embroidery	skiing	gardening	writing	chatting	sewing
netball	stamp collecting	football	music	rugby	basketball

Sport (10)	Handcrafts (10)	Interests (10)
Soccer	knitting	reading
rugby	sewing	cooking
football	card making	music
netball	woodwork	stamp collecting
basketball	weaving	gardening
surfing	jewellery	chess
skateboarding	pottery	computer games
skiing	candle making	writing
swimming	embroidery	collecting
gym	art	chatting

Additional Work

ASSIGNMENT PLANNER

○ MONDAY

○ TUESDAY

○ WEDNESDAY

○ THURSDAY

○ FRIDAY

EXTRA CREDIT WEEKEND WORK

○ SATURDAY / SUNDAY

GOALS THIS WEEK

WHAT TO STUDY

Additional Work

ASSIGNMENT PLANNER

○ MONDAY

○ TUESDAY

○ WEDNESDAY

○ THURSDAY

○ FRIDAY

EXTRA CREDIT WEEKEND WORK

○ SATURDAY / SUNDAY

GOALS THIS WEEK

WHAT TO STUDY

Additional Work

ASSIGNMENT PLANNER

○ MONDAY

○ TUESDAY

○ WEDNESDAY

○ THURSDAY

○ FRIDAY

EXTRA CREDIT WEEKEND WORK

○ SATURDAY / SUNDAY

GOALS THIS WEEK

WHAT TO STUDY

A= Above Standards S=	93-97 A	80-82 B	68-69 D+	
Meets Standards N=	90-92 A	78-79 C+	62-67 D	Track overall daily grade(s)
Needs Improvement	88-89 B+	73-77 C	60-62 D	
98-100 A+	83-87 B	70-72 C	59 & Below F	

Week	Monday	Tuesday	Wednesday	Thursday	Friday
1					
2					
3					
4					
5					
6					
7					
8					
9					
10					
11					
12					
13					
14					
15					
16					
17					
18					

Notes

A= Above Standards S=	93-97 A	80-82 B	68-69 D+
Meets Standards N=	90-92 A	78-79 C+	62-67 D
Needs Improvement	88-89 B+	73-77 C	60-62 D
98-100 A+	83-87 B	70-72 C	59 & Below F

Track overall daily grade(s)

Week	Monday	Tuesday	Wednesday	Thursday	Friday
1					
2					
3					
4					
5					
6					
7					
8					
9					
10					
11					
12					
13					
14					
15					
16					
17					
18					

Notes

A= Above Standards S=	93-97 A	80-82 B	68-69 D+	
Meets Standards N=	90-92 A	78-79 C+	62-67 D	Track overall daily grade(s)
Needs Improvement	88-89 B+	73-77 C	60-62 D	
98-100 A+	83-87 B	70-72 C	59 & Below F	

Week	Monday	Tuesday	Wednesday	Thursday	Friday
1					
2					
3					
4					
5					
6					
7					
8					
9					
10					
11					
12					
13					
14					
15					
16					
17					
18					

Notes

End of the Year Evaluation

Name: ______________________________

Grade/Level: ____________________ Date: ____________________

Subjects Studied: ______________________________

____

____

Goals Accomplished: ______________________________

____

____

____

Most Improved Areas: ______________________________

____

____

____

Areas of Improvement: ______________________________

____

____

Main Curriculum Evaluation	Satisfied		Final Grades
		A= Above Standards S= Meets Standards N= Needs Improvement	
____________________	Yes No	98-100 A+ 93-97 A	____________
____________________	Yes No	90-92 A 88-89 B+	____________
____________________	Yes No	83-87 B 80-82 B	____________
____________________	Yes No	78-79 C+ 73-77 C	____________
____________________	Yes No	70-72 C 68-69 D+ 62-67 D	____________
____________________	Yes No	60-62 D 59 & Below F	____________

Most Enjoyed: ______________________________

____

Least Enjoyed: ______________________________

____

Made in the USA
Coppell, TX
27 July 2023

19622446R00208